Conservative Comebacks
To Liberal Lies

Conservative Comebacks
To Liberal Lies

*Issue by Issue Responses
to the Most Common Claims of the Left
From A to Z*

Gregory Jackson

JAJ Publishing

Conservative Comebacks To Liberal Lies
Copyright © 2007 Gregory Jackson
Published by JAJ Publishing

All rights reserved. No part of this book may be reproduced (except for inclusion in reviews), disseminated or utilized in any form or by any means, electronic or mechanical, including photocopying, recording, or in any information storage and retrieval system, or the Internet/World Wide Web without written permission from the author or publisher.

For further information, please contact:
Annie Fischer at: annie@conservativecomebacks.com

Conservative Comebacks To Liberal Lies
Gregory Jackson
First Printing: July 2006
Second Printing: October 2006
Third Printing: January 2007
Fourth Printing: April 2007

Book design by:
Arbor Books, Inc.
19 Spear Road, Ste 202
Ramsey, NJ 07446
www.arborbooks.com

Printed in the United States

1. Title 2. Author 3. Political/Science

Library of Congress Control Number: 2005907470
ISBN-10: 0-9772279-0-1
ISBN-13: 978-0-9772279-0-7

Acknowledgments

First and foremost, I would like to thank God for planting the dream and vision in my heart which became *Conservative Comebacks to Liberal Lies* and for giving me the energy during the last five years to research and write it when I would rather have been on the couch watching sports. He's helped me clarify my purpose in life and recognize that "I can do all things through Christ who strengthens me" (Philippians 4:13).

Secondly, I would like to acknowledge three very special women:

Barbara Bendall, thank you for providing candid feedback, constructive criticism and wise council. You were an answer to many prayers and I thank you for treating this book as if it were your own. Thank you for all you've done for me, not just as my editor, but more importantly as a friend who helped make my dream into a reality. I will never forget your genuine dedication to this project, as well as your godly wisdom and advice. You are a special person.

Jill Jackson, thank you for being such an amazing mother and raising me to pursue truth—to stand up for my deeply held convictions and beliefs no matter how "unpopular" they may be. You may not have known it at the time, but you helped cultivate a source of confidence I may never have had without your encouragement, support and love. I am blessed and proud to be your son.

Annie Jackson, thank you for all you sacrificed for me while I wrote *Conservative Comebacks*. You helped me research, edit, proofread, organize, re-organize—and you've provided vital editorial feedback. You did all this when you could have been doing other things for yourself. You chose to help me pursue my dream even if it meant that I sat in isolation at my keyboard for hours on end—apart from you (though, at times, you probably thought of it as "peace and quiet"). Thank you for being my best friend, my soul mate, my devoted and unconditionally loving wife and mother to our son.

She is clothed with strength and dignity.
She can laugh at the days to come.

She speaks with wisdom, and faithful instruction is on her tongue.

She watches over the affairs of her household and does not eat the bread of idleness.

Her children arise and call her blessed, her husband also and he praises her:

Many women do noble things but you surpass them all (Proverbs 31:24-29).

Jacob Jackson, my son, I thank God every day for giving me the joy which is you. We prayed for you, impatiently waited for you and excitedly watched your entrance into this world. Already you've taught us so much.

Let love and truth never leave you; bind them around your neck, write them down on the tablet of your heart. Then you will win favor and a good name in the sight of God and man.

Trust in the Lord with all your heart and lean not on your own understanding; in all your ways acknowledge him and he shall direct your paths.

Do not be wise in your own eyes; fear the Lord and shun evil. This will bring health to your body and nourishment to your bones.

Honor the Lord with your wealth and with the first fruits of all your increase; then your barns will be filled to overflowing, and your vats will brim over with new wine.

My son do not despise the Lord's discipline and do not resent his rebuke, because the Lord disciplines those he loves, as a father the son he delights in.

Happy is the man who finds wisdom, and the man who gains understanding (Proverbs 3:3-13).

Finally, special thanks to: the entire crew at Arbor Books, including Larry Leichman, Dennis Gorski, Olga Vladimirov, Adam Berberich, Victoria Colotta and Suzanne Mahle; my long-time friend Jim Quinn; my Pundit Radio co-host and friend Kevin Whalen; and my friend La Shawn Barber. You all helped make *Conservative Comebacks* a reality.

Thank you to everybody for helping me grasp that "the way of a fool seems right to him, but a wise man listens to advice." (Proverbs 12:15)

"One man with courage makes a majority."
Andrew Jackson

Table of Contents

Introduction .... *xi*

Chapter 1 .... *1*
A is for Abortion: *A Woman's Right to Choose Murder?*

Chapter 2 .... *27*
B is for Bill Clinton: *Sex, Lies and Blind Devotees*

Chapter 3 .... *43*
C is for Church and State: *What Our Constitution Says About Religion*

Chapter 4 .... *51*
D is for Democrats: *Why They're Usually Wrong About Everything*

Chapter 5 .... *70*
E is for Economics: *Why it Really is About the Economy, Stupid!*

Chapter 6 .... *90*
F is for Females: *Which Group Really Supports Them?*

Chapter 7 .... *95*
G is for Gun Control: *Why We Have a Second Amendment*

Chapter 8 .... *117*
H is for Health Care: *Do You Really Want National Eighty Percent Taxation?*

Chapter 9 .... *134*
I is for Independent Israel: *Why We Need to Support the Only Middle East Democracy*

Chapter 10 .... *141*
J is for Justice: *Why Criminals Need Discipline*

Chapter 11 .... *154*
K is for Kids: *The Leftist Indoctrination of Our Children*

Chapter 12 .... *168*
L is for Liberal Media: *Agenda, Agenda, Agenda*

Chapter 13 .... *172*
M is for Mega-Watt Energy: *Oil, Tree Huggers and Environmental Yappers*

Chapter 14 .... *191*
N is for 9/11 Attacks: *A New Kind of War*

Chapter 15 .... *206*
O is for Operation Iraqi Freedom: *Why We Had to Fight This War*

Chapter 16 .... *222*
P is for President George W. Bush: *The Man for the Hour*

Chapter 17 .... *234*
Q is for Queer Eye for Same-Sex Marriage: *Why the Family is in Jeopardy*

Chapter 18 .... *259*
R is for Race-Based Preferences: *What's Wrong With Affirmative Action*

Chapter 19 .... *272*
S is for Social Security: *How to Fix it*

Chapter 20 .... *288*
T is for Taxes: *Cut Your Way to Financial Freedom*

Chapter 21 .... *317*
U is for the United States: *What Makes Us Great*

Chapter 22 .... *327*
V is for Vouchers and Public Schools: *How We Can Fix Education*

Chapter 23 .... *343*
W is for Welfare: *What's Wrong With it*

Chapter 24 .... *351*
X is for Xenophobia: *Why Illegal Immigration is Hurting Us*

Chapter 25 .... *360*
Y is for Yankee Doodle Founding Fathers: *They Really Got it Right*

Chapter 26 .... *373*
Z is for Zealot Terrorists: *How Can We Fight Them?*

Endnotes *383*

Introduction

Conservative Comebacks to Liberal Lies provides factual responses from a uniquely conservative perspective to the most common claims the left makes on contemporary issues from A to Z. If Conservatism is to prevail in the ideological and political war of ideas and sustain a substantial majority in our country, those who are dedicated to its preservation and advancement (rule of law, preservation of the Constitution and Bill of Rights, traditional Judeo-Christian principles, limited government, free markets, protection of our borders, language and culture) will have to arm themselves with the facts to overcome the false and misleading claims the liberal left habitually makes.

If patriotic citizens, grassroots organizations and political candidates want to win the war of ideas, influence public policy and maintain lasting political power, they must be prepared to confidently advocate and defend conservative positions. For conservatives to sustain lasting majorities, they must be able to communicate conservative principles not only to their traditional constituencies (middle/upper class whites in suburbia and rural America), but also to minorities (blacks, Jews and especially Hispanics, who now represent the largest minority in America) as well as more "centrist" Democrats and Independents.

Republicans (especially ideological and philosophical conservatives) won the 2002 mid-term and 2004 presidential elections because conservative ideas, by and large, are winning the day. President Bush's popularity and inexorable campaigning for GOP candidates significantly contributed to the historic victories. In the final analysis, however, GOP candidates who won, clearly enunciated conservative principles to the voters. Candidates who made the case that the GOP is the party that's best on defense and national security, the economy, traditional family values and important reforms—such as reforming and strengthening social security, health care and public schools—overwhelmingly defeated Democrats.

In short, traditional conservative principles of a strong national defense, free market capitalism and limited government, attracted more voters than the Democratic Party's status quo, big government platform.

For conservative Republicans to sustain an enduring majority at all levels of state and federal government, they must win the war of ideas and information. Former British Prime Minister Margaret Thatcher once said, "First win the argument, then the vote."

Historically, when conservatives such as Ronald Reagan (the "Great Communicator") or the candidates who ran for and won congressional seats in 1994 under Newt Gingrich's "Contract with America" platform, have a unifying coherent message reflecting clearly enunciated conservative principles, they win almost every time—usually in landslides!

When conservative Republicans dilute conservative themes and principles to pacify the "centrists" and "moderates," or to curry favor with the elite media, they tend to lose the thrust of the message, which only disheartens their grassroots supporters and indirectly gives succor to their opponents.

Grassroots conservatives vote with less frequency and vigor for "lukewarm" RINOs (Republicans In Name Only) than they do for solid conservative candidates.

The left's specious claims have not changed fundamentally in the last half-decade. The liberal "chattering class" and "intelligentsia" have consistently accused conservative Republicans of favoring tax cuts for the "rich," favoring investing senior citizens' retirement on "risky privatization schemes," destroying the environment, imposing their Christian morals on the country and starving children.

Since the liberal left has essentially no new and innovative ideas of their own for reforming the very broken institutions they themselves created, they can only demonize conservative legislative proposals and ridicule conservative advocates.

The left has been fairly successful repeating these slogans often enough so these shibboleths have become indelibly forged on the public psyche. Even though the top half of one percent of taxpayers fork over almost one third of all taxes, while the bottom 50 percent pay less than five percent of all taxes, the notion (I should say myth) that across - the - board tax cuts unfairly benefit the "rich" only, is still perpetuated. This fallacy has been reiterated with such frequency by those on the liberal left that Republicans often only reluctantly support sweeping tax reductions, not wanting to lose the support of middle class voters.

The liberal left has leveraged its pervasive influence in television, print and broadcast media, movies, classrooms and the courts to advance their big-government Socialist agenda.

The left has been fairly successful replacing traditional conservative values and principles which our Founding Fathers enunciated in our founding documents with "secular humanism," "multiculturalism," "diversity training," "anger management," "social justice," "moral relativism," "political correctness" and "cradle-to-grave welfare." This transformation has been achieved by the mass dissemination and perpetuation of the left's distortions, half-truths and overt lies.

However, conservatives have, over the past decade, begun to fight back. Cable news (Fox), A.M. radio (Rush Limbaugh, Sean Hannity, Larry Elder and our show "Pundit Review" which focuses on the new media) and the internet (Newsmax, FreeRepublic and the "bloggers" such as Hugh Hewitt, Powerline, InstaPundit and our blog PunditReview.com) have provided conservatives with a platform to express their beliefs and to publicly rebut the distortions and inaccuracies of the liberal left. The strong ratings and popularity of many of these conservative programs, web sites, radio shows, books and magazines, demonstrate that conservatives possess a widespread appeal with a significant majority of Americans. The 2000, 2002 and 2004 elections revealed that indeed most Americans are right of center on most issues.

In 2004 Republicans successfully increased gains among virtually all voter demographics. Conservatives should expose the failures of the Democratic Party and the institutions they have created. Social Security, government schools, health care, "progressive" taxation and welfare are liberal Democratic legacies which have all been failures.

Most importantly, liberal Democratic policies have significantly weakened our national security, especially during the Clinton administration. Conservatives must make the convincing case that Democrats have not earned the confidence of the American people and can't be trusted to govern based on their abominable track record. Zell Miller, a Democrat, made this case quite emphatically, eloquently and succinctly at the 2004 Republican National Convention. Other conservatives need to make this case just as persuasively and forcefully.

The way to win the war of ideas is to ensure voters know liberals use class warfare, race baiting and personal attacks to disguise the truth with the overriding purpose of gaining political power and advancing their far left agendas. Their major or overriding aim is the acquisition of political power for the advancement of their leftist agenda.

For liberals to achieve and consolidate power, they must ensure that as many people as possible are dependent upon the government. Essentially, the liberal base consists of non-taxpaying citizens (the bottom 50 percent of workers) and are abetted by rich white liberals in the elite media and entertainment industries who have the most to gain by ensuring the vast majority of Americans are kept uninformed and uneducated.

The less Americans understand the history of their country (the founding documents, such as the Declaration of Independence, the Constitution and the Bill of Rights), the less they will object to such blatant constitutional violations as campaign finance reform, gun control, abortion "rights" and "affirmative action"—all of which the elite left routinely promote.

The more individual rights are diminished, the easier it becomes for the political ruling class liberal elites to maintain and consolidate power and achieve their socialist objectives.

The goal of my book is to provide ideological conservatives, independents and conservative Democrats with factual information on key contemporary issues to refute the claims and assertions of the left and ensure the protection of our founding principles and values now under attack from the left.

The liberal Democratic Party is on the proverbial "ropes." However, the opponent is often times most dangerous when he is closest to defeat. We are witnessing a desperate party barely clinging to power. The liberal left will now utilize everything at their disposal to regain political advantage. They will continue to leverage their liberal dominated institutions to shape public opinion and to further advance their big-government Socialist agenda. Perhaps the desperation of this once great political party was most evident when CBS News and Dan Rather attempted to change the outcome of the 2004 presidential election by airing a fraudulent Bush National

Guard document with the knowledge that the authenticity of the document could not be confirmed by any experts.

Liberal Democrats continue to talk about their "new vision for America" which is really just the same old repackaged quasi-socialism. Every liberal institution and policy such as, public housing, government education, social security, forced busing, rehabilitative justice, high taxation, managed health care and welfare have all been colossal failures.

If their vision actually resonated with voters, then Republicans would not control the presidency, both Houses of Congress and the majority of the state legislatures and governorships. Indeed, as Americans proved in the 2002 mid-term elections and 2004 presidential election, our country is right of center philosophically and most citizens favor the Republicans' vision for America: strong national defense, lower taxes and regulations on businesses, as well as choice in matters of schools, medical care and invested retirement funds. At the same time, however, so-called conservatives in the Republican Party have supported expanding Medicare/Medicaid, the Department of Education, race-based preferences, tariffs, and even amnesty for illegal aliens. These are not conservative positions and I hope this book will make the case for genuine conservative principles and ideas for all who cherish liberty and freedom.

Chapter 1

A is for Abortion:

A Woman's Right to Choose Murder?

Claims:
1. "Keep abortion safe, legal, and rare."
2. "Legalized abortion reduces child abuse."
3. "It's not fair to bring unwanted children into the world."
4. "The Fetus is part of the pregnant woman's body, like her tonsils or appendix. A woman has the right to do what she wishes with any 'part' of her own body."
5. "The unborn is an embryo or a fetus – just a simple blob of tissue -- not a baby. Abortion is simply terminating a pregnancy, not killing a child."
6. "It is uncertain when human life begins, therefore it's a religious question, not a scientific one."
7. "A fetus isn't a person until it can survive on its own outside the womb."
8. "Every person has the right to choose. It would be unfair to restrict a woman's choice by prohibiting abortion."
9. "Every woman should have control over her own body. Reproductive freedom is a basic right."
10. "I'm personally against abortion, but I wouldn't impose my beliefs on someone else."

11. "Abortion is legal. Things that are "legal" are OK, aren't they?"
12. "Abortion helps solve the overpopulation problem."
13. "If abortion is made illegal, thousands of women will die from back alley and clothes hanger abortions."
14. "Abortion is a safe medical procedure, safer than full-term pregnancy and childbirth."
15. "Abortions are necessary for women whose lives are threatened by pregnancy or childbirth."
16. "A woman who has been raped should be able to have an abortion."
17. "I can't tell a woman what to do with her body."
18. "Abortion liberates women."
19. "Women have a constitutional right to abortion because the courts have ruled that women have a right of privacy."
20. "I'm pro-choice, but I don't support partial birth abortion."

Perhaps the most paramount and divisive cultural and social issue of the past 30 years has been abortion.

Being "pro-choice" has become almost a pre-requisite for any Democrat seeking public office. So much have "abortion rights" become a sacrament of the Democrat Party that presidential aspirants such as Bill Clinton, Al Gore, Joe Lieberman and John Kerry all renounced their former "pro-life" stances to gain the support of major contributors such as the National Association for the Repeal of the Abortion Laws (NARAL) and other pro-abortion organizations.

The National Organization for Woman (N.O.W.), one of the Democratic Party's major financial donors, has stated in its literature that abortion is the most "fundamental right of a woman"—more important than free speech, self-defense or the right to vote.

In November 2003, President Bush signed a congressional ban

on partial-birth abortion or "late-term" abortion, dealing a severe blow to those on the left who have tirelessly endeavored to keep "abortion safe and legal." The Bush Administration has also proposed a ban on tax-payer funded abortions, as well as parental notification laws. Liberal Democrats have almost unanimously opposed any of these restrictions.

On one side of the political debate are the liberals who claim abortion is a constitutionally protected woman's right based on the settled law of *Roe v. Wade* and that, fundamentally, the government has no right to "tell a woman what to do with her own body." Abortion "rights" activists say, "Keep your laws off my body."

On the other side are pro-life conservatives and even some socially conservative Democrats, such as the late Senator Daniel Patrick Moynihan (D-NY), who maintain all human life is sacred (barring convicted murderers, rapists and child molesters) and must be protected by government.

The main purpose of our Constitution and Bill of Rights is to secure "life, liberty and the pursuit of happiness" for every American—no matter how old or young for that matter. Our Constitution protects the individual's right to life, especially for those who can't speak for themselves in their earliest stages of development. Thomas Jefferson, the primary author of the U.S. Declaration of Independence said on March 31, 1809, "The care of human life and happiness and not their destruction is the first and only legitimate object of good government."

Most importantly, conservatives argue it's a biological fact that life begins at conception. This is not a religious or philosophical belief, but a scientific fact.

As technology rapidly advances, enabling mothers to visualize their baby during the inchoate stages of development, it becomes clear the living fetus growing in the womb is more than an unfeeling "piece of flesh" as is often claimed by abortion defenders. Look at a sonogram of an eight-week-old baby and the baby's humanity becomes patently evident.

Support for abortion is declining, according to the vast majority of polls. *The New York Times* reported on a Gallup Poll conducted on January 21, 2001 showing those who consider themselves to be pro-life, rose from 33 percent to 43 percent.

From 2001-2004, those describing themselves as pro-choice declined from 56 percent to 48 percent,[1] evidence the tide is turning in regard to how Americans view abortion. This trend also demonstrates increasing numbers of Americans are able to discern the truth behind the hackneyed slogans and deceptive propaganda campaign of the left.

<u>CLAIM #1</u>: "Keep abortion safe, legal, and rare."

<u>RESPONSE</u>: Although abortion is "legal," it is neither "safe" nor "rare."

The number of abortion clinics in the United States between 1994 and 1998 decreased by 40 percent due to more and more doctors refusing to perform the gruesome procedure, as well as fewer women asking for them.

The number of abortions performed may be decreasing, but more than a million abortions are still performed in the United States every year. Abortion clinics have decreased, but crisis pregnancy centers have increased significantly—from 500 in 1980 to about 4,000 currently.

There is nothing "rare" about abortion, especially among unmarried teens and women in their early 20s who are most likely to obtain an abortion.

Abortion is never safe for the babies because they always die. There will never be a "safe" way to kill a baby.

For pregnant women, abortion is four times deadlier than childbirth, and often results in infertility and breast cancer—commonly referred to as the "ABC link." Eleven of 12 studies of American women reported an increased risk of breast cancer after having an induced abortion.[2]

Why abortion should even be "rare" contradicts some vital assumptions about abortion in general. If, as many abortion advocates assert, abortion is merely "terminating a potential pregnancy, not an actual human being," why would it matter if the "procedure" were "rare?" After all, if you're not actually doing any harm to a human being and if a fetus is nothing more than a "blob of flesh," why would it matter if the procedure were "rare" or not?

Many on the left have incorrectly concluded there have been positive aspects of abortion on society, such as lower levels of crime and child abuse. If that's true, then shouldn't abortion be even more "rare" than it is?

The assumption implicit in this statement is that by killing a developing baby inside the womb, a woman's health risks will be greatly reduced by keeping the procedure legal.

Those from groups such as NOW and NARAL say by making abortion illegal, many women's lives would be at risk because of abortions performed "in back alleys." Even when abortions are performed "legally," women can and do die, as well as suffering other severe life-long physical and emotional injuries.

There are well-documented emotional and psychological consequences stemming from abortion, such as post-abortion syndrome—with women experiencing symptoms of anxiety, guilt, anger, depression, nightmares and hallucinations.

Since the Supreme Court narrowly decided to make legalized abortions the law of the land in 1973, women have been the victims of many "unsafe" procedures. There are three types of abortion procedures: none of which are "safe" for the baby being killed.

First Trimester (Month 1-3)

The most common type of surgical abortion performed in the first trimester is called suction-aspiration. The abortionist numbs the cervix and stretches it open, then inserts a hollow plastic tube with a very sharp, knife-like edge into the uterus. The baby's body and the placenta are torn apart as the enormous force of the suction pulls the pieces into a bottle.

Another similar method which is performed, is dilation and curettage—the "D & C" method. A loop-shaped steel knife is inserted into the uterus and the abortionist scrapes and cuts the placenta and the baby into pieces, suctioning the remaining body parts into a basin to discard.

The newest method of aborting first trimester babies is through the use of Mifepristone (RU-486). The drug breaks down the lining of a woman's uterus, causing excessive bleeding, which induces contractions and miscarriage by causing the cervix to open and expel the baby.

Side effects can include severe bleeding, nausea, vomiting and pain. In some cases it has even caused death.

Second Trimester (Months 4-6)

The most common abortion technique is called dilation and evacuation (D & E). To accommodate the larger child to be aborted, the cervix must be dilated more widely, because surgical instruments are used to remove larger pieces of the baby's body. Following dilatation of the cervix, forceps are advanced and the baby's body is then methodically cut into pieces.[3]

At Christ Hospital and Medical Center in the Chicago suburb of Oak Lawn, "live birth abortions" are performed on second trimester babies—as late as 23 weeks into a pregnancy. The babies are born alive, then left to die.

Jill Stanek, a nurse who used to work at the hospital, described the gruesome procedure, saying a woman is injected with a drug which relaxes and opens her cervix, allowing the baby to fall out in a form of early labor. Sometimes the baby dies in the process. But many are born alive and are left to die—either in the hands of a nurse ("comfort care") or many times alone. Babies have even been left to die in a dirty utility closet.

The hospital calls the procedure "therapeutic."[4]

Late Second and Third Trimester (Months 7-9)

During this time period, lethal chemicals are injected into the womb, sometimes causing what abortionists call the "dreaded complication"—when the baby is born, but is severely injured.

One of the instillation techniques used after the 16th week is called saline amniocentesis or "salt poisoning" abortion.

A large needle is inserted into the abdominal wall of the mother into the baby's amniotic sac and a concentrated salt solution is injected into the baby's amniotic fluid. As the baby breathes and ingests the poison, it struggles and sometimes convulses. The chemicals burn the baby's outer skin, while its arteries and veins rupture, and tissue and organs hemorrhage. The baby suffers for more than an hour and the mother delivers a dead baby about one day later. The Nazis originally developed this procedure in the concentration camps.[5]

Another common type of third trimester abortion is called "partial-birth abortion," which is preformed on babies from the fifth to ninth month of development.

The cervix dilates for two days and on the third day, the abortionist pulls the baby through the birth canal, feet first, leaving only the head inside. The abortionist then punctures the base of the skull with surgical scissors, inserts a tube and vacuums out the brain tissue, causing the skull to collapse.

CLAIM #2: "Legalized abortion reduces child abuse."

RESPONSE: Child abuse has increased since abortion became legal.

In 1973, the year abortion became legal in the United States, 167,000 cases of child abuse and neglect were reported. In 1980, this number increased by 370 percent to 785,100 cases. In 1987, 2.02 million cases were reported, an increase of 1,112 percent.[6]

Evidence suggests abortion is an important *cause* of child abuse due to the effects the abortion has on the woman's self-esteem and ability to deal with stress, according to a study by Dr. Philip Ney, a practicing child and family psychiatrist in Canada.

Dr. Ney, who directs the International Institute for Pregnancy Loss and Child Abuse Research and Recovery, notes in his study, "...elective abortion is an important cause of child abuse... Recent evidence indicates that women harbor strong guilt feelings long after their abortions. Guilt is one important cause of child battering and infanticide. Abortion lowers women's self-esteem and there are studies reporting a major loss of self esteem in battering parents..."[7]

The landmark study on this issue was done by Dr. Edward Lenoski, Professor of Pediatrics and Emergency Medicine at the University of Southern California School of Medicine. Dr. Lenoski studied 674 children at both the in- and out-patient centers of the U.S.C. Medical Center and interviewed their parents as to whether they wanted and planned their pregnancies.

Dr. Lenoski's studies showed that 91 percent of the abused children had been planned and wanted pregnancies. Of the children *not* abused, only 63 percent were planned and wanted.

Dr. Lenoski also found that 24 percent of the abused children were named after their parents, while four percent of the non-abused children were named after them.[8]

The study shows the majority of abused children were "wanted." Aborting "unwanted" children doesn't stop child abuse.

The late psychiatrist and family therapist Antonio J. Ferreira studied the relationship between unplanned pregnancies and deviant babies and found no relationship between the two. In fact, he found there were more deviant babies, of mothers who had planned their pregnancy than those who did not.[9]

In another study, *How Much Do Mothers Love Their Children*, published in the *Rocky Mountain Psychological Association*, the investigators concluded: "initial feelings about pregnancy are predictive of how a mother will eventually feel about her baby to only a very limited degree."[10]

Much is still not known about the causes of child abuse. But what is known, is the majority of children who are abused are *not* unwanted pregnancies. In fact, most abused children are planned and "wanted."

CLAIM #3: "It's not fair to bring unwanted children into the world."

RESPONSE: It's not fair to stick surgical scissors in a baby's skull, suck out her brains with a vacuum, dismember her and throw her away in a garbage can either.

And since when does an individual's unalienable right to live depend upon somebody else "wanting" them? Whether a child is "unwanted" or not, does not justify killing that child. While it is true there are children who are neglected and abused, it can't be determined with any degree of certainty which babies will be born to loving parents or abusive ones.

Moreover, some who may be nurturing parents when a child is born, become abusive later in the child's life. The most unsuspecting, monied parents have abused their children, while parents from poverty have raised children to be emotionally well-adjusted and productive adults.

Condoning abortion because there are "too many unwanted children" cannot be justified since a person can't determine with any degree of certainty which circumstances or lives their children will have. Even if someone has the ability to make such a determination, it wouldn't justify killing a developing child. The decision to kill a baby should never be the result of somebody's subjective feelings. A woman who might consider her child to be an "inconvenience" is not justified in killing the child.

While nobody would disagree with Planned Parenthood's slogan "Every Child is a Wanted Child," the notion that another human being's right to life is contingent upon another human being's deeming him or her "wanted," harkens back to Hitler's Germany where Jews, Gypsies and Catholics were considered inferior to the Aryan "Master Race" and the "unwanted" were sent to the gas chambers.

Time Magazine reported in 1990 there were at least 6 million unwanted pregnancies in the United States each year. However, that year there were only 4 million births, about 1.6 million abortions and 400,000 miscarriages. The number of "unwanted" pregnancies has been significantly inflated in order to make the case for abortion more reasonable and appealing.[11]

The fact is, there are many more couples in our country who want to adopt (currently 200,000) than babies available for adoption (about 25,000 each year). Many of these families are forced to adopt babies from other countries such as Russia and China, having to spend tens of thousands of dollars to do so. There are many more couples who want children than children available for adoption.

CLAIM #4: "The fetus is part of the pregnant-woman's body, like her tonsils or appendix. A woman has the right to do what she wishes with any 'part' of her own body."

RESPONSE: A baby is a distinct human being apart from his or her mother.

Human beings shouldn't be discriminated against based on where they reside.

A body part is defined by the common genetic code it shares with the rest of the body. An unborn baby's genetic code differs entirely from the mother's. It's not part of the woman's body. The fetus merely resides in the mother's womb.

While the baby does reside physically in the mother's womb,

biologically this unique individual human being is not a physical part or organ belonging to the mother. Therefore, the mother's "right" to "control her own body" ends at the edge of the womb. The mother has the "right" to control the food she chooses to put into her body, but she does *not* have the "right" to kill another distinct human life in her womb.

Carol Everett of Dallas, Texas, after having an abortion herself, ended up running five abortion clinics. She admits she and her staff, like most abortionists, routinely lied to the pregnant girls who came to them.

She wrote in an article for *All About Issues Magazine*, "Every woman [who walks into the clinic] has two questions: Does it hurt? and Is it a baby? No, the counselor assures her. It's a blood clot or ball of cells. Even though these counselors see six-week babies daily, with arms, legs, toes and eyes that are closed like newborn puppies, they lie to the women. How many people would have an abortion, if we told them the truth?"[12]

In a testimonial to students at Vanderbilt University, Everett wrote, "I cannot tell you one thing that happens in an abortion clinic that is not a lie."[13]

Abortion clinic worker Norma Eidelman, who worked with second-trimester patients, admits clinic staff routinely lied to pregnant women about the "humanness" of their fetuses.

"We tried to avoid the women seeing them [the fetuses]," says Eidelman. "They always wanted to know the sex, but we lied and said it was too early to tell. It was better for the women to think of the fetus as an 'it.'"[14]

CLAIM #5: "The unborn is an embryo, a fetus—just a simple blob of tissue—not a baby. Abortion is simply terminating a pregnancy, not killing a child."

RESPONSE: The Latin word "fetus" means "little child" or "young one."

The very word used to describe a baby developing in the womb implies that it *is* a human, not just a blob. And those who have worked in abortion clinics know firsthand they're taking the life of a living human being.

Abortion worker Kathy Sparks, who worked in a Granite City, Illinois abortion clinic, recounts her experiences in *The Conversion of Kathy Sparks* by Gloria Williamson.

"Sometimes we lied," said Sparks. "A girl might ask what her baby was like at a certain point in the pregnancy: Was it a baby yet? Even as early as 12 weeks a baby is totally formed, he has fingerprints, turns his head, fans his toes, feels pain. But we would say 'it's not a baby yet. It's just tissue, like a clot.'"[15]

Those who are pro-abortion should be forced to justify supporting, condoning and encouraging the arbitrary taking of life.

CLAIM #6: "It is uncertain when human life begins. Therefore it's a religious question, not a scientific one."

RESPONSE: It is an undisputed biological scientific fact that human life begins at conception.

While there are a variety of religious and philosophic beliefs and theories pertaining to when life begins, scientifically life begins at conception—at the union of the father's sperm and the mother's ovum—a process called fertilization or "fecundation."

From the very moment of conception, the fetus contains all the genetic information that baby will have for the remainder of his or her lifetime. Any embryology book in any medical school will confirm that this new, unique, human creation is a defined sex and is alive, complete and growing.

At the very moment of conception, this creation is completely human in every one of his or her characteristics, totally unique from any other living organism. The new developing baby has the same forty-six human chromosomes he or she will have until death. Fetuses are living Homo sapiens who contain *separate* and *unique* chromosomal structures from their mothers.

That means they deserve all the same "rights" to life that other individuals enjoy. Even if someone has doubts, there are enough reasonable biological facts to give an unborn baby the benefit of the doubt. If you're not sure if someone's dead or alive, you don't bury them, right?

Dr. Bernard Nathanson, a former abortionist who was personally responsible for 75,000 abortions and co-founded the pro-abortion National Association for the Repeal of the Abortion Laws (NARAL), had a change of heart, rejecting abortion on scientific grounds. Writing in the *New England Journal of Medicine*, Dr. Nathanson admitted he has come to know life begins at conception.

"There is no longer serious doubt in my mind," he wrote, "that human life exists from the very onset of pregnancy."[16]

The sacred protection of life should be the final word on this topic. The United States Declaration of Independence affirms that the first and most sacred right is the right to life: "We hold these Truths to be self-evident, that all Men are created equal, that they are endowed by their Creator with certain unalienable Rights, that among these are Life, Liberty and the Pursuit of Happiness..."

No human being should be discriminated against based on his or her stage of development, place of residence (inside the womb) or arbitrary notion of "when life begins."

CLAIM #7: "A fetus isn't a 'person' until it can survive on its own outside the womb."

RESPONSE: Survival isn't the measure of humanness or a baby's right to live.

The stage of fetal development when the baby is "potentially able to live outside the mother's womb albeit with artificial help," is called "viability" in *Roe v. Wade*, U.S. Supreme Court, 1973.

But "viability" is constantly changing. As technology, knowledge, neonatal intensive care units and doctors improve, the age at which a baby can live outside the womb has decreased from 50 years ago when it was thirty weeks to twenty weeks today.[17]

On June 16, 1985, just outside Fort Lauderdale, Florida, baby Kenya Renee King was born prematurely at four-and-a-half months (twenty-one weeks), weighing just eighteen ounces. After birth, Kenya's weight dropped to thirteen ounces, but by the time she left the hospital, she weighed a life-sustaining five pounds.[18]

Regardless of "viability," the fact remains that a live human being or fetus—no matter how small—is formed at conception (fertilization).

Premeditated destruction of that live human being is legally defined as murder. Legalized murder is still murder.

CLAIM #8: "Every person has the right to choose. It would be unfair to restrict a woman's choice by prohibiting abortion."

RESPONSE: Nobody has the "right" to choose murder.

The fundamental question is not whether the mother has the "right" to choose to end the life of the developing baby inside her womb. The more fundamental question is whether abortion itself is morally and ethically right or wrong.

Most rights—except for the Constitution's guaranteed right to protect innocent life—have limitations. My freedom of speech does not include shouting "fire" in a crowded theatre. Similarly, a woman has certain rights to her own body—but there are limitations. As a matter of fact, the vast majority of Americans do believe there are certain limits to a "woman's right" to choose an abortion. About 80 to 90 percent of Americans in most polls oppose late-term abortions. President Bush signed a federal ban on this procedure, but this issue crosses party lines. The late Democratic Senator Daniel Patrick Moynihan, called it "infanticide."

In 1857, the U.S. Supreme Court ruled in the *Dred Scott* decision by a 7-2 vote, that black people were not "legal persons" and were property of the slave owners who were granted basic constitutional "rights" to own those slaves. Abolitionists were told if they disagreed with slavery, they didn't have to "own a slave" and were told not to "impose their morality on slave owners."

Similarly, in 1973, by a 7-2 decision, the Supreme Court ruled in *Roe v. Wade* that unborn humans were not "legal persons" and that they were, in essence, property of the owner (the mother) who had the constitutional right to kill her unborn baby. Pro-lifers who opposed abortion were told, like the early abolitionists, that if they opposed abortion, they shouldn't have one and shouldn't impose their morality on those who choose to.

Since it is a proven scientific fact that life begins at conception, the question is really whether a mother's so-called right to "privacy" transcends the baby's right to life. Neither the Declaration of Independence nor the Constitution ever mentions the "right to privacy," which has served as the foundation for the "right to abortion" emanating from the *Roe* decision. Both of our founding documents do, however, make it clear the right to *life*, not the right to *death*, is the primary objective of our democratic government.

Ironically, those on the left who support abortion "rights," don't offer pregnant women true "choice." Most, if not all, pro-life organizations which attempt to provide alternative solutions to pregnant woman are viewed as threats to abortion clinics which are hugely profitable, money-making businesses. The choice to abort is rarely, if ever, balanced with alternative options such as adoption.

CLAIM #9: "Every woman should have control over her own body. Reproductive freedom is a basic right."

RESPONSE: Then the 750,000 females aborted every year also should have the same right to control their own bodies.

Abortion takes the lives of approximately 1.5 million developing babies each year in our country. Half are females. Don't these females have the same constitutional "right" to control their own bodies which pregnant women purportedly have? What is the constitutional basis for discriminating against the most defenseless females in our society by robbing them of their right to life?

Nobody enjoys total control of his or her body. In most states, individuals are prohibited from selling their bodies for prostitution. People are also prohibited in most states from taking illegal drugs.

Women already enjoy "reproductive freedom" in the sense that they can control when they engage in sexual activity and reproduce. However, this "right" does not extend to the right to harm another individual (her baby). All freedoms have certain limitations with regard to how these freedoms impact the freedoms and rights of others.

CLAIM #10: "I'm personally against abortion, but I wouldn't impose my beliefs on some one else."

RESPONSE: To be "pro-choice" is to be "pro-abortion" and "pro-murder."

"Pro-choice" is the same as "pro-abortion." It legitimizes and condones it by supporting another's "right" to have or commit an abortion.

It's like claiming to be personally opposed to child abuse, but in favor of the "right" to abuse a child—an attitude which promotes the legitimacy and social acceptance of child abuse.

It's the same with abortion. Those who claim to be "pro-choice" believe they've taken a more "moderate," middle-of-the-road position than those who claim to be either "pro-abortion" or "pro-life." But you can't have it both ways. Either you believe all human life is sacred and deserves legal protection—or you don't.

People who are "pro-choice" vote the same way "pro-abortion" people vote. Both vote against conferring legal protection on the unborn. They condone the murder of developing babies. *You can't be pro-choice and pro-life simultaneously.*

Moreover, those who claim they can't "impose their religious beliefs on others," as John Kerry said during the 2004 presidential campaign, rely on a faulty premise.

The only thing "religious" about abortion is in the general sense that Judeo-Christian principles emphasize life, liberty and justice for the individual.

But abortion is primarily a *civil rights* issue. It's a question of whether or not an entire class of citizens should be deprived of "life, liberty and the pursuit of happiness" guaranteed to all American citizens under our Declaration of Independence. Civilized societies restrict individual freedoms when they harm innocent people.

It is a *biological* fact—not a religious or philosophical one—that human life begins at conception. By opposing abortion, you oppose the intentional destruction of human life.

If any religious beliefs have been "imposed" in our society, it has been the religion of Secular Humanism which primarily comprises the secular left. The "pro-choice" abortion rights movement is primarily comprised of those liberals who have since the early 1970s, attempted to impose their atheism and moral relativism on the rest of our society by supporting the total removal of voluntary school prayer, as well as the Ten Commandments and God from every corner of society, including the Pledge of Allegiance.

Abortion advocates claim to be "pro-choice"—meaning someone is free to either abort or keep their unborn child—but the reality is pro-choicers always fail to support allowing the fetus to develop to full-term and be born.

Those who are pro-life recognize and acknowledge the biological humanity of the human fetus and oppose its destruction at any stage of development. They believe life cannot be arbitrarily destroyed.

The pro-choicers and pro-abortionists say women have a right to choose. But what about the babies? Do they get to choose? Babies certainly don't "choose" abortion, any more than African Americans "chose" slavery, or the Jews "chose" to be killed in ovens in the Holocaust.

CLAIM #11: "Abortion is legal. Things that are 'legal' are OK, aren't they?"

RESPONSE: What is legal is not always ethically or morally right.

Substantial majorities of Americans oppose same-sex marriage, race-based preferences and abortion on demand without restrictions. Yet activist liberal courts have, by judicial fiat, legally recognized these practices. They are technically legal, in spite of the fact the vast majority of Americans deem them immoral and contrary to acceptable modes of behavior.

The fact of the matter is some of our laws are immoral. Just because slavery was "legal" didn't make it ethical. Just because it was "illegal" for women to vote didn't make it moral. Just because activist judges have arbitrarily concluded that women have a "right" to end the lives of their developing babies doesn't make the "procedure" morally right.

Laws may change, but truth and justice don't.

CLAIM #12: "Abortion helps solve the overpopulation problem."

RESPONSE: **The world isn't overpopulated. The reason population is increasing in many Western nations is because of immigration and increased life expectancy of those already here, not because of too many births.**

Birth rates continue to decline significantly, posing a more vital threat to the world than the myth of "overpopulation."

Most Western nations face a rapidly aging population. In 1970, life expectancy in the U.S. was seventy years. In 1993, it was seventy-six years. By 2050, it is estimated to be eighty-two years, primarily as a result of innovations in medical technology, health care and improvements in agricultural production.[19]

Population increases in Western industrialized nations are due to burgeoning immigration, not rising birth rates. The U.S. is becoming more Hispanic and countries such as Germany, France and Greece are becoming more Muslim—while birth rates in these countries continue to decline.[20]

In Italy, for example, the birth rate is 1.2 children per woman— one of the lowest in the world. In 1993, there were 5,265 more Italians buried than were born. If this trend continues, the population in Italy within the next 100 years will decrease from 57 million to 15 million, with half the population over 65 years old.[21] Among non-Muslims in Russia, the trend is even worse. The birth rate in the mid 1990s was 1.0—and deaths exceeded births by more than 1 million per year.[22]

Underdeveloped nations such as India, Mexico, Brazil, South Korea and Indonesia face zero population growth from declining birth rates.

The 1994 analytical report entitled *How Much Land Can Ten Billion People Spare for Nature?*, written by a consortium of thirty major U.S. agricultural societies and published with the cooperation of the Rockefeller Foundation, concluded the earth can feed everyone—even if the population doubles to ten billion people.[23]

No one can say with any degree of certainty how many people the earth can sustain. As technology and productivity increase exponentially, people around the world, on average, continue to enjoy higher standards of living, better health and longer life expectancy. The focus should be to ensure that the people who do populate the planet live the highest quality of life possible by improving technology, education and health care, while promoting democracy, the rule of law and free markets—traditionally the most important determinants of high standards of living. The focus should not be on promoting worldwide "population control" which is a euphemism for abortion.

CLAIM #13: "If abortion is made illegal, thousands of women will die from back alley and coat hanger abortions."

RESPONSE: Women have died from legal abortions.

Prior to legalization, ninety percent of abortions were done by physicians in their offices, not in back alleys. Even today, women still suffer and die from "legal" abortions in America.[24]

In *Aborting America,* Dr. Bernard Nathanson, who co-founded the pro-abortion organization NARAL and who is responsible for 75,000 abortions, admits the statistics as to how many women would die in "back alleys" were "totally false."

Dr. Nathanson said, "In NARAL, we generally emphasized the drama of the individual case, not the mass statistics, but when we spoke of the latter, it was always '5,000 to 10,000 deaths a year.' I confess that I know the figures were totally false and I suppose that the others did, too, if they stopped to think of it. But in the 'morality' of our revolution, it was a useful figure, widely accepted, so why go out of our way to correct it with honest statistics?"[25]

Prior to *Roe v. Wade*, legalizing abortion on demand nation-wide, abortion was permitted in California beginning in 1967 and in New York beginning in 1970. Legalization in these two states should have saved women's lives. However, no decline occurred.[26]

Prior to the 1973 U.S. Supreme Court decision which allowed abortion on demand in all fifty states, the number of illegal abortions declined. In 1973, the year after abortion on demand was made legal, the death rate from illegally performed abortions remained flat according to U.S. Vital Statistics.[27]

Prior to legalization of abortion in the 1950s and '60s, even pro-abortion advocates acknowledged that trained accredited physicians—not "back-alley butchers"—performed the vast majority of abortions.

"Ninety percent of illegal abortions are being done by physicians," said Dr. Mary Calderone, founder of Sexuality Information and Education Council of the United States (SIECUS) and medical director of the Planned Parenthood Federation of America. "Call them what you will, abortionists or anything else, they are still physicians, trained as such...They must do a pretty good job if the death rate is as low as it is...Abortion, whether therapeutic or illegal, is in the main no longer dangerous, because it is being done well by physicians."[28]

As to the "coat-hanger" abortions which abortion rights advocates claim would take place if abortion were illegal, there have never been any documented cases of such a gruesome procedure being performed according to the U.S. Department of Vital Statistics.[29]

In Poland, following the establishment of democratic self-government in 1990, abortion rights advocates warned if abortions were made illegal many women would die from "illegal back-alley" abortions. In fact, not a single death was reported due to any illegal abortion—exactly the opposite of what International Planned Parenthood people in Poland predicted. Not only was the total number of abortions reduced from 59,417 in 1990 to 782 in 1994, but women's deaths connected to pregnancy also declined. In 1990, 90 women died and in 1994, 57 women died. Miscarriages also declined—from 59,454 to 49,970, as well as cases of infanticide which declined from 31 to 17.[30]

CLAIM #14: "Abortion is a safe medical procedure, safer than full-term pregnancy and childbirth."

RESPONSE: Abortion kills the child and can result in significantly higher complications for the mother including death.

Woman can suffer complications such as: injuries to the uterus and cervix; urinary tract infections (Pelvic Inflammatory Disease); hemorrhaging; miscarriages; heart failure; embolisms; sterilizations; ruptured intestines and bowels; comas; subsequent Ectopic (tubal) pregnancies and, in some cases, death. Additionally, women who have abortions suffer mental health declines, while those who deliver their babies actually have improved mental health.

A study from Finland, which analyzed the accuracy of the statistics in pregnancy-related deaths, found that women who had an abortion were almost four times as likely to die as women who gave birth. For every 100,000 pregnancies, twenty-seven women die during full-term live births, compared to forty-eight women who die during miscarriages and 101 women who die during abortions.[31]

There are also a number of serious physical and emotional complications which result from abortion.

Seventeen percent of women participating in a study on the effects of abortion reported they have "experienced physical complications (e.g., abnormal bleeding or pelvic infection) since their abortion." Based on reported abortion statistics, this represents 200,000 women annually experiencing physical complications after an abortion.[32]

Abortion can adversely affect later pregnancies. Research has found that women having abortions are more likely to have a low birth-weight baby in a later pregnancy. There are also indications having an abortion can increase a woman's chances of delivering prematurely and having multiple abortions increases a woman's chance of having a miscarriage in a later pregnancy.[33, 34] All women, especially young teenagers, are at risk for damage to their cervix during an abortion, which can lead to complications with later pregnancies.[35]

Abortion can increase the risk for breast cancer, according to the February 2000 issue of *The New England Journal of Medicine*.[36, 37]

Women who ended their first pregnancy by abortion are five times more likely to report subsequent substance abuse than women who carried the pregnancy to term and they're four times more likely to report substance abuse compared to those whose first pregnancy ended naturally through miscarriage.[38]

According to research published in the *Archives of General Psychiatry*, many women experience post-traumatic stress disorder (PTSD) following an abortion. In one of the longest running studies ever done which followed women after an abortion, researchers found over time, negative emotions increased, including dreams and flashbacks to the abortion. There was also an increased numbing of responsiveness not present prior to the abortion and more difficulty sleeping. Of the women in the study, twenty-eight percent said they were either indifferent about, or dissatisfied with, the abortion and thirty-one percent said they were uncertain or would not have an abortion again.[39]

As many as sixty percent of women experience some level of emotional distress following their abortions. In thirty percent of women, the distress is classified as severe.[40]

Welch researchers examined abortion and suicide and found "our data suggests that a deterioration in mental health may be a consequential side effect of induced abortion."[41]

CLAIM #15: "Abortions are necessary for women whose lives are threatened by pregnancy or childbirth."

RESPONSE: Doctors say there is never a reason for an unborn child to be intentionally destroyed to save the life of the mother.

More than 100 physicians—including former abortionists Bernard Nathanson and Beverly McMillan—signed this statement:

"I agree that there is never a situation in the law or in the ethical practice of medicine where a pre-born [unborn] child's life need be intentionally destroyed by procured abortion for the purpose of saving the life of the mother. A physician must do everything possible to save the lives of both of his patients, mother and child. He must never intend the death of either."

Dr. C. Everett Koop, former U.S. Surgeon General, stated publicly that in his thirty-eight years as a pediatric surgeon, he was never aware of a single situation in which a pre-born child's life had to be taken in order to save the life of the mother. He said the use of this argument to justify abortion, in general, was a "smoke screen."[42]

Ron Fitzsimmons, executive director of the National Coalition of Abortion Providers admitted he "lied through his teeth" when he claimed late-term abortions were uncommon and used only in the most extreme situations. He admitted partial birth abortion was almost always performed on healthy mothers with healthy babies.[43]

CLAIM #16: "A woman who has been raped should be allowed to have an abortion."

RESPONSE: Less than one percent of all abortions are due to rape or incest.

Children shouldn't be punished for the crimes their parents commit. We wouldn't kill a four-year-old child if his father committed a murder, so why should we kill developing babies in the womb just because their biological fathers are guilty of rape or incest? Forced rape or incest is tragic, but in our society we don't kill the children of criminals.

This "what about in cases of rape or incest?" argument is often used by abortion defenders as a way to pander to people's natural sense of sympathy and compassion for victims of sexual crimes and to divert attention away from the developing baby who is killed inside the womb.

Even radical feminist Gloria Steinem in a 1985 interview with *USA Today* said, "To make abortion legal only in cases of rape and incest would force women to lie."[44]

In effect, Steinem acknowledged the rarity of abortions resulting from rape and incest and the likelihood that many women would lie to obtain an abortion if it were only "legal" in cases of rape and incest. In fact, Norma McCorvey ("Roe" in the famous *Roe v. Wade* decision) in order to obtain a legal abortion in Texas, fabricated a story that she had been gang raped at a circus. Now McCorvey says she lied—her baby was conceived "through what [she] thought was love."[45]

In fact, less than half of rape pregnancies are aborted. In one study of thirty-seven rape pregnancies, twenty-eight carried them to term.[46]

A woman who becomes pregnant as a result of rape is more concerned with whether people understand her trauma and support her or whether they will shun her and treat her as if it were her fault.[47]

Instead of encouraging her to kill her child, we should provide love, compassion and concern for both the mother and her baby—whether the mother chooses to raise the child herself or give up the baby for adoption.

Rape is violent, but when the pregnant woman decides to abort and kill her unborn child, she is taking part in a second act of violence. When she destroys that baby, she is destroying someone who is genetically half hers.

CLAIM #17: "I can't tell a woman what to do with her body."

RESPONSE: What about the separate body inside her womb?

What if that unborn baby is a male body—a little boy? Surely that can't be the mother's body because she can't be a man and a woman simultaneously.

If a woman becomes pregnant by her husband and the baby is a boy, then does the father—because he's the same gender, gave the baby life through his sperm and is genetically linked to the child—have some say in whether that developing baby lives or dies? Doesn't a biological father who opposes abortion have every right to proclaim his pro-life values to protect that innocent human life?

If females unilaterally have the "right" to dictate the life and/or death of the child inside her womb, then males certainly have a "right" to stand up for the life of the unborn.

CLAIM #18: "Abortion liberates women."

RESPONSE: Abortion liberates men by absolving them of responsibility for the children they create.

Females are more pro-life than males, according to most polls. Many men have avoided taking responsibility for the lives they helped to create by using abortion as a substitute for birth control.

Abortion allows men to escape responsibility for their sexual behavior, including financial and emotional support. It's not surprising the Playboy Foundation is a major supporter of abortion rights because abortion is a natural consequence of *Playboy Magazine*'s ideal of uncommitted, anonymous sex without consequences. Women are reduced to the status of a consumer item which, if "broken" by pregnancy, can be "fixed" by abortion.

Feminists who have adopted this philosophy that abortion "liberates women" are actually saying a pregnant woman is inferior to a non-pregnant woman. They've additionally embraced the male position that it's acceptable to oppress the weak by utilizing physical violence against women and children.

There's nothing "liberating" about being complicit in the deliberate murder of a pre-born child. The notion perpetuated by the radical leftist feminist movement that true liberation and freedom are synonymous with paying a physician to suck out pregnant women's developing babies, dismember them with surgical scissors and discard the babies in a trash receptacle, is contrary to the larger philosophy of feminism which values all human life.

Feminists who are truly liberated realize all human beings have an inherent net worth. True feminists realize violence used against the smallest and most defenseless is always immoral and contrary to the primary female role as nurturer and giver of life. True feminists oppose any attempt by our male-dominated society to sacrifice children for convenience, refusing to participate in their own oppression and the oppression of their children.

Truly liberated women recognize abortion denigrates the life-giving capacity of women. They realize the Patricia Irelands and Margaret Sangers of the world have lied to them since the counterculture revolution of the 1960s and their "liberation" has resulted in the murder of close to 40 million babies since abortion became legal nation-wide in 1973.

Truly "liberated" women oppose the destruction of children resulting from abortion and are staunchly pro-life.

CLAIM #19: "Women have a constitutional right to abortion because the courts have ruled women have a right of privacy."

RESPONSE: Roe v. Wade is not constitutional law.

That's according to the late John Hart Ely, a pro-abortionist who taught law at Yale, Harvard and the University of Miami, as well as being dean of Stanford Law School.

Ely said, "Roe is a very bad decision. It is bad because it is bad constitutional law, or rather because it is not constitutional law and gives almost no sense of an obligation to try to be."[48]

Roe v. Wade gave women the "right" to have an abortion in any state, but relied on a flawed interpretation of the Constitution—the very definition of judicial activism.

Nowhere in the Constitution is the "right to privacy" mentioned, even though the court ruled just the opposite—that a "right to privacy" exists in the Constitution, which is broad enough to "encompass a woman's decision whether or not to terminate her pregnancy."

The issue is not about the woman's body and her right to privacy as much as it is about the innocent individual life growing inside it.

"Privacy" isn't mentioned in the Declaration of Independence or the Constitution either. Instead, the Declaration of Independence says "all men are created equal…[and] are endowed by their Creator with certain inalienable rights such as life, liberty and the pursuit of happiness."

The most fundamental "right" of every American citizen, regardless of age or size, is and always will be life. The right to *life* trumps the so-called right of *privacy.*

The fact that government can regulate abortions (making late-term abortions illegal) disproves the notion that women have an unlimited "right to privacy." If abortion advocates want to use the "right of privacy" argument to justify abortion, they must also acknowledge the court ruled this so-called "right" is limited.

Norma McCorvey, the original Jane "Roe" in *Roe v. Wade*, is now vehemently pro-life. She has publicly stated abortion rights activists coerced her into bringing her lawsuit against Wade in 1972.

The original case found a "right of privacy" in the "emanations and penumbras" of the Constitution and was based on the fraudulent and coerced testimony of the plaintiff herself. She is currently attempting to have her case heard again in an effort to overturn the initial *Roe v. Wade* decision.

CLAIM #20: "I'm pro-choice, but I don't support partial-birth abortion."

RESPONSE: What's the difference between a developing baby at six months, thirty days,

twenty-three hours and fifty-nine seconds from a developing baby who is one second older at seven months?

Under the law, the second developing baby is protected from being aborted, but the first baby is not. Is the baby who is one second older than the first any more human? How can anybody claim it's inhumane to abort a seven-month-old developing baby, but killing one only seconds younger is morally acceptable? Why is the first baby not entitled to the same protections under the law of life the second baby is entitled to? Don't both babies deserve the same equal protection under the law as guaranteed by our Constitution? Why is it acceptable to discriminate against an entire class of developing babies solely based on some arbitrary demarcation?

If you oppose late term abortion because you recognize it is inhumane to kill the developing baby, you cannot rationalize killing a baby only seconds younger. Doing so makes an arbitrary judgment regarding a human life.

If it's wrong to kill an unborn child at seven or eight months, why is it right to kill an unborn baby at five or six months? Since all of them are live human beings at different stages of development, why is it "murder" to kill the seven to nine-month-old developing babies, but "choice" when babies under seven months old are killed?

The first week a baby starts developing in the womb, the sex and genetic traits are determined; the third week, the heart, brain and intestinal tract develops; the fourth week, the vertebra, eyes, arms and legs are developing and the blood is flowing. The fingers and toes appear in the sixth week, as well as the nose and ears. By the seventh week, the child has all the essential organs and is forming eyelids. By the thirteenth week—three months—the baby has hair, lungs and can move and suck it's thumb. By the seventeenth week, the circulatory system is working, the nails on the fingers and toes are growing and the baby can swallow. Fingerprints form in the twenty-first week—five months—and the baby can hear; by the twenty-fifth week—six months—the baby reacts to light and can probably survive outside the womb.

But legally you can still kill that baby.

Chapter 2

B is for Bill Clinton:

Sex, Lies and Blind Devotees

Claims:

1. "Whitewater never proved anything and exonerated Clinton, and it was a waste of taxpayer money."
2. "The Clinton Administration was no more scandalous than other administrations."
3. "Clinton's legacy was the 'strongest economy in a generation', '20-million new jobs created', and the 'end of welfare as we know it'."
4. "Clinton was guilty of some personal 'scandals' but murder? You crazy right wingers and your conspiracy theories."
5. "Bill Clinton was our nation's first 'black president'."
6. "President Clinton's affair with White House intern Monica Lewinsky was just sex. It's nobody's business what two consenting adults do in private."

There has never been as polarizing a political figure in U.S. history as President William Jefferson Clinton.

Elected president twice without ever achieving a majority of the popular vote, President Clinton became the only elected president in U.S. history to be impeached, disbarred from practicing law and accused by a credible witness of rape.

As chief beneficiary of President Reagan's world vision and the high technology boom of the 1990s, President Clinton enjoyed many of the benefits of presiding over relative peace and prosperity. The economy expanded significantly during his administration (despite the fact the vast majority of "dot-com startups" generated no actual revenues or profits) and America enjoyed a prolonged period of peace (if one ignores the multitude of terrorist attacks on the U.S. around the world which were, for the most part, ignored).

Beneath this thin veneer of economic prosperity, however, existed the most corrupt and scandalous administration in history.

President Clinton raised taxes on the backs of social security recipients, destroyed the morale of the military, unsuccessfully attempted to place one-seventh of the economy under the control of the federal government, increased the size, scope and intrusiveness of government, degraded the rule of law, sent those seeking refuge from Communist dictatorships back to their country of origin and, most tragically, failed to apprehend Osama bin Laden when given the chance.

Many in the press claim liberals hate George W. Bush like conservatives hated President Clinton and they're half right. Liberals do hate Bush—because of his conservative positions such as tax cuts, preemptive force, support for the death penalty, as well as opposition to homosexual "marriage," abortion and judicial activism.

Conservatives on the other hand don't limit their revulsion for President Clinton to his socialist policies and positions, but loath him for his utter lack of respect and regard for the esteemed office of the president, which manifested itself in the lies he told, the political power he abused and the treason many believe he committed.

Although the President Clinton spinmeisters are out in force to legitimize his presidency, a thorough examination of the facts disprove and debunk what the President Clinton apologists proclaim in their efforts to revise history.

> **CLAIM #1**: "Whitewater never proved anything, exonerated Clinton and was a waste of taxpayer money."
>
> **RESPONSE**: Independent Counsel Robert Ray's final report released the week of March 18, 2002, concluded Whitewater was a "serious bank fraud involving numerous Clinton intimates."

A dozen people went to jail. The main Clinton business partners Jim and Susan McDougal were convicted on multiple fraud and conspiracy charges. Former Arkansas Governor Jim Guy Tucker was convicted and so was the Clintons' close friend, Webb Hubbell, whom Mr. Clinton made the number three man at the Justice Department.[1]

<u>**CLAIM #2**</u>: "**The Clinton administration was no more scandalous than other administrations.**"

<u>**RESPONSE**</u>: **The Clinton administration was the most corrupt in the history of the Republic.**

The Clinton apologists constantly attempt to reconstruct and historically revise the "Clinton Legacy." Here is a snapshot of Bill Clinton's corruption and illegalities, in no particular order:

- Lied to the American people regarding the Monica Lewinsky relationship
- Lied under oath in the *Paula Jones* v. *Clinton* case
- Lied to Congress regarding Lewinsky
- Made false claims of memory loss
- Shredded documents
- Whitewater documents mysteriously disappeared and reappeared
- Misused FBI files
- Improperly claimed privileges
- Abused power
- Misused federal agencies
- Politicized the Justice Department, the IRS, the FBI, the BATF, the EPA and the FDA
- Demonized, smeared and destroyed witnesses
- Racked up campaign finance abuses such as the White House "coffees" and the "no controlling legal authority" Buddhist Temple fundraiser
- Laundered money

- Took illegal foreign campaign contributions
- Took donations from drug dealers, spies and international arms smugglers
- Allowed serious national security breaches at Loral Space Corporation and Los Alamos where computer hard drives disappeared
- Bombed Iraq and Kosovo to deflect attention from political problems
- Obstructed justice in *Paula Jones* v. *Clinton*
- Tampered with witnesses in *Paula Jones* v. *Clinton*
- Intimidated witnesses in *Paula Jones* v. *Clinton*
- Violated the Privacy Act
- Blackmailed people
- Repeatedly perjured himself
- Was in contempt of court
- Indulged in ridiculous adolescent sexual escapades
- Had credible accusations of rape brought against him[2]

CLAIM #3: "Clinton's legacy was the 'strongest economy in a generation,' with '20-million new jobs created' and the 'end of welfare as we know it.'"

RESPONSE: President Clinton's tax hikes and new regulations didn't fuel the economic boom of the 1990s.

True, the economy grew rapidly during President Clinton's term in office. However, there was no clear correlation between his economic policies of raising taxes and the strong economy.

The strong economic growth and surplus was the result of the technology boom, which former President Ronald Reagan's marginal tax rate cuts almost a decade earlier initially stimulated, in turn fueling massive risk-taking and capital investment in the private sector.

Entrepreneurs and risk takers, such as Bill Gates of Microsoft and Jerry Yang of Yahoo, aided the '90s economic boom, despite the 1993 Clinton tax hikes (on social security payments and marginal rates on income).

If anything, the private sector was able to flourish *in spite of* the tax increases and multitude of new regulations the Clinton administration imposed. The only major pieces of legislation which stimulated the economy during the Clinton administration were welfare reform and the lowering of the capital gains tax in 1998 (both of which were sponsored by the GOP-controlled Congress). Republicans in Congress were also primarily responsible for minimizing spending growth during the majority of the Clinton years in office.

The 1996 Republican Congress created the Welfare legislation which President Clinton reluctantly signed into law that, as Clinton said, "ended welfare as we know it today."

As for the surplus, President Clinton was the beneficiary of the "peace dividend" created when Ronald Reagan won the Cold War (allowing for defense spending cuts which proved to be too large in retrospect).

Clinton's True Legacy

The Clinton administration holds the all time record for having the greatest number of associates who have: resigned under fire; pleaded the Fifth; fled the country; gone to jail or died under mysterious circumstances.

Despite what liberals say to rehabilitate the Clinton legacy, nothing can change the fact Bill Clinton was the first elected president in U.S. history to be impeached, was the first to be disbarred from practicing law in his home state, was the first to pay $800,000 to settle a sexual harassment claim, was the first president in history to have a credible witness accuse him of rape, the first to pardon a convicted traitor and drug dealer and was the first to have sex with an intern his daughter's age while conducting national-security-sensitive foreign policy. That is the true Clinton legacy!

The U.S. was in bad shape at the end of Bill Clinton's administration. Although he asked in Reganesque fashion at his last State of the Union if "Americans were better off now than they were eight years ago?" it's clear he left the office of the president and the country in far worse condition than when he began his term.

Clinton Started the Recession

The "Bush Recession" actually started during 2000—the final year of the Clinton administration, according to the U.S. Department of Commerce. The U.S. economy shrank in the third quarter of 2000 from five percent GDP growth to negative 0.5 percent.

The panel of economists serving as official timekeepers for the nation's recessions acknowledged the economy started stalling in March 2000 and the recession officially began sometime between October and December 2000—Clinton's final months in office.

The Clinton recession officially ended in November 2001—during President George W. Bush's first year in office.[3]

Clinton's Impact on the U.S. Military

The military was in far worse shape after eight years of Clinton. Morale was at an all time low and there was widespread disdain for him within every branch of the military, especially because Clinton, a draft dodger, used the military as a U.N. police force around the world.

Clinton's Impact on National Security

National security was in bad shape, too. He sold our most sacred nuclear technology to the Chinese for campaign contributions and allowed our Los Alamos Nuclear Facility to suffer well-documented security breaches which included the loss of sensitive security hard drives. He passed up multiple opportunities to capture and kill Osama bin Laden, but chose not to do so because, as he told an audience in Long Island at a fundraiser in 2002, he had never felt there were any "legal" reasons to bring bin Laden to the U.S.

Under the Clinton Justice Department, Assistant Attorney General Jamie Gorelick played a pivotal role in erecting a "wall of separation" between the CIA and FBI—something which significantly weakened the CIA's ability to gather vital intelligence information on terrorists involved in 9/11.

Illegal immigration increased dramatically. Our borders became porous under President Clinton and the U.S. received 15 million new undocumented illegal immigrants, some of whom took part in the 9/11 attacks. At the same time, he sent those seeking freedom in the U.S. back to communist dictators.

On top of that, President Clinton conducted top secret national security while having sex in the Oval Office with an intern his daughter's age.

Clinton's Impact on the Federal Government

After eight years of Clinton, more than 500,000 new employees were added to the federal government's payroll.

The federal budget was bigger, jumping from $250 billion in '92 to $400 billion in 2000. Now that's what I call "reinventing government"—inventing new ways to fatten the government payroll and Democratic voters!

U.S. citizens paid the government more in taxes after eight years of Clinton. He and the Democrats raised taxes on the backs of social security recipients and unsuccessfully attempted to place one-seventh of the economy under the control of the federal government (Hillary Care).

There were more federal regulations and bureaucracy after his presidency, including thousands of regulations on individual small businesses and large corporations.

The environment suffered, too. Forest fires throughout the West caused massive economic and environmental devastation because they spread so fast—a result of Clinton's policy toward logging. The dead and dried brush which fuels forest fires could not be cleared because his administration declared 58 million acres in thirty-nine states off limits. That meant roads couldn't be built on those 58 million acres, which in turn meant firefighters didn't have fast access to battle the fires when they started from the dried brush.

Clinton vetoed tort reform, giving the green light to his trial lawyer cronies and contributors so they could bring lawsuits against private businesses such as tobacco companies, Microsoft and SUV manufacturers.

Drug use was up after eight years of Bill "I-never-inhaled" Clinton. Use of hard drugs such as cocaine, heroin, acid and ecstasy increased dramatically during the Clinton Administration.

CLAIM #4: "Clinton was guilty of some personal 'scandals' but murder? You crazy right wingers and your conspiracy theories."

RESPONSE: **There is a long list of those Bill and Hillary Clinton either intimately knew or were involved with who were murdered, mysteriously died, committed suicide or disappeared.**

Here's a partial list:

James McDougal

The Clintons' convicted Whitewater partner died of an apparent heart attack March 8, 1998 while in solitary confinement. He was a key witness in Ken Starr's investigation into the Clintons and was cooperating with Starr, preparing to give damaging testimony against them. The *Fort Worth Star-Telegram* reported McDougal died when he was denied his heart medication.[4]

Mary Caitrin Mahoney

The twenty-five-year-old former White House intern was murdered execution style along with two co-workers at the Starbucks Coffee Shop in the Georgetown area of Washington D.C. on July 6, 1997. There was no sign of forced entry and none of the $10,000 at the cafe was taken. *Newsweek* reporter Michael Isikoff had written that a former intern whose name was "M" was about to go public with sexual harassment charges. People speculated it was Mahoney, but later it turned out to be Monica Lewinsky.[5]

Vince Foster

The Deputy White House Counsel and Clintons' lawyer who had worked with Hillary Clinton at the Rose Law firm in Little Rock, Arkansas died from a gunshot wound to the head in July, 1993. His suspicious death was officially ruled a suicide, but the person who discovered Foster's body in a Washington, D.C. park said no gun was near his body.[6]

Ron Brown

The Secretary of Commerce and former Democratic National Committee chairman is reported to have died in a plane crash in Croatia on April 3, 1996. But a pathologist close to the investigation reported there was a hole in the top of Brown's skull resembling a gunshot wound. At the time of his death, Brown was being investigated and had spoken publicly of his willingness to cut a deal with prosecutors.[7]

C. Victor Raiser II and Montgomery Raiser

Victor Raiser and his son Montgomery were said to be "major players" in the Clinton fundraising organization. They died in a private plane crash in Alaska on July 30, 1992.[8]

Paul Tulley

The DNC political director and top strategist was found dead in a hotel room in Little Rock, in September, 1992. Clinton described him as a "dear friend and trusted advisor."[9]

Ed Willey

Hunters found the body of the Clinton fundraiser deep in the Virginia woods on November 29, 1993. Willey's death was ruled a suicide by shotgun. He died the same day his wife Kathleen Willey claimed Bill Clinton groped her at the White House in the Oval Office.[10]

Jerry "Luther" Parks

The former head of security for the Clinton-Gore headquarters in Little Rock, Arkansas was gunned down in his car September 26, 1996—two months after Vince Foster's death. Parks' son said he was building a dossier on Clinton's sexual escapades and had allegedly threatened to reveal this information. The files mysteriously disappeared from his house in a burglary a few weeks before his murder.[11]

James Bunch

Bunch reportedly had a little black book with the names of influential people in Arkansas and Texas who had visited prostitutes. He died from a gunshot which was ruled a suicide.[12]

James Wilson

Wilson, a politician in Washington, D.C. who was known as "John" Wilson, reportedly had ties to Whitewater. His death on May 19, 1993 was ruled an apparent suicide from hanging.[13]

Kathy Ferguson and Bill Shelton

Kathy Ferguson's ex-husband, Arkansas State Trooper Danny Ferguson, was a co-defendant with Bill Clinton in the Paula Jones lawsuit. Ferguson herself was a possible witness for Paula Jones. On May 11, 1994, five days after Jones filed her sexual harassment lawsuit against Clinton, Kathy Ferguson was found dead in her fiancé's apartment. The cause of death was a gunshot to her head and was ruled a suicide, even though several packed suitcases were nearby, as if she was getting ready to leave.

Her fiancé, Bill Shelton, a Sherwood, Arkansas police officer, publically objected to his fiancé's death being ruled a suicide. One month after her death, he was found dead on top of her grave. His death, which was from a gunshot wound similar to Kathy Ferguson's, was also ruled a suicide.[14]

Gandy Baugh

Baugh was an attorney for the Clinton's friend Dan Lassater, a convicted drug dealer. Baugh fell to his death from a window of a multi-story building on January 8, 1994.[15]

Florence Martin

Martin, an accountant and subcontractor for the CIA, was linked to arms and drug smuggling being run out of the airport in Mena, Arkansas while Bill Clinton was governor. She died after being shot three times.[16]

Suzanne Coleman

Coleman allegedly had an affair with Clinton when he was Arkansas Attorney General—and her law professor. Her death was ruled a suicide even though she died from a gunshot wound to the back of her head. Coleman was pregnant at the time of her death. The baby was rumored to have been Clinton's.[17]

Paula Grober

Clinton's speech interpreter for the deaf died in a one-car accident December 9, 1992.[18]

Danny Casolaro and Paul Wilcher

Casolaro was a reporter investigating whether drugs and weapons were being smuggled into the airport in Mena, Arkansas while Bill Clinton was governor. He was also investigating the Arkansas Development Finance Authority. Casolaro was found in a West Virginia hotel room August 10, 1991—his wrists slashed. *People Magazine* reported he'd told family and friends he feared his life was in danger.

Paul Wilcher was an attorney working with Casolaro to investigate the alleged corruption at Mena's airport. He was found dead in his Washington D.C. apartment June 22, 1993, three weeks after he'd delivered his report to then Attorney General Janet Reno. He told Reno in the report that he was in grave danger and if sensitive information in the report was leaked to the wrong people, some would be "silenced in the very near future."[19]

Jon Parnell Walker

Walker, a Whitewater investigator for Resolution Trust Corporation, fell to his death from the balcony of his Arlington, Virginia apartment August 15, 1993. He was investigating the Morgan Guarantee scandal.[20]

Barbara Wise

The Commerce Department staffer had worked closely with Commerce Secretary Ron Brown, as well as fund-raiser and Commerce Department employee John Huang, who had extraordinary access to President Clinton. Wise's bruised and partially nude body was found in a locked office at the Department of Commerce on November 29, 1996.[21]

Charles Meissner

Meissner, Assistant Secretary of Commerce under Clinton who gave John Huang special security clearance, died with Ron Brown in a plane crash in Croatia on April 3, 1996.[22]

Dr. Stanley Heard

Dr. Heard, Chairman of the National Chiropractic Health Care Advisory Committee, worked on Clinton's advisory council and personally treated the president's mother, stepfather and brother. Heard and his attorney, Steve Dickson, died in a small plane crash.[23]

Barry Seal

Seal, a CIA pilot who smuggled drugs and arms through the Mena, Arkansas airport while Bill Clinton was governor was murdered in Louisiana in 1986, machine-gunned by three men allegedly connected with the Medellin drug cartel.[24]

Johnny Franklin Lawhorn, Jr.

Lawhorn, a mechanic, found Whitewater documents and a cashier's check made out to Clinton in the trunk of a car left at his transmission shop. He was killed when his speeding car hit a utility pole.[25]

Stanley Huggins

Huggins, an attorney investigating Madison Guarantee Savings and Loan, reportedly died of viral pneumonia in July, 1994. His 300-page report on Madison was never released.[26]

Hershell Friday

The attorney and Clinton fundraiser died March 1, 1994 when his plane crashed and exploded while trying to land. The NTSB said there may have been an electrical failure in his instrument panel which contributed to the crash.[27]

Kevin Ives and Don Henry

Reports say the boys may have stumbled upon the Mena, Arkansas Airport drug and arms smuggling operation. Their bodies were found after they were hit by a train on August 23, 1987. The conductor of the train which hit them, said the bodies were partially covered with a green tarp, lying between the tracks, a shotgun at their side. The boys were first said to have died after falling asleep on the tracks and being run over by the train, but later reports said they'd been killed elsewhere and their bodies then placed on the tracks. Ives' skull had been smashed and Henry had been stabbed in the back.[28]

Seven of those with information about the case died before their testimony could come before a Grand Jury:

Keith Coney died in July, 1988 when his motorcycle hit the back of a truck.[29]

Keith Mcmaskie died in November, 1988 when he was stabbed 113 times.[30]

Gregory Collins died in January, 1989 from a gunshot wound.[31]

Jeff Rhodes was found in a trash dump, on April 1989. He'd been shot, mutilated and burned.[32]

James Milan was found decapitated. The coroner ruled his death was due to "natural causes."[33]

Jordan Kettleson was found shot to death in the front seat of his pickup truck in June, 1990.[34]

Richard Winters, a suspect in the boys' death, was killed in an alleged robbery in July, 1989.[35]

Major William S. Barkley Jr., Captain Scott J. Reynolds, Sergeant Brian Hanley, Sergeant Tim Sabel, Major General William Robertson, Col. William Dansberger, Col. Robert Kelly, Spec. Gary Rhodes, Steve Willis, Robert Williams, Conway LeBleu and Todd Mckeehan.[36]

All twelve of these Clinton bodyguards died of unnatural causes. Coincidence? You decide.

CLAIM #5: "Bill Clinton was our nation's first 'black president.'"

RESPONSE: President Clinton may have been a friend to the rich and powerful Black Establishment, but his policies and positions weren't friendly to mainstream blacks.

Even though President Clinton played the saxophone in black sunglasses on late-night television and was often photographed with his wealthy black lawyer golfing pal, Vernon Jordan, he wasn't always a friend to blacks.

The GOP House and Senate passed legislation which took hundreds of thousands of blacks off the government welfare rolls, giving them the incentive and opportunity to work, but President Clinton only reluctantly signed it into law.

He opposed a voucher pilot program for the worst performing schools in the District of Columbia which would have given about 2,000 black children in under-performing schools the opportunity to attend private or charter school programs. Even though nationally in most polls seventy percent of black parents support these types of programs, Clinton opposed it to appease his financial contributors from the powerful National Education Association (NEA).

President Clinton gave the Medal of Honor to William Allen Fulbright, an ex-segregationist and opponent of the Civil Rights Act of 1964, calling the ex-senator a "visionary."

Clinton didn't select any persons of "color" for his highest level cabinet positions in eight years—with the exception of Secretary of

Commerce Ron Brown who was killed suspiciously while in office—only white, mostly white male liberals.

Clinton's sexual improprieties and indiscretions (adulterous behavior) set a terrible example for the black community where the number one problem they face is illegitimacy and fatherlessness.

Crime, illegitimacy, literacy, drug use and housing became worse for blacks in America during the Clinton administration.

President Bill Clinton represented everything that plagues the black community the most. Because of his irresponsible "if it feels good do it" behavior, he made others feel better about their own failings. Clinton's behavior and actions, if anything, provided a certain moral justification for other black males who acted similarly.

If President Clinton had wanted to really improve the plight of blacks in our country, he would have set a positive example by stressing the importance of fidelity in marriage and responsible, mature and upright behavior. He would have stressed Dr. King's dream of a "color-blind" society, instead of favoring race-based "affirmative action" which uses race to discriminate. He would have supported school choice for black parents.

Instead, President Clinton pandered to the black community and largely ignored their most vital needs and concerns.

He didn't unify our country. He did everything in his power to divide it to maintain a large voting block during election time.

CLAIM #6: "Bill Clinton's affair with White House intern Monica Lewinsky was just sex. It's nobody's business what two consenting adults do in private."

RESPONSE: Consensual sex may be a private matter, but when a sexual relationship influences a public court case involving the president of the United States, the consensual sex becomes publicly relevant.

President Bill Clinton obstructed justice.

Those on the left claim the Lewinsky affair was nobody's business because of its "private nature." Yet, as soon as the affair became public news, it ceased to be a "private matter." The sexual acts between President Clinton and Lewinsky took place in the Oval Office (paid for by taxpayers' money).

Not only that, President Clinton attempted to use his political power to fix a court case where he was the lone defendant. The Clinton apologists who assert it was "just sex" miss the larger point. The issue isn't whether it was legally permissible for the two to engage in sexual acts of perversion with cigars, it's that it wasn't "legal" to hide the relationship from investigators in the Paula Jones' sexual harassment case.

When Jones accused the president—alleging while he was governor of Arkansas, he'd pulled down his pants and told her to "kiss it"—she had to demonstrate he'd exhibited a clear pattern of this type of behavior in the past.

Lewinsky fit the pattern of President Clinton's sexual exploitation of women. When Linda Tripp recorded phone conversations of Lewinsky discussing her affair with Clinton, those recordings became vital to Jones' case. That's why Jones' attorneys called her before the Grand Jury to testify.

But President Clinton, in essence, tried to fix the Jones' court case by persuading witnesses to lie about his relationship with Lewinsky, claiming at first she had only delivered "pizza to the president."

He also made calls to Betty Curry, his secretary, asking her to hide gifts he had previously purchased for Lewinsky. President Clinton lied about the nature of his relationship with Lewinsky—before the tapes and her "blue dress" stained with his semen surfaced. He then asked other witnesses to lie on his behalf in front of the Grand Jury—both of which are federal crimes.

The Lewinsky scandal was much more than a private sexual matter, as those on the left continue to claim even today. The main issue, which this assertion conveniently ignores, is that when the Lewinsky relationship went public, President Clinton had a legal obligation not to interfere with the Jones' case in which he was the defendant. Jones had every legal right to call Lewinsky and other pertinent witnesses to testify to build her case. When Clinton perjured himself, suborned the perjury of others and tampered with witnesses, he obstructed justice.

President Clinton violated his sworn oath to uphold and

defend the Constitution and the laws of our country. What he did in the final analysis was far more destructive than merely conducting an immoral and indiscrete sexual relationship with an intern in the Oval Office (and via the telephone, which, by the way, could have easily been intercepted by a foreign nation hostile to the U.S.).

As the Chief Executive of the United States—arguably the most powerful person in the free world—President Clinton had the sacred and sworn obligation to protect, defend and uphold the Constitution and laws of our country. Because the president is entrusted with seeing the laws of our country are faithfully and properly executed, any breach of that duty and obligation by the president himself can have disastrous consequences for the entire country.

If the president doesn't follow the laws, and he is the chief executive primarily responsible for enforcing them, why should an average citizen comply with the law? Is it any wonder corporate corruption and moral decline in our nation during the Clinton Administration was so pervasive?

Our country was founded upon the rule of law. Lady Liberty is blindfolded to denote the impartiality and equality under the law available to all citizens of our justice system regardless of their status. President Clinton attempted to remove the blindfold to manipulate the legal system in his favor. He attempted to use the power and influence of his government authority to manipulate the outcome of a court case brought against him by a private citizen.

That's what the case was about. "Sex between two consenting adults" had nothing to do with President Clinton's far worse dereliction and violation of his duty as chief executor of the laws of the United States of America.

Chapter 3

C is for Church and State:

What Our Constitution Says About Religion

Claims:
1. "The Constitution mandates the separation of church and state."
2. "America is a secular nation, not a Judeo-Christian one, whose founding documents- the Declaration of Independence and the Constitution- were based on secular principles."
3. "Republicans and conservatives are fascists and Nazis who are always imposing their Christian moral values on others."
4. " Separation of Church and State prohibits any mention of God in public places."
5. "Prayer in schools is unconstitutional."
6. "Government has a responsibility to create and sustain an environment of neutrality so that no citizen is offended by the religious speech of another."

The liberal left has repeated the phrase "separation of church and state" so often the majority of the American public believe the words actually appear in our Constitution.

They don't. That phrase doesn't exist in our Constitution, Bill of Rights or Declaration of Independence. Rather, the phrase appeared in a private letter Thomas Jefferson wrote on January 1, 1802— eleven years after the First Amendment was ratified.

By improperly attributing Jefferson's private words to the Constitution, the left has attempted to revise history and the true meaning of the First Amendment. Their hope, it would seem, is to dismantle the religious underpinnings of America by distorting and manipulating the First Amendment to justify their staunch opposition to conservative federal court nominees, school choice, faith-based initiatives, traditional marriage, voluntary school prayer, recitation of the pledge of allegiance, the flying of the American flag and the posting of the Ten Commandments in schools and courthouses.

Here's what the First Amendment of the Bill of Rights of the U.S. Constitution actually says:

"Congress shall make no law respecting an establishment of religion, or prohibiting the free exercise thereof; or abridging freedom of speech or of the press; or the right of the people peaceably to assemble and to petition the government for a redress of grievances."

A more thorough examination of the First Amendment and those who authored and debated it reveals the Founders never intended there be a wall between church and state. The intent was for individual American citizens to be assured of uninhibited freedom to practice their religion, unencumbered by the constraints of the federal government.

CLAIM #1: "The Constitution mandates the separation of church and state."

RESPONSE: The First Amendment ensures freedom of religion, not freedom from religion.

The First Amendment clearly spells out that "Congress shall make no law respecting an establishment of religion; or prohibiting the free exercise thereof."

The First Amendment was written with the intent of preventing the United States from establishing a national religion, to give American citizens total religious freedom without the fear of being coerced to show devotion to any particular national religion.

"Free exercise" means Americans can profess their religious beliefs—whatever they may or may not be—in any manner, any time and in any place without prohibition from the government and the courts.

C IS FOR CHURCH AND STATE: *WHAT OUR CONSTITUTION SAYS ABOUT RELIGION*

The complete discussions of the Founding Fathers vis-a-vis the First Amendment is contained in the Congressional Records from June 7 to September 25, 1789. Nowhere in these discussions is the term "separation of church and state" ever mentioned.[1]

The term "separation of church and state" originated primarily from two different sources—the Danbury Letter and the Supreme Court case of *Everson v. Board of Education*.

The Danbury Letter is a private letter Thomas Jefferson wrote to the Association of Danbury Baptists, eleven years after the ratification of the First Amendment. He used the term "a wall of separation between church and state" to assure the Baptists the federal government would not establish a federally recognized "state" religion.

In *Everson v. Board of Education*, the Supreme Court ruled in 1947 that a New Jersey law which reimbursed parents for the cost of bus transportation to public and religious schools did not violate the First Amendment. Chief Justice Hugo Black, however, in his majority opinion wrote inaccurately that the First Amendment created a "complete separation between the state and religion." He cited Jefferson's wording from the private Danbury Letter rather than the actual text of the First Amendment which clearly bars Congress from prohibiting the free exercise of religion.[2]

CLAIM #2: "America is a secular nation, not a Judeo-Christian one, whose founding documents—the Declaration of Independence and the Constitution—were based on secular principles."

RESPONSE: America was founded on Judeo-Christian principles by those with the intent of securing religious liberty and who fled from England to escape religious persecution.

The signing of the Mayflower Compact on Nov 11, 1620, marked the first time in recorded history a free community of equal men created a new civil government by means of a social contract. Governmental authority was derived from the consent of the people with equal treatment under the law. The principles in the Mayflower Compact were later incorporated into the Constitution.

Writes historian Paul Johnson: "What was remarkable about this particular contract was that it was not between a servant and a master, or a people and a king, but between a group of like-minded individuals and each other, with God as a witness and symbolic co-signatory."[3]

All the early settlements from Massachusetts to Georgia consisted of Christians of all denominations and all the early American colonies were established on Christian principles.[4]

The Puritans established the concept of biblically based governments modeled on church covenants which served as the foundation for our constitutional form of government.[5]

And that continues today. According to Gallup polls, about eighty-five percent of Americans profess to being Christians. Only a small minority—about three or four percent claim to be secular atheists. America is mainly comprised of self-described Christians—not secular atheists.[6]

Greek and Roman ideas of rights didn't form the foundation of our American system, according to secular humanists Michael Villey and Richard Tuck of England. Their studies concluded these concepts originated from the Bible.[7]

The concept of "inalienable rights," concludes author Gary Amos, is traceable to the Scriptures, not the ideas of the Greeks and Romans. Only in the Bible exists the notion of "all men being created equal" and being "endowed by their Creator with inalienable rights." The Book of Genesis states God created man in His image and likeness—an idea foreign to the Greeks and Romans who practiced polytheism—a belief in many gods.[8,9]

<u>CLAIM #3</u>: "Republicans and conservatives are fascists and Nazis who are always imposing their Christian moral values on others."

<u>RESPONSE</u>: Nazis were not Christians.

Nor did Nazis resemble modern day American conservatives. Their beliefs were the exact opposite. They didn't believe in God and they didn't respect individual life or the rule of law and free market capitalism.

Most Nazis were atheists who esteemed anti-theist nihilists such as Kierkegaard and Nietzche, who had little regard for equality under the law or any form of free trade.

The Nazi Party was called the National Socialist German Workers' Party (*Nationalsozialistische Deutsche Arbeiterpartei*) under Adolf Hitler. It adopted a pagan ideology which rejected the church. Members were "baptized," but not in Christian churches, becoming instead members of the "Church of Germany"—atheist pagans, like many of America's liberals.

Since most on the far left are self-admitted secularists (as opposed to Judeo-Christian monotheists) they actually have more in common with Nazis (from a religious perspective) than the Republicans do. Liberals are famous for claiming their opponents are what they themselves are guilty of being.

Polls show Democrats tend to be less likely to believe in God and attend church regularly than Republicans who have a more theistic world view.

Nazism was a pagan ideology which resulted in the murder of 13 million people, including 6 million Christians and 6 million Jews. As American author and journalist William L. Shirer wrote in his book *The Rise and Fall of the Third Reich,* the Nazis sought to "exterminate irrevocably... the strange and foreign Christian faiths imported into Germany in the ill-omened year 800."[10] Shirer told how the Nazis planned to replace denominations with the "National Church" whose symbol would be a swastika and copy of Adolf Hilter's book *Mein Kampf.*

Most liberal Democrats have attempted to replace our Judeo-Christian heritage with their own religion—Secular Humanism. Both Nazism and Secular Humanism are derived from the same basic assumptions—namely that man is perfectible, there is no divine higher authority or creator (God) and all truth and morals are "relative."

Conservatives tend to be more theistic and believe their rights are unalienable—that they are derived from our Creator and not—as secular humanist Nazis thought—from the state.

Liberal Democrats leverage the mainstream media, courts, public schools, entertainment industry and unions to disseminate their leftist propaganda which closely resembles the Nazis' Ministry of Propaganda run by Joseph Goebbels. The left-wing liberal slant in the mainstream media has been well documented, as has the abundance of movies with a left-of-center tilt put out by Hollywood.

The liberal Democrat's divisive class warfare and race-baiting rhetoric ("tax cuts for the rich," "disenfranchised minorities," "two-Americas") closely resembles the Nazis' use of similar sloganism and demagoguery to incite racial hatred toward the Jews and other "sub-human" groups.

The liberal left's support for abortion-on-demand without restrictions, "therapeutic" genetic cloning, evolution, embryonic stem cell research and assisted suicide is frighteningly reminiscent of the human "experimentation" routinely practiced by the Nazis.

The liberal left's support for race-based preferences ("Affirmative Action") is quite similar to the Nazi belief that the "Aryan master race" was superior to all others and that some races are inferior.

The assault by the liberal left on Christians in the U.S. (Waco, Ruby Ridge, the demonizing of the Catholic church in the mainstream media, the Ninth Circuit Court's removing God from the Pledge of Allegiance and removal of the Ten Commandments from public court houses) is quite similar to the anti-Christian sentiment in Nazi Germany which was a precursor to the millions of Christians the Nazis exterminated.

CLAIM #4: "Separation of Church and State prohibits any mention of God in public places."

RESPONSE: The Declaration of Independence, the Constitution and many of the Founders' public speeches all refer to God, as do many of our public government buildings.

About twenty-five percent of the U.S. Capitol's statuary incorporates a religious message, including a statue of Father Junipero Serra ("The Apostle of California") holding a cross in his hands, as well as Marcus Witman, a missionary, carrying a Bible in his hand.

A 14-by-20-foot painting of the baptism of Pocahontas is located in the Capitol Rotunda, as well as *Pilgrims at Prayer* and Christopher Columbus holding a cross while praying with his crew.

A stained-glassed window showing Washington seeking Divine

guidance is in the Congressional chapel. A line from Psalm 16:1 is etched into the stained glass.

"In God We Trust" is engraved in the Speaker's rostrum.

Moses is depicted in the House of Representatives.

Our currency is engraved with the words "In God we trust."

If the Founders put religious statues, symbols and paintings in our most sacred places of government, how could anybody reasonably conclude they would advocate God's removal from our classrooms, courthouses and other public places?

CLAIM #5: "Prayer in schools is unconstitutional."

RESPONSE: For 185 years, prayer was allowed in public schools.

It wasn't until 1961 that prayer was removed from the public schools, after the Supreme Court ruled in *Engel v. Vitale* that the Constitution prohibits an establishment of religion, and that school officials may not compose any public prayer even if the prayer itself is denominationally neutral.

However, the court, when making its decision, failed to acknowledge an earlier case from 1844—*Vidal v. Girarad's Executors*. In that case, the court ruled "there is an obligation to teach what alone the Bible can teach, viz. a pure system of morality."

The 1962 *Engel v. Vitale* decision which removed God from the classroom has had disastrous social consequences. Since then: birth rates for unwed girls age 15 to 19 have increased; sexually transmitted diseases among 10 to 14-year-olds have increased; premarital sex has increased; violent crime has increased; adolescent homicides have increased significantly; test scores and achievement scores have plummeted.

CLAIM #6: "Government has a responsibility to create and sustain an environment of neutrality so no citizen is offended by the religious speech of another."

RESPONSE: The government can't be "neutral" and has no constitutional responsibility to do so.

When the government prohibits the child who believes in God from expressing himself so as not to offend the atheists, the child who believes in God is offended.

If discussions about sex are not only allowed in public schools, but are, in fact, encouraged, then discussions about God should enjoy the same, considering its relevance and historical significance as the foundation for almost 200 years in American public education.

Since a *Newsweek* poll conducted by Princeton Survey Research Associates found that ninety-four percent of Americans believe in God versus four percent who are self-described atheists, why should the small minority of atheists have a right to inhibit voluntary school prayer? Why should a small minority take precedence over the vast majority of Americans' belief in God and their constitutional right to freely express themselves without government interference or prohibition?

The responsibility of the government is to ensure the Constitution is being faithfully abided by and executed. The government can't trample on each citizen's First Amendment right to freely exercise his or her religion.

Furthermore, the government has an obligation to ensure the prevention of a self-imposed national state sponsored religion (i.e. secular humanism).

Finally, government must allow the states, unimpeded, to deal with religious establishments and aid religious institutions as they see fit.

The government does not have the constitutional authority to prohibit the "Free exercise of religion." There is no constitutional guarantee that protects citizens from being "offended." Government's only duty is to ensure the First Amendment right to free exercise of religion.

Chapter 4

D is for Democrats:

Why They're Usually Wrong About Everything

Claims:
1. "Republican presidents are stupid."
2. "Democrats are the party of human rights and civil liberties."
3. "The Republican Party is intolerant."
4. "The Republican Party is racist."
5. "The religious right dominates the Republican Party."
6. "Democrats are the party of the little guy."
7. "Republicans are the party of rich corporate special interests."

Liberal Democrats claim they represent the little guy in our society—women, minorities, children and working middle-class Americans. They assert their policies on a number of issues—the environment, education, health care, taxes and social security—are superior to conservative Republican prescriptions which tend to benefit only the rich at the expense of everyone else.

But when the positions the left advocates are analyzed and compared with their policies and actions, it becomes clear there's an enormous disconnect between the two.

Far from representing the oppressed and "average working Americans," the Democratic Party's core constituency has increasingly consisted of corporate media moguls, Hollywood movie actors, millionaire trial lawyers, radical environmentalists, billionaire financiers, militant homosexual groups, teachers unions, pacifist organizations, Marxist educators and big government bureaucrats.

By successfully leveraging their dominance in the mainstream media, entertainment industries, academic institutions and courts of law, the liberal left has won the public relations campaign on a number of issues.

The superior public relations campaign of the Democratic Party is to be applauded. During the past fifty years, the Democrats have been successful in demonizing conservatives as intolerant religious extremists, rich elites and gun-toting warmongers.

In spite of this steady barrage of rhetoric, most polls reveal mainstream Americans are right-of-center on most fiscal and social issues. Most Americans are in favor of keeping more of the money they earn, controlling and investing for their own retirement, choosing their own doctors and schools for their children and reducing the size and scope of government. They favor American sovereignty, protecting developing babies in mothers' wombs and maintaining a strong national defense.

Liberals claim the rich don't pay their fair share, but usually these same liberal critics are themselves elite millionaires and billionaires such as John Kerry, John Edwards, Hillary Clinton, Teddy Kennedy, Warren Buffet, George Soros and Michael Moore who are impervious to the high marginal tax rates they blithely advocate on the middle and upper middle class.

These elite liberal money bags are able to shield their income and assets in tax shelters only the mega-rich are able to access, enabling them to avoid paying a significant tax burden.

When you assess the way liberal Democrats describe conservative Republicans, it becomes clear they're more accurately describing themselves.

CLAIM #1: "Republican presidents are stupid."

RESPONSE: Republican presidents have amassed impressive and intelligent achievements.

Republican President Dwight D. Eisenhower, the 34th president

(1953-61), graduated from West Point and was one of the greatest military commanders in history. He masterminded the largest and most successful military alliance in history—the D-Day invasion—which led to the defeat of Nazi Germany and Hitler's allies.

Republican President Gerald Ford earned degrees from the University of Michigan and Yale Law School, was a Navy officer in World War II, then a congressman in the House of Representatives for twenty-five years, serving as House Minority Leader, specializing in military matters and the budget, before becoming vice president, then the 38th president (1974-77).

Republican Ronald Reagan, the 40th president (1981-89), served as governor of California before creating the longest sustained economic expansion in history, restoring pride in America and winning the Cold War without firing a single shot.

He was followed by Republican George Herbert Walker Bush (1989-93). Bush "41" served as a Navy pilot in World War II, graduated from Yale, was a member of Phi Beta Kappa—the honors society for academic excellence—then became a successful businessman. He was elected to Congress, served as ambassador to the U.N. and China, headed the CIA and was selected as Reagan's vice president. As president, he defeated Iraq in less than four days—with only 150 American casualties.

His son, Republican George W. Bush, the 43rd president, scored 1206 on his SATs—in the top ten percent—received his bachelors in history from Yale, his masters in business administration from Harvard Business School (with a 3.6 grade point average), flew fighter jets in the Texas Air National Guard, was a successful business owner and was governor of Texas—winning both times in landslide victories before becoming president—twice.

After his election to the presidency (the second time receiving more votes than any presidential candidate in U.S. history), Bush helped restore economic growth through his successive tax cuts and led the war against Islamo-fascism successfully helping to tranform many tyrannical dictatorships in the middle east into emerging democracies. He also was the major factor in the historic 2002 midterm election and 2004 congressional wins for Republicans nationwide. That's not stupid.

What *is* stupid is getting blowjobs from interns your daughter's age in the Oval Office while conducting sensitive national security business—as President Bill Clinton did.

Since 1968, Americans have elected Republican presidents seven times. They've elected Democrats three times and neither—Presidents Carter nor Clinton—received greater than fifty-one percent of the popular vote.

According to elite liberals, Democratic presidents are all brilliant and have the "gravitas" required for the job. Yet after eight years of big-government socialism, Democratic President Franklin D. Roosevelt failed to get the U.S. out of the Depression.

Democratic President Truman was so smart he got the U.S. involved in the Korean War and couldn't get us out for two-and-a-half years. (Once Eisenhower was elected, the war ended in six months.)

Democratic President Kennedy botched the Bay of Pigs invasion of Cuba in 1961, then four months later rocked in his chair and snoozed while the Russians built the Berlin Wall—preventing those in East Germany from escaping to freedom in the West. To cap it all off, he stepped up the U.S. involvement in the Vietnam War.

While the liberal pundits were busy calling Bush "stupid" during the 2000 campaign, they failed to focus much attention on his opponent's school records.

Former Vice-President Al Gore received mostly C's and B's in English, French and history in high school. He was admitted to Harvard with the extra "boost" of having a father who was a prominent U.S. senator.[1]

In his sophomore year at Harvard, Gore got one D, one C-minus, two C's, two C-pluses and a B-minus, placing him in the bottom fifth of his class for the second year in a row.[2]

Gore failed five of his eight classes at Vanderbilt Divinity School and dropped out of Vanderbilt Law School.[3]

During a tour of Monticello during Clinton's 1993 inaugural festivities, Vice President Al Gore looked at two carvings of Benjamin Franklin and George Washington and asked the curator, "Who are these guys?"[4]

Despite the media's portrayal of Bush during the 2004 election as a "dunderhead" who mangled his sentences and Kerry's comment on election night that, "I can't believe I'm losing to this idiot," Bush's grades at Yale were superior to Kerry's.

Kerry received five D's during his four years there, finishing with a cumulative average of 76. Bush had one D in four years and finished with a cumulative average of 77. Kerry received a 63, 68, 69, 71 and 79 in history courses, averaging a 70. Bush averaged an 88! Bush also outperformed Kerry on military intelligence tests.[5]

CLAIM #2: "Democrats are the party of human rights and civil liberties."

RESPONSE: Liberals have been silent about the massive human rights violations throughout the world.

Millions of Chinese live in slave labor camps under horrendous conditions, yet you rarely hear a peep out of the liberals who claim to fight on behalf of the oppressed. Liberals have only partially and reluctantly supported trade sanctions against China.

To be fair, Republicans have also voted for World Trade Organization membership for the Chinese, but have been far more outspoken in favor of attaching human rights stipulations to any trade agreements.

Liberal Democrats fail to acknowledge the human rights violations associated with communist dictatorships. The left has been silent with regard to Castro's blatant human rights violations. Here we have a communist dictator ninety miles away from Florida who routinely tortures and imprisons his people. Thousands risk their lives and many die attempting to escape to the U.S. to live in freedom. Yet, all we hear from liberals such as Jimmy Carter is how great Castro's health care system is.

Even though communist dictators have killed hundreds of millions of innocent human beings around the world and the utter failure of communism has been thoroughly documented, the left still continues to conciliate and appease these brutal communist dictators.

Liberal Democrats are only interested in human rights within the context of their multicultural-secular ideology. News stories about human rights abuses are prevalent in the mainstream media whenever there is an isolated police brutality incident. But when leftist regimes and militant Islamic fundamentalists in the Arab world and in Africa murder millions of Christians, the left wing media is virtually silent.

When college administrators routinely discriminate against Christian students, there is hardly a mention of these types of abuses in the media. Liberals even condone college admission decisions based on skin color. Apparently human rights don't include discriminating based on race.

The left pays lip service to human rights. Many of the worst human rights abusers in the world sit on the human rights commission at the U.N. (China, Cuba and Saudi Arabia). Yet time and time again the liberals in Congress say we can't act unilaterally to protect our sovereignty without the imprimatur of the very same nations in the U.N. who are the most violent and egregious human rights abusers.

Liberal Democrats have consistently supported partial-birth abortion, which even Democrats such as the late Senator Daniel Patrick Moynihan described as infanticide. What worse offense against humanity could there be than condoning the legalization of taking that baby's life arbitrarily by sticking scissors in the back of the baby's skull and sucking his or her brains out until the head collapses and then discarding the baby in the garbage like trash? Support for the legal protection of this murderous act alone significantly minimizes the liberal lefts' claim to be advocates of human rights.

CLAIM #3: "The Republican Party is intolerant."

RESPONSE: Liberals are among the least tolerant groups in America today.

The liberal left characterizes the majority of Americans as reactionaries or extremists because they believe in: the right to bear arms; the right to life of the unborn; lower taxes; limited government; traditional marriage; voluntary prayer; God as Creator; individual personal retirement and medical accounts; strategic missile defense and school choice.

Few liberals will debate the issues. As tolerant as they claim to be, in reality, they are only tolerant of their own ideology and their own partisan ideologues. They are only "tolerant" of those who subscribe to the "open-minded" post-modern secular humanist world view—moral relativism, Darwinian evolution, homosexual "marriage," and multiculturalism.

Liberals have also fundamentally altered and distorted the meaning of tolerance. Traditionally, tolerance has meant intellectual forbearance, especially concerning the opinions of others. There was a time when individuals could have a discussion with civil disagreement. Now, any form of disagreement can be construed by those on the left as being "intolerant."

If a person believes in accordance with his religious beliefs that homosexuality is immoral and sinful behavior, he would be called by many on the left an "intolerant bigot," guilty of using "hate-speech," in dire need of "sensitivity training."

"Tolerance" has come to mean a general acceptance of all behaviors with the implication that truth and morals are essentially relative.

CLAIM #4: "The Republican Party is racist."

RESPONSE: **The Democratic Party has a long history of racism which is still alive and well today.**

The Republican Party was founded in 1854 to abolish slavery. Slavery was primarily an institution of the Democratic Party. Democrats founded the Ku Klux Klan.

The poll tax, which was enacted in southern states from 1889 to 1910, was a Democrat institution. Because payment of the tax was a prerequisite for voting, it disenfranchised many blacks and poor whites who couldn't afford to pay it.

Democrats instituted Jim Crow laws (laws which imposed racial segregation on blacks) throughout the South.

When black and white student activists made "Freedom Rides" on Greyhound buses through the South in the spring of 1961, Alabama police departments refused to protect them from the KKK and angry white mobs. Many freedom riders were beaten and harassed at bus terminals—including the one in Birmingham, Alabama where Police Chief Eugene "Bull" O'Connor arrested everyone on the bus for violating segregation laws. Chief O'Connor was a Democrat.

Democrats were the original segregationists who opposed de-segregation and the Civil Rights Act of 1964 (including Senator William Allen Fulbright who Bill Clinton awarded the Medal of Honor and Senator Al Gore, Sr. who vehemently opposed equal rights for blacks). If not for the support of white Northern Republicans, former President Lyndon B. Johnson would not have been able to pass the 1964 Civil Rights Act.

Martin Luther King, Jr. supported and endorsed Republican candidates—not Democrats—for Congress in the South.

Democratic Senator Robert Byrd from West Virginia was a Kleagle in the KKK and used the term "white nigger" twice in a TV interview by Tony Snow on the March 4, 2001 broadcast of *Fox News Sunday*.

Democrat Al Sharpton, who ran for the presidency in 2004, has a history of making anti-white and anti-Semitic remarks. In 1987, Sharpton accused Steve Pagones and a group of white men of abducting, raping and smearing feces on fifteen-year-old Tawana Brawley. The crime never happened and Sharpton was ordered to pay Pagones $345,000 in damages. But Sharpton to this day refuses to apologize for the highly-charged incendiary racist remarks.

In 1991, Democrat Sharpton railed against the "diamond merchants"—code for Jews—with "the blood of innocent babies" on their hands. After mobilizing hundreds of protesters to march in a Jewish neighborhood to protest the accidental killing of a seven-year-old black child in Brooklyn's Crown Heights, Sharpton led chants of, "No justice, no peace!" and "Kill the Jews!" The result of Sharpton's incendiary action was that his mob surrounded a Jewish man, Yankel Rosenbaum and stabbed him to death.

Four years after that, Democrat Sharpton used the term "cracker" to describe a white Jewish property owner who raised the rent on a black tenant.

Former Democrat presidential candidate Jesse Jackson used the anti-Semitic term "hymietown" to describe New York City and has admitted publicly to spitting in white peoples' food.

Democrats oppose school choice vouchers which would give minority children in under-performing public schools the ability to attend higher quality private or charter schools. Conservatives, in general, support these school choice reforms.[6]

There are currently more blacks, Hispanics and Asians in the Bush Administration than in any other administration in history. Currently the highest office holder in the Republican Bush Administration is black—Condeleeza Rice, Secretary of State, a position previously held by Bush-appointee Colin Powell.

The Bush administration's former Secretary of Education was black—Robert Page. The head of the Department of Housing and Urban Development, Alphonso Jackson, is black.

The only black sitting on the Supreme Court is conservative Clarence Thomas. Elaine Chow, the Secretary of Labor is an Asian-American. Alberto Gonzales, the president's first term chief legal council and second term attorney general, is an Hispanic-American.

CLAIM #5: "The religious right dominates the Republican Party."

RESPONSE: Voters who consider themselves Christians are fairly evenly divided among Republicans, Independents and Democrats.

Christians, unlike the Democratic constituencies (blacks, Hispanics, Jews, unmarried women and government workers), tend to vote more independently—with only a slight preference for Republicans.

Compared to other groups, Christians "bloc vote" less than any other group. In fact, the "religious right" is merely a contrived bogeyman of the left, is hard to define and exerts relatively little influence on the Republican Party.

Ironically the Democratic Party has become the party of the pagan left, bent on removing any form of God from public places and protecting abortion rights at any cost.

Of Protestant voters: 55 percent voted for Bush in the 2000 Election, 43 percent voted for Gore. Of Catholics: 49 percent voted for Bush, 47 percent for Gore. Of Jews: 79 percent voted for Gore, 19 percent for Bush.

Of whites: 54 percent voted for Bush, 42 percent for Gore. Of blacks: 90 percent voted for Gore, 8 percent for Bush. Of Hispanics: 67 percent voted for Gore, 31 percent for Bush.

Of unmarried women: 63 percent voted for Gore, 32 percent for

Bush.

In the 2004 presidential election: 62 percent of Protestants voted for Bush, 38 percent voted for Kerry. Of Catholics: 48 percent voted for Bush, 52 percent for Kerry. Of Jews: Bush expanded his share to 25 percent—up six percent from the 2000 election.

Of union households: 33 percent voted for Bush, 67 percent Kerry. Of military veterans: 60 percent voted for Bush, 40 percent for Kerry.

Of whites: 57 percent voted for Bush, 43 percent for Kerry. Of blacks: 93 percent voted for Kerry, seven percent for Bush.

Of unmarried women: 64 percent voted for Kerry, 36 percent for Bush.[7]

The special interest groups which liberals are fond of denouncing as exerting disproportionate influence on the political process dictate the actions of the modern day Democratic Party. Groups such as the ACLU, NEA, Trial Lawyers of America, AFSCME, Teamsters Union, UAW, International Brotherhood of Electrical Workers, Laborers Union, Carpenters and Joiners Union and the American Federation of Teachers narrowly control, define and dictate legislation and the policy of the Democrat Party.

The liberal media, however, would rather demonize the religious right—a group which is difficult to define—rather than focus on the radical left, whose core constituencies have very little in common with mainstream Americans.

Take a look at the top twenty Political Action Committee (PAC) contributors to federal candidates, during the 1999-2000 election cycle: pro-choice PACs donated $1,159,966 to federal candidates, while pro-life groups gave $482,789; the total for all Republican/conservative PACs combined was $2,599,663. In contrast, the Trial Lawyers of America alone gave $2,661,000 and funneled ninety-five percent of that to Democrats.

While the Democrats accuse the Republicans of being the party of the religious right, the Democratic Party appears to be the party of the multi-millionaire trial lawyers.[8]

CLAIM #6: "Democrats are the party of the little

guy."

RESPONSE: The Democratic Party primarily consists of rich elites—financiers, academics, heiresses, media moguls, software millionaires and Hollywood entertainers.

Polling company Ipsos-Reid, which compared voters' financial makeup by state counties, found that those who voted for Gore had substantially higher family incomes than those who voted for Bush in 2000.

In pro-Bush counties, only seven percent of voters earned at least $100,000, while thirty-eight percent had household incomes below $30,000.

In pro-Gore counties, fourteen percent had earnings of $100,000 or more, while twenty-nine percent earned less than $30,000.[9]

Federal Election Commission data shows the Democrats obtain most of their money not from average working Americans, but, overwhelmingly, from super-rich trial lawyers, Hollywood entertainment executives and billionaire financiers like George Soros and Warren Buffet.

As of July 2004, trial lawyers had donated $112 million to Democratic political candidates compared to the entire oil and gas industry which donated a mere $15 million to the GOP. Wealthy lawyers give seventy-one percent of their money to Democrats and only twenty-nine percent to GOP candidates.

Wall Street also gave heavily to the Democrats. Six of the top fifteen donations to John Kerry came from partners at firms such as Citibank, Goldman Sachs, Morgan Stanley and J.P. Morgan.

While contributions to the Bush 2004 campaign came from multiple small donors across the country, Kerry received his money from much more well-heeled individuals, such as the Hamptons' beach homeowners who, at the end of August 2004, donated $3 million in one day.[10]

CLAIM #7: "Republicans are the party of rich corporate special interests."

RESPONSE: In 2002, the top ten donors to federal candidates and political parties gave overwhelmingly to Democrats.

That includes all PACs, soft money and large $200+ individual donations and individual contributions made by the organization, its employees, officers and their immediate families.

Of the $59,305,429 donated by the top ten donors, 92.4 percent ($54,798,216) went to Democrats, 7.6 percent ($4,507,212) went to Republicans.[11]

Here's what the top business donors comprising sixty-eight businesses gave from 1990-2002:

TOP BUSINESS DONORS
(68 organizations)

CYCLE	TOTAL $	DEMS	REPUBS
1990	41,251,474	54%	46%
1992	65,517,258	51%	49%
1994	69,663,610	48%	52%
1996	100,601,094	35%	65%
1998	98,060,649	36%	64%
2000	150,609,181	38%	62%
2002	97,116,495	38%	62%
TOTAL	$ 622,819,761	41%	59%

Here's what the top labor organizations donated during that same time period:

TOP LABOR DONORS
(27 organizations)

CYCLE	TOTAL $	DEMS	REPUBS
1990	32,444,126	92%	8%
1992	41,758,146	94%	5%

1994	41,593,795	96%	4%
1996	53,044,585	94%	6%
1998	49,106,707	93%	7%
2000	74,343,018	95%	5%
2002	53,440,214	93%	7%
TOTAL	$ 345,730,591	94%	6%

Here's what the top ideological organizations donated during that same time period:

TOP IDEOLOGICAL DONORS
(5 organizations)

CYCLE	TOTAL $	DEMS	REPUBS
1990	3,184,594	77%	23%
1992	5,422,173	76%	24%
1994	5,162,867	62%	38%
1996	6,061,531	71%	29%
1998	6,789,329	69%	31%
2000	9,226,768	64%	36%
2002	4,544,928	60%	39%
TOTAL	$ 40,392,190	68%	32%

It's clear private business does favor Republicans slightly, but the overwhelming donations from labor unions and ideological organizations go predominantly to the Democrats.[12]

Of the top ten All-Time Donors, all but one organization—the National Association of Realtors—gave predominantly to Democrats:[13]

TOTAL	1989-2004 CYCLES DEMS GOP	2004 CYCLE DEMS GOP

1. Amer. Federation of State, County & Municipal Employees
$35,222,356   98%   2%   98%   1%
2. National Association of Realtors
$24,598,780   50%   49%   46%   53%
3. National Education Association

$23,730,094   88%   11%   94%   6%
4. Association of Trial Lawyers of America
$23,621,116   90%   9%   89%   11%
5. Communications Workers of America
$22,354,566   98%   1%   99%   0%
6. Service Employees International Union
$22,269,375   90%   9%   96%   3%
7. International Brotherhood of Electrical Workers
$21,861,387   95%   4%   97%   2%
8. Carpenters & Joiners Union
$21,168,387   71%   28%   92%   7%
9. Teamsters Union
$21,089,131   87%   12%   92%   7%
10. American Medical Association
$20,841,986   26%   73%   39%   60%

Section 527 of the Internal Revenue Code allows for the creation of "527s"—tax-exempt special interest organizations which influence the nomination or election (or defeat) of candidates for public office.

Of the top ten individual contributors to "527s" in the 2004 election, the vast majority of money spent came from very wealthy liberal donors and went almost predominantly to Democratic organizations.

Only one private donor—Carl Lindner of American Financial Group in Cincinnati, Ohio—gave to GOP organizations.[14] Nine of the top ten contributed to the Democrats.

Rank Contributor	Total Contributions
1. Peter Lewis	$14,230,000
Peter B. Lewis/Progressive Corp, Cleveland, OH	
2. George Soros	$12,600,000
Soros Fund Management, New York, NY	
3. Steven Bing	$8,086,273
Shangri-La Entertainment, Los Angeles, CA	
4. Andrew & Deborah Rappaport	$2,910,000
August Capital, Woodside, CA	
5. John A. & Lawrie Harris	$1,714,000
Changing Horizons Fund, Berwyn, PA	

6. Lewis Cullman $1,650,000
Cullman Foundation/Cullman Ventures, New York, NY
7. Agnes Varis $1,500,000
Agvar Chemicals, New York, NY
8. Alida Messinger $1,158,000
Alida Messinger Charitable Lead Trust, New York, NY
9. Fred Eychaner $1,150,000
Newsweb Corp, Chicago, IL
10. Carl Lindner $1,020,000
American Financial Group, Cincinnati, OH

And here are the details of their contributions:
1. PETER LEWIS
Contributions to 527 Committees 2004 Election Cycle

Recipient	Total Contributions
America Coming Together	$ 5,000,000
Joint Victory Campaign 2004	4,550,000
MoveOn.org	2,500,000
Campaign for America's Future	300,000
Democracy for America	250,000
TOTAL	**$14,230,000**

2. GEORGE SOROS
Contributions to 527 Committees 2004 Election Cycle

Recipient	Total Contributions
Joint Victory Campaign 2004	$ 7,750,000
America Coming Together	2,995,000
MoveOn.org	2,500,000
Marijuana Policy Project	485,000
Young Democrats of America	450,000
PunkVoter Inc.	50,000
TOTAL	**$12,600,000**

3. STEVEN BING
Contributions to 527 Committees 2004 Election Cycle

Recipient	Total Contributions
Joint Victory Campaign 2004	$6,964,846
MoveOn.org	971,427
Americans for Progress & Opportunity	150,000
TOTAL	**$8,086,273**

4. ANDREW & DEBORAH RAPPAPORT
Contributions to 527 Committees 2004 Election Cycle

Recipient	Total Contributions
Music for America	$1,550,000
New Democrat Network	1,100,000
Democrats 2000	200,000
America Votes	50,000
EMILY's List Non-Federal	10,000
TOTAL	**$2,910,000**

5. JOHN A. & LAWRIE HARRIS
Contributions to 527 Committees 2004 Election Cycle

Recipient	Total Contributions
League of Conservation Voters	$1,478,000
State Conservation Voters Action Fund	130,000
Clean Water Action Education Fund	40,000
Defenders of Wildlife Action Fund	28,000
Sierra Club	28,000
MoveOn.org	10,000
TOTAL	**$1,714,000**

6. LEWIS CULLMAN
Contributions to 527 Committees 2004 Election Cycle

Recipient	Total Contributions
Joint Victory Campaign 2004	$1,000,000
America Coming Together	500,000
MoveOn.org	100,000
Americans for Jobs, Healthcare & Values	50,000
TOTAL	**$1,650,000**

7. AGNES VARIS
Contributions to 527 Committees 2004 Election Cycle

Recipient	Total Contributions
Joint Victory Campaign 2004	$1,500,000
TOTAL	**$1,500,000**

8. ALIDA R. MESSINGER
Contributions to 527 Committees 2004 Election Cycle

Recipient	Total Contributions
America Coming Together	$ 500,000
League of Conservation Voters	500,000
State Conservation Voters Action Fund	133,000
Democrats 2000	25,000
TOTAL	**$1,158,000**

9. FRED EYCHANER
Contributions to 527 Committees 2004 Election Cycle

Recipient	Total Contributions
America Coming Together	$ 500,000
Media Fund	500,000
Voices For Working Families	150,000
TOTAL	**$1,150,000**

10. CARL LINDNER
Contributions to 527 Committees 2004 Election Cycle

Recipient	Total Contributions
Progress for America	$ 500,000
College Republican National Committee	300,000
Republican Governors Association	200,000
GOPAC	20,000
TOTAL	**$1,020,000**

*NOTE: This data is based on records released by the Internal Revenue Service on Monday, September 20, 2004. Federal law prohibits the use of contributor information for the purpose of soliciting contributions or for any commercial purpose.

<u>Final Score among the top ten donors:</u>
Big Money to Democratic 527s
from nine of the ten top donors $31,802,503
Big Money to Republican 527s
from one of the ten top donors $1,020,000

That's ninety-seven percent to Democratic 527s and three percent to Republican 527s! So who's really the party of the rich special interests? The Democrats!

The Democratic Party—which receives massive financial support from Hollywood actors, multi-millionaire trial attorneys and billionaires such as Warren Buffet and Ted Turner—has refused to release the average size of the donations it receives. Average donations to the party of the "wealthy and powerful" (the Republicans) are about $50.

Records obtained on the Rush Limbaugh website show the average donation to the DNC to be $600. George Soros, the billionaire financier who has been one of the most outspoken advocates for drug legalization, has given more than $15 million to the Democrat Party and pledged to spend whatever it took to defeat President Bush.

The richest members of the U.S. Senate are almost exclusively multi-millionaire Democrats. The only Senators worth more than $200 million are all Democrats. Eight of the eleven richest Senators are Democrats.

Net worth of fourteen richest Democratic senators in 2004:

Senator John Kerry (D, Massachusetts)	$620 million
Senator Jon Corzine (D, New Jersey)	400 million
Senator Herb Kohl (D, Wisconsin)	300 million
Senator Jay Rockefeller (D, West Virginia)	200 million
Senator Diane Feinstein (D, California)	50 million
Senator Ted Kennedy (D, Massachusetts)	30 million
Senator Mark Dayton (D, Minnesota)	20 million
Senator John Edwards (D, North Carolina)	15 million

Senator Hillary Clinton (D, New York)   8 million
Senator Jeff Binghaman (D, New Mexico)   8 million
Senator Bob Graham (D, Florida)   8 million
Senator Ben Nelson (D, Nebraska)   6 million
Senator Barbara Boxer (D, California)   5 million
Senator Harry Reid (D, Nevada)   2 million

Chapter 5

E is for Economics:

Why it Really is About the Economy, Stupid!

Claims:
1. "Democrats are the party of balanced budgets and fiscal responsibility."
2. "The Democrats support increasing the minimum wage (a.k.a. "living wage" which would help the lowest paid workers.")
3. "Rent controls are humanitarian and help protect renters from greedy landlords."
4. "Everybody has the right to affordable housing."
5. "Human rights are more important than property rights."
6. "Rent controls must be legitimate, they've been voted in by a majority of voters."
7. "Landlords are acting selfishly when they demand higher rents from tenants."
8. "Democrats represent the small business owner."
9. "Budget deficits increase interest rates."
10. "Democrats are the party of union labor."
11. "Reagan was a 'B-movie' actor who only represented his rich and powerful friends."
12. "The 1980s under Reagan were the decade of greed."

13. "Reagan's policies made blacks poorer."
14. "The rich got richer and the poor got poorer under Reagan."
15. "Reagan destroyed the safety net for the poor by cutting needed programs."
16. "To stimulate a slow economy we should increase government spending to pump money into the economy."
17. "We need fair trade, not free trade."

The preservation of a vibrant and robust free market economy comes from a solid understanding of how it functions and responds to government intervention.

Conservatives and liberals envision two fundamentally different economic systems. Liberals tend to view the economy as a zero sum game. They believe rich people acquire wealth at the expense of others who are paid substandard wages, who work in substandard working conditions, with substandard health care. Liberals will reluctantly concede free-market capitalism is good, but still believe it has inherent shortcomings which government has the obligation to rectify. The goal of any economic system, according to liberal Democrats, should ensure "equality" for all citizens. They tend to speak in terms of "economic justice" and the need to "level the playing field" and ensure "living wages."

Liberals often speak of the need to maintain a "progressive tax system" to ensure the "rich pay their fair share." Even though the policies and positions they advocate (raising taxes on the most productive, government wage and price controls and protectionist tariffs) have had harmful effects on the economy in the past, they continue to advance these anti-competitive socialist economic concepts.

The three most notable examples include: Hillary Clinton's attempt to federalize health care in 1993 (Hillarycare); California Governor Gray Davis' government-mandated energy price controls which resulted in numerous statewide blackouts; and various government imposed "living wage" laws which have only resulted in higher prices, increased unemployment for workers and scarcity for consumers.

Fiscal conservatives subscribe to the concept that business and the economy are not about subjective and theoretical notions such as "fairness," but about the efficient allocation of scarce resources to consumers.

Raising workers' wages and standard of living are by-products of economic growth because, first and foremost, businesses exist to provide the highest quality goods and services to consumers at the lowest price.

Liberals bemoan evil corporations such as Wal-Mart, claiming they pay "substandard" wages and benefits, threatening the existence of smaller local businesses. What they fail to acknowledge is Wal-Mart exists primarily to serve their customers.

Wal-Mart has been able to consistently offer their customers variety at low prices because the corporation invests in technology and leverages economies of scale. As a result, consumers have been able to maximize their purchasing power, benefitting lower and fixed income consumers the most.

Yet, liberal Democrats, who continue to demonize Wal-Mart as an evil corporation which "destroys" communities, can't explain why higher prices benefit consumers, which is what they support every time they oppose the construction of a new Wal-Mart.

None of Wal-Mart's 1.5 million employees is forced to work for Wal-Mart. If the wages they receive are "sub-standard," they are free to do what any other individual who wants to earn more money does—get a new, higher paying job. That's the way our free market capitalist system works. People voluntarily provide their labor in exchange for the wages they receive.

Businesses—and the goods and services they produce—exist not for workers, but, first and foremost, for consumers. In other words, no business can exist if it doesn't meet consumers' specific needs (excluding government monopolies and oligopolies such as the U.S. Post Office and IRS which continue to thrive even though they provide an abysmal level of service).

After a business has been established to meet the needs of its customers, the second goal of any business is to generate a profit. The more profits a business generates, the more the business can reinvest those profits in new technologies, infrastructure, hiring and expansion.

As the economy expands, workers benefit from higher wages and a higher standard of living. The role of government, from a conservative perspective, is to create and sustain a healthy and robust environment where companies can compete with one another (i.e. limiting taxes, regulations, trade barriers, wage and price controls, excessive lawsuits and penalizing unlawful business practices). When government interferes in the free market, it has the tendency to distort the true value of goods and services, which often results in contrived scarcities, surpluses and volatile price fluctuations.

Time and again, socialist welfare countries such as Germany, France, the old Soviet Union and our neighbors to the north—Canada—have demonstrated the economic and societal devastation which accompanies command-control run economies. Yet, those on the left continue to advocate these same big governments socialist-style policies here in the U.S.

The Democrats' slogan in 1992 was, "It's the economy, Stupid!" Apparently, it was only a slogan. Eight years of Bill Clinton's presidency and his economic policies only succeeded in sending the U.S. economy sliding into a recession, months before George W. Bush was elected in 2000.

Take a look at some Democratic myths which have proved disastrous for the economy.

CLAIM #1: "**Democrats are the party of balanced budgets and fiscal responsibility.**"

RESPONSE: **Liberal Democrats propose more tax increases, government spending and regulations than Republicans, who tend to vote for tax cuts and spending limits.**

The National Taxpayers Union (NTU) ranks all members of Congress to determine the highest spenders and those deemed taxpayers' friends. The NTU says their ratings are based on "every vote that significantly affects taxes, spending debt and regulatory burdens on consumers and taxpayers."

Congressional members with the highest scores have a strong record of voting for taxpayer interests. Those with low percentage scores have the poorest record.

The top twenty taxpayers' friends in the House and Senate in the 108th Congress in 2004 were all Republicans. The top twenty spenders were Democrats. Hillary Clinton received the third lowest score in both houses at eleven percent.[1]

Government spending has increased dramatically under every Democratic president during the past 100 years. Government spending grew significantly under Franklin Roosevelt's "New Deal"—increasing 697 percent—the largest increase in spending in the history of the United States.

Woodrow Wilson, also a Democrat, had the second largest increase in spending at 292 percent.

Under Lyndon B. Johnson's "Great Society," spending increased thirty-one percent.

Fifty years of Democrat-controlled Congresses have significantly increased the size and scope of the federal government.[2]

The "surplus" during Clinton's final term in office was the result of enormous defense spending cuts, a benefit of the Reagan "peace dividend," a Republican Congress which kept spending in check and a roaring, private sector, high technology economy which dramatically increased government tax receipts.

CLAIM #2: "The Democrats support increasing the minimum wage (or "living wage") which would help the lowest paid workers."

RESPONSE: Studies show government-imposed increases in the minimum wage increase unemployment.

Government mandated wage hikes imposed on private businesses artificially increase labor costs, which unfairly harm small businesses. Because businesses have to allocate more capital to labor costs, they not only cut jobs, but often pass onto the consumer the mandated government cost increases.

Increased labor costs lead to higher prices for consumers, decreasing purchasing power overall. Higher costs of goods and services, which result from government imposed "living wages," only hurt those with lower incomes or those living on fixed incomes.

There are always costs to government intrusion in the free market. The beneficiaries of wage controls are the ones who are fortunate enough to get a job at the government-mandated inflated wage. The losers end up being: teenagers and poor minorities who remain unemployed because of decreased demand for labor; consumers who pay higher prices for goods and services; and shareholders who are forced to accept reduced earnings and equity prices.

The majority of small business owners who bear the burden of wage controls are the very "average" working Americans whose interests liberals claim to represent.

The bottom line is: any time the government interferes with the free labor market, contrived scarcities, inflated prices and inferior quality are usually the result.[3]

CLAIM #3: "Rent controls are humanitarian and protect renters from greedy landlords."

RESPONSE: Rent controls benefit the "rich" and hurt the poor.

The entire concept of "rent controls" and "affordable housing" is deeply rooted in socialist economic theory—pitting the "rich" against the "poor."

Rent controls (when the government arbitrarily sets the maximum price a private property owner can charge to a renter) are especially detrimental to the poor—exactly the opposite of what those on the left claim. Any government-mandated price ceiling for apartments will either result in contrived scarcities or reduced quality. That's the only result when owners are forced to rent their properties for less than they're worth.

When owners' rent incomes are less than what they owe in mortgage payments, taxes and other costs, they either sell their buildings or abandon them—something thousands of owners have done in New York and other cities which have rent controls.

Rent controls—instead of providing more apartments and lower prices—actually end up *decreasing* the supply and quality. Why? Because when property owners lose profits as a result of controls, they are less able to invest in their properties. That means they don't make necessary repairs or provide regular maintenance, which inevitably leads to property deterioration and abandonment.

Housing policy expert William Tucker estimates 30,000 New York buildings *per year* were abandoned between 1972 and 1982 because of rent control—a loss of almost 350,000 apartment units.[4]

Paul Niebanck, a community planner and developer, concluded about thirty percent of rent-controlled housing in the U.S. has deteriorated, compared to only eight percent for apartments which rent at the fair-market value.[5]

Rent controls can also end up protecting rich tenants. Ed Koch, the former Mayor of New York City, benefitted from rent controls at the expense of poorer individuals who couldn't find "affordable" rents.[6]

Since rent "controls" limit profitability by capping rents owners can charge, demand for new apartment buildings decreases and non-controlled dwellings—such as condos and luxury apartments—increases, causing excess demand and inflated prices. At the same time, those who can least afford expensive condos and luxury apartments face reduced availability of quality rental apartments.

Rent controls violate fundamental free market principles. Even though the left likes to use non-threatening terms such as "humanitarian" and "helping the poor," when making a case for rent controls, they are immoral. The government has no right to violate the rights of private property owners to decide what price they can charge for their own property. That type of intrusive coercion is more indicative of socialist-controlled economies than free market capitalistic ones.

Both the prospective tenant and the apartment owner have the moral right to agree on a mutually acceptable price. They also have the moral right to disagree. While the left describes government intrusion into the private affairs of citizens as being "humanitarian," it clearly violates the concept of economic freedom.

Most economists (on both the right and the left) agree controls are generally bad. Right-leaning Nobel Prize winning economists Milton Freidman and Friedrich Hayak and left-leaning Nobel laureate Gunnar

Myrdal are in unanimous agreement that, in the words of Myrdal, "Rent control has in certain Western countries constituted, maybe, the worst example of poor planning by government lacking courage and vision."[7]

Assar Linbeck, a Swedish economist from the "left," asserted that, "In many cases rent control appears to be the most efficient technique presently known to destroy a city—except for bombing."[8]

Clearly, the best way to ensure maximum housing availability at the lowest prices is for the government to allow the free market to function with minimal government intrusion.

CLAIM #4: "Everybody has a 'right' to affordable housing."

RESPONSE: The U.S. Constitution outlines Americans' rights and nowhere is there any stipulation of an individual's "right to affordable housing."

The Declaration states that individuals are endowed by their Creator with certain unalienable rights such as "life, liberty and the pursuit of happiness." Other rights guaranteed by the Bill of Rights include freedom of speech, freedom of the press, freedom of religion, freedom to assemble peacefully, the right to bear arms, the right to trial by jury, the right of due process, freedom against unreasonable search and seizure, the right of just compensation for property from the government, and the right of equal protection of the law. But housing isn't a "right."

Housing is property and property—whether it is money, land, clothing or intellectual property—is exchanged for either goods or services. In most cases, the amount of property people are able to acquire is usually the result of the amount and value of the labor they are willing to exchange for that property—how much they can charge for their goods and services in a free market.

A doctor or CEO possesses more value in our capitalistic free market society than, for example, a bus driver and is able to acquire more property because of the superior societal value of his skills and labor. Their "right" to property is contingent upon their value to society as a whole. Some doctors are more valuable than others and subsequently earn more money (property). That's how a free market works.

The "right" to property is not an inalienable "right." It is an earned privilege. Once a person has earned the right to own property, nobody else has the legal "right" to take that property without just compensation. Governments of men are instituted to protect individual rights to their own private property, not to guarantee all citizens own private property.

"Affordable housing" is an arbitrary and relative term. Proponents argue that low-skilled restaurant workers and their families should be able to live in the city where they work—even expensive cities such San Francisco. But, according to this fallacious logic, anybody working in Beverly Hills as a maid or landscaper could demand that the government reduce the price of Beverly Hills mansions to insure "affordable" prices.

The reality is, everyone faces tradeoffs in our society, whether it's our overall standard of living, cost of living or commuting time. If low-wage workers can't afford to live in a city such as San Francisco and they don't like the commute to get to their jobs, they're free to find jobs closer to their homes.

But no person—regardless of his economic status—has a "right" to confiscate anybody else's property. When governments impose rent controls (below fair market rents) on private property owners, they essentially decrease the value of the owner's property without just compensation.

In a free market, private property owners do have "rights," including how much they choose to charge for rent on their properties. The "rights" of renters include how much they choose to agree to pay for the property. Both have the "right" to reject the offer of the other and negotiate a mutually beneficial price based on their individual needs and circumstances. The "rights" of tenants don't include having the government mandate to private property owners how much they can charge for their own property.

Governments are supposed to secure individual property rights, not violate them.

CLAIM #5: "Human rights are more important than property rights."

RESPONSE: **Property rights are human rights. Humans have rights to property.**

The most important "right" a human being has is the right to his or her own property—guaranteed by the Bill of Rights of the U.S. Constitution. No person may, without due process of the law, be deprived of "life, liberty and property."

The Founders clearly understood what so many liberals today fail to recognize which is, as Ayn Rand wrote in *Capitalism: The Unknown Ideal*, "Without property rights, no other rights are possible. Since man has to sustain life by his own effort, the man who has no right to the product of his effort has no means to sustain his life. The man who produces, while others dispose of his product, is a slave."[9]

CLAIM #6: "Rent controls must be legitimate. They have been voted in by a majority of voters."

RESPONSE: **No government has the right to steal from its citizens, regardless of whether the majority votes to make that theft "legal." Just because something is legal does not make it moral.**

For many years, blacks and women couldn't vote in our country, but that didn't make it moral. For years, leftist politicians and courts have enacted socialist-style legislation to redistribute wealth. In essence, rent controls unfairly aid a select group of renters (those fortunate enough to have housing) at the expense of private property owners and those searching for housing.

Since rent control laws tend, in most cases, to decrease the value of private property without "just compensation," the state is using its coercive power to take property from one group (private property through owners' rents) to redistribute it to another group (renters who pay less).

CLAIM #7: "Landlords are acting selfishly when they demand higher rents from tenants."

RESPONSE: An individual private property owner has the right under the U.S. Constitution not to be deprived of "life, liberty or property without due process of the law; nor shall private property be taken away without just compensation."

The Constitution says nothing about the "selfish" motives of buyers or sellers. Landlords have a right to charge whatever rents the market will bear for their own property. Prospective renters also have a right to act "selfishly"—motivated by their own desire to get the best quality product for the least amount of money. No government agency has the right to dictate the price individuals agree upon for a private transaction.

"Selfishness" is one of the prime underpinning of all free market transactions—the desire to get the most for the least. In our free market capitalistic system, selfishness is not only good, but a necessary ingredient for the system to work and flourish. The desire to get the "most for the least" is what provides the incentive for new technological innovation, which, in the long run, increases individual and business productivity and tends to increase the standard of living across the board.

Rent controls remove that incentive, resulting in contrived scarcities and long lines. A limited number of consumers do get more for less, but many more potential renters are denied access to housing.

Is it "selfish" for renters to squat in their rent-controlled apartments for years at the expense of those who are denied this same privilege? They are only doing what individuals do in a free society. They are getting the most for the least amount of money. Whatever money they save in rent, they use for other "selfish" purposes, such as feeding their families, medical expenses and paying for their children's education.

Because of controls, owners also act "selfishly"—to protect their investments. Both actions decrease the overall supply and quality of housing, which hurts all renters and property owners.

The free market system works best when owners and renters act selfishly. The motivation to get the most housing for the least rent ensures the most effective and efficient allocation of apartments.

CLAIM #8: "Democrats represent the small business owner."

RESPONSE: Democratic support for high taxes and regulatory burdens disproportionately hurts small business owners (who constitute eighty percent of all businesses in the U.S.).

John Kerry called for raising taxes on the "rich" (those earning more than $200,000 a year). Eighty percent of those are small business owners who are taxed at the individual rate. Taxing these small businesses restricts saving, investing and expansion.

The fastest way to financial freedom is through entrepreneurship. The prospect of starting their own business is what attracts so many millions to our country to achieve the "American Dream." So when Democrats advocate higher taxes and more regulations (increased Corporate Average Fuel Economy [CAFE] standards, the Kyoto Treaty, ergonomics standards and the Family and Medical Leave Act, to name a few), they reduce the likelihood the "little guy" will have a shot at the American Dream.

Indirectly, by opposing lower taxes and regulations on individual small businesses, liberals, in essence, protect entrenched corporations from small business competition.

Democrats have supported "living wage" laws and other onerous regulatory burdens which have hurt small businesses. Socialist-style command-and-control economic wage and price controls artificially increase costs for small businesses trying to compete with other larger business entities.

In contrast, Republican tax policies, which tend to reduce the tax and regulatory burden on small businesses, enable those owners to retain more of their own capital for innovation, investment and expansion.

CLAIM #9: "Budget deficits increase interest rates."

RESPONSE: Real interest rates depend on the total debt relative to the gross domestic product

(GDP), not the annual change in budget deficits.

Budget deficits only have a marginal effect on interest rates, according to empirical evidence.

The debt-to-GDP ratio shows whether an economy is large enough to absorb the total level of public debt. America's debt-to-GDP ratio was more than 100 percent after World War II, fifty percent in 1994 and is just thirty-six percent today.

As a general rule, demand for any commodity will drive up its price, including demand for money (i.e. interest rates). The global economy is so large, however, that government borrowing has only a marginal effect on interest rates.

Harvard economist Robert Barro studied the economies of twelve major industrialized countries and found:

- If one country borrows to finance its debt, capital seekers can still find cheap capital in other countries, averting a shortage which would increase interest rates.

- Since 2000, the United States' $236 billion surplus has been replaced by an estimated $300 billion deficit. But, instead of increasing interest rates, rates on the ten-year Treasury bond have dropped from 3.7 percent to 2.3 percent.[10]

- A one percent increase in America's debt-to-GDP ratio raises interest rates by approximately 0.05 percent. If all twelve countries increased their ratios by one percent, interest rates would increase by approximately 0.1 percent.

- These small movements are usually overwhelmed by larger trends affecting real interest rates, such as economic growth and expectations of future inflation.[11]

CLAIM #10: "**Democrats are the party of union labor.**"

RESPONSE: **Democrats oppose the very policies and legislation which would help union labor the most.**

Democrats almost unanimously oppose paycheck protection laws for individual union laborers. Such laws give individual union members the right to designate whether or not they choose to have a portion of their dues appropriated for partisan political purposes.

Yet, they regularly oppose the very type of employment laws which would protect the individual laborer the most, siding instead with Big Labor bureaucrats who provide financial contributions to the Democratic National Committee.

Not only that, Democrats generally oppose right to work laws which bar the firing of workers for refusal to join or pay money to a union.

CLAIM #11: "**Reagan was a 'B-movie actor' who only represented his rich and powerful friends.**"

RESPONSE: **Reagan revived the American economy from the Jimmy Carter recession, defeated communism around the world and raised the standard of living for all Americans across the board, independent of race, sex and class.**

There has never been any conservative figure in America, aside from perhaps Rush Limbaugh and George W. Bush, who has been the recipient of as much derision, venom and unadulterated hatred among liberals as has President Ronald Reagan.

Reagan's unabashed traditional conservative ideas and beliefs on taxes, social and cultural issues, and foreign policy, energized and solidified the Republican Party and antagonized many on the left.

Liberal elites such as Arthur Schlesinger, Jr. and John Kenneth Galbraith considered Reagan stupid for believing his supply-side tax cuts would produce economic growth. But, Reagan's record against the backdrop of history clearly shows these liberal elites were wrong and he was right.

Now that Reagan has died, those on the left reluctantly acknowledge him as an optimist whose good nature, communication skills and humor were central to his success, but they continue to ignore his revolutionary ideas, which were hugely popular with the vast majority of Americans.

The left has never been able to acknowledge the American people were primarily attracted to Reagan's core beliefs in limited government, individual liberty, right to life, peace through strength, lower taxes and genuine love of God and country.

Instead, the left, to this day, claims Reagan's tax cuts caused children to go hungry and the elderly to go without their medicine. They say he was a war monger and a cowboy whose military build up was reckless and irresponsible. A closer analysis of the facts reveals these claims are ignorant and baseless.

He was elected twice, winning forty-four states from incumbent Jimmy Carter in 1980, and forty-nine states in 1984, the largest landslide in presidential election history.

He cut taxes, ended inflation and presided over ninety-six consecutive months of economic growth (1982-1990), with the stock market tripling in value during his administration.

America reached full employment while simultaneously negating inflation, thereby debunking the vaunted Phillips Curve of the Keynesian school of economics which asserted there was a requisite trade-off between unemployment and inflation.

It's also ironic those on the left now claim Reagan was successful and popular with the American people because of his tremendous acting abilities, while simultaneously contradicting themselves by referring to him as a "B-Grade" movie actor.

CLAIM #12: "The 1980s under Reagan was the decade of greed."

RESPONSE: The 1980s were actually the years of giving.

The annual growth rate of giving during the '80s was fifty-five percent higher than the previous twenty-five years. Donations totaled $124.31 billion. As a percentage of national income, total and individual giving reached all-time highs in 1989.[12]

E IS FOR ECONOMICS: *WHY IT REALLY IS ABOUT THE ECONOMY, STUPID!*

CLAIM #13: "Reagan's policies made blacks poorer."

RESPONSE: The black middle class grew rapidly under Reagan.

By the time Reagan left office in 1989, households with yearly incomes of $25,000 or more increased to 3.9 million—up from 2.6 million in 1979. From 1980 to 1990, black household income increased eighty-four percent, whites' income increased sixty-eight percent.

The number of black-owned businesses increased from 308,000 in 1982 to 424,000 in 1987—a thirty-eight percent increase versus a fourteen percent increase in the total number of firms in the U.S. Receipts of black owned firms more than doubled, from $9.6 billion to $19.8 billion.

From the end of 1982 to 1989, black unemployment dropped nine percentage points (from 20.4 percent to 11.4 percent), while white unemployment was reduced by only four percent.[13]

From 1977 to 1981, under Democrat Jimmy Carter's administration, the number of poor blacks rose by more than 2 million. From 1982 to 1989 under Republican Ronald Reagan's leadership the number of poor blacks fell by 400,000, while the poorest twenty percent of Americans' real incomes grew by almost twelve percent, meaning the "poor" blacks got richer under Reagan.[14]

CLAIM #14: "The rich got richer and the poor got poorer under Reagan."

RESPONSE: From 1983 to 1989, the total population under the poverty line decreased by 3.8 million people, with unprecedented numbers of people entering the work force.

Reagan inherited from Jimmy Carter twenty-one percent interest rates, fourteen percent inflation, twelve percent unemployment and falling incomes.

Under Reagan, 20 million new jobs—eighty-two percent of

which were higher-skilled, higher-paying jobs—were created in the private sector—real long-term jobs (as opposed to the millions of "dot-com" jobs during the Clinton Administration).

The Kemp-Roth Tax Cut (The Economic Recovery Tax Act) successfully reduced marginal tax rates across the board, increased individual and business investment and fueled enormous economic growth. Interest rates fell and the stock market rose in value.

In fact, the 1980s represented the longest peace-time expansion in the history of the United States (ninety-six continuous months of economic growth from 1982-1990). The "misery index," which measured how bad off people were under Jimmy Carter, took a nose dive under Reagan. According to the U.S. Census Bureau, average real incomes for all Americans increased more than fifteen percent from 1982-1989.

During Reagan's administration, tax-payers were five times more likely to increase their incomes than to have them fall. All income groups experienced real income gains. Under Carter only the top one percent grew. The rich got richer under Carter, not Reagan![15]

Less than twenty-five percent of families in 1980 under Carter earned more than $50,000 a year. By 1990 under Reagan, the number had increased to thirty-one percent of families and that economic boom was responsible for a rapidly expanding middle class.

Of the bottom twenty percent of income earners in 1979, sixty-five percent jumped at least two income brackets during the 1980s.

All income groups paid less in taxes as a percent of their income during the Reagan years, with the poor receiving the most relief, the middle class the next and the rich the least.

The "rich" also paid a greater share of total taxes under Reagan than under Carter![16]

CLAIM #15: **"Reagan destroyed the safety net for the poor by cutting needed programs."**

RESPONSE: **According to the Congressional Research Service, federal spending for social programs increased from $344.3 billion in 1981 to $412 billion in 1989, representing a 19.7 percent increase using 1982 dollars.**

Social spending as a percentage of GNP averaged 1.73 percent during Reagan's two terms.

Under Carter, social spending averaged 1.65 percent.

Under Reagan, from 1983 to 1989, federal spending for the poor increased—providing income, food, housing, education and social services.[17]

CLAIM #16: "To stimulate a slow economy, we should increase government spending to pump money into the economy."

RESPONSE: Lower government spending leads to higher economic growth.

Higher government spending decreases business investment, reducing the economy's growth opportunities, according to a study of investment and growth in industrial economies conducted by Professors Silvia Ardagna and Fabio Schiantarelli of Boston College, Alberto Alesina of Harvard University and Roberto Perotti of Columbia University.[18]

Two decades of data demonstrated that not only do stock market averages track remarkably well with inflation levels and interest rates, but also with the size of government, according to a study Lowell Gallaway conducted for the Joint Economic Congress.

When federal spending (as a percentage of total output) grows, the stock market falls considerably. The rise in market averages from 1994 to 1999 reflects, in large part, the decrease in federal spending as a percent of the gross domestic product (GDP), thanks mostly to Newt Gingrich and the other Republicans in Congress who limited Democrat pork-barrel spending.[19]

The private sector is, on average, dollar for dollar, more productive than the public sector. The former is forced to face the market discipline in its decisions while the government does not.

Aggregate productivity falls when the government crowds out private activity. To "get the economy moving," government should create the best possible environment for the private sector to flourish (i.e. lower tax rates on individuals and businesses, less burdensome regulations and free trade guidelines).

Government spending does not create new income. It merely

shifts existing income and has little effect on GDP. The claim that the government can "inject" money into the economy to stimulate growth is based on an outdated Keynesian economic theory which asserts government purchases of goods and services expand GDP. This supposition, however, is based on fallacious logic. Since the government doesn't create its own money, every dollar it "pumps" into the economy is first either taxed or borrowed. Government spending doesn't create new income, it merely shifts existing income. These direct purchases displace private purchases, using tax dollars to acquire goods and services from the private sector to stimulate economic growth. Total economic activity is unchanged.[20]

<u>CLAIM #17</u>: "Free trade agreements such as the North American Free Trade Association (NAFTA) and the General Agreement on Tariffs and Trade (GATT) result in high wage countries such as the U.S. losing jobs to lower wage countries. We need 'fair trade' not free trade."

<u>RESPONSE</u>: Jobs have increased since NAFTA and GATT were signed.

Democrats (and some Republicans) oppose free trade policies and support the very same protectionist tariffs which have historically resulted in less jobs for labor. Most liberal Democrats have been vocal opponents of global free trade in an effort to be perceived as being on the side of the "American worker." They claim they're for "fair" trade and American workers have to be protected from the export of American jobs overseas or "outsourcing."

Yet, passing NAFTA, GATT and other free trade agreements did not result in the massive layoffs liberal Democrats direly predicted. Unlike Clinton, who pushed for and signed these free trade bills into law, the extreme left wing of the Democratic Party continues to ignore the long-term net economic benefits and gains for workers when our trading partners and markets expand internationally.

Since NAFTA went into effect in 1993, the number of jobs in the United States has increased steadily and the unemployment rate has fallen to low levels not seen in years prior. U.S. unemployment is below the thirty-year average at 5.6 percent of the workforce.[21]

The inability to understand the efficiencies of free trade agreements stems from not understanding the difference between wage rates per unit of time and labor costs per unit of output. When workers are paid twice as much per hour, but are able to produce three times as much per hour, the labor costs per unit of output are lower. This explains why high wage countries such as the U.S. have been exporting to low-wage countries for centuries.

The countries which have the comparative advantage (whether they are a high wage or low wage country) are able to produce the most for less. Even though some manufacturing and service jobs are being exported to countries abroad which have higher comparative advantages, foreign companies such as Siemens and Toyota still employ tens of thousands of American workers. In 2004, Toyota produced their ten-millionth car in the U.S.[22]

Economist, journalist and management guru Peter Drucker claims the U.S. imports far more jobs than it exports and nobody is contradicting his findings.[23]

There are always dislocations of jobs in a vibrant world economy. Some years the U.S. loses jobs and in other years they gain them. But the end results of globalization are lower cost products and services, which in turn raise living standards, provide jobs, opportunities and create a prosperous global economy. When underdeveloped countries with a comparative advantage in one area can produce a product or service more efficiently and less costly, U.S. companies who employ their services can become more competitive in the global market.

Yes, some American jobs may be lost in the short run, but in the long run, as workers employed by American companies earn more and increase their standard of living; they have more money to purchase those same goods and services. Not only does free trade make sense from a micro and macro economic standpoint, but by exporting jobs and opportunities abroad, it is the best way to promote democracy, the main by-product of free markets and free trade.[24]

Chapter 6

F is for Females:

Which Group Really Supports Them?

Claims:
1. "The Democratic Party best represents women."
2. "Abortion rights are fundamental to the advancement of women."

Liberal Democrats have consistently captured the majority of women voters over the past thirty years. Since the 1960s, the feminist movement has liberated many women from their traditional roles as housewives and stay-at-home moms, with millions entering the workforce.

Yet, women—especially those married with children—are moving away from the Democratic Party. Increasingly these "security moms" have chosen to stay at home with their children and have leaned toward the Republicans.

Democrats say their party best represents women because they protect women's "reproductive rights" from conservative Republicans who seek to violate them by "imposing their morality" on them.

Yet, most polls among women have shown a gradual shift toward the pro-life position. While liberal Democrats generally oppose restrictions on abortion on demand and parental notification laws, most mainstream American women support such limitations. Democratic presidential nominee John Kerry voted against a ban on partial-birth abortion, even though national polls show approximately eighty percent of women oppose this grisly "procedure."

F IS FOR FEMALES: *WHICH GROUP REALLY SUPPORTS THEM?*

Liberal Democrats wax eloquent about how much concern they have for women and protecting their "rights." Yet, for eight years these same people basically ignored the many instances of sexual harassment, including a credible rape allegation, committed by the sitting commander and chief Bill Clinton.

CLAIM #1: "The Democratic Party is the party which best represents women."

RESPONSE: The Democratic Party supported Bill Clinton, who, on numerous occasions, groped and fondled women in the Oval Office.

Rather than show concern for women, Democrats showed a permissive attitude and slavish support for Clinton's persistent abuse of women.

They elected a president who had sex with an intern in the Oval Office while conducting national security, then voted against removing him. They continued to support a man who was charged with rape (a credible allegation by Juanita Broaddrick which Bill Clinton has never denied).

How can a party which claims to care so much for the rights of women blatantly disregard the top elected Democrat's wanton treatment and general disrespect for women?

Not only that, but the Democratic Party has been reluctant to oppose the worst abusers of women in the world—Islamic Fundamentalist terrorist countries and organizations. Many of these countries engage in brutal treatment of women including genital mutilation, forced abortions and death for any woman who exposes any part of her body. Indeed, women have virtually no rights and are basically sex slaves for the male population.

Yet the liberal Democrats who claim to be the "party of women" have fought Bush and the Republicans at every turn on disarming Iraq and other countries who sponsor terrorism or harbor terrorists. Even though millions of women have been liberated from the oppression under which they have lived as a result of "regime change," the liberal Democrats continually advocate appeasement and containment which would do nothing to free the millions of women living under severe oppression and terror.

Saddam Hussein's oldest son was well-known as a rapist throughout Iraq. He frequently kidnapped women, then tortured, raped and even killed them. Yet Democrats, even after 9/11, vociferously opposed the immediate removal of Saddam and his murderous regime.

CLAIM #2: "Abortion rights are fundamental for the advancement of women. Feminists support the 'right to choose.'"

RESPONSE: The founding feminists were pro-life, not pro-choice.

The National Organization for Women (NOW) and politicians such as Hillary Clinton and Barbara Boxer may claim abortion is "the most fundamental right of women," but the original "feminists" didn't agree.

Reformer and suffragist Susan B. Anthony referred to abortion as "child murder" and viewed it as a means of exploiting both women and children.[1]

"We want prevention, not merely punishment," she said. "We must reach the root of the evil... It is practiced by those whose innermost souls revolt from the dreadful dead."[2]

She also said, "All the articles on this subject that I have read have been from men. They denounce women as alone guilty and never include man in any plans for the remedy."[3]

Feminist and women's rights leader Elizabeth Cady Stanton classed the killing of newborns as "infanticide" and said, "When we consider that women are treated as property, it is degrading to women that we should treat our children as property to be disposed of as we wish."[4]

Stanton and Anthony's newspaper *The Revolution* and most other feminist publications of the early 1900s refused to join in the common practice of printing advertisements for thinly-disguised patent medicine abortifacients.

Matilda Gage, president of Stanton and Anthony's organization National Woman Suffrage Association (NWSA) said about abortion, "The crime of abortion is not one in which the guilt lies solely or even chiefly with the woman... I hesitate not to assert that most of this crime of 'child murder,' 'abortion,' 'infanticide,' lies at the door of the male sex."[5]

F IS FOR FEMALES: *WHICH GROUP REALLY SUPPORTS THEM?*

She went on to say, "When a man steals to satisfy hunger, we may safely conclude that there is something wrong in society. So when a woman destroys the life of her unborn child, it is an evidence that either by education or circumstances she has been greatly wronged."[6]

Victoria Claffin Woodhull, the first female stockbroker on Wall Street and the first woman to run for president of the United States, was a strong opponent of abortion. In December 1870, she wrote in her publication *Woodhull's and Claffin's Weekly*, "The rights of children as individuals begin while yet they remain in the fetus."[7]

Sarah Norton, the first woman to attend Cornell University, wrote in Woodhull's publication that same year, "Child murderers practice their profession without let or hindrance and open infant butcheries unquestioned... Is there no remedy for all this ante-natal child murder?... Perhaps there will come a time when... an unmarried mother will not be despised because of her motherhood... and when the right of the unborn to be born will not be denied or interfered with."[8]

A few years later in 1875, Woodhull again wrote on the subject of abortion, this time for Wheeling, West Virginia's *Evening Standard*, "Every woman knows that if she were free, she would never bear an unwished-for child, nor think of murdering one before its birth."[9]

Emma Goldman, a nurse, knew how to induce abortions, but refused to do them. In 1906 she founded and edited the magazine *Mother Earth* to express her views. She wrote in 1911 about how pervasive, even at that time, the practice of abortions was. "The custom of procuring abortions has reached such appalling proportions in America as to be beyond belief... So great is the misery of the working classes that seventeen abortions are committed in every one hundred pregnancies."[10]

Alice Stokes Paul, the author of the original Equal Rights Amendment (1923), also opposed abortion. Evelyn Judge, a colleague who worked with her in the 1940's, recalled Paul frequently expressing the opinion that, "Abortion is the ultimate exploitation of women."[11]

English author and feminist Mary Wollstonecraft decried the sexual exploitation of women. In 1792, she wrote in her book *A Vindication of the Rights of Women*, "Women becoming, consequently, weaker, in mind and body, than they ought to be... have not sufficient strength to discharge the first duty of a mother; and sacrificing to lasciviousness the parental affection, that ennobles instinct, either destroy the embryo in the womb, or cast it off when born. Nature in every thing demands respect and those who violate her laws seldom violate them with impunity."[12]

Many of today's active feminists still oppose abortion, so what happened?

Well, for one, abortion rights activists tied abortion to "women's rights" in the 1960s as a profit motive. (Feminists for Life was started in the early 1970s to counter the misdirected mainstream feminist movement's change to pro-abortion.)

The Democratic Party is the party of pro-abortion. If killing 750,000 females a year (half of the 1.5 million abortions) is what you're looking for, then the Democratic Party is the best party for women.

Abortion has become the "sacrament" of the Democratic Party. If you're a women and aren't in favor of abortion on demand, there's little room for you in the party. In fact, if you're a pro-life Democrat, your party won't tolerate you. Just ask Democrat Zell Miller.

Chapter 7

G is for Gun Control:

Why We Have a Second Amendment

Claims:

1. "The 2nd Amendment does not guarantee an individual right to own a gun. It was intended to guarantee a 'collective' right of the states to maintain militias."
2. "Gun possessions increase violent crime."
3. "Gun control laws eliminate guns and prevent crime."
4. "The Democratic Party supports common sense gun control."
5. "Military and war kill innocent people with guns."
6. "Concealed carry laws threaten to bring back the chaos of the frontier days."
7. "Most Americans favor more restrictive 'common sense' gun control laws."
8. "Crime has decreased because of the the Brady Act's five day waiting period and the assault weapons ban."
9. "Guns are dangerous. Gun accidents are at an all time high. We need trigger locks."
10. "Foreign countries such as Japan and England have

less crime and violence than the U.S. has because they have more restrictive gun control laws."

11. "Pulling a gun on a criminal endangers you more than the criminal."
12. "Guns kill children in epic numbers."
13. "You need a license to drive a car. You should have one to own a gun."
14. "Guns are more likely to injure or kill fifteen-to-twenty-four year old black males than white males in the same age group."
15. "Having a gun in the home makes the home less safe."
16. "We need laws which mandate the storage of firearms to protect children."
17. "Guns should only be legal for legitimate 'sporting' purposes such as hunting."
18. " Gun violence is at all time high epidemic proportions."
19. "We need to close the 'gun show loophole.'"
20. " The NRA is a fringe group that opposes 'moderate' and 'reasonable' gun control regulations."

Liberal "gun-control" advocates, in their well-financed and concerted effort to rewrite the Second Amendment, argue the right to bear arms should be limited and restricted to enhance public safety. To bolster these positions, liberal leftists such as Michael Moore point to Columbine and other public tragedies as evidence America needs to enact more restrictive "gun control" laws.

Bill Clinton stated publicly that Al Gore lost the 2000 election primarily because of the Democrat's support for "gun control."

John Kerry tried to win some of those gun-supporter votes in the 2004 election with a much publicized, duck hunting trip in Pennsylvania, further underscoring how influential and powerful gun owners are in America.

This conclusion rests on the faulty premise that more laws will decrease gun violence. In reality, more gun laws have had marginal impact on gun violence in our society. What's proved more effective in reducing violence is stricter enforcement of the more than 20,000 *existing* federal gun laws.

The left has consistently opposed more stringent programs and penalties for repeat gun offenders such as Project Exile and other such programs. Yet those programs have dramatically reduced gun crime by getting off the streets those criminals most likely to commit gun related crimes.

While some on the left may be well intentioned, those who advocate more restrictive gun control laws are really talking about measures which would make it more difficult for average law abiding citizens to protect themselves and their property. Since more than 90 million Americans own a gun, those on the left know gun-control is a loser politically if put to a vote of the people through the constitutionally prescribed legislative process.

After all, the right to bear arms is in the Constitution and Americans don't like to mess with one of their founding documents.

The Second Amendment of the Bill of Rights stipulates every citizen of the United States is endowed by God with the inalienable right to protect their own liberty and property. Here's what it says:

"A well regulated militia, being necessary to the security of a free state, the right of the people to keep and bear arms, shall not be infringed."

If Congress renounces this God-given, inalienable right, what other constitutional freedoms can the state arbitrarily take away from its citizens? The Bill of Rights was written to limit governmental authority. If those on the left feel the Second Amendment is evil, they should try to amend the Constitution in the legally prescribed manner. Put it to a vote of the people.

Gun control advocates have attempted to revise the Second Amendment through the courts by bringing class action lawsuits against gun manufacturers. They have also attempted to use the mainstream media and Hollywood to shape public opinion in support for more restrictive gun control laws. The left-wing, anti-gun bias has been well documented. A 2000 Media Research Center study showed that television news stories calling for stricter gun laws outnumbered those opposing such laws by a 10-1 ratio.[1]

Like many of the dangerous ideas of the left, the specious central arguments in support of gun control can easily be debunked with empirical evidence. While the Hollywood elites and liberal intelligentsia in Washington—many of whom have armed bodyguards and live in homes protected by iron gates and security systems—call for more restrictive "gun control" laws—including registration and confiscation—they ignore the 3 million times each year Americans use firearms to protect themselves. How many would be violently attacked, raped or killed if they were disarmed?

The most dangerous aspect of the gun-control agenda is it ultimately criminalizes the legal ownership of guns, making law-abiding citizens more prone to being the victims of gun violence. Consider countries such as Canada and Great Britain, (as well as the State of California) where licensing, registration and other restrictive "gun control" measures have been instituted. The result has been sharp increases in gun-related crime overall.

The "gun control" debate is more than a discussion about "safety." It's really about individual liberty. The Founders were keenly aware that any nation's citizens unable to defend themselves are more susceptible to a tyrannical government. They understood the Second Amendment was vital in the defense of liberty and freedom.

> **CLAIM #1**: "The Second Amendment does not guarantee an individual's right to own a gun. It was intended to guarantee a 'collective' right of the states to maintain militias."

> **RESPONSE**: The Federal Court of Appeals for the Fifth Circuit on October 16, 2001 issued a landmark decision in *U.S.* v. *Emerson* affirming the constitutional right of individuals to own a gun.

In *Emerson*, the court ruled, "The plain meaning of the right of the people to keep arms is that of an individual, rather than a collective, right and is not limited to keeping arms while engaged in active military service or as a member of a select militia such as the

National Guard...We conclude that [*United States* v.] *Miller* (the legal precedent by which the court considered *Emerson*) does not support the [Clinton Administration's] collective rights or sophisticated collective rights approach to the Second Amendment. Indeed to the extent that *Miller* sheds light on the matter it cuts against the government's position."

The court then iterated the history and text of the Second Amendment with regard to individual rights: "There is no evidence, in the text of the Second Amendment, or any other part of the Constitution, that the words 'the people' have a different connotation within the Second Amendment than when employed elsewhere in the Constitution. In fact the text of the Constitution, as a whole, strongly suggests that the words 'the people' have precisely the same meaning within the Second Amendment as without. And as used throughout the Constitution, 'the people' have 'rights' and 'powers,' but federal and state governments only have 'powers' or 'authority,' never 'rights'."

Finally, with regard to the Second Amendment only pertaining to militia power, the court concluded: "We have found no historical evidence that the Second Amendment was intended to convey militia power to the states, limit the federal government's power to maintain a standing army, or applies only to members of a select militia while on active duty. All of the evidence indicates that the Second Amendment, like other parts of the Bill of Rights, applies to and protects individual Americans. We find that the history of the Second Amendment reinforces the plain meaning of its text, namely that it protects individual Americans in their right to keep and bear arms whether or not they are a member of a select militia or performing active military service or training. We reject the collective rights and sophisticated collective right models for interpreting the Second Amendment. We hold consistent with *Miller*, that it [the amendment] protects the right of individuals, including those not then actually a member of any militia or engaged in active military service or training, to possess and bear their own firearms."[2]

In 1990, the Supreme Court recognized in *U.S.* v. *Verdugo-Urquidez* that rights belonging to the "people" are undeniably the rights of individuals.

The court concluded: "'The people' seems to have been a

term of art employed in select parts of he Constitution. The Preamble declares that the Constitution is ordained and established by 'the People of the United States.' The Second Amendment protects 'the right of the people to keep and bear arms,' and the Ninth and Tenth Amendments provide that certain rights and powers are retained by and reserved to 'the people' protected by the Fourth Amendment and by the First and Second Amendments and to whom rights and powers are reserved in the Ninth and Tenth Amendments, refers to a class of persons who are a part of a national community or who have otherwise developed sufficient connection with this country to be considered part of that community."

On May 6, 2002, the U.S. Department of Justice officially adopted the historically correct interpretation that the Second Amendment guarantees an individual right. Solicitor General Theodore B. Olson wrote that the position of the United States is that "the Second Amendment more broadly protects the rights of individuals, including persons who are not members of any militias or engaged in active military service or training, to possess and bear their own firearms."[3]

The individual right to keep and bear arms is well documented in our founding documents. It has been unanimously affirmed in *Federalist Number 46* (by James Madison); *Federalist Number 29* (by Alexander Hamilton); Thomas Jefferson's Proposed Virginia Constitution in 1764 ("No free man shall ever be debarred the use of arms."); and George Mason at Virginia's U.S. Constitution ratification convention in 1788 ("I ask, sir, what is the militia? It is the whole people... To disarm the people is the best and most effectual way to enslave them.").[4]

Various United States Supreme Court decisions have affirmed the individual right to keep and bear arms, including *Logan* v. *the U.S.* (1892), *Miller* v. *Texas* (1893), *Robertson* v. *Baldwin* (1897) and *Maxwell* v. *Dow* (1900).[5]

This individual rights view is also supported by the vast majority of academic legal scholars on both sides of the political spectrum: William Van Alstyne of Duke University, Akhil Reed Amar of Yale, Sanford Levinson of Yale, Harvard's Laurence Tribe—a liberal gun-control advocate—and Don B. Kates, Jr., formerly of Stanford University. All concur the Second Amendment protects individuals' right to keep and bear arms.[6]

CLAIM #2: "Gun possessions increase violent crime."

RESPONSE: Countries who have banned firearms have higher crime rates than the U.S.

Australia and England have already banned personal ownership of guns, but it hasn't made their countries any safer.

In Australia, violent crime is up in every category. From 1997-1999, murders rose 6.5 percent and attempted murders 12.5 percent. Increases in assaults, kidnappings and armed robberies also increased.

England ranks second among industrialized nations in violent crime. Between April and September 2000, street crime in London rose thirty-two percent over the same period in 1999.[7]

Switzerland has the highest per capita firepower in the world, but is one of the most peaceful countries in the world. The Swiss avoided both world wars and have a considerably lower murder rate than Canada, England, Australia, or New Zealand where guns have been either outlawed or severely restricted.[8]

The United States, where gun ownership is legal, is not even in the top 10 most violent nations and the number of those who privately own guns has grown. Since 1991, the number of private firearms grew by about 70 million guns and the number of states with Right-to-Carry laws has more than doubled—from seventeen to thirty-seven states.

That means since 1991, we have more guns, more gun owners, more gun owners carrying guns and more citizens living among citizens carrying guns and yet total violent crime has decreased by thirty-five percent—dropping every single year to a thirty-year low. Murder is down forty-three percent, rape is down twenty-two percent, aggravated assault down twenty-eight percent and robbery down forty-seven percent.[9]

About 99.8 percent of firearms and more than 99.6 percent of handguns in the U.S. will *not* be used to commit violent crimes in any given year.[10]

CLAIM #3: "Gun control laws eliminate guns and prevent crime."

RESPONSE: Violent crime has increased in areas where gun control laws have been enacted, making it more likely law-abiding citizens have been unable to defend themselves from armed criminals.

While strict gun control laws and registration often reduce the number of guns owned by law-abiding citizens, they don't reduce the number of guns owned by *criminals*. Since criminals will always have access to guns and don't obey laws in the first place, more laws and restrictions on law-abiding citizens only reduce their ability to defend themselves against criminals.[11]

As author Richard Poe points out in his book *The Seven Myths of Gun Control: Reclaiming the Truth About Guns, Crime and the Second Amendment*, "The only question is who has access to the guns and who doesn't. That question, in large part, determines who lives and who dies."[12]

There are currently thousands of federal, state and local gun laws on the books, but no matter how severe and restrictive "gun-control" laws, they have failed to decrease crime. In many cases, crime has increased.

That was the case in Washington D.C. A ban on handgun sales in 1987 led to a tripling of the murder rate by the early 1990s, with handguns used to commit most of the violent crime in the city.[13]

In 1968, officials in Chicago instituted handgun registration. Murders with handguns *increased*. In 1982, Chicago imposed a D.C. style ban which, over the next decade, resulted in a doubling of handgun related murders.[14]

Since 1975, California's annual murder rate has averaged thirty-two percent higher than the rate for the rest of the country, even though the state has: increased its waiting period on retail and private sales of handguns from five to fifteen days; outlawed "assault weapons" in 1989 and subjected rifles and shotguns to waiting periods in 1990.[15]

Officials in Maryland imposed a gun purchase limit and a waiting period, restricted "assault weapons" and regulated private transfers of firearms between family members. The result? During the last decade, Maryland's murder rate has been about forty-four percent higher than the rest of the country and has the highest robbery rate among any state in the country.[16]

The New York handgun licensing law on the books since 1911 has done little to reduce one of the highest violent crime rates in the country.[17]

The signing of the Federal Gun Control Act of 1968, which imposed massive restrictions on firearms nationwide, did little to reduce violent crime. The national murder rate was almost fifty percent higher the first five years after the law went into effect, seventy-five percent higher over the next five years and eighty-one percent during the five years after that.[18]

In 1993, Congress passed the Brady Act which provided for a waiting period prior to the purchase of a handgun and for the establishment of a national instant criminal background check system prior to the transfer of any firearm. States where the Brady Act's waiting periods were imposed experienced worse violent crime trends than other states.[19]

The only thing which has reduced violent crime has been strict law enforcement for criminals. From 1980 to 1994, the ten states with the greatest increases in prison population experienced an average decrease of thirteen percent in violent crime. The ten states with the smallest increase in prison populations experienced an average fifty-five percent increase in violent crime.[20]

And what happens when those criminals are released from prison? In 1991, 162,000 criminals released on parole committed 46,000 violent crimes while under supervision.[21] Nineteen percent of persons involved in the felonious killings of law enforcement officers over the last decade were on probation or parole at the time of the officers' killings.[22]

Virginia's Project Exile—a federal, state and local effort led by the U.S. Attorney's Office in Richmond—sentenced felons convicted of illegally possessing guns to a minimum of five years in prison. Following enactment of Project Exile, Richmond's firearm murder rate dropped nearly forty percent. Members of Congress were so impressed with those statistics that in 1998 they approved $2.3 million to implement Project Exile in Philadelphia and in Camden County, New Jersey.[23]

CLAIM #4: "The Democratic Party supports 'common sense' gun control."

RESPONSE: Liberals advocate more restrictive "gun control" laws, which would make obtaining a gun more difficult for average American citizens, but would do very little to prevent criminals from obtaining firearms.

Project Exile, sponsored by the NRA and instituted in Virginia, dramatically reduced crime by taking off the streets and putting in jail, criminals who tried to obtain guns illegally. This program, which focused on robust enforcement of existing laws, reduced gun-related crimes. Yet, almost unanimously, liberal Democrats opposed this program.

The Clinton Administration did everything in its power to dilute the Second Amendment. Clinton confiscated guns in the Chicago projects from law-abiding citizens as part of a public relations campaign to compensate individuals for turning in illegal firearms. This program, which was intended to reduce crime, led to increased crime because the law-abiding citizens could no longer protect themselves from the criminals.

The vast majority of available data supports the fact that in states where gun ownership and concealed carry permits are granted to law-abiding citizens, crime is dramatically lower. By opposing these tough crime measures, liberal Democratic "gun-grabbers" oppose the very measures which protect average law abiding citizens the most.

Liberals actually oppose more "common sense" strict enforcement of the thousands of gun laws already on the books—the very measures which would have taken violent offenders off the streets.

Members of the Democratic Party and organizations such as Hand Gun Control have stated their ultimate goal is for complete gun confiscation in America. Liberal Democrats continue to propose legislation which incrementally restricts individuals' rights to acquire and use firearms for defensive purposes, even though the vast majority of citizens consider those bills intrusive and misguided.

CLAIM #5: "War and the military use guns to kill innocent people."

RESPONSE: Tyrannical governments are responsible for the murders of more people than combat.

More people die violently in countries with strict gun control laws than in countries without them.

In his 1994 book *Death By Government,* Rudolph J. Rummel, Professor Emeritus of Political Science at the University of Hawaii, found that in the 20th century, governments murdered 170 million of their own people while combat claimed 38.5 million lives.[24]

CLAIM #6: "Concealed carry laws threaten to bring back the chaos of the wild west days."

RESPONSE: States with the largest increase in gun ownership also have the largest decrease in violent crime, especially in high crime urban areas and neighborhoods where minorities are allowed to carry concealed handguns.[25]

Thirty-eight states now have right-to-carry laws permitting law-abiding citizens to carry concealed firearms for protection against criminals. Half the U.S. population, including sixty percent of handgun owners, live in right-to-carry states.

Professors and legal scholars John R. Lott, Jr. and David B. Mustard of the University of Chicago conducted one of the most comprehensive studies of firearm laws ever, analyzing gun ownership and FBI crime data for each of the nation's 3,045 counties during an eighteen-year period—1977 to 1994.

Their report, *The Right-to-Carry Concealed Guns and the Importance of Deterrence,* concluded, "Non-discretionary concealed handgun laws are the most effective means of reducing crime."

Their study also found, "Allowing citizens to carry concealed weapons deters violent crimes and it appears to produce no increase in accidental deaths. If those states which don't have right-to-carry concealed gun provisions had adopted them in 1992, approximately 1,570 murders; 4,177 rapes; and over 60,000 aggravated assaults would have been avoided yearly...[T]he estimated annual gain from allowing concealed handguns is at least $6.214 billion...[W]hen state concealed handgun laws went into effect in a county, murders fell by 8.5 percent and rapes and aggravated assaults fell by five percent and seven percent."[26]

Lott found a negative relationship between the number of law-abiding citizens with permits and the crime rate. As more people obtain permits, there is a greater decline in the violent crime rates. Each year a concealed handgun law stays in effect, the murder rate declines by three percent, rape declines by two percent and robberies by more than two percent.[27]

Murder rates decline when both men and women carry concealed handguns, but the effect is especially pronounced for women. Lott writes, "An additional woman carrying a concealed handgun reduces the murder rate for women by about three or four times more than an additional man carrying a concealed handgun reduces the murder rate for men."[28]

Right-to-carry laws lead to lower murder rates without increasing the number of accidental deaths or suicides by handguns.[29]

Child murders have also dropped following adoption of non-discretionary concealed carry laws.[30]

Lott and Mustard's report continues, "States that have RTC laws have lower violent crime and homicide rates on average, compared to the rest of the country. RTC states have a 24 percent lower total violent crime rate, a 19 percent lower aggravated assault rate, a 39 percent lower robbery rate and a 19 percent lower aggravated assault rate, on average compared to the rest of the country."[31]

They also concluded, "People who obtain carry permits are by far more law abiding than the rest of the public. In Florida, for example, only a fraction of 1 percent of carry licenses have been revoked because of gun-related crimes committed by license holders."[32]

Survey research by criminologist Gary Kleck shows at least 2.5 million protective uses of firearms each year in the U.S. In his book *Targeting Guns: Firearms and Their Control*, Kleck writes, "[T]he best available evidence indicates that guns were used about three to five times for defensive purposes as for criminal purposes."[33]

Most protective uses do not involve discharge of a firearm. In protective gun uses only about 0.1 percent of criminals are killed and only one percent of criminals wounded. A Department of Justice survey found forty percent of felons chose not to commit at least some crimes for fear their victims were armed and thirty-four percent admitted being scared off or shot at by armed victims.[34]

CLAIM #7: "Most Americans favor more restrictive gun control laws."

RESPONSE: Eighty-five percent of Americans believe people should have the right to use firearms to defend themselves in their homes.

That's according to Lawrence Research's survey of American voters. The survey also found sixty-four percent of Americans favor allowing law-abiding citizens to carry firearms for personal protection outside their homes and seventy-two percent favor stiffer sentences for criminals who use a gun in crime rather than more gun laws.[35]

CLAIM #8: "Crime has decreased because of the the Brady Act's five-day waiting period and the assault weapons ban."

RESPONSE: Waiting periods have seldom reduced crime.

Historically, crime and murder rates have been worse in states with waiting periods and other laws which delay handgun purchases than in states which don't.

Despite California's ten-day waiting period and an "assault weapons ban," California's violent crime rate averaged forty-five percent higher than the rest of the country in the 1990s. The murder rate was thirty percent higher.[36]

In the Brady Act's first two years, the overall murder rate in states subject to its waiting period declined only nine percent versus seventeen percent in other states.[37]

Anti-gun researcher David McDowell writes, "Waiting periods have no influence on either gun homicides or gun suicides."[38]

The Brady Act five-day waiting period has resulted in fewer arrests of prohibited purchasers compared to NRA-backed instant check systems.

For example, from November 1989 to August 1998, Virginia's instant check led to 3,380 arrests—475 of those already wanted by law enforcement. Contrast that with what the General Accounting Office (GAO) discovered: in seventeen months of the Brady Act, only seven individuals were convicted of illegal attempts to buy handguns.[39]

States which had the Brady Act's waiting period imposed on them had worse violent crime trends thereafter, compared to other states. And today most violent crime occurs in states which delay firearm sales.[40]

Legal scholar John R. Lott, Jr. writes in his book *More Guns Less Crime: Understanding Crime and Gun Control Laws* that the Brady law has failed to reduce crime.

Waiting periods don't get criminals off the streets. Instead the longer the waiting period, the longer the criminal gets to walk the streets. Instant background checks are far more effective in determining if the person attempting to purchase the firearm has a criminal record.

Waiting periods needlessly delay law-abiding citizens from buying guns, a dangerous situation when a gun is needed immediately for protection. The debate over waiting periods has only served to distract America from concentrating on policies which would lead to the arrest, prosecution and imprisonment of violent criminals.

Violent crime started to decline nationally in 1991 prior to the Brady Act (which didn't take effect until February 1994) and the "assault weapons law" (which didn't take effect until September 1994). The Brady Act has never proven it reduces crime. Crime has declined for other reasons.

In New York, where one in ten violent crimes are committed, implementation of more severe police strategies and a more broad crackdown on crime dramatically reduced crime.[41]

Another reason crime has decreased is because the incarceration rate has doubled nationally.[42]

Finally, gangs, which accounted for a significant portion of gun crime in the United States, became less prevalent during the 1990s.[43]

CLAIM #9: "Guns are dangerous. Gun accidents are at an all-time high. We need trigger locks."

RESPONSE: **According to the National Center for Health Statistics, the fatal firearm accidents per capita rate fell to an all-time low in 1996.**

The new rate of 0.4 per 100,000 population represents an eighty-eight percent decrease from the all time high recorded in 1904.[44]

Fatal gun accidents are well below rates for other types of fatal accidents:

Motor vehicles—16.3 per 100,000 population
Falls—5.6 per 100,000 population
Poisonings—3.6 per 100,000 population
Drowning—1.3 per 100,000 population
Fires—1.4 per 100,000 population
Choking—1.2 per 100,000 population
Medical mistakes—1.1 per 100,000 population[45]

CLAIM #10: "Foreign countries such as Japan and England have less crime and violence than the U.S. because they have more restrictive gun control laws."

RESPONSE: **England, Wales and Australia, which have the most restrictive gun laws, actually have the highest rates of crime and violence among any of the top seventeen industrialized nations.**[46]

Countries which have banned gun ownership have, in essence, disarmed law abiding citizens and have made them more prone to gun violence.

Japan has both restrictive gun control laws and low crime, but only at the cost of imposing a virtual police state, something which couldn't be imposed in the U.S. Japanese citizens have fewer individual liberties and legal protections than Americans. Government officials in Japan routinely search citizens' homes (called "home visits")—without a warrant. The Tokyo Bar Association says police routinely engage in torture or illegal treatment. Even Amnesty International says Japan's police custody system represents a "flagrant violation of the U.N.'s human rights principles."[47]

CLAIM #11: "Pulling a gun on a criminal endangers you more than the criminal."

RESPONSE: According to Florida State University criminologist Gary Kleck, citizens use guns to defend themselves from criminals about 1 million times per year.

Kleck says in ninety-eight percent of "reported cases, criminals flee the moment they realize their intended victim is armed."[48]

Gun control expert John Lott studied fifteen national polls and organizations such as the *L.A. Times*, Gallup and Peter Hart Research Associates and concluded defensive gun uses run anywhere from 760,000 to 3.6 million per year.

Regardless of the figures, it's obvious the data demonstrates criminals are more "endangered" than law-abiding gun owners.[49]

CLAIM #12: "Guns kill children in epic numbers."

RESPONSE: The number of children age ten and under killed by guns is 0.4 times per day lower than the number of children killed each day by automobiles (in 1995 the number was 2,900), drowning (950) or burns (1000).[50]

Anti-gun activists consider anybody under the age of twenty-one a "child," adding into their statistics young men involved in drug trafficking.

The reality is there is no safety "crisis" as gun grabbers such as Democratic Senator Chuck Schumer of New York and comedian Rosie O'Donnell have suggested. Policy analyst David Kopel wrote in April 2000, "The number of fatal gun accidents is at its lowest level since 1903."[51]

Children who are trained in using and respecting guns are less likely to be harmed accidentally by a gun.

ABC News videotaped an experiment in which two different groups of children were left alone in a room with an unloaded gun. The kids who had gone through the NRA sponsored Eddie Eagle gun safety course left the gun alone. The course teaches that if you encounter a gun you should "Stop. Don't touch. Leave the area. And tell an adult."

The second group of kids, who had not taken the course, immediately began playing with the gun, pointing it at each other and pulling the trigger.[52]

CLAIM #13: "You need a license to drive a car. You should have one to own a gun."

RESPONSE: Licensing cars has not stopped the high number of fatalities on our nation's highways and the licensing of guns will not stop criminals who break the law.

Driving a car is not a constitutional right, as is the right to keep and bear arms.

Licensing every legally-owned gun in America will do nothing to stop criminals who commit crimes with firearms. It will only violate the individual right to keep and bear arms as guaranteed in the Bill of Rights of the U.S. Constitution.

Gun licensing leads to registration and ultimately to confiscation as it did in Nazi Germany and, more recently, in Great Britain and Australia where gun crime has dramatically increased.

The U.S. government has no constitutional authority to limit or revoke any individual amendment in the Bill of Rights, including the Second Amendment, unless three-quarters of the states vote on and pass an amendment to the Constitution.

But our constitutional rights weren't granted in exchange for "good behavior," which means they can't be withdrawn for bad behavior. That's what it means for a right to be inalienable.

As Patrick Henry said, "Guard with jealous attention the public liberty. Nothing will preserve it but downright force. Whenever you give that force up, you are ruined."

CLAIM #14: "Guns are more likely to injure or kill fifteen-to twenty-four-year-old black males than white males in the same age group."

RESPONSE: **Black males are more likely to commit violent crimes than any other group in America.**

Guns are inanimate objects. Guns are no more the cause of violence within the black community than McDonalds is the cause of obesity.

Blacks make up only twelve percent of the population, yet they account for more than forty-six percent of all violent crime and more than ninety percent of murders of blacks.[53]

So it's not illogical that guns are more likely to injure or kill black males—especially members of gangs—than whites of the same age group.

Black criminals—not white racist gun manufacturers—kill other blacks. And whites are the victims of black perpetrators in ninety percent of interracial crimes, according to Justice Department figures.[54]

Massive illegitimacy, teen pregnancy, drug use, unemployment and illiteracy are the primary causes of the continued plight of blacks in our inner cities. A strong and more plausible argument can be made that the Democrats' "Great Society" and resulting welfare programs of the 1960s, '70s and '80s greatly contributed to the rampant violence in the black community—not gun manufacturers.

CLAIM #15: "Having a gun in the home makes the home less safe."

RESPONSE: **Fatal shootings of criminals occur in only a fraction of one percent of protective firearm uses nationwide.**

Firearms are used for protection as many as 2.5 million times annually, according to research conducted by Gary Kleck, award winning Florida State University criminologist.[55]

Even gun-control advocate Marvin E. Wolfgang couldn't fault the methodology used in Kleck's research. He admitted using a gun in self-defense against a criminal perpetrator can be helpful.[56]

Gun-control advocates Arthur Kellermann and Donald Reay published an article in the June 12, 1986 issue of the *New England Journal of Medicine* claiming a gun in the house is "43 times more likely to be used" to kill a family member than an intruder. But what they didn't mention is suicides constitute thirty-seven out of every forty-three firearm related deaths. Nationwide, fifty-eight percent of firearm related deaths are suicides which are not solved with more gun control laws. Gun owners accidentally kill family members less than two percent of the time, or about once for every 90,000 defensive gun uses.[57]

CLAIM #17: "We need laws which mandate the storage of firearms to protect children."

RESPONSE: Firearm accidents account for only one percent of fatal accidents among children.

Trigger locks and safes have been on the market for years and individual gun owners can use them if they wish. Mandatory storage laws and locks, however, cannot take the place of responsible firearm handling.

Mandatory storage laws would also be almost impossible to enforce given the Fourth Amendment's protection against unreasonable searches.

Mandatory storage laws in Great Britain only led to the country's prohibition on handgun ownership, registration and ultimate confiscation.

CLAIM #17: "Guns should only be legal for legitimate 'sporting' purposes such as hunting."

RESPONSE: The Second Amendment of the U.S. Constitution gives individual citizens the right to own firearms.

This constitutional guarantee does not distinguish between the "legitimate" uses for which firearms ought to be used. This refrain of the left is merely used to make their position sound more "reasonable" and is primarily intended to pacify hunters, while simultaneously restricting guns not specifically intended for hunting, such as handguns and semi-automatics.[58]

Criminologist and long-time gun control supporter Phillip Cook rejected the "illegitimate" gun theory.

"Any gun that can be used in self-defense has a legitimate purpose and therefore is not 'useless,'" he said. "Similarly, any gun that can be used in crime can also be used in self-defense."[59]

Outlawing "Saturday Night Specials," as gun control advocates refer to the smaller caliber and often inexpensive handguns, would reduce the availability of these guns for low income people. Criminologist Gary Kleck observed "most SNSs are not owned or used for criminal purposes. Instead, most are probably owned by poor people for protection." Outlawing firearms not specifically intended for hunting would severely restrict those most at risk of being attacked (low income, law abiding, poor people mostly in inner cities).[60]

A study from the National Institute of Justice concluded, "There is no evidence anywhere to show that reducing the availability of firearms in general likewise reduces the availability to persons with criminal intent, or that persons with criminal intent would not be able to arm themselves under any set of general restrictions on firearms."[61]

CLAIM #18: "Gun violence is at all time high epidemic proportions."

RESPONSE: Gun violence has been declining rapidly for more than a decade.

Only a fraction of one percent of firearm owners ever use their guns in crimes and only a fraction of one percent of guns are used to commit crimes.[62]

The number of privately owned firearms has increased to an all-time high, while the violent crime rate has decreased every year since 1991 and is now at a twenty-three-year low.[63]

According to FBI crime statistics, firearm-related violence is less prevalent in many states and cities where firearm ownership is the greatest.[64]

Guns deter violence. This is a fact demonstrated by decreasing crime rates in states which allow citizens to carry firearms for protection and by surveys of felons which indicate the fear of encountering an armed law abiding citizen serves as a deterrent for committing crime.[65]

Research from the 1990s shows there were as many as 2.5 million self-defense uses of firearms annually—three to five times the number of crimes committed with firearms.[66]

CLAIM #19: "We need to close the 'gun show loophole.'"

RESPONSE: There is no gun show "loophole."

Since 1938, persons engaged in selling firearms have been required by law to register with the federal government. In 1968, all such persons were required to register to obtain a federal firearms license. Since 1998, dealers have been required to submit all prospective gun buyers to the National Instant Check System (NICS) background check conducted by the FBI or a state agency. This requirement is applicable for all gun shows all the time.

Guns used in crimes are rarely purchased at gun shows. According to the Bureau of Justice Report, less than one percent of criminals obtain guns from gun shows. This study was based on interviews conducted with 18,000 prison inmates representing the largest and most extensive study ever conducted by the federal government. And the National Institute of Justice study showed less than two percent of criminals' guns came from gun shows.[67]

CLAIM #20: "The NRA is a fringe group which opposes 'moderate' and 'reasonable' gun control regulations."

RESPONSE: The NRA has consistently supported many gun laws focused on making it more difficult for criminals to obtain firearms.

The NRA has supported state and federal laws prohibiting convicted violent criminals from possessing firearms and juveniles from being able to buy guns.[68]

The NRA assisted in drafting the 1986 law which prohibited the manufacture and importation of armor piercing ammunition.[69]

The NRA supported the 1988 Hughes-McCollum bill which prohibited the manufacture and production of any firearm that would be undetectable by airport detectors and enhanced airport security systems to counter terrorism.[70]

The NRA worked with slate legislators to write laws requiring computerized "instant" criminal records checks on firearms purchasers.[71]

The NRA worked with various legislators and citizens' groups to increase sentencing for violent criminals, to sentence violent criminals to prison rather than probation, to prevent the parole of the most violent criminals and to expand prison capacity.[72]

In sharp contrast, anti-gun activist groups like Handgun Control have supported restrictive laws which have had little impact in reducing violent gun crime, while making it more difficult for law-abiding citizens to protect and defend themselves and their property.[73, 74]

Chapter 8

H is for Health Care:

Do You Really Want National Eighty Percent Taxation?

Claims:
1. "No American should go without health care. Universal health care should be a guaranteed right of every American."
2. "Too many Americans don't have health care."
3. "We need to ensure health care for all Americans and need to institute a government health care single payer systems like they have in Canada, Europe, and Cuba so that all Americans can receive quality affordable health care."
4. "We need to spend more on health care."
5. "We need to roll back 'tax cuts for the rich' and 'invest' that money for health care for the poor."
6. "Health Care Savings Accounts (HSAs) will only benefit the rich and will result in higher costs to those who wish to remain in the traditional program which will hurt the elderly and the poor."
7. " The vaccine shortage proves that government has to be in control of health care to ensure universal vaccinations. This is too important to allow profits to come before health for the children and the elderly."

Health care is one of the few sectors of the American economy where costs and prices continue to rise—even though in almost every other sector of the economy they're declining due primarily to technology efficiencies and productivity gains.

Exorbitant health care costs, which consistently exceed inflation, have resulted in millions of Americans not being able to afford health insurance. It's vital for the American health care system to transform itself to meet the needs of an aging population and to give more consumers greater individual choice at affordable prices.

Americans are now directly dependent upon the government for about forty-five percent of their health care payment, with most of the rest provided by employers. The result is basically a giant tax-subsidy for the middle-class.

Projections show Medicare alone will consume about thirty-five percent of the entire federal budget within twenty-five years. By 2006, health care will be consuming $1 out of every $7 the American economy produces. Experts predict the government-run health care system will worsen significantly as the baby boomers continue to retire.

The major problem our system faces is price tags have virtually been removed from health care goods and services, concealing the true cost of health care from consumers, but not relieving them of paying higher costs.

In the 1940s, the IRS allowed companies to pay their workers in untaxed health care benefits. This subsidy has meant high-end workers now obtain a forty percent discount on health insurance and low-end workers end up getting nothing.

According to Clark Havighurst, Duke University's health care expert, "the systematic hiding of health-care costs from those who pay them" gives rise to the ultimate "moral hazard," allowing politicians to spend the public's money on health care in ways the public would never choose for itself—in the marketplace or the voting booth.

He further wrote, "the consequence of the shell game in which costs are moved wherever employees/consumers/voters are not looking" is regulated in ways "that make sense only because price tags have been generally removed. Several whole percentage points of the nation's gross domestic product are thus diverted wastefully to health care from other uses."

Havighurst also notes the regressive nature of the transfer.

"The United States has structured things so that lower and middle-income premium payers bear heavy burdens," he said, "so that the elite classes can continue to enjoy the style of health care to which they are accustomed."

This third-party payer system in the form of government, employers or insurance companies insulates consumers of health care from its true cost and encourages over-consumption and inflated costs.[1]

America had the best health care system in the world until the federal government moved into the field in the late 1960s. Medical care cost a fraction of today's prices, health insurance was significantly less expensive and doctors were a lot more accessible.

The tax code allows employers to deduct health care costs, but has never enabled individuals to deduct the majority of their medical expenses or all the cost of their health insurance. Employers paid these higher expenses in place of higher wages for their employees. The result was coverage not only became more expensive for employers, but also induced employees to take advantage of what seemed like "free" health care—putting greater demands on the health care providers and driving up the price for everyone.

Government has also made insurance more expensive by forcing insurance companies to provide benefits individuals may never need, but that companies have to offer employees in the price of the premiums they pay.

Because state and federal government have consistently mandated insurers to cover more benefits, employers have had to raise employee premiums, which has increased the price of health insurance dramatically over the last quarter century. Those rising costs have caused many employers to drop health insurance coverage for their employees. In 1980, ninety-seven percent of employees working for companies with 100 or more employees had medical coverage. By 1995, only seventy-seven percent were covered.

Then there's government-sponsored health care—Medicare and Medicaid.

Medicaid has inflated the cost of health care to such an extent that officials in Oregon were forced to ration care to Medicaid recipients. Tennessee officials increased taxes to pay for Medicaid overruns. On top of that, federal and state governments have imposed numerous regulations on doctors, hospitals, insurance companies and managed-care providers.

Hospitals by law are forced to admit anyone who shows up at the door—whether those patients have money to pay for treatment or not. These costs are passed along to consumers in the form of higher premiums.

The "Medicare + Choice" bill in 1997 stated managed-care providers had to add more services without being compensated for them. This has resulted in a loss position for so many providers that more than a hundred of them have had to leave the Medicare system entirely. That, in turn, has forced more than 400,000 senior citizens to search for new plans, resulting in less choice for seniors—not more.

Medicare routinely turns down roughly twenty percent of all procedures physicians decide are needed. The guidelines cover 111,000 pages and have resulted in higher health care costs by overloading doctors with regulations, forcing them to undercharge for their services and driving many of them out of the medical profession entirely.

Some physicians have decided to beat the problem by refusing to accept patients who use Medicare and Medicaid—usually the elderly and the poor. By doing so, doctors have been able to reduce by half or more their fees to their remaining patients.

President Bush and the GOP, as part of the Medicare Modernization Act of 2003, created Health Savings Accounts (HSAs) tax-free, high-deductible, health insurance plans for individuals and families under the age of sixty-five. People spend their own money on routine or minor health issues and unused funds in the HSAs accumulate tax free to be withdrawn in retirement at normal tax rates. By negotiating better prices for minor medical problems, health care expenses are reduced.

The administration also proposed the creation of a national marketplace for health insurance which would enable individuals from one state to purchase less expensive health insurance from other states—something which is now prohibited. Those in favor of allowing Americans to purchase lower cost drugs from Canada should surely support Americans' being able to cross state lines to purchase lower cost insurance policies.

Small businesses create seventy percent of all new jobs in America and account for more than half the output of the American economy. Employees of small businesses also represent the single largest segment of the uninsured population.

But HSAs have already dramatically reduced health care costs for them and have increased the availability of affordable health care to those who were previously uninsured. Small businesses realized an average of forty to fifty percent savings on health insurance premiums in 2004.[2]

To further aid individuals and families who work for small businesses, the Bush Administration proposed a federal tax credit to fund HSAs.

Yet, liberal Democrats continue to advocate "universal" government-run health care and oppose the very free market reforms which have resulted in lower health care costs. They continue to assert that Republican plans to "privatize" health care unfairly benefits the "rich, HMOs and the pharmaceutical industry" at the expense of the "poor" and "uninsured."

Those on the left, such as 2004 Democratic presidential candidate Senator John Kerry, have proposed increasing government spending by more than a trillion dollars in the next decade, with plans to pay for it by increasing taxes on the "rich." Unfortunately, Kerry's plan is not fundamentally different from most of socialist Europe's government-run health systems which have resulted in rationing and inferior care, especially for low- and middle-income workers.

Kerry's Universal Health Plan called for more government bureaucracy and the creation of an Office of Public Health Preparedness within the FDA. It also advocated more government price controls, which removes any incentive for companies to innovate and develop vaccines and other life-saving drugs and therapies. Senator Kerry and the Democrats proposed adding more uninsured (including many non-elderly and non-poor) to the government rolls and shoring up the faltering employment-based insurance system with more taxpayer subsidies.

While it's true far too many Americans don't have access to affordable health insurance, the left ignores the fact that increasing the size and scope of the federal government in the health care system has only stifled free-market innovation and competition—resulting in inferior care, contrived scarcities, price controls, less choice for consumers and higher costs.

A thorough examination of the claims the liberal left makes about health care uncovers many inaccuracies and distortions—a vital moral issue. It is crucial Americans evaluate and consider the facts. The future of health care in America is much too important to be decided by demagoguery, campaign soundbites and scare campaigns.

<u>CLAIM #1</u>: "No American should go without health care. Universal health care should be a guaranteed right of every American."

<u>RESPONSE</u>: Health care is never mentioned in the U.S. Constitution's Bill of Rights. The only "rights" outlined in our founding documents are rights to action.

Americans have the right to "pursue" happiness. They don't have the "right" to have somebody else pay for it or achieve a level of "happiness" at the expense of someone else's happiness.

The Constitution is the foundation which undergirds the laws governing our country. The Founders recognized the principle Thomas Jefferson clearly enunciated in the Declaration that man has been endowed with certain fundamental, inalienable rights which preexist government—namely life, liberty and the pursuit of happiness—not food, clothing and health care.

Our Constitution establishes justice, insures domestic tranquility, provides for the common defense, promotes the general welfare and secures "the Blessings of Liberty."[3]

But it doesn't decide who is "deserving" and who is not. Health care isn't a "right." That's because the American Founders recognized that type of "right" would require one person to work for, or serve, another person and they knew that wasn't liberty. An individual's freedom is diminished significantly when his money is confiscated to subsidize someone else's health care, food or anything else.

The very purpose of our government is to protect our rights. The government is not the *source* of these rights, but the *protector* of them. While we need to provide for the general welfare of society and should, as a compassionate society, care for those in poverty who cannot afford health care, it is not the constitutional jurisdiction of the government to provide health care to every American citizen.

A compassionate society provides charity for the less fortunate (and in dollar terms we in the United States are the most compassionate in the world), so there is no constitutional basis for taxing individuals' money to provide government run health care for the citizenry.

The way in which money is appropriated for constitutionally mandated programs has nothing to do with who is "deserving" and who isn't. Whether people are "deserving" is highly subjective and arbitrary.

It would be preferable for every American to have affordable health care insurance, however, it shouldn't be the responsibility of the government, any more than auto insurance should be a universal "right." Both are things individuals should be responsible for obtaining on their own. That's what it means to live in a free society.

Regardless, everyone in America does have universal access to health care. According to federal law, hospital emergency rooms are required to treat anybody, including the uninsured and illegal aliens.

Communist and socialist countries have universal health care, but freedom is at a premium in those countries. If you want to live in communist Cuba, Fidel Castro's constitution states people there have a "right" to health care and it is the duty of the government to provide hospitals, physicians and medicine to the citizenry.

If liberal Democrats want health care to be a "universal right" for all Americans, they can propose a constitutional amendment to the Bill of Rights to include the "right for every citizen to get free government-sponsored health care"—right along with the right to freedom of speech, the right to bear arms and due process of the law.

But based on the overwhelming opposition to Clinton's attempt to socialize health care in 1993, this scenario seems unlikely in the United States.

CLAIM #2: "Too many Americans don't have health care."

RESPONSE: While there are about 45 million Americans who don't have health insurance, not one U.S. citizen (and, by law, non-citizens) can by law be turned away from any emergency room in any hospital in America.

Every American (and even an illegal immigrant) has access to health care at any emergency room in America.

Many Americans, especially the self-employed and those who tend to be in general good health, choose not to purchase insurance and instead pay cash anytime they visit the doctor. Should Americans who pay for their own health care insurance be forced to subsidize with their tax dollars other Americans who can afford to purchase insurance but choose not to?

Many Americans spend their money on things such as clothing, trips, cars and electronics instead of insurance. If individuals could realize the same tax benefits businesses currently enjoy, many experts argue that more Americans would choose to purchase coverage. President Bush's health savings accounts (HSAs) enable individuals to save tax free for their own health care needs and purchase coverage at significantly reduced costs.

The Census Bureau shows the total number of Americans with health care insurance rose to a record 243.3 million in 2003. It also shows there are 45 million Americans without health care insurance. As a percentage, the number of those without insurance is 15.6 percent lower than it was in 1997-1998 under the Clinton administration and within the same range it's been for the past decade. Why was Bill Clinton not able to make health care more affordable in his eight year presidency?[4]

What many don't realize is that one third of those who are uninsured are eligible for Medicaid and the State Children's Health Insurance Program (S-CHIP), but are not enrolled. More than 14 million Americans who are eligible for insurance can apply for health care assistance if and when they require it.[5]

There are, according to 2003 Census Data, almost 15 million uninsured people in households considered "wealthy"—with incomes above $50,000 (7.6 million of them in households over $75,000). While some may dispute that somebody earning $75,000 is considered "rich," it is reasonable to assume those individuals who are earning these types of incomes can afford to purchase the health care which best fits their needs.[6]

There are another 18.8 million uninsured between the ages of eighteen and thirty-four who voluntarily forgo coverage because many states offer "guaranteed issue" laws which enable individuals to put off purchasing insurance until they get sick and need it. This law actually encourages the irresponsible to delay buying insurance. The fact remains, however, that these 18.8 million citizens have access to health care insurance. They choose to forgo purchasing it until they are sick enough to need it.[7]

While the number of uninsured is high, there are ways to make health insurance more readily available at a lower cost to consumers which don't include expanding government or raising taxes.

One way is for Congress to end the fifty-state insurance market by proclaiming there shall be nationwide commerce in health care like there are for other goods and services.

Another way to lower the price of coverage, as President Bush has proposed, is to equalize the tax treatment for employer-purchased and individually-purchased health care.

Finally, Congress should pass legislation to deny any illegal immigrant unlimited health care access and treatment. Health care prices would drop substantially if we didn't reward non-U.S. citizens who enter our country illegally with free health care.

CLAIM #3: "We need to ensure health care for all Americans and institute government health care single payer systems like they have in Canada, Europe and Cuba so all Americans can receive quality affordable health care."

RESPONSE: Government run, Socialist-style health care has been a dismal failure everywhere it has been instituted.

Even though there are many problems with our current managed care health care system, it is far superior to any other country in the world.

Many on the left claim medical care is superior in other countries.

However, in each country they allude to, costs are higher, waiting times for treatment longer, quality of care inferior and patient choice significantly reduced.

Canadian socialized medicine does not have enough money to provide care for all its citizens. Socialism always leads to price controls, reduced innovation and rationing. Because the government runs health care in Canada, it must compete with other government programs for funding and is therefore dependent upon politicians and bureaucrats who determine the quantity and quality of the health care citizens receive.

Some of the problems with Canada's socialized medicine are:

- Hospital money shortages

The *Toronto Star* reported on Dec. 24, 1999 "The Ontario government is bailing out deficit ridden hospitals to the tune of $196 million." This infusion "marked the second year in a row the Tory government has come to the rescue of about half of the province's hospitals."

- Doctor shortages

On Dec. 23, 1999, the *Toronto Star* ran the headline: "Ontario Government Report Calls For Up To 1,000 More MDs."[8]

Canadian socialized medicine does not provide "universal access to care." On Jan. 18, 2003, the *Canadian Press* carried the headline: "Send Cancer Patients to U.S, Alberta MDs Urge." The story begins, "Breastcancer patients whose wait to see a specialist has jumped up to eight weeks from less than four should be sent out of province for treatment, the president of Alberta Medical Association says."

In a story about a proposal to allow private day surgeries in Vancouver, BC to reduce waiting times, the *Vancouver Province* reported on June 11, 2003: "But even when the (Richmond) hospital was at its most efficient 40 percent of patients were waiting three months or more (for elective surgery)."[9]

The overall quality of care in Canada is inferior to health care in the U.S.

The British Columbia Medical Association has released a paper calling for "the establishment of maximum wait times or 'care guarantees' for various medical procedures," according to the story. The report "proposes that patients not helped within the guaranteed time frame should be able to seek care out of province —in a public or private facility—at no cost to themselves."

That's because it's against the law for a citizen to pay out of pocket for care provided by the government-run health care system. The only other countries which criminalize privately paying for health care are North Korea and Cuba.[10]

Canadians are increasingly seeking medical care in the United States. Are they crossing the border to receive inadequate health care?

On January 16, 2000, a *New York Times* article titled "Full Hospitals Make Canadians Wait and Look South" concluded, "As a result, Canada has moved informally to a two-tier, public-private system. Although private practice is limited to dentists and veterinarians, 90 percent of Canadians live within 100 miles of the United States and many people are crossing the border for private care."[11]

Socialized health care results in rationing, which disproportionately hurts the poor. According to the leftward-leaning Brookings Institution, thousands of British citizens are denied medical attention. Each year in Great Britain, 7,000 who need hip replacements, between 4,000 and 20,000 who need coronary bypass surgery and some 10,000 to 15,000 who need cancer chemotherapy don't get the help they need.

Why? For one, age discrimination is particularly apparent in all government-run regulated systems of health care.

Consider the treatment of chronic kidney failure in the U.K. Those who are fifty-five years old are refused treatment at dialysis centers thirty-five percent of the time; sixty-five-year-olds are denied treatment forty-five percent of the time; and patients seventy-five or older rarely receive any medical attention.

Consider the following headlines from British and Canadian newspapers:

- "Am I Too Old To Be Treated?" *The Sunday Times*, April 17, 1994.
- "Kidney Patients Die As Costly Dialysis Machines Lie Idle," *The Times*, July 26, 1993
- "Too Old To Be Cured Of Cancer," *The Times*, August 16, 1993.

- "For Dogs, A Scan Can Be Arranged Within 24 Hours. Humans Wait in Pain, Dogs Don't," *Canadian Press*, June 14, 1991.[12]

And Britain isn't the only country with socialized medicine to discriminate against the elderly. In Russia, patients older than sixty are considered worthless parasites and those over seventy are often denied even elementary forms of health care.

The rich and well-connected always get better treatment in Britain and Canada, according to a Heritage Foundation study.

Heritage cites a survey sent to Ontario cardiologists showing that "the politically powerful, the rich, and the potentially litigious received preferential treatment. Over eighty percent of doctors and fifty-three percent of hospital administrators had been involved personally in a case involving preferential treatment."[13]

Most of the doctors said they gave preferential treatment to those they personally knew, as well as those who were well-known where delayed treatment would embarrass the hospital, such as basketball star Shareef Abdur-Rahim who received an MRI scan for his knee—jumping ahead of almost 1,000 others who were waiting for MRIs. The Canadian doctors also said they favored patients whose political or social standing would be helpful to their hospitals and tended to give prompt treatment to those more likely to sue for slow service.

CLAIM #4: "We need to spend more on health care."

RESPONSE: We need to spend LESS on health care.

In order to decrease health care costs, increase quality and consumer choice, we need to empower individuals to be directly responsible for their own health care. When costs are removed from the decision making process, consumers will always choose to use more health care services, even if they are not required, since they are not directly responsible for paying for those services. When millions of Americans go to the emergency room for routine non-emergent reasons, overall health care costs increase dramatically.

Health savings accounts (HSAs) enable individual Americans to save tax free for their own health care at half the cost of the third party system. Individuals are given the incentive to spend this money more wisely. HSAs decrease the overall cost of health care insurance. Increased government spending has only made the system less efficient and more expensive by distorting the true value of health care services.

CLAIM #5: "We need to roll back 'tax cuts for the rich' and 'invest' that money for health care for the poor."

RESPONSE: Raising taxes on the most productive members of society would only exacerbate the situation.

The problem with our current government-run health care system is that costs are hidden from consumers.

Since consumers are limited to only choosing doctors and services "in their plan," and since the vast majority of health care dollars come from the government, the consumer is no longer the "customer." The high cost has made it disproportionately more difficult for the poor to purchase affordable health care.

Eighty percent of those who earn more than $200,000, work for or own small businesses who pay taxes at the individual tax rate. Raising taxes on small businesses will leave less money for them to hire more workers and less money to provide insurance for them.

The United States can have vibrant economic growth and low-cost, high-quality health care simultaneously. HSA plans have allowed small businesses to realize an average forty to fifty percent immediate savings on health insurance premiums in 2004.

The Center for Health Transformation has collected thirty-one examples of small businesses which have saved money adopting HSA plans. Twenty-seven of these small businesses are saving an average of forty-four percent on their health insurance premiums. The complete list of these examples can be found at http://www.healthtransformation.net/Transforming_Examples/Transforming_Exampl es_Resource_Center/.[14]

CLAIM #6: "Health Care Savings Accounts will only benefit the rich and will result in higher costs to those who wish to remain in the traditional program which will hurt the elderly and the poor."

RESPONSE: Universal government-run health care disproportionately hurts the poor.

As previously discussed, government price controls and regulations hamper innovation, competition and choice, and lead to rationing and artificially high prices.

The rich will always be able to afford high-quality medical care. Exorbitant health care insurance costs penalize those who can least afford it. Socialism is intended to more equitably distribute society's wealth, but it always results in inefficient allocations of scarce resources, arbitrarily high prices and scarcities. History is replete with examples of the misery, destruction and death socialism has wrought.

The early results of the transformation to health savings accounts has been extraordinary in terms of cost savings for individuals, small businesses, family farms, large employers and governments as well as expansion of health care to previously uninsured Americans.[15]

For example, in 2004:

- Ohio Waste Water, a small business with sixty-six employees, saved $207,566 (37 percent) on health insurance premiums with an HSA Plan.

- Herve Riel, a self-employed small business owner in New Hampshire, saved $6,600 (sixty-six percent) on his individual health insurance coverage after choosing an HSA plan.

- An Iowa small business counseling service with eight employees saved $14,740 (thirty-two percent) on health insurance premiums with an HSA plan.

- An Iowa OB-GYN clinic with thirteen employees saved $40,608 (thirty-eight percent) on health insurance premiums when the owner switched to an HSA plan.

- Mercury Office Supply, a Minnesota small business with fifteen employees saved $12,000 with an HSA plan.

- A Minnesota small business with eighteen employees saved $20,000 (twenty-three percent) with an HSA Plan.

- Dr. Jeffrey Wilder, a Wisconsin small business owner, saved $8,400 (seventy percent) on his family health insurance coverage in the first year with an HSA plan.[16]

<u>CLAIM #7</u>: "The vaccine shortage proves that government has to be in control of health care to ensure universal vaccinations. This is too important to allow profits to come before health for the children and the elderly."

<u>RESPONSE</u>: The shortage demonstrates how government price controls cause shortages.

A fundamental cause of the problem is that the U.S. government purchases fifty-five percent of the childhood vaccine market at forced discount prices, according to a report the National Academy of Science's Institute of Medicine issued in August 2003. The result has been "declining financial incentives to develop and produce vaccines."[17]

Hillary Clinton is largely to blame. In August 1993, a Democrat-controlled Congress passed Mrs. Clinton's Vaccines for Children program which used federal power to ensure universal immunization. The government agreed to purchase sixty percent of the national pediatric vaccine supply (the Clintons pushed for 100 percent) at a forced discount of about fifty percent, to be delivered to doctors, the poor, the under-insured and uninsured, even though vaccines are already free for the needy through programs such as Medicaid.

The result of Hillary's program was that the *government* instead of *doctors* became the direct purchaser for most children's vaccines. That meant the government was dictating the price to the drug manufacturers and it was so far below cost that many suppliers were forced out of business. Thirty years ago, twenty-five companies produced vaccines. Today, there are only five.

That's what has caused numerous shortages of vaccines in recent years.[18]

The tort trial lawyers are also largely to blame for the vaccine shortages. In 1986, Congress created the Vaccine Injury Compensation Program which required injured parties to seek redress prior to suing in the regular courts. But the plaintiff's bar has circumvented the VICP mostly by claiming damages due to the discontinued, but harmless, additive thimerosal. Similar lawsuits have significantly driven up production costs for these companies and have forced many of them to exit the vaccine market, further exacerbating the dearth of manufacturers and the subsequent shortage of vaccines.[19]

The vaccine shortage demonstrates the failure of government price controls and the need for a return to a free market system. Private companies are willing to invest and innovate if they can realize an adequate profit. Vaccines are a predictable cost, not a variable cost, and according to Jack Calfee of the American Enterprise Institute, constitute less than two percent of the pharmaceutical market or less than 0.2 percent of U.S. health costs.

The $400 to $600 cost can be spread out over sixteen years and the needy can obtain these vaccines through Medicaid or the federally funded State Children's Health Insurance Program. It is vital the government enable companies to compete in the free and open market instead of setting price controls. That only stifles innovation and competition, and invariably leads to shortages and rationing, as was the case with the October 2004 vaccine shortages.[20]

Liberals advocate less choice for the individual and more centralized power and authority for the state in medical matters. Democrats consistently advocate "single payer/universal health care" which limits individual patient choice and gives most of the power and decision-making authority to federal government bureaucrats. The Clintons tried to incorporate one-seventh of our economy under the control of the federal government by creating "Hillary-Care" in 1993. The voters revolted the following year and elected Republican majorities in both houses of Congress for the first time since Calvin Coolidge was president in 1930.

Similar socialized "universal health care" legislation has been rejected by the voters in many individual states such as Oregon (one of the most liberal states in the country). While liberals have advocated federalization of health care, conservatives have proposed legislation which gives more autonomy and authority to individual health care consumers.

Chapter 9

I is for Independent Israel:

Why We Need to Support the Only Middle East Democracy

Claims:
1. "The Jews illegally occupy Palestinian land."
2. "A Palestinian state is needed because Arabs were forcibly removed from their property in the 1948 war."
3. "Militant Islamists attacked the U.S. because we support Israel."
4. "Israel is the real terrorist in the Middle East."

Since the September 11, 2001, terrorist attacks on the U.S., many on the left have claimed America invited the terrorism mainly because of its support for Israel.

As the argument goes, "If America didn't side with Israel, we wouldn't have antagonized the Arab and Islamic world."

Or they say if Israel would end its "illegal occupation" of Palestine, "peace in the Middle East" would finally be achieved.

However, critics who suggest Israel's presence in the Middle East and U.S. support for Israel are primary causes of terrorism and other violence, base their arguments on faulty logic. With the leftward leaning international media organizations by their side, those who blame Israel for most of the world's ills do so by misrepresenting the facts and distorting many important truths.

<u>CLAIM #1</u>: "The Jews illegally occupy Palestinian land."

RESPONSE: Asserting an "illegal" occupation implies there has been a violation of the law.

Which law has Israel broken? The nation state of Israel was created as a legal entity in 1948.

This claim is nothing more than strategic deception and propaganda used to justify the murder of Jews in Israel by state-sponsored terrorist organizations such as the Palestine Liberation Organization (PLO), Hamas and Islamic Jihad. The stated goal of many of the surrounding Arab countries is the complete destruction of the state of Israel and the Jewish people. The 1964 PLO manifesto calls for the "obliteration of Israel as the Zionist entity" and Palestinian leaders have never abandoned or renounced this manifesto.

The name Palestine was first used in 70 A.D. when the Romans committed genocide on the Jews, destroyed the temple in Jerusalem and declared the land of Judea would be no more. From that point forward, the Romans decided the land would be called Palestine, which was derived from the word "Philistines"—a people the Israelites had conquered more than 1,000 years earlier.

Prior to the 1967 Arab-Israeli War, no serious movement existed for a Palestinian homeland. It was not until after the Six Day War in 1967 that the Israelis captured Judea, Samaria and East Jerusalem—not from the Palestinians, but from Jordan's King Hussein—that this movement began.

Palestine never existed as a nation state. It was ruled by Rome, Islamic and Christian crusaders, the Ottoman Empire and the British—but never by Arabs.

There is no language known as Palestinian. There is no distinct Palestinian culture and there has never been a land governed by Palestinians.

When the kingdom of Jordan ruled Palestine, the "Palestinians" never accused Jordan of "occupying" Palestinian land. Where were the Palestinians when Jordan occupied the entire West Bank, including Jerusalem? Why didn't they make claims of wanting their own state then?[1]

CLAIM #2: "A Palestinian state is needed because Arabs were forcibly removed from their property in the 1948 war."

RESPONSE: There was never a Jewish conspiracy to drive Arabs from their homes.

Arabs during that time period placed much of the blame on Arab countries and not on the nation state of Israel.

On September 6, 1948, Emile Ghoury, secretary of the Palestinian Arab Higher Committee, was quoted in an interview with the *Beirut Telegraph* as saying, "The fact that there are these refugees is the direct consequence of the act of the Arab states in opposing partition and the Jewish state. The Arab states agree upon this policy unanimously and they must share in the solution of the problem."

A few months later on the February 19, 1949, the Jordanian daily newspaper *Falastin* reported, "The Arab state which had encouraged the Palestinian Arabs to leave their homes temporarily in order to be out of the way for the Arab invasion armies, have failed to keep their promise to help these refugees."

The Beirut Muslim weekly *Kul-Sahy* on August 19, 1951 reported, "Who brought the Palestinians to Lebanon as refugees, suffering now from the malign attitude of newspapers and communal leaders, who have neither honor nor conscience? Who brought them over in dire straits and penniless, after they lost their honor? The Arab states and Lebanon amongst them, did it."

The Cairo daily *Akhbar el Yom* on October 12, 1963 reported, "The 15th May, 1948, arrived... On that day the mufti of Jerusalem appealed to the Arabs of Palestine to leave the country, because the Arab armies were about to enter and fight in their stead."

The Jordanian daily newspaper *Al Urdun* on April 9, 1953 reported, "For the flight and fall of the other villages it is our leaders who are responsible because of their dissemination of rumors exaggerating Jewish crimes and describing them as atrocities in order to inflame the Arabs... By spreading rumors of Jewish atrocities, killings of women and children, etc., they instilled fear and terror in the hearts of the Arabs in Palestine, until they fled leaving their homes and properties to the enemy."[2]

Most of the surrounding Arab nations have also failed to absorb the "refugees" into their under-populated, wealthy nations.

Following World War II, there were approximately 100 million refugees around the world. The Palestinian Arab group is the only one in the world not absorbed or integrated into their own people's lands.

A bill was introduced in Lebanon's Parliament in 2002 which denied Palestinian-Arabs the right to own property. Those who owned property would not be able to give it to their children.

While Israel has bent over backwards to accommodate the Palestinians—offering them ninety-five percent of the West Bank in 1999 as part of the peace plan—other Arab nations continue to exploit the misery and poverty of the Palestinian people in order to justify their belligerent opposition to Israel and the Jewish people.[3]

CLAIM #3: "Militant Islamists attacked the U.S. because we support Israel."

RESPONSE: Islamo-fascists attacked the United States because they hate our way of life and the democratic values we promote around the world.

Terrorism cannot be justified by any rationale.

It's disingenuous to assert the U.S. has "sided" with Israel unfairly because the U.S. doesn't solely support Israel. America gives billions of dollars each year to the Palestinians and has repeatedly attempted to broker "peace" deals which have included provisions for a Palestinian state.

Palestinian terrorist organizations such as the PLO, Hamas and Islamic Jihad have purposefully targeted innocent civilians, including pregnant women and children in their homicide "bombings." Only the Palestinians have committed these blatant acts of terrorism against innocent civilians in Israel. One cannot equate Israel's fundamental right to protect herself from such terrorist attacks by targeting terrorist organizations and other military installations with egregious acts of terror. Attributing moral equivalence is dangerously misguided.

Arabs who live in Israel are treated better and have more political, religious and economic freedoms than most Arab citizens in any of the other twenty-two Arab states—all of which are varying degrees of police states.

Not only that, Israel is the largest employer of Palestinians in the world. The approximately one million Arabs living in Israel can practice their own religion (unlike Jews living in Arab countries), can vote in elections and serve in Israel's legislative body the Knesset.

Arab women living in Israel are granted greater liberty and freedom than women living in Arab countries—where they're treated as men's property and have few, if any, individual liberties.

If Israel treats Palestinians better than Arab countries do, with more individual freedoms and economic opportunities, how can the Arab world hate the U.S. for its support of Israel?

What about the other Islamic and Arab terrorist atrocities around the world—many times Arabs committing terrorist acts against other Arabs?

- Syria committed terrorist acts against Lebanon.
- Saddam Hussein unleashed a bloodbath against Iran and invaded Kuwait.
- Kuwait expelled hundreds of thousands of Palestinians.
- Muslim terrorists murdered hundreds of thousands of Christians in Sudan.
- Muslim terrorists murdered 202 people in Bali.
- Muslim terrorists encouraged church bombings in Pakistan.[4]

The United States' support for Israel is not the primary cause of the Islamic terrorism and violence the world has witnessed over the past twenty years—and for that matter, 9/11 itself. The Islamic terrorists hate—above all else—liberal democracies, religious freedom and the rule of law. Shifting blame on the U.S. as though we provoked these barbaric acts fails to acknowledge the root cause of terrorism—which is pure unadulterated evil.

Arab states actively promote bigotry toward Jews and Christians. Here are some examples of the flagrant intolerance and hatred found in some Muslim textbooks:

- "Jews subscribe to a belief in racial superiority... Their religion even teaches them to call down curses upon the worship places of non-Jews whenever they pass by them."
- "Judaism and Christianity are deviant religions."
- "Befriending the unbelievers, through loving and

cooperating with them while knowing that they are unbelievers, makes those who are their friends the same as them."

- "Many (Jews and Christians) lead such decadent and immoral lives that lying, alcohol, nudity, pornography, racism, foul language, premarital sex, homosexuality and everything else are accepted in the society, churches and synagogues."

CLAIM #4: "Israel is the real terrorist in the Middle East."

RESPONSE: **Israel does not promote terrorism, house terrorists, or aid and abet terrorist organizations.**

Any military action Israel has taken has been in defense of its country and its citizenry. Although in some cases, innocent Palestinian civilians have been killed, the vast majority of Israeli attacks have narrowly focused on military targets and terrorist organizations as retribution for past terrorist attacks in an effort to prevent future attacks.

Palestinians, in contrast, promote terrorism—the intentional targeting and murder of innocent civilians. They harbor terrorist organizations and reward families of terrorists. Whether these "suicide bombings" are perpetrated in the name of "peace" or "justice" or in the name of "Allah," the fact is, Palestinian "freedom fighters" intentionally target and murder innocent Israeli citizens.

These violent and murderous acts are not committed in response to other intentional atrocities against innocent Palestinians. One never sees young Israelis strapping bombs to themselves and killing innocent women and children in pizza parlors in Palestinian neighborhoods.

Palestinian terrorist acts are committed to instill fear and to intimidate the Jewish people into leaving Israel. The Palestinians have rejected virtually every offer to live in peace, side-by-side with their Jewish neighbors. The Palestinians and their Arab neighboring countries only want to see the complete removal or subjugation of the Jewish people and the Jewish state of Israel in the Middle East.

Trying to equate Israel's self-defense with the intentional terrorist attacks of Islamic militants is merely an attempt to gain sympathy from the rest of the world for the plight of the Palestinian people. Reasoning that Palestinians are "martyrs" and Israel "terrorists" completely distorts reality.

Chapter 10

J is for Justice:

Why Criminals Need Discipline

Claims:
1. "If you conservative Republicans believe that every life is sacred, how can you justify the death penalty?"
2. "Criminals should be rehabilitated not locked up. We need to build more hospitals not more prisons."
3. "Crime is predominantly the result of failures of societal institutions and poverty not individuals."
4. "The death penalty doesn't deter crime."
5. "Life imprisonment is just as bad if not worse than the death penalty."
6. "Many found guilty of murder and sentenced to death are later found to be innocent. Innocent people are executed."
7. "The Bible opposes killing, and there is no scriptural foundation for the death penalty."
8. "The death penalty is cruel and unusual punishment."
9. "The death penalty is racist. A disproportionate number of prisoners on death row are black (40%) while they account for only twelve percent of the American population."

Liberals and conservatives differ significantly with regard to the causes of crime and the appropriate manner to deal with criminals.

Many on the liberal left say crime is primarily a result of failed social institutions. In other words, those who commit crimes do so because the state has not done enough to deal with the root causes of crime—meaning the government hasn't done enough to achieve "economic justice." They say the capitalist system has resulted in a fortunate, but small, group of rich people, a dwindling middle class and vast lower class, who are victims of the callous system. The left asserts government should offer social programs so the poor won't feel the need to commit crime.

The left suggests that the purpose of the criminal justice system should be rehabilitative, because incarceration and the death penalty are inhumane and inherently racist.

There are many causes of crime, including failed public schools, the meteoric rise of sex and violence in the media, activist federal courts and rampant illegal immigration. But many conservative leaders argue crime is fundamentally the consequence of the disintegration of the family. The link between illegitimacy, welfare dependence, poverty and crime has been well documented. Because of that, conservatives primarily advocate policies which strengthen the family as opposed to more government social programs.

Decades of government welfare programs have only exacerbated government dependence, especially among minorities, resulting in a rapid rise of illegitimacy, poverty and violent crime.

Conservatives argue that in the short term, violent criminals should be locked up in order to protect law-abiding citizens. But the long-term solution for reducing violent crime can only be achieved by strengthening the family and enabling faith-based institutions and schools, to promote the morals which under-gird individual and community growth.

Liberals support the "right" of an abortionist to kill a woman's unborn baby; of the state to terminate life (euthanasia); and the intentional destruction of human embryos for scientific research (embryonic stem cell research), but don't support the death penalty for convicted murderers because they say *that* is cruel, unjust and inhumane. The advocates of "choice" claim "innocent" people could unfairly die.

However, they show no similar concern for the destruction of the 40 million innocent developing babies who have been aborted since 1973.

If there is one issue which most clearly reveals the hypocritical liberal mindset, it is definitely the issue of crime and punishment.

CLAIM #1: "If you conservative Republicans believe every life is sacred, how can you justify the death penalty?"

RESPONSE: The life of the unborn is sacred. A convicted murderer renounces this "right" when he or she takes an innocent life.

Putting convicted murderers to death affirms the sanctity of life by making sure those murderers will never kill again. It simultaneously assures society justice will be done.

CLAIM #2: "Criminals should be rehabilitated, not locked up. We need to build more hospitals, not more prisons."

RESPONSE: The purpose of our penal code is not rehabilitative. It's to punish those who break the law so law-abiding citizens are protected from those who may harm them.

Liberal Courts and politicians have already experimented with "rehabilitative justice" by reducing prison terms and increasing the number of parolees. The result? Crime skyrocketed.

Over the last fifty years, prison sentences have decreased sixty percent, while the U.S. population has increased forty-one percent. The number of violent crimes (rapes, robberies, murders and aggravated assaults) have increased 550 percent, according to FBI statistics.

The idea that punishment has no effect on criminals contradicts the data.[1] The ten states which had the greatest *increases* in their incarceration rates reaped the benefit of an eight percent *decrease* in their crime rates, according to the American Legislative Exchange Council's findings.

In contrast, the ten states with the *lowest* incarceration rates experienced about a fifty percent *increase* in crime.[2]

Michigan in the early 1980's instituted an early-release program when prison funding dried up. From 1981 to 1986, violent crime rose twenty-five percent while national rates fell.[3]

A 2002 Department of Justice study concluded approximately sixty-eight percent of criminals released from federal prison are rearrested for a felony or serious misdemeanor within three years of their release. Almost half are convicted of a new crime.[4]

Some states have tried the softer, rehabilitation way only to return to a stricter incarceration policy. In North Carolina, state officials decided they would pursue alternative punishments such as probation and parole instead of building new prisons. The idea was to rehabilitate criminals by taking them out of the "dehumanizing" conditions of the state prison system. By 1990, eighty percent of the state's convicts were enrolled in "alternative" programs and only twenty percent were actually serving prison time.

What was the result of this more "humane" policy of "rehabilitative justice?" Many violated their probation and parole and ended up in prison once again while crime continued to rise twenty-five percent—the second highest rate in the nation.[5]

North Carolina's Governor Jim Hunt decided to take action. He enacted "structured sentencing" which increased the time criminals served in prison. The new law abolished parole for violent offenders and set aside more money for additional prison construction. As a result of this law, crime decreased dramatically—from 6,000 crimes per 100,000 people in 1990 to 4,800 crimes per 100,000 people in 2002, according to U.S. Bureau of Justice statistics.[6]

CLAIM #3: "**Crime is predominantly the result of failures of societal institutions and poverty, not individuals.**"

RESPONSE: **Throughout history, neither reductions in poverty, nor increases in government spending for social programs, nor reductions in unemployment have ever led to lower crime rates.**

Crime rates during the Great Depression were much lower than they are today. The Chinese in San Francisco in the mid-1960s had the lowest family income of any ethnic group (less than $4,000 per year), but virtually zero crime. Only five Chinese were in prison during that time.

Even during the 1982 recession, crime dipped slightly.[7]

On the other hand, crime *increased* during America's long period of economic growth from 1905 to 1933. It also rose as the economy was booming and incomes rising from 1965 to 1974.

The most dramatic increases in crime in the past fifty years have coincided with the largest appropriations of federal and state aid to cities. More than $5 trillion has been spent since the "War on Poverty" was declared in 1965 and the number of major felonies has increased.

From 1960 to 1970 when government social spending was the greatest, the murder rate increased almost 200 percent as did rapes, and property crimes such as burglary and car theft almost tripled.[8]

Crime is the result of many factors, including: government dependency; escalating images of violence and sex in the media and in our culture; high rates of illegal immigration; and activist courts who have made it increasingly more difficult to punish criminals.

The root cause of crime, however, is the breakdown in traditional moral values, especially the disintegration of the family. Research shows an increased likelihood that children born out of wedlock will grow up to be criminals.

The "root cause of violent crime thus is found in failed intimate relationships of love and marriage in the family," writes family therapist and clinical psychologist Patrick F. Fagan in *The Real Root Cause of Violent Crime: The Breakdown of Marriage, Family and Community*. "The breakdown of stable communities into crime-infested neighborhoods flows directly from this failure. In contrast, addressing the root causes of crime requires an understanding of the crucial elements of supportive family and community life."[9]

Fagan, a William H. G. Fitzgerald Research Fellow in Family and Cultural issues at the Heritage Foundation, served as Deputy Secretary of Health and Human Services during the George H.W. Bush (41) Administration.

He concludes, "It is no coincidence that one of the central rules in the traditional moral code of all communities at all times, in all places and in all cultures is the prohibition against giving birth to children outside of marriage. Societies all over the world have recognized that this prohibition is essential to social stability and to raising members of each new generation with the proper respect for their community and their peers. Unfortunately and with disastrous consequences, this prohibition is ignored today in American society at all levels but mostly especially in central-city neighborhoods. Having a child outside of marriage virtually guarantees a teenage woman and her children a life of poverty, low education, low expectations and low achievement. It gradually puts into place the conditions which foster rejection and, ultimately, crime."

To reduce crime, Fagan says the family needs to be rebuilt and that "institutions in the community, such as the church and the school, have demonstrated their importance in helping to restore stability."[10]

With regard to more government social programs as a solution to crime, Fagan says, "Government agencies, on the other hand, are powerless to increase marital and parental love; they are powerless to increase the ability of adults to make and keep commitments and agreements. Instead, thanks to policies that do little to preserve the traditional family and much to undermine it, government continues to misdiagnose the root cause of social collapse as an absence of goods and services. This misdiagnosis is government's own contribution to the growth of crime. Having misdiagnosed it misleads."[11]

Fagan cites a few major studies to support his contention that the root cause of crime is the breakdown of the traditional family. For example, criminologists Dr. G. Roger Jarjoura, a professor at Indiana University and the late Dr. Douglas A. Smith, in their major 1988 study of 11,000 individuals found that "the percentage of single-parent households with children between the ages of 12 and 20 is significantly associated with rates of violent crime and burglary."[12]

Harvard sociologist Dr. Robert J. Sampson in his study of the differential effects of poverty and family disruption on crime writes, "Overall the analysis shows that rates of black violent offences, especially by juveniles are strongly influenced by variations in family structure. Independent of the major candidates supplied by prior criminological theory (e.g. income, region, size, density, age, race composition) black family disruption has the largest effects on black juvenile robbery and homicide. The effects of family structure are strong and cannot be easily dismissed by reference to other structural and cultural features of urban environments...The effect of family disruption on black violence is not due to the effect of black violence on family structure."[13]

A significant cause of crime during the past forty years has been activist judicial courts making it easier for criminals to commit crimes. For example, the liberal Warren Court concluded in 1966 in *Miranda v. Arizona,* "The police did not undertake to afford appropriate safeguards at the onset of the interrogation to insure that the statements were truly the product of free choice."

Even though the defendant Ernesto Miranda—who had previously been arrested for rape and for peeking in ladies' windows half-a-dozen times—had confessed to raping a woman and stealing her car, the Warren Court concluded he had not signed the confession "voluntarily, knowingly, or intelligently."

Even though nobody ever claimed, including Miranda himself, that the police had tortured, coerced or beaten him, the Warren Court, in essence, re-wrote the Fifth Amendment by proclaiming that criminals are entitled to "safeguards at the onset of the interrogation to insure that the statements were truly the product of free choice."

Whether the Supreme Court was correct in its analysis or not, the role of the judiciary branch is not to rewrite law, it is to interpret the Constitution. Judicial employees do not have the constitutional authority to rewrite constitutional law based on their own ideological bents. As a result of Miranda, law professor Paul Cassell estimates that "Miranda warnings" prevent police from solving up to 359,000 crimes each year. Every unsolved crime keeps a criminal out on the street committing more crimes.[14]

When Ronald Reagan was elected to the presidency in 1980, he began to appoint more strict constructionists to the federal bench and slowly began to reverse some of the Warren Court's permissive rulings—which resulted in a dramatic increase in criminal incarcerations. During the 1980s and '90s, when criminal incarcerations *increased* by about 1.5 million, crime *decreased* dramatically nationwide.[15]

Crime has continued to fall even though millions of former

welfare recipients have come off the welfare roles courtesy of the enactment of the 1996 Welfare Reform Act.

The best way to reduce crime is to: focus on rebuilding the family; reward work and responsibility; and keep criminals behind bars where they belong.

CLAIM #4: "The death penalty doesn't deter crime."

RESPONSE: **The primary purpose of the death penalty is punishment, not deterrence.**

The death penalty always deters those who have murdered from ever murdering again.

Penalties exist primarily to punish offenders who break the law, but there will always be those who choose to "take their chances." Just because they ignore the law and are not "deterred" by it, doesn't mean others don't consider the penalty and are deterred from breaking the law.

The argument could be made that speed limits fail to "deter" drivers from speeding since millions of speeding tickets are issued each year. The tickets are issued as a penalty for breaking the law. Just because others won't be "deterred" from speeding doesn't mean offenders shouldn't be punished for their unlawful behavior.

Stricter enforcement of capital punishment does, in fact, deter crime. From 1990 to 2000, the number of murders in the U.S. dropped as the number of executions increased.

Political analyst William Tucker in the *National Review Online* states, "The most dramatic decline in murders over the last decade has been precisely in those regions that have had the most executions...Since 1990, [Texas, Oklahoma, Louisiana and Arkansas] have performed half the nation's executions...[and] murder rates in these four states have fallen faster than anywhere else in the country."[16]

Of 432 executions during a twenty-year period, *each execution* prevented about 5.5 murders, according to a 2001 University of Colorado study which examined the deterrence effect of the death penalty. That's 2,376 murders which didn't happen! The study, conducted by Dr. H. Naci Mocan and graduate student R. Kaj

Gittings, analyzed the U.S. Justice Department records of 6,143 death sentences imposed between 1977 and 1997.[17]

Dr. Mocan's findings demonstrate what most people know intuitively—punishment deters crime. Does it prevent all future crimes? Of course not. But evidence shows the harsher the penalty, the more crimes will be prevented.

CLAIM #5: "Life imprisonment is just as bad, if not worse, than the death penalty."

RESPONSE: If this were true, then criminals wouldn't plead guilty or plea bargain to avoid the death penalty.

Convicted murderers who are sentenced to life in prison are still free to enjoy the very things they denied their victims. They are still free to watch cable television, eat three square meals a day, work out, read, pursue higher education, surf the internet and even get married.

CLAIM #6: "Many found guilty of murder and sentenced to death are later found to be innocent. Innocent people are executed."

RESPONSE: There has never been a single case in the United States in which an innocent person has been executed.

One of the primary reasons the innocent are protected from execution in our country is because we have an abundance of legal safeguards. Prior to a murderer being executed, a grand jury indicts him, a jury of his peers presided over by a judge then tries, convicts and sentences him to death. In most states, what follows is several years of appeals in which lawyers for the defendant can revisit the case. Moreover, DNA testing now further protects the innocent from being mistakenly convicted.

But those opposed to the death penalty still try to sway public opinion. Columbia University professor and anti-death penalty criminal defense attorney James S. Liebman conducted a study between

1973 and 1995 which concluded, "More than two out of every three capital judgments reviewed by the courts during the 23-year study period were found to be seriously flawed."[18]

After Liebman's report *Broken System: Error Rates in Capital Cases, 1973-1995*, was released in 2000, however, Paul G. Cassell of the *Wall Street Journal* wrote, "The study's authors (like other researchers) were unable to find a single case in which an innocent person was executed. Thus, the most important error rate—the rate of mistaken executions—is zero."[19]

Reg Brown of the Florida governor's office also rebutted Liebman's study, saying, "The study defines 'error' to include any issue requiring further review of the lower court...Using the authors' misleading definition, the 'study' does, however, conclude that 64 Florida post-conviction cases were rife with 'error'—even a 'not guilty' verdict, a pardon, or a dismissal of murder charges."[20]

CLAIM #7: "The Bible opposes killing and there is no scriptural foundation for the death penalty."

RESPONSE: Both the old and new covenant provide a firm foundation for capital punishment.

"Do not pollute the land where you are. Bloodshed pollutes the land and atonement cannot be made for the land on which blood has been shed, except by the blood of the one who shed it." (Numbers 35:33-34)

"Show him no pity. You must purge from Israel the guilt of shedding innocent blood, so that it may go well with you." (Deuteronomy 19:13)

God made it clear in the scriptures that if people tolerated taking of human life, the whole community would share the guilt and suffer the consequences.

God holds life in high regard and requires payment for those who casually snuff it out.

"But if there is serious injury you are to take life for life, eye for eye, tooth for tooth, hand for hand, foot for foot, burn for burn, wound for wound, bruise for bruise." (Deuteronomy 19:20)

This balanced approach to retribution has served as the foundation for our Western legal system.

"If anyone takes the life of a human being, he must be put to death...Whoever kills a man must be put to death." (Leviticus 24:17-22)

In the book of Romans, the apostle Paul writes that the state's retribution of capital punishment is the retribution of God, "If you do wrong, then you may well be afraid; because it is not for nothing that the symbol of authority is the sword: it is there to serve God, too, as his avenger, to bring retribution to wrongdoers." (Romans 13:4)

The "authority" of the state is empowered to put evil "wrongdoers" to the "sword."

CLAIM #8: "The death penalty is cruel and unusual punishment."

RESPONSE: The death penalty is neither cruel nor unusual.

The taking of innocent human life is the worst crime a human being can commit and our penal code should reflect it by ensuring the penalty reflects the crime. When the punishment fails to fit the crime, citizens stop believing in the system. Abolishing the death penalty for convicted murderers takes away society's justice.

The death penalty has been on the law books in just about every nation since recorded history. Today, it's on the statutes of about half.

The death penalty was also on the statute books of every single state when the Constitution was adopted. The Founding Fathers who adopted the Bill of Rights banning "cruel and unusual punishment" did not have a problem implementing the death penalty.

The same compassionate liberals who consider the death penalty to be "cruel and unusual" treatment of convicted murderers are the very same compassionate leftists who support partial-birth abortion where a baby is forcefully removed from the mother's birth canal, then punctured in the head with scissors and has his brain sucked out.

These are the same compassionate liberals who condone and advocate the intentional creation and destruction of human life for the purpose of scientific experimentation. These are the same compassionate liberals who opposed the reinsertion of feeding tubes into Terri Schiavo as the entire nation watched her slowly die of hunger and thirst—one of the most slow and painful deaths imaginable.

CLAIM #9: "The death penalty is racist. A disproportionate number of prisoners on death row are black (forty percent) while they account for only twelve percent of the American population."

RESPONSE: Blacks commit capital crimes out of proportion with their numbers in the general population.

Statistics show those who commit the most murders are disproportionately male, young and black.

"Males between the ages of 14 and 24, less than 8 percent of the population, commit almost half the nation's murders," says Heather MacDonald, a John M. Olin fellow at the Manhattan Institute. "Black males of the same age, less than 1 percent of the population, committed some 30 percent of the nation's homicides in the 1990s."[21]

The majority of those executed since 1976 have been white, even though black criminals commit a majority of murders. If the death penalty is "racist," it is racist against whites, not blacks, since blacks commit the largest number of murders. Blacks committed 51.5 percent of murders between 1976 and 1999, while whites committed 46.5 percent, according to the U.S. Census Bureau of Justice Statistics.

Even though blacks committed the majority of the murders, the Bureau of Justice Statistics reports, "Since the death penalty was reinstated by the Supreme Court in 1976, white inmates have made up the majority of those under sentence of death."

In 2000, whites continued to comprise the majority on death row (1,990 whites to 1,535 blacks and 68 others). In 2000, 49 out of 85 people put to death were whites.[22]

Capital charges are less frequently brought against blacks (79 percent of the time from 1995 to 2000 versus 81 percent of the time for whites, according to a June 2001 Justice Department Report which scrutinized the death penalty system for evidence of racial bias). The report concluded the attorney general approved seeking the death penalty for 27 percent of white defendants, but only 17 percent of the black defendants and 9 percent of the Hispanic defendants.

Whites do outnumber blacks in this country by a seven to one ratio, yet the number of each race murdered each year is virtually identical—about 7,300 blacks and 7,300 whites.[23]

A credible argument could be made that since whites are more likely to be put to death by the death penalty, even though they commit proportionally less murder, the system favors minorities and is unfairly biased against whites.[24]

Chapter 11

K is for Kids:

The Leftist Indoctrination of our Children

Claims:

1. "We need to spend more on pre-school, day care and after-care government funded programs. It takes a village."
2. "America needs government-sponsored national child day-care."
3. "Some children are better off in day care-particularly those who have cold, insensitive mothers."
4. "Legislation providing for more day-care had to be passed because parents demanded Congress deal with the 'crisis.'"
5. "Abstinence-only education is old fashioned, unrealistic and ineffective."
6. "Sex education and health based clinics in schools reduce the number of unplanned pregnancies and sexually transmitted diseases."
7. "Using condoms promotes safe-sex."
8. "There is no liberal bias on college and university campuses."

"In history it is always those with little learning who overthrow those with much learning," said Chinese communist leader Mao Tse-tung in 1958. He went on to say, "When young people grasp a truth, they are invincible and old people cannot compete with them."

Mao could have been describing America's young people today. Indeed, there is an educational crisis in America. Study after study confirms how woefully inept our children are in reading, writing, math, U.S. history and science.

Our public schools have become indoctrination camps, much like our colleges and universities, where students are taught a curriculum of secularist new age pap. Kids are taught that homosexuality and bisexuality are "normal" behaviors and are even encouraged in many school districts to experiment with these behaviors. They are taught to engage in "safe sex" and practice putting condoms on cucumbers. The theory of Darwinian Evolution is routinely taught as if it were based on sound scientific evidence.

At the same time, unelected judges have ruled that the recitation of the Pledge of Allegiance, the display of the Ten Commandments and voluntary prayer violate the "separation of church and state."

On our nation's college campuses, liberal professors use the classroom to advance their political ideology even though institutions of higher learning are supposed to be places where intellectual *diversity* is encouraged, cultivated and nurtured. Students are supposed to think critically and be exposed to a wide berth of thoughts and ideas. But when they receive a predominantly leftist ideology, they're not being exposed to opposing traditionally conservative perspectives and principles. Instead of diverse ideas, students are receiving incomplete educations.

In a survey of college students at fifty-five elite colleges and universities, only a third of students were able to identify the U.S. Constitution as establishing the division of power in our government and forty percent could not place the Civil War in the correct half-century, according to the National Endowment for the Humanities.

At the high school level, seventy-five percent of students perform at or below a basic level of achievement. More than fifty percent of those who took the National Assessment of Education Progress (NAEP) history test thought Italy, Germany or Japan was a U.S. ally in World War II.

Leftist ideology is so pervasive in our public schools that students are rarely, if ever, exposed to the more traditional and evidentiary teachings of creationism/intelligent design (versus evolution) and abstinence (versus "safe-sex").

CLAIM #1: "We need to spend more on pre-school, day care and after-care government funded programs. It takes a village."

RESPONSE: Children do better when at least one parent is home providing them with love and nurturing.

Liberals' answer to any problem is always the same: more government funded programs at taxpayers' expense. Calls for more "universal preschool day care" are really just code for increasing the power of the state in child development and decreasing the amount of time children spend at home. Liberals have tried to persuade voters that day care before and after school will improve learning and keep kids out of trouble while Mom and Dad are working. The calls for government day care are nothing more than attempts to limit children's time spent at home. It is an effort on behalf of liberal government bureaucrats to increase the influence of the state on our youth's minds. The more time children spend away from home at government schools, the more they can be indoctrinated with the leftist ideology of "diversity," "multiculturalism," "gay-rights," "moral relativism" and "social justice."

We don't need more government-funded baby-sitters.

What we do need is a tax code which doesn't penalize families and allows them to afford to have one parent at home caring for the children. High taxes—which Democrats love to advocate—to pay for all those government programs make it more difficult for families to afford that. If the average family didn't have to pay almost half of their earnings in taxes, they might be able to afford to have one parent stay home to love and nurture the children.

Being a housewife has been viewed as weak. Since the 1960s, feminists have told women they could be a wife, mother and worker simultaneously. The absence of the mother in the home, in addition to the increased divorce rate (which has also removed millions of fathers from the home) has had disastrous consequences on our nation's children.

The Census Bureau estimates that in the mid-1990s there were 4.5 million "latchkey children"—kids who care for themselves after school.

But children shouldn't be left home alone without parental supervision. They're more likely to get into trouble, have sex and give birth out of wedlock.

Girls who give birth during their teen years are less likely to finish high school or graduate from college than teens who don't give birth says Dr. Duane Alexander, Director of the National Institute of Child Health and Human Development at the National Institutes of Health.

A baby's health is more likely to be adversely affected if the mother is a teen. The baby has an increased chance of having low birth weight, dying during infancy or, if they do live, have health problems such as deafness, blindness, mental illness, retardation or cerebral palsy.

In 1970, fewer than five percent of girls under age fifteen—about one in twenty—had had sex. By 2004, about twenty percent of ninth grade girls—one in five—were having sex and fifty-one percent of those in the 12th grade (compared to almost twenty-six percent of freshmen boys who had had sex and more than forty-four percent of those who were seniors). In 2000, about 4.5 million teenagers were affected with a sexually transmitted disease—almost a fourth of all new STD infections.[1]

The good news is the number of teens giving birth has started to decline, after reaching all time highs in the 1990s. Teen pregnancies and abortions are also decreasing. In 2005, for the sixth consecutive year, the adolescent birth rate among unmarried teenagers reached a record low, dropping more than two-fifths what it was in 1991.[2]

Divorce is on the rise, causing numerous problems for children. Suicide rates among children from broken homes have increased. From 1979-88, the suicide rate for girls between the ages of ten and fourteen rose twenty-seven percent. For boys it was even more frightening, rising a staggering seventy-one percent. Children in one-parent homes are twice as likely to attempt suicide and have psychiatric and alcohol-related diseases compared to kids with both Mom and Dad at home. Children whose parents have divorced are more than three times more likely to abuse drugs than those with both parents at home.[3]

Children are more likely to be abused by cohabitating males—live-in boyfriends not biologically related to the children—who are, many times, predatory child abusers.

The number of sexual abuse cases in America increased by 350 percent from 1980 to 1997 and many of those were at the hands of a male cohabitating with single mothers.

Mary Eberstadt, fellow at the Hoover Institute and author of the book *Home-Alone America: The Hidden Toll of Day Care, Behavioral Drugs and Other Parent Substitutes* reports, "The increasing absence from home of biological mothers...effectively increases the access of would-be predators."[4]

Leftist politicians and mainstream media elites continue to ignore and suppress the damage done to our children because it is not politically correct to acknowledge that the absence of mothers in the home has been the primarily cause of this epidemic crisis.

Liberal Democrats avoid this issue because they're beholden to the radical feminist organizations such as NARAL and NOW who have basically told women they don't need men, that a father isn't necessarily required to successfully parent a child and that a woman is just fine working while her child is sent off to day care because, after all, it "takes a village."

But the facts show that increased childcare only further alienates children from their mothers and dilutes the importance of the mother-child relationship.

CLAIM #2: "America needs government-sponsored national child day care."

RESPONSE: The family is the primary instrument for social instruction.

Institutionalized day care has caused psychological harm to many children. Psychologist Jay Belsky, founder and director of the Institute for the Study of Children, Families and Social Issues at Birkbeck College at the University of London, says, "It looked like kids who were exposed to 20 or more hours a week of non-parental care in their first year of life—what I call early and extensive non-parental care—and here comes the critical phrase, of the kind that was routinely available to families in the United States today seemed to be at elevated risk. They were more likely to look insecure in their relationship to their mothers, in particular at the end of their first year of life."[5]

Dr. Belsky found, "[C]hildren in any of a variety of child care arrangements, including center care, family day care and nanny care, for 20 or more hours per week beginning in the first year of life, are at elevated risk of being classified as insecure in their attachments to their mothers at 12 or 18 months of age and of being more disobedient and aggressive when they are from 3 to 8 years of age."[6]

Psychologist J. Conrad Schwarz, who with his collegues studied three- and four-year-olds, concluded that children who spend excessive time in day care as infants are more physically and verbally aggressive with other children and adults, as well as being more physically active. They're also less likely to cooperate with adults.[7]

Bryna Siegel, a psychologist at Stanford University, concluded in her nine-year study encompassing more than 1,000 hours of observation that children in day care are "15 times more aggressive...a tendency toward more physical and verbal attacks on other children." Siegel believes those same children, growing up without a close bond to their mothers, will choose to marry less and divorce more than those who had close ties with their mothers while they were infants.[8]

Author and scholar Dr. Brenda Hunter said, "Just as the 'attachment theory' predicts, babies are at risk psychologically if separated from their mothers for 20-plus hours per week during the first year of life."[9]

In Bermuda, a study of three-to five-year-olds found that children who had been in day care since they were infants were more maladjusted than those who were cared for at home.[10]

In one study, teachers noticed that three- and four-year-olds who were placed in day care before they were a year old were "more likely to cry," "more likely to be troublemakers," "more likely to withdraw and internalize," and "more likely to be loners."[11]

Psychologist Urie Bronfenbrenner, a professor at Cornell University in Ithaca, New York, has found through his studies that children need "a strong, mutual, rational, emotional attachment [with someone] who is committed to the child's well-being and development, preferably for life." For children to develop into healthy teens and adults, they need people caring for them who adore them.[12]

Day care can be hazardous to children's health. Dr. Reed Bell, a pediatrician and pediatric endocrinologist in Florida, writes, "Children in day care, especially infants and toddlers, are at increased risk for acquiring and spreading infectious diseases, compared to children not in day care. They have more respiratory, gastro-intestinal, skin and epidemic childhood infections, e.g., meningitis, than are children in home care. Infectious diseases are more common and more severe and more complications occur in the younger ages. Important also is the fact that day care-related illnesses, e.g., hepatitis A, may be spread to members of the household and to the community at large."[13]

Attending day care is the most significant factor associated with the increased incidence of bacterial meningitis, according to Dr. Ron Haskins and Dr. Jonathan Kotch in an article appearing in *Pediatrics* magazine showing the negative effects of day care.[14]

Other diseases, such as cytomegalovirus, the leading cause of congenital infections in newborns, has also been linked to day care centers. Given the close physical proximity and intimate contact of so many unrelated children in day care centers playing, sleeping, eating and using toilet facilities, it's not surprising infectious diseases are three to four times more common than in children who are cared for at home.[15]

Children having close contact in day care is responsible for recent "outbreaks of enteric illness—diarrhea, dysentery, giardiasis and epidemic jaundice—reminiscent of the pre-sanitation days of the seventeenth century," according to Dr. Stanley Schuman an epidemiologist at Medical University of South Carolina in Charleston writing in the *Journal of the American Medical Association*.[16]

CLAIM #3: "Some children are better off in day care—particularly those who have cold, insensitive mothers."

RESPONSE: Even bad mothers are better than day care.

Child development researchers have theorized for years that

children of unfeeling, unloving mothers are better off in day care because they say at least there the infants can receive "well-trained, high-quality" care.

But studies demonstrate just the opposite. When an infant of a cold, unloving mother is in day care for more than ten hours a week, the child becomes significantly more insecure says psychologist Dr. Jay Belsky of the University of London, who helped direct the National Institute of Child Health and Human Development (NICHD) study. The study followed 1,153 infants until they were seven years old.[17]

The conclusion: the *less* time a child spends in day care, the *more* secure that child will be.

Even a bad mother beats day care.

CLAIM #4: "Legislation providing for more day care had to be passed because parents demanded Congress deal with 'the crisis.'"

RESPONSE: Democrats created the day care crisis.

Congressman George Miller, a Democrat from California who worked for eight years to get the Clinton childcare plan passed in Congress, admitted in an interview with *Mother Jones Magazine* in the May/June 1991 issue that, "At its zenith, there was never a child-care movement in the country. There was a coalition of child-advocacy groups and a few large international unions that put up hundreds of thousands of dollars and we created in the mind of the leadership of Congress that there was a child-care movement—but there was nobody riding me. And not one of my colleagues believed that their election turned on it for a moment. There wasn't a parents' movement."[18]

The real "crisis" is that many on the liberal left believe the primary instrument for social instruction is the state—specifically the public schools.

By contrast, social conservatives and even many conservative Democrats believe the family is the primary instrument for social instruction.

CLAIM #5: "Abstinence-only education is old fashioned, unrealistic and ineffective."

RESPONSE: Abstinence until marriage is the only 100 percent effective way to avoid STDs and out-of-wedlock pregnancy.

Whether it's "old fashioned" or not, the free-love of the 1960s and '70s has only resulted in a record number of STDs, virtually assuring that most people who have sex outside of marriage will contract a sexually transmitted disease.

Schools which teach sex education emphasizing saving sex until marriage experience a dramatic decrease in teen pregnancies in as little as one year.

At one high school in San Marcos, California, out of 600 girls, the number of teen pregnancies dropped from 147 to 20 pregnancies within two years of instituting "Teen Aid"—a federally funded program which emphasizes saving intercourse until marriage.[19]

Delaying sex until marriage is realistic. More than fifty percent of females and forty percent of males between the ages of fifteen and nineteen have not had intercourse. Of those who have had at least one sexual experience, only twenty percent had sex in the past, but were not sexually active. That means only a minority of students are sexually active.[20]

Parents and children strongly favor abstinence-only education programs. One national poll by the University of Chicago found that sixty-eight percent of adults surveyed said premarital sex among teenagers is "always wrong." A poll for *USA Weekend* found seventy-two percent of teens and seventy-eight percent of adults agree with the pro-abstinence message.[21]

The 1960s "counter-culture" movement has had a significant cultural and societal impact. The moral relativism which accompanied the "free love" generation set the stage for the removal of the teachings of God and the Bible in our schools—replacing it with the philosophy that human beings are nothing more than fully "evolved" animals with "urges" which should be satisfied.

This radical philosophical shift led to courses in sex education, which indirectly encourages sexual promiscuity among children—including homosexual and group sex.

Liberals sneered at Reagan's call for abstinence teaching, labeling it outmoded and unrealistic. Yet sexually transmitted diseases are at epidemic proportions, despite courses in "safe sex."

CLAIM #6: "Sex education and health-based clinics in schools reduce the number of unplanned pregnancies and sexually transmitted diseases."

RESPONSE: Sex education has been a dismal failure. Teenage pregnancies and abortions continue to rise.

Even though $3 billion has been spent on federal Title X family planning services, the number of pregnancies among non-married, fifteen- to nineteen-year-old teens increased eighty-seven percent and the number of births increased sixty-one percent.[22]

The ratio of teenage births to unwed mothers increased from sixty-seven percent in 1980 to eighty-four percent in 1991.[23]

Condom education does not significantly change sexual behavior. An article which appeared in the *American Journal of Public Health* concluded that a year-long effort at condom education in San Francisco schools resulted in only eight percent of the boys and two percent of the girls using condoms every time they had sex.[24]

School-based health clinics do not lower the teen pregnancy rate and pregnancies increased among teens who visited community-based clinics, according to a national study done by the Institute for Research and Evaluation.

Douglas Kirby, former director for the Center for Population Options, admitted, "We have been engaged in a research project for several years on the impact of school-based clinics... We find basically that there is no measurable impact upon the use of birth control, not upon pregnancy rates or birth rates."[25]

A Louis Harris poll conducted by Planned Parenthood found the highest rates of teen sexual activity were among those who had comprehensive sex education as opposed to those who had less.[26]

A 1980s congressional study concluded that a decade-and-a-half of comprehensive sex education resulted in a doubling in the number of sexually active teenage women.[27]

Douglas Kirby wrote in the *Journal of School Health*: "Past studies of sex education suggest several conclusions. They indicate that sex education programs can increase knowledge, but they also indicate that most programs have relatively little impact on values, particularly values regarding one's personal behavior. They also indicate that programs do not affect the incidence of sexual activity. According to one study, sex education programs may increase the use of birth control among some groups, but not among others. Results from another study indicate they have no measurable impact on the use of birth control. According to one study, they are associated with lower pregnancy rates, while another study indicates they are not. Programs certainly do not appear to have as dramatic an impact on behavior as professionals once had hoped."[28]

CLAIM #7: "Using condoms promotes safe sex."

RESPONSE: Condoms can reduce the risk of HIV, but do little to stop the spread of sexually transmitted diseases (STDs).

As Meg Meeker explains in her book *Epidemic: How Teen Sex Is Killing Our Kids*, "Every STD has its own characteristics, its individual personality. Gonorrhea behaves differently from chlamydia, which behaves differently from herpes and HIV. Some STDs are viruses, some are bacteria. Some live on skin, some in blood, some only in genital fluids. The amount of germs needed to cause an infection varies from one disease to another. Ways of transmitting the disease also vary. Some sexual practices put certain parts of the body in contact with other parts of the body in contact with other parts of a partner's body. But condoms don't protect against all forms of disease transmission. Condoms only prevent contact with some bodily fluids and only the skin of the genitals themselves."[29]

A Florida study evaluating the effect of condoms on spreading the HIV infection found that after a year-and-a-half, seventeen percent of the previously uninfected partners were HIV positive.

The National Institute of Health evaluated the effectiveness of condoms on stopping the spread of HIV/AIDS in June 2000 and concluded there wasn't enough evidence to determine whether they were effective in reducing the risk of most other STDs.[30]

Some of NIH's other findings were:
- When condoms were used 100 percent of the time, they reduced sexually-transmitted HIV infection in

both sexes and the risk of gonorrhea in men by only about eighty-seven percent.[31]
- Even when a condom was used correctly 100 percent of the time, there was still a thirteen percent chance of transmitting HIV or gonorrhea.
- There is no conclusive evidence condoms are effective in preventing STDs.[32]

Overall, the NIH summed up the evidence as "inconclusive."

In Uganda, where HIV and gonorrhea are at crisis levels, research shows that people who always wear condoms during sex reduce their risk of getting gonorrhea and syphilis by only about fifty percent.[33]

Those aren't very good odds. That means half of the people wearing condoms "responsibly" still contract gonorrhea and syphilis!

Saying condoms promote "safe sex" gives people a false sense of security which actually encourages more sex in the future—increasing a girl's risk of exposure to human papilloma virus and perhaps cervical cancer in later childbearing years.

Studies show condoms have no impact on the risk of sexual transmission of HPV in women.[34] A study published in the *Journal of American Medical Association* in June 2001, found when condoms are worn, "only the women's risk of getting herpes was reduced. Using condoms didn't help the men reduce their risk of getting the disease at all."[35]

Studies evaluating the effectiveness of condoms show "they may or may not reduce the risk of chlamydia in men," and reduce the risk of syphilis only if they're worn all the time.[36] One study of prostitutes showed condoms reduced their risk of contracting syphilis by only fifty percent.[37] That means half the prostitutes who wore condoms still contracted syphilis.

Studies show teenagers are less likely to use condoms the longer they're involved in a relationship[38]—and few use them consistently or correctly.[39] Plus, the earlier a girl becomes sexually active, the more likely she is to have a greater number of partners, reducing her insistence on condom use.[40]

Condoms don't provide 100 percent pregnancy protection. One

study from the School of Medicine Family Planning Clinic at the University of Pennsylvania reported twenty-five percent of patients using condoms as birth control conceived during a one year period.[41]

<u>CLAIM #8</u>: "There is no liberal bias on college or university campuses."

<u>RESPONSE</u>: More than ninety percent of college professors described themselves as Democrats.

Ivy League professors lean heavily to the left according to a poll conducted by Luntz Research. More than eighty percent of Ivy League professors who voted in 2000, voted for loser Al Gore and only nine percent voted for George Bush. Only three percent of those teachers polled described themselves as Republicans. The majority of professors voted for Bill Clinton as the best president over the past forty years.

Here are some of the other results of the poll:

- More than seventy percent of the professors named a Democrat as their pick for best modern-day president. Only eight percent named a Republican.
- Only fourteen percent support missile defense, compared with seventy percent of the public.
- Only twenty-six percent are pro-choice on school vouchers compared to sixty-two percent of the public.
- At least forty percent favor taxpayer-provided slavery "reparations" for blacks compared with eleven percent of the public.[42]

Ideological diversity among college faculty is mostly nonexistent according to the American Enterprise Institute. The organization published a study in 2002 which surveyed professors and checked voter registrations of humanities and social science instructors at nineteen universities. The study found:

- At Cornell University, 166 of 172 faculty members were either Greens or Democrats. Six were either Republicans or Libertarians

- At Stanford University, liberal professors outnumbered conservatives by a ratio of 151-to-17.
- At San Diego State, liberals on the faculty outnumbered conservatives by a ratio of 80-to-11.
- At State University of New York (SUNY) at Binghamton, liberal-to-conservative faculty ratio was 35-to-1.
- At University of California at Los Angeles (UCLA), the ratio was 141-to-9.
- At the University of Colorado at Boulder, the ratio was 116-to-5.[43]

Democratic professors outnumber Republicans at least 7-to-1 in the humanities and social sciences according to a national survey of more than 1,000 academics featured in a *New York Times* article.

In a separate study of professors in engineering and the hard sciences at Berkeley and Stanford, the ratio of Democrats to Republicans is 9-to-1.[44]

One party domination in academia stifles independent thinking, causes minority thought to be discriminated against and betrays the commitment to intellectual diversity which should be at the core of any institution of higher learning.

Mark Bauerlein, an English professor at Emory University in Atlanta writes, "Any political position that dominates an institution without dissent deteriorates into smugness, complacency and blindness. ...Groupthink is an anti-intellectual condition."

The American Council of Trustees and Alumni conducted a survey of students' perceptions of faculty partisanship. Of 658 students polled at the top fifty U.S. colleges, forty-nine percent said some "presentations on political issues seem totally one-sided," and forty-six percent said "professors use the classroom to present their personal political views."[45]

Chapter 12

L is for Liberal Media:

Agenda, Agenda, Agenda

Claims:

1. "The mainstream media isn't biased."

For the past half-century, the primary sources of news and information for the vast majority of Americans has been the mainstream media, which includes the major networks (ABC, NBC and CBS) and major metropolitan newspapers such as the *New York Times, Washington Post, Chicago Tribune* and *Los Angeles Times*.

Technological innovations have revolutionized the way news and information is disseminated. The internet "bloggers," AM radio and cable television, have enabled Americans to access a multitude of diverse thoughts, opinions and beliefs. These alternative media sources, moreover, have provided some much needed balance to the major news conglomerates who for years monopolized the news, analysis and information business.

Liberals have dominated news and journalism. Some prominent in the media have acknowledged the overwhelming liberal bias, others still deny it.

But liberals through the mainstream media for years have attempted to influence public policy by supporting their own agendas. By slanting news coverage to support their ideology, they've managed to sway public opinion.

The elite media's viewership and print circulation continues to plummet, however, as increasing numbers of Americans grow tired of leftist-agenda-driven journalism camouflaged as objective news.

CLAIM #1: "The mainstream media isn't biased."

RESPONSE: Journalists in the mainstream media are predominantly liberal.

That's according to the 1996 findings of The Freedom Forum, an independent foundation which examines media related issues and The Roper Center, an opinion research firm.[1]

Prominent liberal journalist Evan Thomas of *Newsweek* attests to the bias in the media. Appearing on the syndicated political roundtable *Inside Washington* in 1996, he said, "There is a liberal bias. It's demonstrable. You look at some statistics. About 85 percent of the reporters who cover the White House vote Democratic, they have for a long time. There is a—particularly at the networks, at the lower levels, among the editors and the so-called infrastructure—there is a liberal bias. There is a liberal bias at *Newsweek*, the magazine I work for. Most of the people who work at *Newsweek* live on the upper West Side in New York and they have a liberal bias."[2]

Consider these poll results from the 1992 presidential election between Bill Clinton and then-President George H. W. Bush:

- 89 percent of journalists said they voted for Bill Clinton compared with just 43 percent of non-journalist voters who voted for Clinton.
- 7 percent of journalists voted for President George H. W. Bush; 37 percent of the voters did.
- 2 percent of news people voted for Ross Perot while 19 percent of the electorate did.
- 50 percent of journalists said they were Democrats.
- 4 percent of journalists said they were Republicans.[3]

The political leanings of the mainstream media are out of touch with mainstream Americans.

In his *New York Times* best seller *Bias*, former CBS correspondent Bernard Goldberg documents the mainstream media's leftward bent. He writes, "A poll back in 1972 showed that of those reporters who voted, 70 percent went for McGovern, the most liberal presidential nominee in recent memory, while 25 percent went for Nixon—the same Richard Nixon who carried every single state in the union except Massachusetts."[4]

In 1985 the *LA Times* conducted a nationwide survey of about

3,000 journalists and the same number of people in the general public to gauge their feelings on important issues:

- 23 percent of the public said they were liberal compared to 55 percent of journalists.
- 56 percent of the public favored Ronald Reagan compared to 30 percent of journalists.
- 49 percent of the public were for a woman's right to have an abortion; 82 percent of journalists were pro-choice.
- 74 percent of the public were for prayer in public schools compared to 25 percent of journalists.
- 56 percent of the the public were for affirmative action compared to 81 percent of journalists.
- 75 percent of the public were for the death penalty compared to 47 percent of journalists.
- 50 percent of the public were for stricter hand gun controls compared to 78 percent of journalists.[5]

The late ABC News anchor Peter Jennings admitted a liberal media bias.

"Historically in the media," he said, "it has been more of a liberal persuasion for many years. It has taken us a long time—too long in my view—to have vigorous conservative voices heard as widely in the media as they now are."[6]

In his book *Weapons of Mass Distortion*, Brent Bozell, founder of the Media Research Center, chronicles media bias with regard to taxation, environmental issues, gun control, religion and abortion.

Bozell references the three broadcast networks' coverage of the Bush tax-cut proposal of January 2003. Between January 2nd and January 15th of that year, he and his colleagues found twenty-eight stories about the proposal on ABC, CBS and NBC. In these he says, "the liberal mantra was repeated over and over. Bush's tax cuts comforts only the rich."[7]

Americans' trust of the mainstream media continues to decline.

A July 2003, Pew Center report showed fifty-three percent of Americans "believed that news organizations are politically biased," and "twice as many say news organizations are 'liberal' (fifty-one percent) than 'conservative.'"

An August 2003, Gallup survey showed forty-six percent of Americans, when asked how much trust they have in the news media, said, "not very much" or "none at all."[8]

Chapter 13

M is for Mega-Watt Energy:

Oil, Tree Huggers and Environmental Yappers

Claims:

1. "Global warming is occurring and is the result of human activity."
2. "If global warming gets worse, the environmental effects will be devastating."
3. "Signing the Kyoto Global Warming Treaty won't devastate the economy as conservative Republicans claim."
4. "Kyoto will stop global warming."
5. "Increased human economic activity is causing massive environmental pollution and damage."
6. "We are running out of oil and face a global energy crisis."
7. "Drilling in Alaska's Arctic National Wildlife Reserve Refuge (ANWR) will cause environmental degradation and will kill wildlife."
8. "Democrats are the party of the environment."
9. "Our planet is grossly overpopulated."
10. "Nuclear power is too risky and potentially hazardous to the environment."
11. "Deforestation is primarily the result of Western

capitalistic plundering and is an enormous threat to the environment."

12. "We need to preserve the environment by setting aside federally-controlled parks and ecosystems making them off limits to humans."

The traditional home of the Communist Party in America used to be labor unions. Since the number of these unions has diminished since 1980, the Socialists and Communists have found a new home in the environmental movement.

Those on the left use environmental concerns to oppose free market capitalism and expanded industry, justifying it as a great evil largely responsible for the economic inequalities throughout the world.

Al Gore claimed the internal combustion engine posed the single greatest threat to the environment—a greater threat than even Islamic terrorism.

Like Gore, those in the modern day enviro-movement claim they're protecting the environment from the greedy capitalists who they say blithely abuse and degrade it. Enviros say capitalists are placing profits over concern for the surrounding habitat.

Those on the left who bemoan SUVs and power plants are the same people who support abortion and who believe overpopulation is destroying the earth. They see man as the ultimate polluter of the earth. Nature has become their god.

The godfather of the environmental movement Paul Ehrlich fans the flames of this eco-hysteria. According to "environmentalists" such as Ehrlich, the American people are "a cancer to the planet."

He also claimed the problem with the "environment worldwide was the Western way of life: capitalism, consumption, industry and technology." For years, liberals such as Mr. Ehrlich have predicted similar catastrophic consequences of "global warming."[1]

These apocalyptic predictions, however, contradicted past predictions of global cooling. In 1970, the year of the first Earth Day, University of California professor Kenneth E. F. Watt claimed, "If present trends continue, the world will be about four degrees colder for the global mean temperature in 1990, but 11 degrees colder by the year 2000... This is about twice what it would take to put us in an ice age."[2]

His predictions were wrong.

Conservatives believe economic growth through free market capitalism can be achieved without compromising natural resources. They believe environmental policy should be based on sound science, not emotional and political ideology.

The left argues free market capitalism causes environmental degradation, but the scientific evidence shows just the opposite—the environment continues to improve, especially in countries where economic growth is the greatest.

The bottom line is the environmentalists from the left have predicted environmental disaster after environmental disaster. They have also warned we are "overpopulated" and are "running out of food and oil." Yet the rhetoric lacks solid evidence.

For those on the left, our capitalist society harms the environment. But when environmental conditions in free market societies are compared to highly controlled socialist style economies, it is evident the free market capitalist societies are far less polluted.

CLAIM #1: "Global warming is occurring and is the result of human activity. It emits dangerous greenhouse gasses, causing surface air temperatures and subsurface ocean temperatures to rise, which threatens to destroy the environment."

RESPONSE: Carbon dioxide, the primary greenhouse gas produced by burning fossil fuels, is not a toxic pollutant.

In fact, carbon dioxide—CO_2—is vital for life on earth. Agricultural experts estimate there has been a ten percent increase in crop growth in the last decade due to the fertilization effect of increased carbon dioxide in the air.[3]

Environmentalists from the left claim the earth is heating up and the ozone layer is disappearing, but evidence of a cooling trend debunks the theory of global warming. The snow-covered continent of Antarctica has cooled over the past thirty-five years, according to scientists with the National Science Foundation's Long Term Ecological Research project. Researchers say "that long-term data from weather stations across the continent, coupled with a separate set of measurements from the Dry Valleys, confirm each other and corroborate the conditional cooling trend."[4]

According to Accu-Weather, the world's leading commercial forecaster, "Global air temperatures as measured by land-based weather stations show an increase of about 0.45 degrees Celsius over the past century. This may be no more than normal climatic variation... [and] several biases in the data may be responsible for some of this increase."

Clinton Administration officials conceded global warming was not conclusive. Tim Wirth, President Clinton's top advisor on economic issues, admitted, "We've got to ride the global-warming issue. Even if the theory is wrong, we will be doing the right thing in terms of economic and environmental policy."[5]

Indeed, Mr. Wirth is correct. The theory is unsubstantiated and not based on sound science. Additionally, the economic effects of signing the proposed Kyoto Treaty would be disastrous, especially for the poor and middle classes in the U.S. and developing countries around the world.

Even the National Academy of Sciences report from 2001, which the environmental left used as proof of a global warming trend, stated there is no conclusive link to human activity and "global warming."

An excerpt from the report reads, "Because of the large and still uncertain level of natural variability inherent in the climate record and the uncertainties in the time histories of the various forcing agents (and particularly aerosols), a causal linkage between the buildup of greenhouse gasses in the atmosphere and the observed climate change during the 20th century cannot be unequivocally established. The fact that the magnitude of the observed warming is large in comparison to natural variability as simulated in climate models is suggestive of such a linkage, but does not constitute proof of one because the model simulations could be deficient in natural variability on the decadal to century time scale."[6]

The vast majority of the scientific community does not support the claim that there is a link between human activity and "global warming." Only seventeen percent of the members of the American Meteorological Society and the American Geophysical Union thought the warming of the 20th century was the result of an increase in greenhouse gas emissions, according to a Gallup poll.

Projections of future climate changes are uncertain. Although some computer models predict warming in the next century, these models are very limited. The effects of cloud formations, precipitation, the role of the oceans, or the sun, still are not well known and often inadequately represented in the climate models—although all play a major role in determining our climate. Scientists who work on these models are quick to point out they are far from perfect representations of reality and are probably not advanced enough for direct use in policy implementation. Interestingly, as the computer climate models have become more sophisticated in recent years, the predicted increase in temperature has been lowered.[7]

Average global surface temperatures actually fell during the greatest increase in man-made fossil fuels. There was a strong warming trend of about .5 degrees Celsius which began in the late 19th century and peaked around 1940. Then there was a cooling trend from 1940 to the late 1970s and a modest warming trend which occurred from the late 1970s to the present. About eighty percent of the CO_2 from human activities was added to the air after 1940, which cannot account for the pre-1940 warming trend. The trend, therefore, had to be largely natural. Then, as the air's CO_2 increased most rapidly, temperatures dropped for nearly forty years.[8]

CLAIM #2: "If global warming gets worse, the environmental effects will be devastating."

RESPONSE: There is no conclusive evidence "global warming" is anything other than natural temperature variations which existed before mankind and have very little to do with man-made fossil fuel emissions.

The idea that global warming would melt the ice caps and flood coastal cities seems to be mere science fiction. A slight increase in temperature—whether natural or human induced—is not likely to lead to a massive melting of the earth ice caps, as sometimes claimed in the media. Rising sea levels over the centuries are due more to warmer, expanding oceans, than to melting ice caps.

Larger quantities of CO_2 in the atmosphere and warmer climates would not necessarily be bad. Thomas Gale Moore, a Senior Fellow at the Hoover Institution and author of *Climate of Fear: Why We Shouldn't Worry About Global Warming* concludes a warming earth might be a good thing. Moore explains a warming planet could give a "rising world population longer growing seasons, greater rainfall and an enriched atmosphere."

He also says, "Transportation would benefit generally from a warmer climate, since road transport would suffer less from slippery or impassable highways. Airline passengers, who often endure weather-related delays in the winter, would gain from more reliable and on time service."[9]

During warm periods in history, vegetation flourished, at one point allowing the Vikings to farm in now-frozen Greenland and Iceland.

CLAIM #3: "Signing the Kyoto Treaty won't devastate the economy as conservative Republicans claim."

RESPONSE: **In order to achieve the reductions of carbon dioxide emissions the Kyoto agreement requires, the United States would have to reduce its projected energy use by about 25 percent.**

When the Kyoto Treaty came up for a vote in the U.S. Senate, it was rejected ninety-five to zero. Not one senator—Republican or Democrat—voted for ratification of the Kyoto Treaty. They recognized the problems associated with it.

That's because it calls for a worldwide five percent cut from 1990 levels of carbon dioxide emissions which would affect only a minimal change in world temperatures—to .94 degrees Celsius—which translates into an insignificant .06 degrees Celsius averted temperature increase.

Not only that, Kyoto's expensive. Most economic studies indicate the cost of cutting emissions would amount to between $100 billion to $400 billion per year.[10]

And it would affect the growth of U.S. companies. Stabilizing emissions at 1990 levels by 2010 would reduce the growth of U.S. per capita income by five percent per year, according to Gary W. Yohe of Wesleyan University.[11]

The Kyoto Protocol also has the potential to worsen international relations. The U.S. is the engine of economic growth for the rest of the world. Any treaty such as Kyoto would significantly hamper America's economic growth, which in turn would significantly reduce the amount of aid and economic opportunity we provide to our global trading partners. Our inability to promote global economic growth would likely lead to global instability, which in this day and age of terrorism could make poor countries more susceptible to terrorism.

And it would cause massive job losses in the U.S. According to a report by the Department of Energy, stringent reduction of fossil-fuel emissions in the U.S. will cause energy-intensive industries—including steel, iron, chemical, rubber and plastic—to flee from developed countries to undeveloped countries, taking with them hundreds of thousands of jobs. Since undeveloped countries such as China, India and Mexico would be exempt from Kyoto, our ability to maintain manufacturing jobs in our country would be significantly threatened.[12]

Those such as Senator John Kerry who bemoan "outsourcing" of U.S. jobs should carefully consider Kyoto's intrinsic incentives to "outsource" jobs.

Carbon taxes will cause relatively large income losses in the poorest one-fifth of the population. The poor, because they spend a greater proportion of their income on necessities, would have fewer ways to cut back to compensate for higher living costs.

The tax burden of the treaty would fall unfairly and unevenly on many individuals and families. Taxes would be determined from energy use patterns and circumstances, such as distance from work, condition and energy efficiency of homes, automobiles and appliances—not income, wealth or ability to pay.

Senior citizens on fixed incomes would find their energy costs escalating and their income dwindling. Since emissions taxes would increase dramatically as a result of entering into the Kyoto Protocol, those who would suffer most would be seniors and the poor who would be forced to choose between heat and air conditioning, food or prescription drugs.

The Kyoto Treaty would devastate American sovereignty and contradicts the general principles enumerated in the Declaration of Independence. Signing Kyoto would, in essence, make U.S. private industry answerable to the "global community." If global organizations such as the U.N. can set the environmental standards by which U.S. companies have to comply, what will stop them from using their authority to set other guidelines, such as discrimination laws and even imposition of a global tax?

There is nothing in any of our founding documents that gives our government constitutional jurisdiction to enter into any treaty which permits foreign organizations to regulate private industry. Signing such a treaty would significantly violate American liberty.

CLAIM #4: "Kyoto will stop global warming."

RESPONSE: Only severe reductions in global CO_2 emissions—on the order of 60 percent or more—will alter the computer forecasts.

The resulting economic losses would be tremendous, potentially outweighing the negative impacts of even the most apocalyptic warming scenario.

If the policies do not include developing nations, the result will likely be a reallocation of emissions to developing nations, not a reduction of emissions.

If the entire world is included and CO_2 emissions are severely restricted, the science is not clear what impact, if any, it would have on the world's climate. No conclusive evidence demonstrates temperature changes are the result of human activity or increased fossil fuel emissions.

Liberal Democrats support the Kyoto Global Warming Treaty which Al Gore signed without regard to science or the economic damage ratification of such a treaty would cause. Aside from the fact there is no conclusive scientific evidence supporting global warming and that countries such as China, the largest polluter in the world, would be exempt from complying with emissions restrictions, the costs to the U.S. economy would be disastrous. It's been estimated that complying with the treaty would devastate the U.S. economy to the tune of a loss of $4 trillion dollars in GDP. Radically extreme environmental policies would, in effect, result in a massive loss of jobs and wealth for average working Americans.[13]

Contrary to some groups' fear mongering about the threat of diseases, temperature changes are likely to have little effect on the spread of diseases. Experts say deterioration in public health practices—such as rapid urbanization without adequate infrastructure—has forced large-scale resettlement of people and increased drug resistance.

Higher mobility through air travel and lack of insect-control programs have the greatest impact on the spread of vector-borne diseases—not "global warming."

CLAIM #5: "Increased human economic activity is causing massive environmental pollution and damage."

RESPONSE: Major pollutants declined 25 percent.

That's according to a 2003 Environmental Protection Agency report with collected data from 30 agencies over the course of 30 years. Pollution levels are trending down in 212 out of 260 metropolitan areas—in spite of population increases, more cars and more economic activity.

And consider these facts:

- Pollution violations decreased to three percent in 2001, down from ten percent in 1988.

- Toxic chemicals volume released into the environment decreased by nearly half over 15 years.

- Only 4.3 percent of the nation's total land area is developed. The vast majority of our land is not even inhabited by human beings. Forests cover one third of America and forests *increased* by two million acres from 1997 to 1999.

- Bald eagle nests in the Great Lakes region increased from 50 to 366 from 1961 to 2000.

- 94 percent of our nation's drinking water meets all health standards—up from 79 percent in 1993 under Bill Clinton.[14]

Although our government has a role to play in environmental regulations, it is private industry which will be primarily responsible for keeping our environment clean with future inventions— such as hydrogen cars and cheap, efficient power which harnesses the wind and sun.

CLAIM #6: "We are running out of oil and face a global energy crisis."

RESPONSE: We are not running out of oil. Oil reserves are growing.

Between 1948 and 1992, oil reserves increased a whopping 1,400 percent. How much was that? Well, by 1990, those reserves exceeded one trillion barrels.[15]

"Energy and other natural resources have become more abundant, not less so," said Bjorn Lomborg, a Danish professor of statistics named one of the world's 100 most influential people in *Time Magazine*. Lomborg, a former Greenpeace member and author of *The Skeptical Environmentalist*, added, "The price of oil is half what it was 20 years ago."[16]

"A century of growing world oil production and reserves and a hundred years of being wrong have not stopped the myth-makers," said Dr. Arjun Makhijani of the Institute for Energy and Environmental Research. "All resources are finite. But some are more finite than others. There is a great deal of oil in the world with an estimated trillion barrels of ultimately recoverable reserves in Saudi Arabia alone, which is about 35 years of global consumption at present rates. One fourth of that is proven reserves. Iraq has a hundred billion barrels of proven reserves and much more in undeveloped areas. Persian Gulf proven reserves cost less than a nickel a gallon to pump out of the ground. If the world had higher oil prices driven by true oil depletion, the world would quickly move to using natural gas, gasified coal, liquefied coal, even to hydrogen from wind energy."[17]

Global oil production is not in danger of "peaking" as some have predicted. Oil production is subject to a significant number of artificial constraints—chief among them the Organization of Petroleum Exporting Countries (OPEC). This monopolistic oil cartel deliberately constrains the supply of oil from the Middle East to keep crude at monopolistic prices. Any trends in global oil probably have less to do with actual technological limits on how much oil can be extracted from the ground and everything to do with OPEC's monopoly and supply constraints.

Oil wells are not the only sources of oil. Although large underground reservoirs of crude oil have been the cheapest source of oil by far, there are new technologies which enable us to extract oil from other, more abundant sources. For instance, it has been estimated we could extract at least 500 billion barrels of oil from sand and shale for about $30 a barrel. That alone would increase known reservoirs to more than one trillion barrels of oil.

Thermal depolymerization is another promising new technology being developed which can obtain oil at prices near the cost of ground extraction by converting it from biomass—fuel from recently living organisms such as trees, plants and animal waste.

Alternative energy sources such as coal, uranium, ethanol, solar and other renewables are also being developed to reduce the demand and cost of oil.

Productivity growth must also be taken into consideration. Proponents of an imminent "oil crisis," fail to factor in productivity gains which, as a result of more advanced technology, enable us to consume energy more efficiently, reducing both demand and costs.

CLAIM #7: "**Drilling in Alaska's Arctic National Wildlife Refuge (ANWR) will cause environmental degradation and will kill wildlife.**"

RESPONSE: **Drilling in ANWR will make us less dependent on Middle Eastern oil and can be accomplished in an environmentally friendly way.**

Scientists estimate there are between 6 and 18 billion barrels of recoverable oil in ANWR—an amount which would dramatically reduce our dependence upon foreign oil.

Seventy-five percent of Alaska residents support exploration and production of oil in ANWR. That's because exploration in ANWR would create between 250,000 and 735,000 new jobs. Similar projects have added tens of billions of dollars to the nation's economy in the past. Even the left-of-center *New York Times* and *Washington Post* have editorialized in favor of ANWR exploration and production.[18]

We imported 36 percent of our oil from the Middle East in the 1970s. We now import 56 percent! Excessive dependence on foreign oil threatens our national security, making us more susceptible to foreign blackmail and forcing us to engage with unstable countries bent on our destruction.[19]

Today, we import almost 50 percent of our oil from unstable Arab countries such as Iran and Saudi Arabia. The oil we could obtain from ANWR is equivalent to about 30 years worth of imports from Saudi Arabia (where 19 of the 20 Al Qaeda 9/11 terrorists originated).

By purchasing large amounts of oil from countries where terrorism is breeding, we, in essence, are funding tyrannical dictatorships and terrorism. The more we rely upon unstable countries for oil, the more our country is susceptible to the economically destructive effects of embargoes and massive price hikes by OPEC.

In addition to the national security and economic benefits of becoming more energy self-sufficient, drilling in ANWR can be done in an environmentally friendly way. Of the 530 Fish and Wildlife Service's refuges, drilling is permitted in 29. For more than 60 years, oil and gas development in this country have been done with little environmental degradation.

The Nature Conservancy of Texas, which runs a small reserve for the endangered Attwater's prairie chickens, uses proceeds from oil and gas development on their property to acquire more wildlife habitat.

"Being in Texas, we're used to working with the petroleum industry," says Robert Potts, director of the Nature Conservancy. "We have production on several of our preserves and we know that oil and gas operations are compatible with the environment because they're typically limited in scope."[20]

The same critics from radical environmental organizations who claimed the caribou population in Prudhoe Bay would decrease if oil and gas development took place, now say the same type of development would damage ANWR.

But operations in Prudhoe Bay have not damaged the caribou population. Drilling has been underway for more than 25 years and the result has been a production of more than 10 million barrels of oil—while the caribou herds increased from 3,000 in 1970 to 27,000 in 2000 and almost 32,000 in July 2002.[21]

ANWR is about the size of the State of Delaware and the proposed site for oil development roughly the size of Dulles National Airport. Even if we are only able to develop half the oil and natural gas estimated to be present, we could make ourselves far less dependent upon foreign supply.

Domestic energy development has been and can continue to be, done in an environmentally safe manner. Opposition to domestic drilling—whether in ANWR or off the coasts of California, Florida, Texas and Louisiana—is really an effort to impede economic growth. Those on the enviro-left claim to oppose drilling to protect the environment, but their real goal is to make driving as cost prohibitive as possible for the American consumer.

Leftist elites fundamentally believe that American capitalism is the driving force behind economic "inequality" and enviromental degradation. Therefore, opposition to domestic drilling is really the left's concerted effort to impede free market economic growth. The left's main goal is to oppose economic development and capitalism at any cost. The environmental movement has become the new home of the Communist Party in the United States. They understand that by becoming less dependent upon foreign oil, energy costs will likely decrease. As a result, they will not be able to scare Americans into smaller, less safe automobiles.

Al Gore himself wrote in his book *Earth in the Balance* that the internal combustion engine—not terrorism—posed the most imminent threat to the world!

By opposing environmentally responsible domestic development and production of oil and natural gas, however, the far left environmental organizations not only make us less secure, but also lower the overall standard of living by increasing the costs of oil and gas the most for those who can least afford it.

Artificially high energy costs and shortages which result from contrived scarcities lead to economic slowdowns and lost jobs. Small and medium businesses employ more than half the American workforce. These businesses are more vulnerable than larger corporations which can better absorb higher energy costs. It's the little guy—the small business owner who suffers most from excessive energy costs—the very same constituency liberals claim to represent.

CLAIM #8: "Democrats are the party of the environment."

RESPONSE: **Democrats advocate extreme positions on environmental issues, even when it financially harms the poor.**

Liberals place environmentalism above our energy independence. By taking extreme positions on the environment, those belonging to extreme environmental and animal rights organizations are indirectly driving up the cost of energy (oil and gas) for U.S. citizens.

Poor and middle class working Americans are often the victims of leftist environmentalist ideology which tends to put radical environmental concerns above regard for the livelihood of average citizens.

Paying $2.50 a gallon for unleaded gasoline doesn't effect Woody Harrelson's, Robert Redford's or Susan Sarandon's budget, but for an average worker who only earns $30,000 per year, paying an extra $10 to $20 in gas per week adds up, taking away available funds needed for things such as their children's school, clothes and food. Yet, liberal "environmentalists" continue to oppose domestic oil production and development in spite of the fact it would significantly decrease our dependence on Middle East oil and would lead to lower energy prices and more American jobs.

The Democrat Party's close affiliation with radical leftist environmental groups, who are among their major financial contributors, actually makes it more difficult for blacks to obtain "affordable housing."

That's because Democratic support for environmental organizations who push restrictive "land use laws" and "open space laws" actually drives the price of land and real estate up in many cities, making it more difficult for poorer black citizens to afford to live. By limiting the supply of land, the "rich"—who already own land and homes—actually benefit from seeing the value of their property increase as a result of these restrictive enviro-regulations at the expense of their poorer black "constituents."

The Democrat's addiction to environmental organizations' campaign cash makes it more difficult for blacks in the inner city to achieve the "American Dream" of home ownership and makes them more dependent upon government.

The Democrats believe that to reconcile the contrived scarcity of new development, the government should tax citizens to provide government funded "affordable housing" (housing which is underwritten by the taxpayers).

CLAIM #9: "Our planet is grossly overpopulated."

RESPONSE: There's plenty of room for everyone.

If the entire population of the world were placed in a land area the size of Texas, each person would have an area equivalent to the floor space of a typical American home, with a population density roughly equivalent to Paris, France.[22]

The left has for years, since T. R. Malthus published his treatise on population in 1798, contended the exponential growth of people and their demands will eventually exceed the earth's capacity. They say the situation demands immediate attention to avoid catastrophic consequences, including famine, poverty and death for millions.

There are many problems with this assumption.

First, human beings are not like animals. The Malthusian proposition ignores the fact that human beings use problem-solving techniques to expand the natural resource base and temper the environment in which we live. Over the past century, we have experienced a significant "health explosion" as the result of decreased mortality rates and higher life-expectancy rates.

The benefits of living longer and healthier lives have been the result, primarily, of improved scientific and technical knowledge. The world's population almost quadrupled from 1900 to 2000. Today, people enjoy a better diet and overall health than they did when the population was one quarter as large.[23]

Even though the world's population is growing, it continues to do so at a slower pace. The growth rate of the world's population seems to have peaked around 1970 when the annual rate of growth was 2.09 percent. By 1980, annual population growth slowed to 1.73 percent and by 1990 to 1.7 percent. By 1995, the annual increase slowed to 1.5 percent.[24]

In fact, there is a worldwide fertility decline. According to the U.S. Census Bureau, 83 countries and territories are now experiencing below-replacement fertility. Those areas account for nearly 2.7 billion people—roughly 44 percent of the world's total population. It's estimated that, with current projections, by 2025 fewer babies will be born worldwide than at any point during the last 50 years.[25]

Under-population could have a devastating societal impact. Between 2000 and 2025, the median age of China's population will soar. By 2025 about 200 million Chinese will be 65 or older. Add to this the fact that 40 countries will have lower life expectancies in 2010 than they enjoyed in 1990. Many of these countries include sub-Saharan African countries that are victims of the HIV/AIDS epidemic. Even in urbanized countries such as Russia, life spans today are shorter than they were 40 years ago.[26]

The "overpopulation myth" continues to be promulgated by the left mainly as a way to justify the "need for worldwide family planning" (code for taxpayer abortion on demand). The left tries to frighten people into believing overpopulation will destroy the environment and we will all perish in some apocalyptic "last days."

However, the Malthusian claims are not based on sound logic or empirical evidence. Because technology has improved vastly during the past century, people are able to produce more food in less time, requiring less land. We use fewer natural resources to feed people than were required in the past. While it is clear we must manage our natural resources judiciously and focus on conservation whenever possible, we must use sound science as a guide.

Population growth is slowing throughout the world in both more developed nations and less developed ones. The overpopulation myth has been used as a front for abortion organizations. However, no government should be able to dictate "acceptable" population levels as justification for murder. In countries such as China, women are coerced into having forced abortions for this purpose.

Liberals are correct when they contend there has been a population explosion due to declining mortality rates. The human population has increased from 1.7 million people in 1900 to 6 billion in 2000. By most estimates, the population will continue to climb until 2050 when it will peak around 9 billion. Other studies predict the world's population will peak around 7.5 billion in 2040. It's impossible to conclude with any degree of empirical certainty, however, that the earth cannot sustain this human population.

CLAIM #10: "Nuclear Power is too risky and potentially hazardous to the environment."

RESPONSE: Currently 103 nuclear power plants supply 20 percent of our electricity in the U.S.

Aside from Pennsylvania's Three Mile Island nuclear meltdown in 1979, there has never been any major environmental destruction caused by nuclear power in the U.S. Nuclear power is extremely environmentally friendly which tends to decrease carbon dioxide emissions. In 1999, natural gas cost 3.52 cents per kilowatt hour compared to 2.07 cents for coal and 1.83 cents for nuclear!

Nuclear power is not only environmentally friendly, but is significantly more cost efficient and effective than fossil fuels. Even the European Green countries such as Germany and France are massive consumers of nuclear power. Again, this is another prime example of whacko environmentalism, which is not based on science. To liberals, anything which doesn't bring us back to the dark ages is too "risky."

CLAIM #11: "Deforestation is primarily the result of Western capitalistic plundering and is an enormous threat to the environment."

RESPONSE: There are more acres of forestland in America today than when Columbus discovered America in 1492.[27]

There are 730 million acres of forestland in our country today and the growth on these acres is denser than at any time, with about 230 billion trees—780 trees for every American.[28]

According to Jonathan Adler of the Competitive Enterprise

Institute, New England has more forested acres than it did in the mid-1800s. Vermont is twice as forested as it was then. Almost half of the densely populated northeastern United States is covered by forest.[29]

There are several reasons why we have actually experienced a growth in the number of trees in the U.S:

- Technology in the form of wood preservatives has reduced the need for timber.
- Automobiles have reduced the need for timber previously required by the rail industry.
- Chemical fertilizers and pesticides have made possible growing more food on less land, decreasing the overall amount of clearing (deforestation) which used to take place.[30]

CLAIM #12: "We need to preserve the environment by setting aside federally-controlled parks and ecosystems, making them off limits to humans."

RESPONSE: The environment doesn't always manage itself well. Fires can easily destroy land when humans have no access to them to save them.

The policy of the Clinton administration for eight years was that humans are predisposed to damage and ravage the environment, making it necessary to put as much land as possible off limits to those people.

According to the laws the Clinton administration enacted regarding the management of these federal lands, there could be no logging or fire roads built. As a result, millions of acres of wild brush grew out of control, becoming, in essence, kindling for the raging fires. Since even access roads were not permitted to be built on the land, it was increasingly difficult for fire trucks to gain access to contain and put out the fires.

The Clinton administration's forest-management policy led directly to the destruction of millions of acres of forestland, especially in the western United States, as well as the destruction of private property (land and homes) in the paths of the many forest fires which blazed out of control.

Bush's 2003 forestry management legislation has only recently restored a semblance of responsible stewardship by allowing for some clearing of dead tinder brush and the construction of fire-roads to enable fire trucks increased access to these natural forests in the event of future fires.

Democratic environmental policies during the Clinton administration failed to recognize the importance of stewardship and has had devastating consequences on the environment.

Bill Clinton even went so far as to sign the international biodiversity treaty to set up these protected "ecosystems" around the world to stop development. This treaty, like the Kyoto Treaty, was never ratified by the U.S. Senate.

Chapter 14

N is for 9/11 Attacks:

A New Kind of War

Claims:

1. "The attacks of 9/11 occurred because of the failure of George W. Bush to take the threat of terrorism seriously."
2. "Islam doesn't advocate violence. It is a religion of peace. Islamic fundamentalists like Bin Laden bastardize the Qu'ran and don't represent true Islam."
3. "The 9-11 attacks occurred because of the United States' support for Israel."
4. "America's wealth is responsible for breeding the global poverty which creates terrorism."

With the exception of perhaps abortion and judicial nominations, there has not been a single issue as divisive and acrimonious among conservatives and liberals as much as the War on Terror. The vast majority of those on the liberal left have argued that the United States' hegemonic foreign policy provoked the 9/11 attacks. Others have suggested that America's support for and alliance with Israel was another major factor which contributed to the 9/11 attacks.

Furthermore, those on the left argued that, although going after Osama bin Laden and al Qaeda was justified, Bush overstepped his authority. Liberals in the U.S. don't want us to protect ourselves by preemptively and, if necessary, unilaterally seeking out and destroying organizations and nations who either sponsor terrorism directly or harbor terrorist organizations.

Those such as Senator's John Kerry and Ted Kennedy claim the best way to win the war on terror is to treat it generally as a law enforcement issue. They say containment, sanctions and diplomacy are superior to preemptive force in spite of the failure of 12 years of failed sanctions and flouted U.N. resolutions. Kerry mentioned in his first debate with President Bush that the U.S. under a Kerry administration would have to pass the "global test" before defending itself against foreign terrorist threats. In other words, conciliatory liberals such as Kerry and others were poised to "outsource" our national security to the United Nations.

Conservatives, in sharp contrast, argue that global organizations such as the U.N. lack the credibility required to be effective in defeating global terrorism. That was demonstrated with the "oil-for-food" program scandal which revealed U.N. Security Council members such as France and Germany were receiving bribes and kickbacks in the form of lucrative oil contracts in return for their support of Saddam's murderous regime.

The conservative position has almost unanimously been that the United States was attacked on 9/11, not because of anything America did to the Islamic world, but because radical Islamic fundamentalists despise our liberal democratic way of life and our export of freedom and liberty abroad—especially to other Arab countries. Conservatives believe the United States is neither required to "seek a permission slip" nor pass a "global test" from any international organization or country to defend ourselves unilaterally. We need to aggressively take the fight to the terrorists who have declared war on the United States of America.

Still, liberals continue to deny the Clinton administration's repeated failures to apprehend the mastermind of 9/11, Osama bin Laden. They also deny the negligence, poor decision making and denigration of the U.S. military which left America extremely vulnerable to the attacks of 9/11.

<u>CLAIM #1</u>: "**The attacks of 9/11 occurred because of the failure of George W. Bush to take the threat of terrorism seriously.**"

RESPONSE: **Preparations leading up to the 9/11 terrorist attacks began well before Bush was even elected to office.**

In fact, it took President Bill Clinton two years subsequent to the 1993 al Qaeda terrorist organization's bombing of the World Trade Center which killed six people, to issue a directive declaring terrorism "a potential threat to national security" and pledged to "deter and preempt" would be terrorists.[1] The Clinton administration was ineffective in combating the numerous terrorist attacks which occurred in the following eight years. These attacks were permitted to continue and culminated on September 11, 2001 killing thousands of innocent Americans.

In November 1995, a van bombing at army training headquarters in Riyadh, Saudi Arabia, killed seven people—including five Americans—and injured 31.[2]

In January 1996, the U.S government asked Qatar for help in capturing Kahlib Sheikh Mohammed, suspected of plotting to plant bombs on U.S. airliners. He disappeared and later became a key planner of the 9/11 attacks.[3]

In 1996, U.S. ally Qatar offered bin Laden to the U.S. as he and 150 of his top aides and family were refueling on their way to Pakistan. According to best-selling author Gerald Posner, author of *Why America Slept: The Failure to Prevent 9/11*, "And the word comes back from the Clinton administration 'let him land and proceed on to Pakistan.'"

Clinton himself admitted, during a speech in Long Island, that he turned down an offer by Sudanese authorities to have bin Laden extradited in 1996. Posner, who voted for Clinton twice, told NBC's Katie Couric during an interview on Wednesday September 3, 2003, "We just were not focused on Islamic militants…You had President Clinton in an eight-year period, there were two years he met with the head of the CIA twice. That was it. He just wasn't attuned to foreign policy or the issue of terrorism."[4]

While speaking with Fox's Bill O'Reilly, Posner said, "I was infuriated. My blood kept boiling as I realized that eight of the ten years leading up to 9/11 were under his [Clinton's] watch- and the job that was done was just terrible."[5]

On June 25, 1996, a truck bomb destroyed the Khobar Towers in Dhahran, Saudi Arabia killing 19 Americans and injuring 372.[6]

In February of 1998, bin Laden declared jihad (holy war) against Americans, military or civilians, anywhere in the world.[7]

On August 7, 1998, truck bombings at U.S. embassies in Kenya and Tanzania killed more than 200 and injured more than 4,500.[8]

In December 1998, intelligence reports showed that bin Laden was in Kandahar, Afghanistan, but no strikes were ordered due to fears of civilian casualties and faulty intelligence.[9]

In February 1999, a military strike against bin Laden was aborted due to concerns that officials from the United Arab Emirates might be harmed.[10]

In May 1999, another opportunity to strike bin Laden was called off due to concerns over civilian casualties and intelligence.[11]

On October 12, 2000, 17 U.S. soldiers were killed and 39 injured when an explosive laden boat rammed the USS Cole in the harbor at Aden, Yemen.[12]

Clinton claimed in 1998, "We will use all the means at our disposal to bring those responsible to justice, no matter what or how long it takes." Yet Lisa Myers, Senior Investigative Correspondent for NBC News, reported on March 17, 2004, "NBC has obtained, exclusively, extraordinary secret video, shot by the U.S. government. It illustrates an enormous opportunity the Clinton administration had to kill or capture bin Laden. Critics call it a missed opportunity."[13]

Myers went on to report that in the fall of 2000, "in Afghanistan, unmanned unarmed spy planes called Predators flew over known al Qaeda training camps. The pictures that were transmitted live to CIA headquarters show al Qaeda terrorists firing at targets, conducting military drills and scattering on cue though the desert...Also, that fall the Predator captured even more extraordinary pictures—a tall figure in a flowing white robe. Many intelligence analysts believed then, and now, it is bin Laden."[14]

Yet even though the Clinton administration was purportedly pursuing bin Laden a year prior to 9/11, the tapes prove the administration failed to take action against him when they had opportunities.

NBC military analyst General Wayne Downing stated, "We were not prepared to take the military action necessary." He added, "We should have had strike forces prepared to go in and react to this intelligence, certainly cruise missiles—either air or sea-launched—very, very accurate could have gone in and hit those targets."[15]

Former CIA station chief in Pakistan, Gary Schroen, said the White House required the CIA to attempt to capture bin Laden alive rather than kill him, which, according to Schroen, "Reduced the odds (of getting bin Laden) from, say 50 percent chance to say 25 percent chance that we were going to be able to get him."[16]

The 9/11 Commission Report gives credence to Schroen's observation. "The United States preferred that bin Laden and his lieutenants be captured, but if a successful capture operation was not feasible, the tribals were permitted to kill them. The instructions (from CIA Director Tenet to the Afghani tribals) added that the tribals must avoid killing others unnecessarily and must not kill or abuse bin Laden or his lieutenants if they surrendered. Finally, the tribals would not be paid if this set of requirements was not met." If the tribals captured bin Laden, the matter would be conducted like a law enforcement issue and bin Laden would "receive a fair trial under U.S. law and be treated humanely." The tribals noted that if they had not had been bound by the requirement to capture bin Laden alive without casualties that "we would have finished the job long before."[17]

According to the 9/11 Commission Report, even though Clinton and his administration policymakers wanted bin Laden dead, "the intent was never well communicated or understood within the CIA. Tenet told the commission that except in one specific case, the CIA was authorized to kill bin Laden only in the context of a capture operation. CIA senior managers, operators and lawyers confirmed this understanding. 'We always talked about how much easier it would have been to kill him,' a former chief of the bin Laden unit said."[18]

Further in the 9/11 Commission Report, "Lieutenant General William Boykin, the current deputy undersecretary of defense for intelligence and a founding member of Delta Force, told us that 'opportunities were missed because of an unwillingness to take risks and a lack of vision and understanding.'"[19]

According to former Democratic Senator Bob Kerry who served on the 9/11 Commission, Clinton treated capturing bin Laden as a law enforcement matter, "The most important thing the Clinton administration could have done would have been for the president, either himself, or by going to Congress, asking for a congressional declaration to declare war on al Qaeda, a military-political organization that had declared war on us."[20]

According the findings of the 9/11 Commission Report, "The United States did not, before 9/11, adopt as a clear strategic objective, the elimination of al Qaeda."[21]

It's also important to note that when Clinton should have been maniacally focused on capturing Osama bin Laden and dismantling the al Qaeda terrorist network, he was embroiled in the Lewinsky scandal which consumed a significant amount of time in 1998 and the first few months of 1999. When his apologists were claiming that consensual oral sex in the oval office with an intern was a private matter, it was clear that Clinton put his childish sexual obsessions above national security concerns for the United States of America, thus putting our country at great risk.

Even though bin Laden's al Qaeda terrorist network had committed numerous terrorist attacks against Americans worldwide since 1993, according to the 9/11 Commission Report, a National Intelligence Estimate on terrorism in 1997 "had only briefly mentioned bin Laden and no subsequent national estimate would authoritatively evaluate the terrorism danger until after 9/11. Policy makers knew there was a dangerous individual, Osama bin Laden, whom they had been trying to capture and bring to trial. Documents at the time referred to bin Laden 'and his associates' or bin Laden and 'his network.' They did not emphasize the existence of a structured, worldwide organization gearing up to train thousands of potential terrorists." Clearly, the Clinton administration failed to recognize the potential enormity of the al Qaeda terror threat despite numerous attacks and declaration of war on the United States by Bin-Laden and al Qaeda since 1993.[22]

According to the 9/11 Commission Report, the last "and most likely the best opportunity for targeting bin Laden with cruise missiles before 9/11," occurred in Kandahar in May of 1999. "CIA assets in Afghanistan reported on bin Laden's location in and around Kandahar over the course of five days and nights. The report was very detailed and came from several sources. If this intelligence was not 'actionable,' work level officials said at that time and today, it was hard for them to imagine how the intelligence on bin Laden in Afghanistan would meet the standard. Communications were good and the cruise missiles were ready. 'This was in our strike zone,' a senior military official said. 'It was a fat pitch, a home run.' He expected the missiles to fly. When the decision came back, that they should stand down, not shoot, the officer said, 'We all just slumped.' He told us that he knew of no one at the Pentagon or the CIA who thought it was a bad gamble. Bin Laden 'should have been a dead man' that night, he said."[23]

Clearly, the Clinton administration missed or intentionally passed up numerous opportunities to kill bin Laden time and time again. The record clearly shows the Clinton administration failed repeatedly to deal effectively and decisively with the greatest terrorist threat posed to our country. Senior military officials acknowledge that terrorism was treated as a law enforcement issue and Clinton administration officials, including President Clinton himself, were reluctant to kill Osama bin Laden, even when intelligence was highly credible and actionable. While Clinton talked tough, it is clear from his actions he underestimated bin Laden and al Qaeda repeatedly, allowing the terrorist threat to mount.

In regard to the culpability of the Bush administration for the 9/11 attacks, it's important to note that Bush had only been in office for about eight months prior to 9/11. Bill Clinton had almost a decade to capture or kill Osama bin Laden and which would have likely prevented the attacks.

Secretary of State and former National Security Advisor Dr. Condoleeza Rice in her testimony to the 9/11 Commission iterated the Bush administration's intense focus on Osama bin Laden and al Qaeda. She noted that President Bush "revived the practice of meeting with the director of Central Intelligence almost every day in the Oval Office—meetings which I attended along with the vice president and the chief of staff. At these meetings, the president received up-to-date intelligence and asked questions of his most senior intelligence officials."[24]

According to Secretary Rice, "From January 20 though September 10, the president received at these daily meetings more than 40 briefing items on al Qaeda and 13 of these were in response to questions he or his top advisors had posed. In addition to seeing DCI Tenet almost every morning, I generally spoke by telephone every morning at 7:15

with Secretaries Powell and Rumsfeld. I also spoke regularly with the DCI about al Qaeda and terrorism."[25]

Liberals have asserted President Bush ignored terrorism and the gathering signs. Yet Secretary Rice explained the president had developed a new strategy for dealing with terrorism in the spring and summer of 2004 and it was approved by the president's national security officials on September 4.

"It was the very first major national security policy directive of the Bush administration—not Russia, not missile defense, not Iraq, but the elimination of al Qaeda...The strategy set as its goal the elimination of the al Qaeda network," she said.[26]

As to specific threat information which Bush critics have claimed he ignored, Secretary Rice explains, "The threat reporting that we received in the spring and summer of 2001 was not specific as to time, nor place, nor manner of attack...More often it was frustratingly vague. Let me read you some of the actual chatter that we picked up that spring and summer. 'Unbelievable news coming in weeks,' 'Big event...there will be a very, very, very, very big uproar,' 'There will be attacks in the near future.' Troubling yes. But they don't tell us when; they don't tell us who; and they don't tell us how."[27]

Nevertheless, Secretary Rice explains that every possible precaution to "detect, protect against and disrupt any terrorist plans or operations that might lead to an attack," including: meeting regularly with the Counterterrorism Security Group (CSG) chaired by Richard Clarke; asking the FAA, the INS, Customs and the Coast Guard to increase security and surveillance; issuance of at least five urgent warnings from the Department of Defense to U.S. military forces that al Qaeda might be planning a future attack and placed them on heightened alert; State Department issuance of at least four urgent security advisories and public worldwide cautions on terrorist threats; issuance of at least three nationwide warnings from the FBI to federal, state and local law enforcement agencies specifying the potential for domestic attacks; FBI increased surveillance of known or suspected terrorists; issuance of at least five Civil Aviation Security Information Circulars to all U.S. airlines and airport security personnel, including warnings about potential plane hijackings; the CIA working "around the clock" to "disrupt threats worldwide" including launching "a wide ranging disruption effort against al Qaeda in more than 20 countries."[28]

One of the primary reasons 9/11 occurred, according to Secretary Rice was due to a vital intelligence failure.

"In hindsight, if anything might have helped stop 9/11, it would have been better information about threats inside the United States, something made difficult by structural and legal impediments that prevented the collection and sharing of information by our law enforcement and intelligence agencies," she said.[29]

Secretary Rice, refers to the "wall of separation" created by the Clinton Justice Department under Jamie Gorelick. The wall made it virtually impossible for domestic law enforcement (the FBI) to communicate and share vital intelligence and threat information with foreign intelligence agencies (the CIA). The fact that these two agencies could not communicate with one another regarding terrorists cannot be understated. Winning the global war on terror is contingent upon achieving the best possible intelligence information and requires all our intelligence gathering organizations to communicate freely amongst themselves.

The Clinton administration's official policy which created this wall of separation significantly hampered our ability to elicit intelligence which could have prevented 9/11. Enabling these organizations to freely share intelligence in terrorist related investigations was the single most significant achievement of the USA Patriot Act *(discussed in greater detail in chapter 26 "Z is for Zealot Terrorists").*

CLAIM #2: "Islam doesn't advocate violence. It's a religion of peace. Islamic fundamentalists like bin Laden bastardize the Qu'ran and don't represent true Islam."

RESPONSE: The holy scriptures of Islam, most notably the Qur'an, advocates violence (jihad) against non-believers (Christians, Jews and Pagans) and anybody who does not submit to Islam.

Perhaps not all Muslims are terrorists, however, the word "Islam" means war, death and persecution—not peace—according to the *Hans Wehr Dictionary of Modern Written Arabic.* The word for peace in Arabic is "salaam."

Jihad is defined as the subjugation and forcible conversion of all people to Islam and world domination, and are central tenants of Islam. Jihad is the sixth pillar of Islam.

Consider some specific teachings from the sacred texts of Islam—the Qur'an and Hadith:

- The Qur'an, Sura 5, verse 82 describes the inevitable enmity between Muslims and non-Muslims: "Strongest among men in enmity to the Believers wilt thou find the Jews and the Pagans."
- Surah 8, verse 39: "And fight them [Unbelievers] on until there is no more tumult or oppression and there prevail justice and faith in Allah altogether and everywhere.
- Surah 9, verse 5 adds: " Then fight and slay the Pagans (the unbelievers) wherever you find them and seize them, beleaguer them and lie in wait for them in every stratagem of war." Then nations no matter how mighty must be fought "until they embrace Islam."
- Sura 9:29: "Fight those who believe not in Allah nor the last day, nor hold that forbidden which hath been forbidden by Allah and his apostle nor acknowledge the religion of truth of the people of the Book (the Jews and the Christians) until they pay Jizya (tax on non-Muslims) with willing submission and feel themselves subdued."
- Qur'an 9:123: "Fight the unbelievers in your surroundings and let them find harshness in you."
- Qur'an 48:29: "Those who follow Mohammed are merciless for the unbelievers but kind to each other."
- Hadith, 4633: "You (the Jews) should know the earth belongs to Allah and His Apostle and I wish to expel you from this land (Arabia).
- Hadith Sahih 4366: "I will expel the Jews and Christians from the Arabian Peninsula and will not leave any but Muslims."

The Qu'ran clearly advocates killing non-Muslims (Jews, Christians and Pagans). This fact is unequivocal. It's not just bin

Laden and other fundamentalist terrorists who bastardize the Qu'ran as is often claimed by leftist apologists. Any Muslim advocating the Qu'ran to be sacred is in essence advocating the same position. Islam means submission, not peace.

Islam rules by force in Africa, Nigeria, Sudan, Indonesia and elsewhere around the globe. Non-Muslims are given a choice between conversion or death. This flagrant lack of individual liberty and freedom is endemic to Islam. It is not an anomaly like the Crusades were to Christianity.

The first five tenets of the Qur'an are of sweetness and light. The sixth tenet is the jihad (holy war). Anybody who denigrates the prophet Mohammed, the Qur'an, or the Muslim faith is marked for jihad.

If a fatwa is decreed against an individual, any Muslim is authorized to kill him and by doing so he is the executioner for what is considered the sentence of Allah.

In 1989, Ayatollah Ruhollah Khomeini issued a fatwa against British author Salman Rushdie because he considered Rushdie's book *The Satanic Verses* blasphemous against Islam. Rushdie was forced into hiding and British police blocked a couple of attempts on his life.

Those associated with the book also were attacked. A man who translated the book into Japanese was stabbed to death in July 1991. The same month, an Italian translator was wounded when he was stabbed. Two years later, a Muslim mob chased a Turkish publisher into a hotel, then torched the building, killing 37 people. Three months later, a man who translated the book into Norwegian was shot three times.

If Islam is really a religion of peace as many claim, why are Muslim countries embroiled in the vast majority of wars on planet Earth? In Indonesia, the Philippines, Chechnya and India radical Muslims are trying to kill non-Muslims or convert them.

Why, if Islam is a religion of "peace" and tolerance, are children taught to hate Christians and Jews in school and use themselves as homicide bombers? Why if Islam is a religion of peace, are Arabic women enslaved and bereft of basic human rights in just about every Muslim country on earth? If Islam is fundamentally a religion of "peace," why have Islamic clerics not formally condemned any and all jihad and formally recognize the existence of Israel?

The vast majority of Muslims are victims of Islamists from Iran, Pakistan, Afghanistan, Sudan, Egypt, Turkey and Algeria. Even though the majority might be peaceful, we have every right to find out if there are people in our country who want to kill and maim Americans and contribute to our downfall.

CLAIM #3: "The 9/11 attacks occurred because of the United States' support for Israel."

RESPONSE: Islamo-fascists attacked the United States because they hate our way of life and the democratic values we promote around the world.

In the 22 Arab states—all of which are varying degrees of police states—Muslim textbooks promote a flagrant intolerance and hatred toward Jews and Christians, such as:

- "Jews subscribe to a belief in racial superiority...Their religion even teaches them to call down curses upon the worship places of non-Jews whenever they pass by them."
- "Judaism and Christianity are deviant religions."
- "Befriending the unbelievers, through loving and cooperating with them while knowing that they are unbelievers, makes those who are their friends the same as them."
- "Many (Jews and Christians) lead such decadent and immoral lives that lying, alcohol, nudity, pornography, racism, foul language, premarital sex, homosexuality and everything else are accepted in the society, churches and synagogues."(In other words everything advocated and supported by the liberal left.)[30]

Terrorism cannot be justified by any rationale. Some on the left have attempted to incorrectly rationalize the 9/11 attacks as backlash for the U.S. support for Israel, saying if the U.S. didn't "take Israel's side" against the "helpless" Palestinians, 9/11 would never have happened.

The truth is the U.S. has given money to both Israel and the Palestinians (billions of dollars each year) and has repeatedly attempted to broker "peace" deals which have included provisions for a "Palestinian state." It's disingenuous to assert the U.S. has "sided" with Israel unfairly. Only the Palestinian terrorist organizations such as the PLO and other Arab terrorist organizations, such as Hamas and Islamic Jihad, have purposefully targeted innocent civilians—including pregnant women and children—in their homicide "bombings." Only the Palestinians have committed these blatant acts of terrorism against innocent civilians in Israel. One cannot equate Israel's fundamental right to protect herself from such terrorist attacks by targeting terrorist organizations and other military installations with egregious acts of terror. Attributing moral equivalence is dangerously misguided.

Arabs are treated better in Israel than in other Arab countries. Arabs who live in Israel have more political, religious and economic freedoms that most Arab citizens in other Arab countries have. Arabs living in Israel (about 1 million of them) can practice their own religion (unlike Jews living in Arab countries), can vote in elections and serve in Israel's legislative body the Knesset. Arab women in most Arab countries have few, if any, individual liberties and freedom. Most are treated as property of men. Arab women living in Israel are granted greater liberties and freedom then women living in Arab countries. The largest employer of the Palestinians in the world is Israel. If Israel grants the Palestinian people more individual freedoms and economic opportunities than do their surrounding Arab countries, who refuse to absorb the Palestinians into their countries, how can the assertion that the Arab world hates the U.S. for its support for Israel have any credibility?

The United States' support for Israel had nothing to do with many other Islamic and Arab terrorist atrocities around the world.

- Syria committed terrorist acts against Lebanon since the early 1970s.
- Saddam Hussein used chemical weapons against Iran during the '80s
- Saddam Hussein invaded Kuwait in 1990.
- Kuwait expelled hundreds of thousands of Palestinians.

- The Taliban destroyed the Bamiyan Buddha statues in Afghanistan in 2001.
- Muslim terrorists have murdered over two million black Christians in Sudan.
- Muslim terrorists murdered 202 people in Bali in 2003.
- Muslim terrorists encouraged church bombings in Pakistan in 2000.[31]

The United States' support for Israel is not the primary cause of the terrorism and violence the world has witnessed over the past 20 years—and for that matter 9/11 itself. The terrorists hate, above all else, liberal democracies, religious freedom, and the rule of law. While it's true Judeo-Christian nations such as Israel and the United States top the list of countries the terrorists hate, it's also evident that shifting blame onto the United States as though we provoked these barbaric acts is misguided.

CLAIM #4: "America's wealth is responsible for breeding the global poverty which creates terrorism."

RESPONSE: Osama bin Laden's al Qaeda terrorist organization had millions of dollars at its disposal.

Bin Laden was a multi-millionaire who grew up a child of privilege. Muslim and Arab countries who sponsor terrorism against the U.S. are also oil rich countries that have more pronounced wealth disparities than do Americans. The assertion that poor Muslim men join together to terrorize the U.S. because of our wealth and high standard of living is preposterous. The fact is that approximately two-thirds of al Qaeda members are college educated. In Muslim countries, only the wealthy have access to colleges and universities.

Terrorism is rooted in a fundamental hatred of Western-style liberal democracy. Those in the Muslim and Arab world who sponsor terrorism against the U.S. and other Western Democracies, such as Israel, are threatened by the values we promote. In his book *What's So Great About America*, Dinesh D'Souza explains that Islamic countries view the United States as a "subversive idea," which poses a threat to the existence of Islam.[32] Islam means "submission." In order for Islam to thrive, there must be a total submission to Allah. Since Western-style democracy promotes religious freedom and toleration, radical Islam cannot peacefully co-exist. Therefore terrorism is the weapon the Islamo-Terrorists have chosen to destroy our Westernized free way of life.

America is the financial engine of the global economy. America buys more of the products and services provided by foreign countries than any other country in the world. We provide more jobs to foreign countries than any country in the world. American taxpayers donate more money to developing countries than any other country in the world. If anything, America has done more to promote economic egalitarianism than any other nation in the world.

The U.S. provides more taxpayer money to the Palestinians than any other Arab country. The U.S. gives billions in "aid" to Palestinian "N.G.O.s" to promote economic opportunity and the wealthy Arab countries from whom the "Palestinians" originated refuse to assimilate them back into their countries.

Who is more "responsible" for a Palestinian homicide bomber who kills innocent Israeli women and children in a disco or pizza parlor—the American taxpayers who give them billions or terrorists such as Yassar Arafat who misdirected the funds and kept his people in permanent squalor?

What about the Arab countries which refuse to absorb the Palestinians into their countries? Are they not responsible for some of the economic inequalities from which the Palestinians suffer?

Chapter 15

O is For Operation Iraqi Freedom:

Why We Had to Fight This War

Claims:
1. "Iraq didn't attack us on 9-11, was not an imminent threat, and was not part of the real war on terror."
2. "Bush went it alone unilaterally in Iraq and failed to get the support of our allies."
3. "Bush should have given the inspectors more time in Iraq. He rushed to war. Sanctions were working"
4. "Republicans spent $200 billion in Iraq which diverted funds from fighting the 'real war' on terror and from domestic programs such as school lunches and health care for the uninsured."
5. "Bush should not have acted preemptively in Iraq."
6. "Bush exaggerated the case for war in Iraq by lying about WMD."
7. "We invaded Iraq for oil."
8. "Invasion of Iraq has not made us any safer."
9. "U.S. occupation of Iraq will only create more terrorists."
10. "Violence in response to violence has never achieved anything. Evil cannot be destroyed by destroying evil people."

11. "War has never solved anything."
12. "Conservative Republicans are war mongers."

Liberal Democrats have, for the most part, opposed the Iraq war. Most of the Democrats in Congress voted for the war, but many, including 2004 presidential candidate John Kerry who equivocated that he only voted to give the president authority to go to war, but didn't directly vote for the war itself, have been in opposition. Other Democrats have attempted to take both sides in an attempt to hedge their bets and satisfy their anti-war base.

Kerry originally argued, in an effort to defeat then-popular anti-war candidate Howard Dean, that America must deal with Saddam Hussein aggressively and that for any presidential candidate to allow Saddam to remain in power would, in his mind, preclude that candidate from being president.

Kerry then voted for the war, then voted against the money to fund the troops in harm's way, then said he would have voted for the war even if Saddam had not possessed WMD, then called the war "the wrong war, at the wrong place, at the wrong time," then said that as president he would fight the war on terror more intelligently and would attract more of our allies to join us in the fight.

Other Democrats, such as former President Clinton, also publicly acknowledged the extreme threat posed by Saddam Hussein and the importance of removing the man who posed such an imminent threat to the United States' national security.

President Bush agreed. Given the events surrounding 9/11, it was obvious to him and those in his administration that the man who had declared war on the United States and who had used chemical and biological weapons against his own citizens posed a significant threat to the United States. The president received information from British and Russian intelligence agencies which confirmed that indeed Saddam was in the process of acquiring enriched uranium for his nuclear weapons program. After Hussein failed to comply with 12 separate U.N. resolutions to allow weapons inspectors back into the country, the decision was made to disarm him.

Conservatives contend that, given the intelligence the Bush

administration received from numerous international agencies, it would have been irresponsible to allow Saddam Hussein to continue to develop his weapons programs—especially given the attacks of 9/11 and Hussein's track record of ignoring U.N. resolutions and the international community in general.

The fact that no actual WMD were found in Iraq has led many on the left to claim that invading Iraq was based on a "lie" and that Saddam had "nothing to do with 9/11."

While it's true that no large stockpiles of WMD were found, it's not true anybody in the Bush administration "lied" about anything. What is known is that one of the most dangerous homicidal maniacs in the world was removed from power and one of the largest hotbeds of terror in the world—Iraq—held democratically free elections in which 12 million citizens voted for their elected representatives.

Tyrannical regimes are the most susceptible to radical Islamic rule, but, as President Bush noted in his 2005 State of the Union address, the best way to win the war on Islamic terror is to plant the seeds of liberty and freedom. The rapid increase in individual freedom and decrease in terrorism in the Ukraine, Palestine, Iraq, Afghanistan and Lebanon seems to have validated the president's long-term vision.

Despite the success of Iraqi Freedom and the reconstruction of the country, liberals continue to deride Bush, his motives for invading Iraq and the manner in which the war has been prosecuted.

CLAIM #1: "Iraq didn't attack us on 9/11, was not an imminent threat and was not part of the real war on terror."

RESPONSE: The Germans didn't attack us in World War II either. The Japanese did.

Yet both the Germans and the Japanese posed a threat to the security of the United States. Should the United States have only attacked Japan because Germany "never did anything to the United States?" If the United States had not joined the allied coalition in World War II and the Germans had taken over Europe, an entire continent would have been under the control of the Nazis.

While the Nazis didn't directly attack America, Roosevelt recognized the Germans were part of the larger war on totalitarianism, which, left unchecked, would pose a significant and imminent threat to our country. The U.S. acted preemptively by attacking the Germans after it became clear appeasement and conciliation had become a feckless policy to combat the spread of Nazism. Acting proactively, millions of lives would be spared in the future.

Bush made clear as part of his Bush Doctrine, the war on terror would not be fought like other conventional wars of the past. The United States would preempt another attack, such as the one on 9/11, by attacking those countries which sponsored terrorism, harbored terrorists or had plans to attack the United States.

Even though Hussein didn't directly attack the U.S. on 9/11, his documented past associations with terrorist organizations qualified Hussein as a very likely terrorist threat. Hussein made $25,000 payments to families of Palestinian homicide bombers and harbored al Qaeda terrorists. He had a well-known commitment to obtain WMDs and use them to attack the U.S.

To deny Saddam Hussein was not "part of the war on terror" would be to deny his past terrorist actions. Hussein was a well-known terrorist who used WMD and poison gas against his own people, killing hundreds of thousands of Kurds in the 1980s and burying them in mass graves. He routinely tortured his own citizens with electric shock and castration. He raped women and killed them in front of their families. Hussein long harbored one of the terrorists who bombed the World Trade Center February 26, 1993. He had already attempted to assassinate a sitting U.S. president (Bush, 41) in 1993 and many intelligence agencies around the world believed he actively pursued enriched uranium (yellowcake) for his WMD program.

According to the Duelfer Report of the Iraq Survey Group (ISG) released in October 2004, Saddam posed an imminent threat to the United States and to the rest of the world.

While it is true there were no actual facilities found producing chemical or biological agents on a large scale, there were many smaller scale clandestine laboratories operating under the Iraqi Intelligence Services which were engaged in small scale production of chemical nerve agents, sulfur mustard, nitrogen mustard, ricin, aflatoxin and other unspecified agents. Moreover, these laboratories were analyzing whether various poisons would alter the texture, smell and appearance of foodstuffs.

Did these findings not constitute an imminent threat? Should we have waited for these chemical and biological weapons to be smuggled into the country and used against our domestic population to murder millions of citizens before we considered these weapons an "imminent threat?"

The report also noted Iraqi Intelligence Service M-16—Saddam's Directorate of Criminology which conducted "special substances" research and development—"had a plan to produce and weaponize nitrogen mustard in rifle grenades and a plan to bottle sarin and sulfur mustard in perfume sprayers and medicine bottles which they would ship to the United States and Europe."

The ISG was told "ricin was being developed into stable liquid to deliver as an aerosol" in various munitions.

"Such development was not just for assassination," wrote Richard Spertzel, head of the biological weapons section of UNSCOM from 1994 to 1999 and a member for the ISG. "If Iraq was successful in developing an aerosolizable ricin, it made a significant step forward. The development had to be for terrorist delivery. Even on a small scale this must be considered as a WMD."[1]

Documentation from the Duelfer Report indicated Iraq was training non-Iraqis at Salman Pak—training Palestinians, Yemenis, Saudis, Lebanese, Egyptians and Sudanese in terrorist techniques, including assassination and homicide bombings.[2]

CLAIM #2: "Bush went it alone unilaterally in Iraq and failed to get the support of our allies."

RESPONSE: The United States successfully went to war against the Taliban in Afghanistan, as well as Saddam Hussein in Iraq with a coalition of more than 30 countries, including Great Britain, Italy, Australia, Poland and Spain.

Those on the left, such as Kerry, who made this accusation, only consider multilateral support of the French and Germans. Not only were both these countries involved in the U.N. oil-for-food scandal, but both stated that even if John Kerry were to be elected, they would not send troops to Iraq.

While procuring multi-lateral support to combat terrorism is often preferable to unilateral and preemptive force, the United States is a sovereign nation who never needs to seek permission from any other country to defend itself.

The United States also has, by far, the most technologically advanced and powerful military in the world. No other country comes close to the military might of the USA, certainly not Canada, France or Germany with their diminutive militaries and equipment.

The fact that Democrats continue to assert the U.S. "went it alone" fails to acknowledge the efforts of the many countries such as Australia, Poland and England who did send troops and experienced casualties. The left's "unilateral" claim also fails to recognize the courageous efforts of the members of Iraqi's civilian army who have given their lives to achieve freedom and democracy in their country. John Kerry referred to these nations as the "coalition of the coerced and the bribed."

CLAIM #3: "Bush should have given the inspectors more time in Iraq. He rushed to war. Sanctions were working."

RESPONSE: The United Nations weapons inspectors were given 12 years to find weapons of mass destruction. During that time, Saddam Hussein violated 16 U.N. Security Council Resolutions.

Saddam failed to prove he had disarmed during that twelve-year inspection period. Only the threatened use of force by the United States and the "coalition of the willing" made Saddam destroy a handful of illegal missiles he denied ever having. Inspectors also discovered Saddam had drone airplanes which could have been used for distributing poison gas or biological agents.

"Hussein continued to seek and develop chemical, biological and nuclear weapons brutalizing the Iraqi people, including committing gross human rights violations and crimes against humanity; supporting international terrorism; refusing to release or account for prisoners of war and other missing individuals from the Gulf War era; refusing to return Kuwaiti property; and working to circumvent UN's economic sanctions," according to the White House document entitled *A Decade of Deception and Fraud*.[3]

According to the Iraq Survey Group's Duelfer Report, there were multiple informants working within UNSCOM and UNMOVIC which kept the Iraqi Intelligence Service informed as to what sites were going to be inspected by the U.N. weapons inspectors. In late 2002 and early 2003, equipment and materials were removed from several sites 24 hours prior to U.N. inspections.

The report says there were multiple accounts of bribery of officials from several countries in exchange for their advocating either lifting or weakening sanctions against Iraq. Inspectors could not be effective, according to the report, without the full support of the U.N. Security Council which was non-existent from late 1996 onward.[4]

CLAIM #4: "**Republicans spent $200 Billion in Iraq, which diverted funds from fighting the 'real war' on terror and from domestic programs such as school lunches and health care for the uninsured.**"

RESPONSE: **Senator Kerry and the vast majority of Democrats voted for the Iraq War Resolution.**

To then claim, as John Kerry did, that Iraq was not part of the "real war on terror" was disingenuous and contradictory since he publicly declared on the day commemorating the 1,000th American casualty in Iraq, that these men and women gave their lives courageously "in the war on terror."

Economists have estimated that the cost of the 9/11 terrorist attacks on the U.S. economy exceeded a trillion dollars in lost GDP, resulting in the loss of one million jobs.

But a strong argument can be made that the U.S. show of military force in Iraq contributed significantly to Muammar Gaddafi's decision in 2003 to rid Libya of its weapons of mass destruction. These weapons could have been used against the U.S. in a terrorist attack.

Both Republicans and Democrats have joined with President Bush, saying they're willing to spend as much is required to win the war on terror. The $200 billion for the war in Afghanistan and Iraq looks cheap when it's compared to the potential costs of nuclear, chemical or biological attacks on our shores in the future. The money becomes a drop in the bucket when you consider those kinds of attacks could very easily cost millions of U.S. lives and trillions of dollars in losses for the U.S. economy.

The money spent in Afghanistan and Iraq had no effect on tax money earmarked for other domestic programs, such as Medicare and education, as is evidenced by President Bush's signing of the largest health care and education spending bills in U.S. history—while fighting the war on terror. Claiming greater military spending siphons money from domestic spending programs is a favorite canard of the left to confuse voters.

CLAIM #5: "Bush should not have acted preemptively in Iraq."

RESPONSE: Should he have waited for another massive attack on U.S. soil instead?

Bush made it clear to the world after the United States was attacked on 9/11 that our country's next response would be a counterattack against any nation which sponsored or harbored terrorists.

Intelligence from our agencies and other countries indicated Saddam Hussein—who had already used WMD on his own people, as well as other nations and was in the process of developing his own WMD programs—posed a potential imminent threat to the United States. When Hussein himself failed to comply with U.N resolutions numbers 1441 and 1442 and numerous attempts were made to disarm him through the U.N., it was necessary for Bush and the U.S. to act preemptively with—as John Kerry called it—the "Coalition of the Coerced and Bribed" to disarm Saddam and liberate Iraq from his rule.

CLAIM #6: "Bush exaggerated the case for war in Iraq by lying about WMD."

RESPONSE: Bush made the decision to go to war in Iraq based largely on findings of the U.N. and International Atomic Energy Agency weapons

inspectors, as well as those of other governments.

In fact, President Bush's harshest critics from the Democratic Party made a case for war with Iraq, nearly identical to the president's.

President Clinton, addressing the nation on December 16, 1998 after ordering a strike on military and security targets in Iraq, said, "The mission is to attack Iraq's nuclear, chemical and biological weapons programs and its military capacity to threaten its neighbors. The purpose is to protect the national interest of the United States and indeed the interests of the people throughout the Middle East and around the world. Saddam Hussein must not be allowed to threaten his neighbors or the world with nuclear arms, poison gas or biological weapons."[5]

Vice President Gore, on that very same day said, "If you allow someone like Saddam Hussein to get nuclear weapons, ballistic missiles, chemical weapons, biological weapons, how many people is he going to kill with these weapons? He's already demonstrated a willingness to use these weapons. He poison-gassed his own people. He used poison gas and other weapons of mass destruction against his neighbors. The man has no compunction about killing lots of people. So the U.S. bombing is a way to save lives and to save the stability and peace of a region of the world that is important to the peace and security of the entire world."[6]

Senator Tom Daschle said in 1998 that a use of force resolution would "send as clear a message as possible that we are going to force, one way or another, diplomatically or militarily, Iraq to comply with international law."

He then went on to further defend Clinton's decision to use force saying, "We have exhausted virtually our diplomatic effort to get the Iraqis to comply with their own agreements and with international law. Given that, what other option is there but to force them to do so? That's what they're saying. This is the key question. And the answer is we don't have another option. We have to force them to comply and we are doing so militarily."[7]

Senator John Kerry on February 23, 1998, said, "If there is not unfettered, unrestricted, unlimited access per the U.N. resolution for inspections and UNSCOM cannot in our judgment appropriately perform its functions, then we obviously reserve the rights to press the case internationally and to do what we need to do as a nation in order to be able to enforce those rights...Saddam Hussein has already used weapons and has made it clear that he has the intent to continue to try, by virtue of his duplicity and secrecy, to continue to do so. That is the threat to the stability of the Middle East."[8]

Richard Butler, who headed the team investigating Iraq's weapons programs, said, "The fundamental problem with Iraq remains the nature of the regime itself: Saddam Hussein is a homicidal dictator who is addicted to weapons of mass destruction."

In his book *The Greatest Threat: Iraq, Weapons of Mass Destruction, and the Growing Crisis of Global Security,* Butler wrote, "It would be foolish in the extreme not to assume that [Saddam Hussein] is developing long-range missile capabilities, at work again on building nuclear weapons and adding to the chemical and biological warfare weapons he concealed during the UNSCOM inspection period."[9]

Saddam's son-in-law, Lieutenant General Hussein Kamel—who was in charge of Iraq's chemical, biological and nuclear weapons programs—defected to Jordan in 1995, then provided information to UNSCOM, IAEA and foreign intelligence agencies about Iraq's WMD programs. (Saddam Hussein had both Kamel and his brother executed a year later.)

Iraqi officials later admitted they had hidden more than 100,000 gallons of botulinum toxin, more than 22,000 gallons of anthrax, more than 500 gallons of aflatoxin, four metric tons of VX nerve gas and 2.7 gallons of ricin.[10]

Even prominent Democrats, along with American, British and Russian intelligence agencies and the U.N., shared the Bush administration's view that Iraq posed a grave and imminent threat to America's security. All knew sanctions and resolutions weren't working. Force was necessary to disarm and remove Saddam from power.

Two British Paliamentary reports—one of them being the Butler Report—found there was credible intelligence Iraq had attempted to acquire 500 tons of uranium oxide—yellowcake—from Niger in 1999.

Valerie Plame, who worked in the CIA's nonproliferation unit, recommended her husband—former Ambassador Joseph C. Wilson IV—be sent to Niger to fact check the British intelligence, telling her husband it was a "crazy report."

Wilson has stated that Vice-President Dick Cheney asked him to go to Niger on a "fact finding" trip. But the authorization didn't come from the White House. It came from the CIA at the recommendation of Wilson's wife—Valerie Plame.

Plame sent a memo on February 12, 2002 to the CIA's operations division saying her husband "has good relations with both the PM [prime minister] and the former Minister of Mines (not to mention lots of French contacts), both of whom could possibly shed light on this sort of activity."[11]

CIA operations accepted her recommendation and authorized Wilson be sent to Africa.

Yet Wilson later lied about it and wrote in his memoirs published in 2004, "Valerie had nothing to do with the matter. She definitely had not proposed that I make the trip."[12]

An article in the *Washington Post* stated, "Former ambassador Joseph C. Wilson IV, dispatched by the CIA in February 2002 to investigate reports that Iraq sought to reconstitute its nuclear weapons program with uranium from Africa, was specifically recommended for the mission by his wife, a CIA employee, contrary to what he has said publicly."[13]

Wilson returned in February 2002 and said the claim Saddam tried to buy yellowcake was "probably false."

The British stood by their intelligence, no matter what Wilson said. On September 24, 2002, British Prime Minister Tony Blair said in a speech to his Parliament, "We *know* Saddam has been trying to buy significant quantities of uranium from Africa."[14]

The same day, a bipartisan Senate report stated the CIA instructed the White House it could say, "We also have intelligence that Iraq has sought large amounts of uranium and uranium oxide, known as yellowcake, from Africa."[15]

While the Senate Intelligence Committee's report on pre-war intelligence found that information the CIA provided was mistaken, they also found that neither Bush nor any of his administration officials, "attempted to coerce, influence or pressure analysts to change their judgments related to Iraq's weapons of mass destruction capabilities."[16]

British government officials stood by their findings (and still do to this day), even after the Butler Report said in 2002 that, in order to discredit the intelligence, someone *forged* documents and "openly" distributed them, saying Saddam had tried to buy the yellowcake.[17] By badly forging the documents, they hoped to make the truth appear to be a lie. Some took the bait.

The British saw through the forgeries and stood by their claim. The White House trusted their ally's intelligence and included that now famous sixteen-word statement in President Bush's January 28, 2003 State of the Union address: "The British government has learned that Saddam Hussein recently sought significant quantities of uranium from Africa."

The Senate report from September 2002 concludes, "no Central Intelligence Agency (CIA) analysts or officials told the National Security Council (NSC) to remove the '16 words'" from the State of the Union address.

Moreover, the Senate report concluded there was no evidence any administration official "attempted to coerce, influence or pressure analysts to change their judgments related to Iraq's weapons of mass destruction capabilities."[18]

President Bush didn't mislead Americans with regard to the threat Saddam posed to the United States. The British government finally publicly released this information in a July 2004 pre-Iraq war intelligence report which concluded, "It is accepted by all parties that Iraqi officials visited Niger in 1999. The British government had intelligence from several different sources indicating that this visit was for the purpose of acquiring uranium. Since uranium constitutes almost three quarters of Niger's exports, the intelligence was credible."

CLAIM #7: "We invaded Iraq for oil."

RESPONSE: If that were the case, we wouldn't be paying record highs for oil now.

The "blood for oil" claim is ridiculous. If America wanted to use its military might to seize Iraq's oil, we could have captured Iraq's oil fields and kept them with the half million troops who were deployed during the Gulf War. The notion is ludicrous because all the evidence contradicts this claim.

CLAIM #8: "The invasion of Iraq has not made us any safer."

RESPONSE: There have been no terrorist attacks on American shores since September 11, 2001.

The Department of Homeland Security and the United States military have thwarted thousands of potential terrorist attacks.

Saddam Hussein, a homicidal maniac and one of the world's most dangerous terrorists, is out of power and now sits in a prison cell awaiting his trial. Uday and Qusay Hussein, his two terrorist sons who ran the rape rooms and torture chambers, have been killed.

American, British and coalition troops have captured 85 percent of al Qaeda's leaders.

In 2003, Muammar Gaddafi of Libya gave up weapons of mass destruction in response to force used in Iraq.

Democratically held elections and the seeds of democracy have been planted in Afghanistan and Iraq—two of the most dangerous terrorist nations in the world.

Under Bill Clinton, before we aggressively pursued terrorists, we were attacked numerous times and failed to respond decisively. Instead, we pursued a strategy of benign neglect, created a wall between the FBI and CIA which made it more difficult to share intelligence information, cut intelligence spending and turned down multiple opportunities to capture and bring to justice Osama bin Laden.

CLAIM #9: "U.S. occupation of Iraq will only create more terrorists."

RESPONSE: There may be more insurgencies from the desperate terrorists who are fighting to retake control of Iraq, but these instances are likely to be short-lived.

The terrorists know if Iraq and Afghanistan become representative democracies, they will effectively be out of business. It shouldn't come as a surprise that the leftovers from Saddam's regime will desperately attempt to recruit other terrorists to replace the ones we kill. It's more realistic to assume that once the Iraqi people experience peace, liberty and freedom, they will band together to fight the terrorists to ensure their own domestic tranquility.

Terrorists were emboldened by the U.S.'s apathetic response to terrorist attacks during the 1990s. They saw America as weak and thought they could significantly damage our country on 9/11 based on this perception.

Reagan's philosophy of "peace through strength" has been the most effective way to protect American citizens. Belligerent organizations such as al Qaeda can only be defeated with force. Any show of pacifism only creates the perception of weakness. There is no negotiating with murderous homicidal maniacs who seek to destroy the United States and Western civilization in general. They can only be defeated by aggressively destroying their networks and bringing them to justice.

During World War II, we didn't rationalize that killing Nazis was going to produce more Nazis. This is a ridiculous line of reasoning. Killing terrorists who are bent on the permanent destruction of the United States is the only 100 percent deterrent that those terrorists will not pose a threat to the United States.

While we may never rid the world completely of all terrorists, destroying as many terrorist cells around the world and planting the seeds of democracy in terrorist hotbeds is the best way to combat Islamic terrorism worldwide and export Western values of free markets, rule of law and democracy.

CLAIM #10: "Violence in response to violence has never achieved anything. Evil cannot be destroyed by destroying evil people."

RESPONSE: Peace conceptually is a good idea, but force is justified depending upon the circumstances—as Democrats have shown throughout America's history.

Since the 9/11 terrorists' attacks, we have heard from liberals that the way to deter violence is through peaceful negotiations and containment. It seems odd that although this non-violent approach seems to be the standard liberal mantra, most of the wars and major conflicts the United States has been involved in came during Democratic administrations, including World War I, World War II, Korea and Vietnam. In fact, the disarmament pacts and appeasement policies of the late '20s and '30s only *encouraged* Germany's Adolf Hitler to spread more violence.

Bill Clinton's administration got us involved in conflicts in Somalia, Kosovo and Iraq.

Nixon got us out of Vietnam and Reagan ended the Cold War without firing a single shot.

CLAIM #11: "War never solved anything."

RESPONSE: War eradicated Communism, Nazism and fascism.

Nobody enjoys having to resort to using military force. However, history has clearly demonstrated that the only way to preserve peace on earth is through the use of military force, to combat those who have no regard for human life. When all other means of peaceful negotiation fail, it's sometimes necessary to use force as a way to defeat militant forces bent on destruction and annihilation of their enemies.

CLAIM #12: "Conservative Republicans are 'war mongers.'"

RESPONSE: During the 20th century it has been almost entirely liberal Democrats who have involved our country in just about every major world conflict.

Democrat Woodrow Wilson ran on the peace platform of "he kept us out of war." He won a close reelection in 1916, then asked Congress for a declaration of war on Germany after concluding America could not remain neutral. In World War I, 116,608 U.S. soldiers were killed; 204,002 wounded.

Democrat Franklin D. Roosevelt ran on the promise he would keep the U.S. out of war by seeking neutrality legislation. In World War II, 407,316 Americans were killed; 786,301 wounded. Worldwide, 55,000,000 people died in the war.

Democrat Harry S. Truman dropped two atomic bombs on two Japanese cities populated primarily by elderly men, women and children. After that, he led the U.S. into Korea. The total number killed in the Korean War—more than one million, of which more than

55,000 were Americans.

Democrat John F. Kennedy was the first U.S. president to commit U.S. ground troops in Vietnam in 1962. In that war, 55,000 U.S. soldiers lost their lives.

Democrat Bill Clinton launched the U.S. military around the world on numerous "peace keeping" missions in places like Somalia and Kosovo and used our men and women as the world's police officers. As a result of his lax defense and military policies (including gays in the military, intelligence cuts and defense cuts), the U.S. defense was severely weakened and U.S. soldiers died as a result.

There was only one major Republican to lead the country into a major conflict in the 20th century. George H. W. Bush (41) destroyed Saddam Hussein's million-man army in less than a week (100 hours), resulting in a relatively minute loss of U.S. lives—148 U.S. casualties.

Now who are the doves and just who are the hawks?

Chapter 16

P is for President George W. Bush:

The Man for the Hour

Claims:

1. "Gore actually won the 2000 election. Bush stole the election by disenfranchising and intimidating voters in Florida, particularly blacks."
2. "Gore got more of the popular vote. Bush is therefore 'illegitimate' and has no clear mandate."
3. "The Supreme Court decision to stop the selective recounts in Florida gave Bush the election by overriding the 'will of the American people'."
4. "Bush didn't get a mandate in the 2004 Election."
5. "Bush needs to moderate his positions to unite the country and to be representative of the 47 million who didn't vote for him."
6. "Bush won because of the smear campaign that Karl Rove coordinated with the Swift Boat Vets."
7. "Bush won because he used social wedge issues such as homosexual marriage to appeal to the religious right and get out the vote."
8. "Bush won the '04 presidential election because of uneducated and intolerant predominantly white Christian Conservatives."
9. "Bush is stupid."

P is for President George W. Bush: *The Man For The Hour*

Like the president who preceded him, George W. Bush is considered by many to be among the most controversial presidents in U.S. history. Rarely has a president received as much simultaneous devotion and admiration on one hand and so much scorn, contempt and ridicule on the other. The hatred and vitriol for Bush was so intense that Democrat voters in 2004 were more motivated by their dislike for Bush than for their support for Kerry. "Anybody But Bush" (ABB) adorned many car bumpers and pins.

The left still has not gotten over the 2000 election, asserting the Supreme Court "gave" the election to Bush, that voters (especially minorities) were "disenfranchised," and that Bush is, therefore, "illegitimate." They argue Bush has never received a clear "mandate" of the people, justifying the left's indignation and maniacal hatred for him.

Those on the left label Bush "stupid" and detest his common references to the Almighty. They mock his communication skills and ridicule his confident "cowboy-like" swagger and demeanor. They cringe every time Bush talks in plain terms about "good and evil" and consider him to be a simpleton who fails to see the intricate complexities and "nuances" of domestic and foreign policy.

Bush represents everything the liberal elites detest. He is staunchly pro-life, frequently and unabashedly speaking of the importance of protecting the unborn. He has also advocated supply side, pro-growth tax cuts which those on the left claim have predominantly benefited "the rich."

Bush's goal of promoting an "ownership society" directly threatens the very underpinnings of the liberal, Democrat, big government, welfare state. In particular, President Bush has proposed to reform the current government-controlled social security system by adding the option of individual personal accounts.

Liberal Democrats have claimed these privatization proposals will "endanger the system" and "risk senior citizens' retirement funds in the volatile stock market."

In fact, the accounts would restore solvency to the system and enable younger workers to earn a higher rate of return for their retirement. Not only that, people would be able to own and pass on these accounts when they die.

President Bush has also promoted Health Savings Accounts

(HSAs) which would allow individuals to realize the same tax benefits businesses enjoy to give them access to lower cost health care insurance coverage. Bush, in the spirit of "bipartisanship," signed into law the largest single entitlement in history—the Medicare Prescription Drug Benefit. Yet, liberal Democrats, even those who voted for the bill, complained the president didn't go far enough.

Nothing Bush has done to reach "across the aisle" to Democrats has mitigated the inexorable tsunami of criticism directed at him.

Any reform or initiative the president has proposed enabling individuals to have more control, influence and authority over their own income, health care, retirement and education for their children, has been routinely opposed by those on the left who believe the government can do it better.

Yet, time and time again, President Bush has proven his critics wrong and has made many of them apoplectic by remaining determined and calm in the face of frequent attacks.

Despite inheriting the Clinton recession, the bursting of the "Dot Com bubble," corporate scandals and the 9/11 terrorist attacks, President Bush has been able to simultaneously lead the global war on terror and promote economic policies which have resulted in consistent economic growth domestically. He has spoken eloquently about the 21st Century being "liberty's century" and has been a seminal cause of burgeoning freedom and democracy around the world—especially in the Middle East.

The challenges facing President Bush have been like none any president in recent memory has had to confront. When you consider the record of this president, it becomes clear he, like Washington, Lincoln, Roosevelt and Reagan before him, is indeed the right man at the right moment in our nation's history.

Nevertheless, those on the left continue to disparage him, his accomplishments and his supporters.

CLAIM #1: "**Gore actually won the 2000 election. Bush stole the election by disenfranchising and intimidating voters in Florida, particularly blacks.**"

RESPONSE: Every individual recount, including ones conducted by the media, concluded Bush was the winner in Florida.

Although the left-leaning Florida Supreme Court improperly attempted to aid Gore in illegally recounting votes in select Democrat precincts, their judicial activist ruling was overturned 7-2 by the Supreme Court and nullified.

Bush got more votes in Florida on election night, following the automatic recount and after all absentee ballots were counted. Seven media publications, including *USA Today* (hardly a rightward-leaning newspaper), sponsored recounts and concluded that, under any proposed standard of methodology, Bush won every recount.

There was never any evidence of illegal voter disenfranchisement or voter intimidation by the Bush campaign or anybody affiliated with the GOP. Far from being "disenfranchised," black turnout nationwide shattered all previous records. In Florida, blacks comprised a larger percentage of the voter pool than of the total population of the state. Blacks voted in record numbers in Florida in the 2000 presidential election. In other areas, such as St. Louis which is heavily populated by blacks, polls were kept open past the 7:00 p.m. closing. Voter turnout reached 100 percent in some precincts.

It was Gore and the Democrats who attempted to "steal" the election by selectively recounting the votes only in heavily populated Democratic precincts and attempting to throw out the votes of overseas military personnel—who tend to vote Republican.

Gore attempted to nullify thousands of U.S. military absentee ballots. Party operatives issued a five-page memo which detailed in depth how to disqualify military ballots. Gore wanted "every vote to count," excluding, of course, those in the military who tend to vote Republican.

In the final analysis, it was the Democrats who were guilty of the very ethical violations they themselves accused Republicans of committing.

In June 2001, the U.S. Commission on Civil Rights issued a report which found no evidence of voter intimidation, no evidence of voter harassment and no evidence of intentional or systematic disenfranchisement of black voters. This commission, which was headed by overtly-partisan Democrat Mary Frances Berry, found "no basis for the contention that officials conspired to disenfranchise black voters."

Another separate investigation was conducted by the Justice Department's Civil Rights Division and concluded, "The Civil Rights Division found no credible evidence in our investigations that Floridians were intentionally denied their right to vote during the November election."[1]

According to the Civil Rights Commission, blacks were more likely than whites to spoil their own votes by a ratio of 10-to-1. In 24 of the 25 Florida counties with the highest spoilage rates, county supervisors overseeing the makeup of the ballots were themselves Democrats. In the 25th county, the supervisor of elections was an independent. Not one supervisor in any of the 25 counties with the highest spoilage rates among black voters was a Republican.[2]

Even prominent liberal Democrats have stated publicly Democrats engaged in highly suspect political means to win the 2000 election.

According to long-time Democratic political operative Pat Caddell, "I'm a liberal Democrat. I started in Florida politics. I worked for George McGovern. I worked for Jimmy Carter. I worked for Ted Kennedy, Mario Cuomo. Nobody can question, I think, my credentials and my convictions. But I have to tell you, at this point it's hard to believe, but my party, the party that [my family has] belonged to since my great-grandfather, has become no longer a party of principles, but has been hijacked by a confederacy of gangsters who need to take power by whatever means and whatever canards they can."[3]

It was the mainstream leftward-leaning media outlets who called Florida for Gore *an hour before the polls closed* in the heavily populated Republican panhandle, which analysts such as the polling company John McLaughlin & Associates say resulted in a suppression of voters—costing Bush about 10,000 votes. Bob Beckel, a Democrat strategist, concluded Bush suffered a net loss of about 8,000 votes in the Panhandle.[4]

Others, such as economist John Lott, say it cost Bush even more votes—between 10,000 to 37,000. He studied voting patterns in the 2000 election and compared the 10 voting counties in the Panhandle to the rest of the state and found there was an "unusual drop-off in Republican voting rates in the 10 Panhandle counties in 2000."[5]

CLAIM #2: "Gore got more of the popular vote. Bush is therefore 'illegitimate' and has no clear mandate."

RESPONSE: The Electoral College system in our country, not the popular vote, determines presidential elections.

The fact that Gore received more of the popular vote is irrelevant. According to our system, each state chooses a number of electors equal to the total number of state senators and representatives. The Founders established the Electoral College to insure the most populous states would not have too much concentrated power in presidential elections.

Bush won a higher percentage and total number of the popular vote than Clinton received in both the '92 and '96 elections. Few, if anybody, in the mainstream press ever claimed Clinton lacked a "clear mandate of the people." In fact, many liberals still trying to rewrite history claim Clinton was incredibly popular with the public in spite of his "personal scandals." They fail to acknowledge he never received more than 50 percent of the popular vote.

CLAIM #3: "The Supreme Court decision to stop the selective recounts in Florida gave Bush the election by overriding the 'will of the American people.'"

RESPONSE: If Bush is "illegitimate" and "lacks a clear mandate" because of a 5-4 Supreme Court vote, then other 5-4 decisions are illegitimate as well.

It was the late Supreme Court Justice William Brennan who said, "With five votes you can do anything."

To claim 5-4 Supreme Court decisions are legitimate when the courts have ruled in their favor, but "illegitimate" when they fail to aid them politically—as was the case in the 2000 election—is both hypocritical and disingenuous.

Consider some other 5-4 votes and decide if they're "invalid:"

- *Miranda v. Arizona* which gave people the "right to remain silent."
- *Planned Parenthood v. Casey* extending *Roe v. Wade*, which legalized abortion.
- *Stenberg v. Carhart* striking down partial-birth abortion laws.
- *Texas v. Johnson* and *U.S. v. Eichman*, both of which protect flag burning.
- *Mapp v. Ohio* giving criminals the right to skate if evidence used for their conviction is improperly obtained.
- *Furman v. Georgia* which struck down all state and federal death penalty statutes.
- *West Coast Hotel v. Parrish* which upheld a state minimum wage law for women.

The Supreme Court ruled 7-2 that the Florida statewide manual recount was unconstitutional in that it violated Floridians' constitutional rights by not explicitly defining what would comprise a valid "vote" during the recount.

The Supreme Court had the legal authority to intervene in the Florida recount because it was a federal presidential election. The Constitution mandates that state *legislatures*—not a state's *Supreme Court*—have jurisdiction for creating a process whereby the states' electors are to be selected.

The Florida Supreme Court violated the Constitution.

It was the constitutional duty of the U.S. Supreme Court to override the activist Florida Supreme Court's decision authorizing the initial recount.

CLAIM #4: "Bush didn't get a mandate in the 2004 Election."

RESPONSE: Bush won by almost four million votes nationwide and received the most votes of any president in U.S. history.

Bush won states previously won by Al Gore in 2000, including New Mexico and Iowa and only narrowly lost blue states Wisconsin, Minnesota, Michigan and Pennsylvania.

Bush received the majority of the popular vote for the first time any presidential candidate has done so since 1988. (Clinton never received 50 percent of the vote. Did he not have a mandate?)

Republicans gained in the Senate, House and statewide in governorships nationwide. The leader of the Senate Democrats was also defeated.

In 2004, Bush also received a greater percentage of demographic votes, including: 24 percent of Jews compared to 19 percent in 2000; 42 percent of Hispanics versus 35 percent in 2000; and 51 percent of the Catholic vote versus 47 percent in 2000.

The last time a Democratic presidential candidate received 51 percent or more of the popular vote was Lyndon B. Johnson in 1964.

<u>CLAIM #5</u>: "**Bush needs to moderate his positions to unite the country and to be representative of the 47 million who didn't vote for him.**"

<u>RESPONSE</u>: **Bush attempted to "reach out" to Democrats during his first administration and almost got his hand bitten off.**

Bush worked closely with Senate Democrats, such as Ted Kennedy, on the No Child Left Behind education bill which garnered bipartisan support and was signed into law. How was he rewarded for reaching out to Senate Democrats such as Senator Ted Kennedy? Senator Kennedy complained No Child Left Behind was underfunded and President Bush was a "liar."

Bush was elected to advance the positions he advocated during the campaign. That is how our constitutional democracy works. The winning political party receives a "mandate" of the people which indicates the direction the majority of American citizens want to move the country.

In Bush's case, he ran on reforming social security (individual voluntary retirement accounts), health care reform (tort reform, medical liability lawsuit limits and individual health savings accounts), tax reform (tax simplification and tax cut permanence), the war on terror (aggressive use of unilateral and preemptive force—the "Bush Doctrine") and nomination of strict constructionist judges to the federal courts (judges who strictly interpret the Constitution—not judicial activists who legislate from the bench).

The bottom line is Americans support and vote for candidates who advocate the positions they believe in. Americans expect their representatives to passionately support and advance these issues when they arrive in Washington. That's how the Founding Fathers intended our representative democracy to function. It's illogical to assume our representatives would contradict the stated positions they took when campaigning to support an opposite stance.

CLAIM #6: "Bush won because of the smear campaign Karl Rove coordinated with the Swift Boat Veterans."

RESPONSE: No documented connection between the White House, the RNC and the Swift Boat Veterans for Truth has ever been established.

Nor have any critics of the Swift Boat Veterans documented any inaccuracies in the vets' allegations. However, there was a well-coordinated connection between the Kerry campaign, Democrat partisan Bush-hater Bill Burkett, and the release of the phony Bush National Guard documents.

Bush-hating billionaire George Soros funded Moveon.org—which compared Bush to Hitler—outspending the Swift Boat Veterans for Truth 100 to one.

And then there was Michael Moore's "documentary" *Fahrenheit 9/11*, which was replete with documented inaccuracies, deceptions and outright lies. No member in the Kerry campaign or the DNC ever condemned the film—which defined the word "smear."

Leading Democrats such as Terry McAuliff and Ted Kennedy publicly called Bush "MIA," "AWOL," and a "liar." They made these references to the president without any basis of fact and made them about a sitting Commander and Chief during war-time. Not only was this a smear campaign, but these comments no doubt aided and abetted our sworn enemies by creating the perception U.S. citizens were not united in the war on terror.

An Accuracy in Media study showed the mainstream media aired favorable Kerry stories three to one over Bush stories.

Democratic 527s (tax-exempt, special interest organizations) outspent Republican 527s approximately 25 to one. It's pretty difficult to accuse Republicans of a "coordinated smear campaign," given how little money was spent by Republican 527 organizations.

The Swift Boat Veterans for Truth advertising and book *Unfit for Command* documenting the real Kerry record in Vietnam was arguably the most effective political advertising. Since Kerry himself never rebutted any of the allegations in the book and even admitted he had lied about not being in Cambodia in 1968, as he had claimed for approximately 30 years, and that he committed war crimes, it's unclear why critics call the Swift Boat Veterans for Truth advertising a "smear" campaign.

CLAIM #7: "Bush won because he manipulated social wedge issues such as homosexual marriage to appeal to the religious right to get out the vote."

RESPONSE: Republicans have been winning elections for the past decade without homosexual marriage being a defining campaign issue.

Bush and Republican congressional candidates won in 2004 largely as a result of moral issues such as homosexual marriage ballot initiatives which were on the ballots in 13 states.

Aside from proposing a constitutional marriage amendment which would define marriage as the union of one man and one woman, Bush rarely mentioned homosexual marriage on the campaign trail.

As most polls have demonstrated, voters are opposed to legalizing homosexual marriage, including civil unions. Most Americans are opposed to redefining traditional marriage and are especially opposed to having unelected judges legislate from the bench. Activist judges have unilaterally redefined marriage without allowing the voters to have a say, but those who felt strongly about protecting traditional marriage voted overwhelmingly for Bush and other Republicans who are perceived to be more supportive of protecting traditional family values.

CLAIM #8: "Bush won the '04 presidential election because of uneducated and intolerant, predominantly white Christian conservatives."

RESPONSE: The majority of educated voters voted for Bush.

A post 2004 election survey revealed Bush led Kerry among educated voters who comprised 80% of the electorate. Among those with post-gradurate degrees (16% of the electorate) Bush did trail Kerry by 11%.

Voters with post-graduate education (16% of the vote)
Voted for Bush—44%
Voted for Kerry—55%

Voters with college education (no post grad) (26% of vote)
Voted for Bush—52%
Voted for Kerry—46%

Voters with some college (32% of vote)
Voted for Bush—54%
Voted for Kerry—46%

Voters with high school or less (22% of vote)
Voted for Bush—52%
Voted for Kerry—47%[6]

CLAIM #9: "Bush is stupid."

RESPONSE: Bush (43) scored a 1206 on his SATs and graduated from Yale and then from Harvard Business School where he received a 3.6 GPA.

He also flew fighter jets in the Texas Air National Guard during

Vietnam; was a successful business owner; became governor of Texas twice in landslide victories; became president of the United States twice; led the war against Islamo-fascism successfully and capably; has enjoyed record high approval ratings, even among women and minorities; was the major factor in the historic 2002 mid-term election wins for Republicans nationwide and received more votes than any other president in the history of the United States in 2004 when he defeated Senator Kerry by almost four million votes.

Chapter 17

Q is for Queer Eye for Same-Sex Marriage:

Why the Family is in Jeopardy

Claims:

1. "Banning homosexual marriage is a form of discrimination similar to the past banning of interracial marriages which makes homosexuals into second class citizens."
2. "Jesus never said that homosexuality was wrong."
3. "Homosexuality is a normal sexual orientation that God intended for some people and is not perversion of normal sexuality."
4. "Jesus preached tolerance-not passing judgment. Who are we to pass judgment on homosexuals to say that they cannot marry?"
5. "How are two men or women getting married threatening or damaging a heterosexual couple's marriage? In other words, How does Bill and Bob's marriage directly hurt Mary and Joe's marriage?"
6. "Homosexuals didn't choose to be homosexual and should have the same rights that heterosexuals enjoy."
7. "Fifty percent of all heterosexual marriages fail. It's hypocritical to talk about how 'sacred' the institution is when 50% of all marriages end up in divorce."

8. "Children need loving parents. Love can come from men and women."
9. "Children who are raised in same-sex homes fair as well if not better, than children raised in divorced or stepfamily homes."
10. "Children raised by homosexual parents adjust socially and psychologically as well as those raised by heterosexual parents."
11. "Marriage is an old-fashioned and outmoded institution. It is merely a piece of paper which doesn't really impact our lives."
12. "Preaching against homosexuality causes gay teenagers to commit suicide."
13. "We don't need to amend the U.S. Constitution to ban same sex marriage. This is an individual state's rights issue (federalism) and each state should vote individually."
14. "Homosexuality is a healthy and comfortable lifestyle."
15. "Ten percent of the population is homosexual."
16. "Homosexuals are born gay. Homosexuality is immutable. It can't be reversed."

Many in America today consider the question of homosexual "marriage" to be among the most vital social, cultural and political issues of the day.

The institution of traditional marriage has been under attack since no-fault divorce laws swept state legislatures in the 1970s. Simone de Bouvier, a prominent leader of the feminist movement who authored the book *The Second Sex*, described marriage as "an obscene bourgeois institution."

Betty Friedan, another leader in the women's "liberation" movement called the home a "comfortable concentration camp."

Lyndon B. Johnson's "Great Society" welfare system channeled massive amounts of welfare money to mothers, making fathers almost irrelevant and encouraged illegitimacy and single parent households. The subsequent high rates of divorce and illegitimacy have resulted in increased poverty, crime, teen pregnancies, drug use, welfare dependency and many other mental and physical problems.

Yet, there are many signs marriage is enjoying a modest, but significant, recovery. Divorce rates are declining, illegitimacy rates are leveling off, teen pregnancy and sexual activity are declining and marital fertility seems to be increasing.

Advocates of homosexual "marriage" argue that most marriages fail anyhow—considering the current 50 percent divorce rate in the U.S.—so it would be hypocritical to limit marriage to one man and one woman. They argue homosexuals should not be denied the same "equal protection" under the law that heterosexual couples enjoy and that what is really important is not the specific family configuration (one man and one woman), but "love" between two "committed" individuals.

Traditional marriage preservationists reason the exclusive marriage between one man and one woman has been the cornerstone of Western civilization, predating America and our common law and must be legally protected for the general health and welfare of our society.

Every society since the earliest civilizations have had some sort of marriage relationship between one man and one woman. Traditional marriage proponents claim marriage is not a "right," but a privilege—one the state can and should regulate. They say that homosexual marriage devalues marriage because if marriage is not confined to one man-one woman, then the "slippery slope" will make possible the legal recognition of any number of potential configurations which ultimately render traditional marriage meaningless.

A stable two-parent biological husband and wife is the optimal family configuration for the rearing of healthy children—protecting them from poverty, sexual abuse and physical violence. It improves their physical and mental health. It helps them in every measure of academic achievement and ultimately helps them go to college.

Traditional marriage helps children avoid violent, criminal and sexual behaviors and protects them from substance abuse. For advocates of traditional marriage, the preservation and strengthening of traditional marriage is paramount to the effective health and general welfare of our children and ultimately the future of Western civilization as we know it.

It's vital to preserve marriage—the oldest social institution known to man.

CLAIM #1: "Banning homosexual marriage is a form of discrimination similar to the past banning of interracial marriages, making homosexuals second class citizens."

RESPONSE: All laws "discriminate" in one way or another.

Laws are enacted by societies which reflect natural law and the moral preferences of the citizenry. Practices such as incest, bigamy, polygamy and pedophilia are all sexual "relationships" which society has deemed to be immoral—and without legal justification and protections.

The analogy between banning homosexual marriage and laws which banned interracial marriage is not an accurate comparison. The Supreme Court struck down anti-miscegenation laws in 1967 (*Loving v. Virginia*) because they frustrated the core purpose of marriage in order to sustain a racist legal order. In *Loving v. Virginia* the institution of marriage was not redefined. The court concluded that using race to deny a couple the right to legally marry was discriminatory. Yet, it did not change the legal definition that marriage be confined to an exclusive union of one man and one woman.

While advocates of homosexual "marriage" claim to be the victims of discrimination, they have no legal precedent to reinforce their central position. It is fallacious reasoning to draw a parallel between racial discrimination and illegality of the so-called "same-sex marriage."

Marriage laws were not invented to persecute or deny specific rights to homosexuals. Marriage laws in our country reinforce an institution which over thousands of years in thousands of cultures provided the foundation for stable societies.[1]

CLAIM #2: "Jesus never said homosexuality was wrong."

RESPONSE: Jesus spoke in specific terms about how He had created intent heterosexuality.

He said, "From the beginning of the creation God made them male and female. For this cause shall a man leave his father and mother and cleave to his wife; and the two shall be one flesh...What therefore God has joined together, let no man put asunder."(Matthew 19:4-6)

And since 2 Timothy 3:16 says, "All scripture is God breathed," those scriptures also include the Old Testament.

In the Old Testament and Torah, Leviticus 18:20 states, "Do not lie with a man as one lies with a woman; that is detestable."

And in the New Testament, Romans 1:27 states, "In the same way men also abandoned natural relations with women and were inflamed with lust for one another. Men committed indecent acts with other men and received in themselves the due penalty for their perversion."

CLAIM #3: "Homosexuality is a normal sexual orientation God intended for some people and is not perversion of normal sexuality."

RESPONSE: There is not one single place in the Bible where God approves of homosexuality. Rather, every place it is mentioned, it is condemned as wrong.

From a biblical perspective, homosexuality is a consequence of the sinful nature all people share. At man's fall in Genesis Chapter 3, God's perfect creation became marred—something which has set the course and affected all mankind from that point forward—physically, emotionally, spiritually, intellectually and sexually.

In Matthew 19:4-5, quoting Genesis, Jesus says, "He who made them at the beginning made them male and female and said, for this reason, a man shall leave his father and mother and be joined to his wife and the two shall become one flesh."

That means, according to the Bible, God's plan for all His creation is *heterosexuality*, making homosexuality a perversion of that. Even if homosexual tendencies are indicated prior to birth, as some researchers theorize, that predisposition still does not make the behavior "normal" in God's eyes.

If, as medical science believes, alcoholics are predisposed to drinking, it is easier for them to become drunks. It's not wrong to want to drink, but it is wrong to drink to excess.

There is no specific gene linked to homosexuality. Even though years ago some thought they'd found a link, other geneticists quickly debunked this notion. There has never been any conclusive evidence demonstrating such a genetic causation.

Some may believe they are genetically predisposed sexually to those of the same sex or to little children or to being a transvestite, but that doesn't give us the license to cross over from temptation to sin.[2]

Even if there is a genetic disposition to it, that doesn't make the behavior right or "legal" in God's eyes. God gave man free will. We either choose to stand against wrong influences in our lives or we choose to let those influences control us.

CLAIM #4: "Jesus preached tolerance, not judgment. Who are we to pass judgment on homosexuals—to say they can't marry?"

RESPONSE: Jesus never preached acceptance of wrong behaviors.

Obviously we shouldn't "judge" another person too quickly or critically as in "passing judgment" on that person. This is what Jesus was talking about during his Sermon on the Mount when He said, "Do not judge [condemn] or you too will be judged. For in the same way that you judge others you too will be judged and with the measure you use, it will be measured to you." (Matthew 7:1-2)

However, you have to understand the entire context of what Jesus is saying. He stressed that humans are, by their very nature, sinful beings and should be understanding of one another's faults. He is saying we should all take a good look at ourselves before being critical of others.

But He has not precluded human beings from making judgments about specific actions or behaviors they find to be counter to God's moral law. Jesus wasn't saying human beings should never use their God-given intellectual faculties of discernment or judgment in order to make moral determinations. He never said all relationships and behaviors were equivalent. In fact, the Gospels are replete with scriptural evidence to the contrary.

There is a difference between personal condemnation of somebody who is a homosexual and agreeing with the scriptures that condemn homosexuality as being morally wrong.

Those who use the Matthew 7 verse as justification for allowing homosexuals to marry are seriously manipulating and distorting Jesus' words and accepted meaning of the passage itself.

To deny that we render judgments thousands of times a day would be to deny reality and human nature. To further deny that the judgments we routinely make have no influence on the course of action we choose by our own volition, is nonsensical.

As an example, no sane person would stand idly by while a child is molested in broad daylight. Most citizens would attempt to rescue the child. Most citizens wouldn't say it was not their place to "pass judgment." The reason we have laws in our society is to place boundaries on human behavior. Society doesn't condone theft and has subsequently passed certain laws which protect citizens by penalizing those who steal.

Similarly, there are certain relationships which society "judges" to be immoral and has subsequently made "illegal" (marrying your brother or sister, marrying more than one person, marrying an animal, marrying a child, etc.).

We as a society have made certain specific judgments on which types of relationships we will condone and those we consider to be immoral and won't condone. We're not "judging" any specific individuals by placing certain restrictions on specific relationships. We're merely placing boundaries between moral and immoral behaviors. We're making judgments to maintain a degree of societal order.

By maintaining marriage is solely between one man and one woman, we're making a moral judgment based on thousands of years of tradition which predated America and our common, natural law.

It's ironic that the same homosexual activists who are trying to redefine the institution of marriage which has existed for 5,000 years claim that those who endeavor to preserve traditional marriage are "intolerant." What about the flip side?

Could it be possible the homosexual-deconstructionist left is imposing its atheistic views on the rest of society despite the overwhelming opposition to homosexual "marriage?" Could these same paragons of "tolerance" be the ones who are the least tolerant of traditional marriage and the values and shared traditions of the vast majority of Americans?

CLAIM #5: "How can two men or women getting married threaten or damage a heterosexual couple's marriage? How does Bill and Bob's marriage directly hurt Mary and Joe's marriage?"

RESPONSE: Legalizing same-sex "marriages" would contradict evidence which shows monogamous, heterosexual marriage is the best family setting for the rearing of children.

Same-sex partnering would enshrine into law that adults' sexual desires are more important than the needs of children for mothers and fathers. Motherless and fatherless families would be deemed socially acceptable. Marriage between a man and a woman is the ideal family unit which promotes procreation and ensures the benefits of child rearing by the distinct attributes of both the father and the mother.[3]

Legalizing homosexual marriage violates the religious beliefs of the vast majority of Christians, Jews and Muslims who comprise about 90 percent of the U.S. population.

By allowing homosexual marriage, society as a whole makes a statement that it's no longer immoral—that the marriage of two men is equal to a marriage of one man and one women.

We would be saying homosexual marriage is an equally conducive environment in which to raise kids. Homosexual marriage has the effect of diluting the moral significance of hetero marriage. That immediately sets up a conflict between what the majority hold as unacceptable conduct based on religious authority and what society says is now acceptable.

You can't have it both ways. If you're a practicing Jew or Christian and believe in the God of the Bible, then you cannot in good conscience support homosexual marriages.

While the direct impact of homosexual marriage on traditional heterosexual marriage may seem benign, there are many unforeseen effects on society we have to consider.

First, when the almost 6,000-year-old assumption that marriage is the exclusive covenant between one man and one woman is redefined to include same sex couples, traditional marriage is no longer an exclusive arrangement. If marriage is no longer exclusive, then homosexual marriage opens the door for other nontraditional marital configurations.

If the standard for marriage becomes "committed loving people," why should this arrangement be limited to two people? What about polygamy, incest and bigamy? What about a man who "loved" his dog? Could they marry one another? Sound ridiculous? Well, what would be the rationale for preventing the dog from attaining the same benefits any "spouse" would receive?

At first, Bob and Peter's "marriage" seems harmless enough. After all, why should Jim and Alice across the street care what "two consenting adults who love one another" do in the privacy of their own home? Unfortunately, Bob and Peter's marriage does not exist in a vacuum. The very foundation of civilization—predating our own Western civilization—has always been traditional marriage and the traditional family. In no other time in the history of the world has any society been able to sustain itself and prosper by condoning the marriage of homosexuals.

While Joe and Mary might not feel the direct effects of Bill and Bob's "marriage," they will certainly experience the lasting impact of a radically different society and culture. Joe and Mary's children will be taught in school that their Christian notion that homosexual behavior is sinful, is "hate speech and hate thought" and not "tolerant." Joe and Mary will have to cede their sacred religious beliefs at the altar of secular humanism which teaches homosexual behavior is normal and should be encouraged and experimented with.

If homosexual marriage is legalized, it is only a matter of time when other non-traditional "marriage" unions are allowed. When four men and four women move in next door to Jim and Alice in a "legal" polyamour "marriage" and each of the polyamours have children together (with different partners) although their arrangement won't directly effect the quality of Joe and Mary's marriage, it could strongly effect the well being of Joe and Mary's children who now live next door to the polyamours.

What will be the effects on children when they are told the octet next door is just another type of "family" and there are a great many diverse families in our country, that each person must decide what is "right" for them, that exclusive marriage between one man and one woman is outdated, intolerant and homophobic?

What about when Mary, who is a third grade teacher, is told by her teacher's union she must teach homosexuality is normal, even though her biblical beliefs dictate otherwise?

And for parents who don't want their children viewing homosexuals hugging and kissing on television, the battle with Hollywood is already lost. It's on the airwaves for young, impressionable minds to see.

If homosexual marriage is legalized and given the same moral standing as heterosexual marriage, what will be the "rights" of the 90 percent of Americans who claim to be Christian who believe homosexuality is sinful behavior? Do the "rights" of a very small minority of radicals transcend hundreds of millions of citizens in this country who don't want to have the homosexual agenda imposed on them?

Every country which has legalized same sex marriage has experienced a significant decline in traditional marriage and the breakdown of the traditional family. During the past decade, same sex marriage has become law in Denmark, France, Hungary, Iceland, the Netherlands, Norway, Sweden and, most recently, Canada. Each country has seen a sharp increase in cohabitation, out of wedlock births, fatherless children, poverty and drug use.

The claim that a homosexual's "marriage" doesn't "hurt" anybody else is based on false logic. The same assertion could be made about other modes of behavior such as pedophilia, child pornography, bigamy, incest or sex with animals. As long as there is mutual consent and none of these behaviors are unlawful, shouldn't everyone be able to enjoy all the same legal protections traditional marriages enjoy? After all, "how does a threesome or person wanting to marry his animal affect the married couple across town?" the cynic might ask.

Anytime we as a society condone specific models of behavior, we tacitly acknowledge it as acceptable. Just because we may never come into direct contact with a pedophile doesn't mean we must condone such behavior by granting it legal approval. Citizens can oppose and restrict certain legal relationships based upon the perceived morality of that behavior. I need not live next door to a polyamorous couple to oppose the legality of this type of family configuration.

CLAIM #6: "Homosexuals didn't choose to be homosexual and should have the same rights heterosexuals enjoy."

RESPONSE: There are no credible peer reviewed studies which conclude people are born homosexual.[4]

There are three ways to test for inborn traits: twin studies, brain dissections and gene linkage studies.

Since about half the identical twins studies didn't have the same sexual preference, twin studies demonstrate that something other than genetics must account for homosexuality. If, as many claim, homosexuality is inherited, then identical twins should either be both straight or both gay.[4]

Another study which attempted to demonstrate a link between homosexuality and the X-chromosome has yet to be replicated and a subsequent study actually contradicted the findings of the first.[5]

Even if homosexuality was found to be an "inborn" inherited trait, it would not necessarily mean it would be "normal." Some children are born with cystic fibrosis or spina bifida, but that doesn't make it a normal condition. Behaviors and inborn proclivities toward alcoholism, violence, obesity and homosexuality are now thought to have some connection to genetics, but are not good behaviors. There are a number of "normal" and "natural" predispositions we are born with, but we as individuals also have the power to overcome these predispositions.

Whether homosexuality is the product of nurture or nature, homosexuals already have the same basic legal constitutional "rights" heterosexuals enjoy.

Marriage has always been understood to be the legal union between one woman and one man. It's governed by the law. Homosexual men are not prohibited from marriage nor are homosexual females. They're merely prohibited from marrying someone of the same sex. The law requires that those wishing to enter into holy matrimony be limited to one male and one female of the legally required age.

Some homosexuals are attempting to radically change thousands of years of accepted normative practice. The question really is: does this small minority of homosexual activists' rights supercede the "rights" of the vast majority of Americans who wish to maintain the current legal definition of traditional marriage as being exclusively limited to one man and one woman?

CLAIM #7: "Fifty percent of all heterosexual marriages fail. It's hypocritical to talk about how 'sacred' the institution is when 50 percent of all marriages end up in divorce."

RESPONSE: Just because there is a high divorce rate, doesn't mean we need to change the standard by which marriage is defined.

It only means we need to focus more attention on the problem of why such a high percentage of marriages fail and focus on changing behavior. Some of the reasons behind the high divorce rate have been "no fault" divorce laws, the rise of radical feminism, increasing cohabitation rates, promiscuity, pornography, adultery and out of wedlock births.

Yet, to say we should change the definition of marriage because some marriages fail, is ludicrous. Just because a high percentage of students fail a test is not evidence the test is flawed. Marriage between one man and one woman has been the cornerstone of civilization for almost 6,000 years.

Traditional marriage remains a sacred institution in spite of those who advocate the homosexual agenda—claiming it's outdated and has become a dismal failure.

CLAIM #8: "Children need loving parents. Love can come from two men and two women. The

> quality of commitment, dedication and love—not the family structure—is what is really important for children."

> **RESPONSE**: **Family structure is the single most important factor in a child's development. The optimal environment for a child is one in which the child's biological mother and father are married to one another.**

If marriage isn't an exclusive arrangement between one man and one women, then shouldn't it also include two women or two men? Shouldn't the equal protection clause protect all types of marriage arrangements (polygamy, bigamy, marrying animals, marrying siblings, marrying children and marrying roommates)?

While it's true men and woman are capable of providing love for children, it's also true no child should deliberately be deprived of either a mother or father—which is what occurs as the result of homosexual "marriage."

Men and women are uniquely different. Research has shown the presence of a father in the household affects children's cognitive and verbal skills, academic performance, involvement in or avoidance of high-risk behaviors, crime, emotional and psychological health.[6] A plethora of evidence exists which also demonstrates the importance of the mother-child bond.[7]

A major study published in the *Journal of Marriage and Family* found that boys and girls who lived with both biological parents had the lowest risk of becoming sexually active. Teens living with only one biological parent had the highest risk of becoming sexually active at younger ages.[8] Children raised by homosexuals are more likely to develop homosexual tendencies themselves.[9]

The stability of a two-parent, male-and-female home impacts children's economic situation, years later. David T. Ellwood, dean of Harvard University's Kennedy School of Government notes that, "The vast majority of children who are raised entirely in a two-parent home will never be poor during childhood. By contrast, the vast majority of children who spend time in a single parent home will experience poverty."[10]

The liberal think tank, The Progressive Policy Institute, states, "It is no exaggeration to say that a stable, two parent family is an American child's best protection against poverty."[11]

Former Clinton domestic policy advisor Bill Galston explains that avoiding poverty requires three things: finish high school; marry before having children; marry after the age of 20.

Only eight percent of the families who do this are poor, while 79 percent of the families who *fail* to do this are poor. Children from married homes are more likely to do all three things and less likely to raise children who are in poverty.[12]

<u>**CLAIM #9**</u>: "Children who are raised in same-sex homes fair as well, if not better, than children raised in divorced or stepfamily homes."

<u>**RESPONSE:**</u> There is little hard clinical data to suggest "same-sex" family configurations would be a healthy environment for children.

The small amount of research available regarding children raised in same-sex couple households reveals those children are comparable in terms of well being to those in *single parent* households.[13] But single parent households, though necessary sometimes, are not the ideal—financially or emotionally.

Of all the essential elements which lead to a child's proper development—access to health care, nutrition, good schools, safe neighborhoods and love—the most important factor is the marital status of the parents.

"The most essential socio-cultural patterning of a newborn human organism is achieved by the family," said Dr. Pitirim Sorokin, founder and first chair of the Sociology Department at Harvard. "It is the first and most efficient sculptor of human material, shaping the physical, behavioral, mental, moral and socio-cultural characteristics of practically every individual...From remotest past, married parents have been the most effective teachers of their children."[14]

"Regardless of which surveys are looked at," said Sara McLanahan of Princeton University, "children from one parent families are about twice as likely to drop out of school as children from two-parent families."[15]

Children from divorced homes are 70 percent more likely than those living with biological parents to be expelled or suspended from school. Those living with never married mothers are twice as likely, according to the research, to be expelled or suspended. Additionally, children not living with both biological parents are 45 to 95 percent more likely to require parent/teacher meetings to deal with the performance or behavior problems than those who live with married parents.[16]

The Progressive Policy Institute, the research arm of the Democratic Leadership Council, reports that "the relationship between crime and one-parent families" is "so strong that controlling for family configuration erases the relationship between race and crime and between low-income and crime. The conclusions show up time and again in the literature."[17]

"Research exploring the diversity of parental relationships among gay and lesbian parents is just beginning," reads an inconclusive 2002 American Academy of Pediatrics' (AAP) report.[18]

The report goes on to caution that "the small and non-representative samples studied and the relatively young age of most of the children suggest some reserve."

Yet, in spite of the report saying the studies are just beginning and those studied were small in number, the report's conclusion still read, "a growing body of scientific literature demonstrates that children who grow up with one or two gay or lesbian parents fare as well in emotional, cognitive, social and sexual functioning as do children whose parents are heterosexual."

The report concludes same-sex families closely resemble stepfamilies formed after heterosexual couples divorce. But how healthy is that?

Step-parents provide less warmth and communicate less with their children than do biological parents.[19]

Children living with stepfamilies are likely to have significantly greater "emotional, behavioral and academic problems" than children living with their biological mother and father.[20]

Instead, the evidence suggests children fare better with a single biological parent than in a stepfamily.

Preschool children who live with one biological parent and one step-parent are 40 times more likely to become a victim of abuse than children living with a biological mother and father.[21]

Compared to children in biological homes and even single-parent homes, "stepchildren are not merely disadvantaged, but imperiled."[22]

Children residing in a home with a step-parent are eight times more likely to die from maltreatment than children living with two biological parents.[23]

In one of the most comprehensive studies ever completed on the impacts of divorce, Dr. Judith S. Wallerstein, an author, psychologist and researcher with the University of California at Berkeley's School of Social Welfare and Dr. E. Mavis Hetherington, a professor of psychology at the University of Virginia, concluded divorce impacts children more dramatically and for longer periods of time than most scholars and child psychologists ever conceived.[24]

Dr. Wallerstein found in her 25-year extensive study on the effects of divorce on children that "divorce is a long-term crisis that was affecting the psychological profile of an entire generation."[25] Almost half the children she observed were "worried, underachieving, self-deprecating and sometimes angry."[26]

National studies show that children from divorced and remarried families are more aggressive toward their parents and teachers, experience more depression, have more learning difficulties and are two to three times more likely to be referred for psychological help at school than their peers from intact families. More of them end up in mental health care clinics, have earlier sexual activity, have more children out of wedlock, have less marriage, more divorce and experience more psychological problems than children of intact marriages.[27]

The bottom line is there is little hard clinical data to suggest "same-sex" family configurations would be a healthy environment for children.

CLAIM #10: "Children raised by homosexual parents adjust socially and psychologically as well as those raised by heterosexual parents."

RESPONSE: The research is inconclusive.

There is no basis to the assertion that children raised by homosexual families are as socially and psychologically adjusted as those raised by heterosexual parents according to research conducted by Dr. Robert Lerner and Dr. Althea Nagai, professionals in quantitative analysis.[28]

Dr. Lerner and Dr. Nagai analyzed for the Marriage Law Project in Washington D.C., the results from 49 empirical studies on same-sex partnering and found major research errors in all 49 studies. The main flaw was that most of the studies were conducted by gay or lesbian researchers or were funded by gay-friendly foundations who wished to influence public policy in support of homosexual families.[29]

Dr. Lerner and Dr. Nagai found most of the studies they analyzed were small and were unrepresentative samples with non-existent or inadequate comparison groups.

Steven Nock, Professor of Sociology at the University of Virginia and a member of the editorial board of the *Journal of Marriage and Family* concluded, "The current literature on lesbian mothering is inadequate to permit any conclusions to be drawn. None had a probability sample. All used inappropriate statistics given the sample sizes obtained. All had biased samples. Sample sizes were consistently small... I do not believe that this collection of articles indicates that lesbian and heterosexual mothers are similar. In fact, from a scientific perspective, the evidence confirms nothing about the quality of gay parents."[30]

Research comparing the outcomes of children raised in homosexual homes and in traditional heterosexual homes is young, plagued with methodological problems and therefore inconclusive. Homosexual marriage and adoption are unproven social experiments which are historically and culturally radical.

The vast majority of data shows two heterosexual biological parents provide the optimal environment for the healthy development of children.

CLAIM #11: "Marriage is an old-fashioned and outmoded institution. It is merely a piece of paper which doesn't really impact our lives."

RESPONSE: A good marriage is one of the best ways for both men and women to live long and healthy lives.

Forty years of clinical research show men and women in their first marriages, on average, enjoy significantly higher levels of mental and physical health than those who are single, divorced, or cohabitating.[31]

"One of the most consistent observations in health research is that the married enjoy better health than those of other statuses," was the conclusion of research at the University of Massachusetts.[32]

"Married people are happier than unmarried ones of the same age," agreed James Q. Wilson, professor of public policy at Pepperdine University, "not only in the United States, but in at least 17 other countries where similar inquires have been made. And there seems to be good reason for this happiness. People who are married not only have higher incomes and enjoy greater emotional support, they tend to be healthier. Married people live longer than unmarried ones, not only in the United States but abroad."[33]

Dr. Robert Coombs of UCLA reviewed more than 130 empirical studies published in the past century dealing with the impacts of marriage on well-being. The studies indicated "an intimate link between marital status and personal well-being."[34]

Dr. Coombs found that 70 percent of chronic problem drinkers were either divorced or separated, and only 15 percent were married. Single men are more than three times more likely to die of cirrhosis of the liver.

His findings also showed that in virtually every study of mortality and marital status, unmarrieds of both sexes had higher death rates in every country that maintains accurate health statistics.[35]

"Married people have the lowest morbidity rates, while the divorced show the highest," was the finding of research conducted in the Netherlands at Rotterdam's Erasmus University.[36]

In 1995, Professor Linda Waite of the University of Chicago in her presidential address to the Population Association of America reported that the health benefits of marriage are so strong, a married man with heart disease can be expected to live, on average, 1,400 days longer that an unmarried man with a healthy heart. The longer life expectancy is even greater for a married man who has cancer or is 20 pounds overweight compared to his healthy, but unmarried, counterpart. The advantage for women is similar.[37]

One of the most consistent findings in psychiatric epidemiology is that married persons enjoy better health than unmarried ones. That was the conclusion of a joint study Yale and UCLA's researchers conducted. Researchers have consistently found the highest rates of mental disorder among the divorced and separated, while the lowest rates are among the married and intermediate rates among the single and widowed. They also found cohabitating partners could not replicate these benefits of marriage.[38]

A study published from the *Journal of Marriage and the Family* looked at the link between personal happiness and marital status in 17 industrialized countries which had "diverse social and institutional frameworks." They study found "married persons have a significantly higher level of happiness than persons who are not married. This effect was independent of financial and health oriented protections offered by marriage and was also independent of other control variables including ones for socio-demographic conditions and national character."[39]

Published studies show other benefits of marriage are:

- Protection against feelings of loneliness.[40]
- Protecting women from general and domestic violence.[41]
- Enhancing a parent's ability to parent.[42]
- Helping create better, more reliable employees.[43]
- Increasing general earnings and savings.[44]

CLAIM #12: "Preaching against homosexuality causes gay teenagers to commit suicide."

RESPONSE: There is no credible research available to prove this statement.

Gay and mainstream publications often use this argument, which was derived from a 1989 report by a special federal task force on youth and suicide. Gay activist Paul Gibson wrote the report, but it was based on such shoddy research and questionable data and figures that Dr. Louis Sullivan, the former Secretary of Health and Human Services, officially distanced himself and his department from it.

Many experts have criticized Gibson's report. Professor David Shaffer, a Columbia University psychiatrist who specializes in teen suicides, concluded Gibson's numbers seemed "more hocus-pocus than math."[45]

Gibson's report allegedly showed that: gay and lesbian youths accounted for one third of all teenage suicides; suicide was the leading cause of death among gay teenagers; and gay teens who commit suicide do so because of "internalized homophobia" and violence directed at them.[46]

Gibson claimed as many as 3,000 gay youths kill themselves each year. But that figure exceeded by 1,000 the *total number* of annual teen suicides. His "one-third" figure came from looking at gay surveys taken at drop-in centers for troubled teens which revealed gay teens had two to four times the suicidal tendencies as straight kids. Gibson then multiplied this higher figure by the disputed and debunked "Kinsey 10 percent homosexual population" figure to produce his "30 percent of all teen suicides are gay."[47]

Another problem with Gibson's study was he didn't use a heterosexual control group—something which skewed the statistics and conclusions of the trial.

Researchers at the University of California-San Diego interviewed the survivors of 283 suicide attempts for a 1986 study and found of the 133 of those under 30 who died, only seven percent were gay—and they were all over 21.[48]

In another study of 107 boys' suicides at Columbia University, only three were known to be gay and two of those died in a suicide pact.[49]

Gay teens who had come close to killing themselves cited other problems or low self-esteem, but "internalized homophobia" was never mentioned.[50]

<u>CLAIM #13</u>: "We don't need to amend the U.S. Constitution to ban same sex marriage. It's something each individual state should vote on because it's a state's rights issue (federalism)."

RESPONSE: Un-elected activist judges and elected politicians continue to ignore the DOMA (Defense of Marriage Act)—passed by 37 state legislatures—which defines marriage as the union of one man and one woman.

The "full faith and credit" clause of the Constitution requires states to recognize a compact made in another state *if* it does not conflict with their own laws.

That means homosexual couples have strong legal ground to go to the District of Columbia or any of the 13 states which do not have DOMA—such as Massachusetts, whose Supreme Court ruled in November 2003 homosexual couples have a constitutional "right" to marry—to demand legal recognition of their "marriage." They can also make the argument the 37 other states which *have* passed DOMA laws would have to recognize their "marriages" under the "equal protection" clause of the U.S. Constitution.

What's needed is a federal DOMA, to ensure activist courts and local officials respect the law. States' rights must be respected and recognized. However, when the laws of the individual states are routinely ignored and over-ridden by activist state courts who rule from the bench, the federal government is left with no other choice than to amend the Constitution of the United States.

Because activist courts like the one in Massachusetts, as well as local officials such as liberal Democrat and San Francisco Mayor Gavin Newsom, have flouted state marriage laws, a Federal Marriage Amendment (H.J. Resolution 56 in the House of Representatives and S.J. Resolution 26 in the Senate) has been introduced in Congress.

The Amendment states, "Marriage in the United States shall consist only of the union of a man and a woman. Neither this Constitution, nor the constitution of any State, shall be construed to require that marriage or the legal incidents thereof be conferred upon any union other than the union of a man and a woman."

Homosexual proponents of gay marriage want it both ways. It is ironic that the same people on the left who claim homosexual marriage is a "states' rights issue" are the same people who also claim homosexual marriage is a "civil right" no group of voters from any individual state can restrict.

On one hand they claim homosexual marriage is a sovereign states' rights issue, while simultaneously asserting it is a federal "civil-rights" issue protected by the U.S. Constitution.

These states' rights activists assert *Roe v. Wade*, which legalized abortion nationwide, was a woman's constitutionally protected "right of privacy." They say no individual state could in any way restrict that privacy despite the fact that *Roe* negated the will of the people in 38 sovereign states to prohibit or strictly limit abortion.

Liberals advocate states' rights when activist courts rule in their favor, but prefer federal involvement when either state legislators or courts vote contrary to their liberal agenda.

CLAIM #14: "Homosexuality is a healthy and comfortable lifestyle."

RESPONSE: Homosexuality is neither a healthy "lifestyle" for homosexuals nor for children.

Homosexuals die much earlier than heterosexuals and have significantly higher rates of suicide, rectal cancer, liver cancer, HIV and other infectious diseases than heterosexuals.

An Oxford University study found that men who have engaged in sodomy by the time they're 20 have about a 50 percent chance of living to be 65.[51]

The median death age for homosexual males is 42 years old—39 if they have AIDS. The median death age for homosexual women is 49 years old. Less than two percent of homosexual males live until age 65.[52]

Researchers found in one study that 43 percent of white homosexual males had had sex with 500 or more men and 28 percent had had sex with 1,000 or more. Seventy percent admitted half their sexual partners were one-night stands.[53]

Another study reports that the average homosexual has between 20 and 106 partners *per year*. In contrast, the average heterosexual has eight partners in a lifetime.[54]

A University of Pennsylvania study found that 95 percent of

boys sexually abused for pornography, prostitution or trafficking are molested by homosexuals.[55]

In one study, 86 percent of convicted child molesters said they were homosexual or bisexual.[56]

Homosexuals commit more than 33 percent of all reported child molestations in the United States, which, assuming homosexuals make up two percent of the population, means that one in 20 homosexuals is a child molester, while one in 490 heterosexuals is a child molester.[57]

In the book *The Gay Report: Lesbians and Gay Men Speak Out about Sexual Experiences and Lifestyles*, researchers Karla Jay and Allen Young report that 73 percent of the homosexual men they surveyed admitted they'd had sex with boys younger than 19 years old.[58]

Thirty-seven percent of homosexuals engage in sadomasochism. The CBS documentary "Gay Power, Gay Politics," reported that in San Francisco, sadomasochistic sex is the cause of about ten percent of accidental deaths among young homosexual men.[59]

Homosexuals account for about four percent of all gonorrhea cases, 60 percent of all syphilis cases, and 17 percent of all hospital admissions (other than for STDs) in the United States. They make up only one to two percent of the population.[60]

Homosexuals live unhealthy lifestyles historically accounting for the bulk of syphilis, gonorrhea, Hepatitis B, the "gay bowel syndrome" (which attacks the intestinal tract), tuberculosis and cytomegalovirus.[61]

The Centers for Disease Control in Atlanta reports that outbreaks of sexually transmitted diseases in major U.S. cities are on the rise among the homosexual population. The CDC says 25 to 73 percent of gay men with syphilis and 25 to 54 percent with gonorrhea are also co-infected with HIV. Gay men—even though they make up less than three percent of the population—account for 42 percent of all new HIV infections in the United States.[62]

The Cleveland Clinic in Fort Lauderdale, Florida found that because of anal intercourse, "up to 55 percent of homosexual men with anorectal complaints have gonorrhea; 80 percent of the patients with syphilis are homosexuals. Chlamydia is found in 15 percent of asymptomatic homosexual men, and up to one third of homosexuals have active anorectal herpes simplex virus. In addition, a host of parasites, bacterial, viral, and protozoan are all rampant in the homosexual population."[63]

The CDC reports that hepatitis A among homosexuals is on the rise in the U.S., Canada, and Australia. One study found gay men in comparison to heterosexual males made up a disproportionate number of new hepatitis cases: 68 percent in San Francisco, 78 percent in New York City, 56 percent in Toronto, Canada, 42 percent in Montreal, Canada and 34 percent in Melbourne, Australia.[64]

CLAIM #15: "Ten percent of the population is homosexual."

RESPONSE: Current research shows about three percent of the population is homosexual.

The ten percent homosexual statistic comes from the 40-year-old Kinsey Report which has been discredited by just about every study ever done in this area.

Recent studies from the University of Chicago show that 2.8 percent of males in the United States are homosexuals and 1.4 percent of women are lesbians.

The maximum percent of the population from any peer-reviewed study ever done is five percent. And many scholars agree this number is on the high side.

CLAIM #16: "Homosexuals are born gay. Homosexuality is immutable. It can't be reversed."

RESPONSE: Homosexuality is a lifestyle choice. It can be reversed.

There are thousands who are living proof homosexuals can change their sexual desires to heterosexual.

Dr. Robert L. Spitzer—the renowned gay-activist psychiatrist who in 1973 successfully managed to have homosexuality removed from the American Psychiatric Association's list of mental disorders—has published results of his new study which show homosexual orientation can be changed to heterosexual.

Dr. Spitzer's findings which were published in the *Archives of Sexual Behavior,* show how 200 homosexuals (143 males and 57 females) responded to therapy, changed their desires and maintained their new lifestyle for a minimum of five years (the length of the study).[65]

Dr. Spitzer only accepted for reparative therapy those who had had predominantly homosexual desires for many years. The majority of those who participated in the therapy reported a change of orientation. But they aren't the only ones.

In 2004, testimonials from 850 *former* homosexuals appeared as full page advertisements in *USA Today* and the *New York Times.* The 850 wrote that they had turned their backs on their prior homosexual lifestyles and were now living as heterosexuals.

Chapter 18

R is for Race-Based Preferences:

What's Wrong With Affirmative Action

Claims:

1. "Race Based Preferences/affirmative action 'levels the playing field' and provides less advantaged minorities with a 'fair' chance to compete."
2. "Affirmative action helps disadvantaged minorities achieve economic success."
3. "There is widespread public support for affirmative action. Opposition to affirmative action is an extreme position."
4. "Without affirmative action, minorities would be relegated to inferior colleges."
5. "Affirmative action is necessary to promote diversity on college campuses and creates a better learning environment."
6. "Affirmative action benefits society as a whole, even though 'more deserving' students and applicants are denied college admission or jobs."
7. "Alumni legacies receive points for admission which is a form of preferences. Minority preferences are no different."
8. "While it may not be legal for state colleges and universities to consider race in admissions decisions, private institutions, such as Harvard can, if they feel there is a compelling reason to do so."

9. "Affirmative action ensures that if two applicants have equivalent grades and test scores that blacks and Hispanics will be 'fairly' represented."

The question as to whether race should be taken into consideration in hiring and admissions decisions has been quite controversial since the 2003, University of Michigan's affirmative action decision in *Grutter* v. *Bollinger*. The decision upheld racial discrimination in law school recruitment for the purpose of "diversity."

Those on the left have argued that blacks, Hispanics and other "minorities" are routinely discriminated against, and hiring and admissions policies which take race into consideration will, in effect, "level the playing field" and minimize any "institutional" racism which exists.

While it would be naive to deny discrimination and bigotry exist in our pluralistic society, conservatives fundamentally adhere to the notion that it's improper to institutionalize racism in an effort to end it. They argue that race-based preferences and quotas violate the very core of the Declaration of Independence and U.S. Constitution, especially the 14th Amendment "equal protection" clause which prohibits all state discrimination based on race.

Conservatives oppose any quota system based on race, regardless of whether these programs are intended to achieve a more diverse campus, or to make up for past "oppression" or "injustices."

Instead, the conservative approach has been to focus on and reform the "root" causes primarily responsible for the endemic underachievement of blacks and Hispanics.

For example, conservatives have consistently opposed bilingual education because English immersion programs have proven to increase test scores among Hispanics. Similarly, conservatives have supported school vouchers for poor urban minorities who have been trapped in under-performing government schools. Both English immersion and voucher programs have been enormously successful and have been opposed almost unanimously by liberal Democrats.

In both cases, politicians who receive substantial financial contributions from teachers' unions and other left-wing organizations, have vigorously opposed conservative efforts to promote, sustain and develop these successful and popular initiatives. Yet those reforms would better prepare minorities to compete for positions in top-level colleges and universities.

Conservatives argue that preferences based on skin color, regardless of the purported justification, is itself racism. There are more effective and legitimate remedies to help the most disadvantaged in our society, promote intellectual diversity and maintain a merit based system that is colorblind.

CLAIM #1: "Race-based preferences and affirmative action 'level the playing field' and provide less advantaged minorities with a 'fair' chance to compete."

RESPONSE: Race-based preferences have the potential of harming the very same minorities which they claim to help.

Instead of aiding minorities by providing more opportunity, affirmative action helps a few minority groups at the expense of others.

In 2000, the University of California at Berkeley rejected 17-year-old Yang-pat Au from San Jose, California, even though he graduated first in his class, received straight A's and scored in the top two percentile on his SAT. On top of that, Au was a member of Junior Achievement, had two varsity letters, a seat on the student council and numerous awards and scholarships.

But UC Berkeley rejected Au because the university had already fulfilled its quota of Asians and had admitted other minorities—even though their qualifications were inferior to Au's. Hundreds of students with far less impressive credentials were admitted that year over Au.

He was the victim of blatant discrimination. His rejection had nothing to do with his achievements. Because he had the wrong skin color, he was not admitted. While some on the left might argue that this case is an extreme and isolated one, the law which is supposed to protect the individual from discrimination is still being broken.[1]

Race-based admissions set up minority students to fail. At the University of Michigan, the Center for Equal Opportunity in a 2003 study found that 90 percent of white students graduated within six years, but only two-thirds of black students did. Similar patterns existed throughout the country according to the results of the study. The study concluded that in the vast majority of cases, minorities who failed to graduate at U of M had a very difficult time meeting the minimum expectations and standards set by the university.[2]

The role of government is to create a level playing field for all individuals, not to guarantee successful outcomes for select groups. Government preferential programs make certain minority groups more dependent upon government. Because the success is guaranteed beforehand, the affirmative action or hiring quota tends to diminish the sense of self-achievement and self-reliance.

CLAIM #2: "Affirmative action helps disadvantaged minorities achieve economic success."

RESPONSE: In many cases, affirmative action hinders minorities from achieving economic success and fails to acknowledge the deeper, more pronounced failure of the public school system to adequately prepare minorities for higher education.

While some minorities might be able to benefit from going to a better college or getting a certain job or promotion which they wouldn't have gotten without special consideration given to their skin color, affirmative action often covers up educational failure at the primary and secondary level.

American public schools are not preparing black and Hispanic students to succeed at the college level and beyond. Only one quarter of high school age blacks in our country read and write proficiently. Admitting a "token" number of blacks into prominent colleges might mollify white liberal guilt, but it does nothing fundamentally to fix the more serious problem—the failure of these minorities to receive foundational reading, writing and math skills in primary and secondary levels.

Minorities from countries around the world achieve higher degrees of economic success in the United States—without race-based preferences—than do domestic blacks with it.

Asians, Hispanics, Middle Easterners and even black immigrants from Africa, Haiti and the Caribbean come to America, without knowing English in many cases and are able to get an education and start their own businesses without the help of race-based government preference programs.

Asians represent only three percent of the American population, but at most colleges and universities, they represent 10 to 15 percent of the student population. Yet, the Census Bureau reports 42.4 percent of Asian-Americans possess a college degree—even though colleges like Harvard, Cal-Berkely, Brown and Stanford place limits on the number of Asian students admitted.

Yet, in spite of affirmative action which has penalized them because of their non-preferred racial status, Asian-Americans have done remarkably well. Their median income is $50,000 per year compared to blacks, Latinos and Native Americans whose median income is less than $30,000 per year.[3]

Many Asians are first-generation Americans and have faced the same kind of prejudice blacks and other minorities have faced at one time in our country. Japanese-Americans were interned during World War II. Irish immigrants were treated like second-class citizens and confronted "Irish need not apply" signs. Jewish immigrants faced similar religious persecution and bigotry. Yet all of these groups have been able to overachieve without the help of race-based preferences.

"Many of these immigrants come from countries where government is not trusted," writes James Robinson in his article in *Human Events* entitled *Why Blacks Should Loathe Government*. "They have a tradition of self-help and problem solving within their own group."

Robinson's article continues, "Some blacks have credited Asian success to preference for these people over indigenous blacks. Whites are less racist toward Asians they say. If that is so, why do black immigrants from the West Indies or the Caribbean have higher incomes than indigenous American blacks?"

In Los Angeles, for example, Asians who are relatively late arrivals to America have higher per capita incomes than blacks and are on par with whites. According to the Los Angeles Chamber of Commerce, in the black sections of L.A., Asians—mostly Koreans—own and operate 60 to 70 percent of all businesses. One in ten Koreans own businesses there compared to one in 57 blacks.

Robinson concludes that the difference is attitudes and explains that immigrants from other countries come to the U.S. to escape tyrannical governments which deprived them of the ability to pursue what we call the American Dream. He believes American blacks are too dependent upon government "even though such dependency is harmful to them."[4]

CLAIM #3: "There is widespread public support for affirmative action. Opposition to affirmative action is an extreme position."

RESPONSE: Support for race-based preferences is actually the "extreme" position because it's not representative of the vast majority of minorities.

A 2001 *Washington Post*/Harvard/Kaiser Foundation survey asked 1,709 Americans this question: "In order to give minorities more opportunity, do you believe race or ethnicity should be a factor when deciding who is hired, promoted, or admitted to college, or that hiring, promotions and college admissions should be based strictly on merit and qualifications other than race or ethnicity?"

Ninety-two percent—including 86 percent of African Americans—said decisions "should be based strictly on merit and qualifications other than race/ethnicity."[5]

It is an "extreme" position to deny a person college admission or a job based on his or her skin color.

It is *not* "extreme" to consider skin color and race when profiling terrorists.

Many on the left are quite vehement in advocating "affirmative action" which discriminates based on skin color, while simultaneously opposing "racial profiling"—a process which uses skin color and race as one component of a physical description of a potential criminal or terrorist.

As many as 70 percent of blacks in some polls agree racial profiling should be used in airports. Equal numbers of blacks in most polls also agree race should not be a factor in hiring and college admissions decisions. In a Gallup Poll, 71 percent of black respondents supported the idea of requiring Arabs, including U.S. citizens, to undergo extra security checks before boarding airplanes. Fifty-seven percent of whites liked that idea.[6] A Zogby International poll found that 54 percent of blacks favored singling out Arab Americans for special scrutiny at airport check-ins.[7]

CLAIM #4: "Without affirmative action, minorities would be relegated to inferior colleges."

RESPONSE: Minority admissions in the California University system increased after Proposition 209 was voted into law in California in 1996.

Proposition 209 ended race-based college admissions and hiring. It outlawed discriminating against or giving preferential treatment to any individual or group on the basis of race, sex, color, ethnicity or national origin in the operation of public employment, education or public contracting.

While critics would argue fewer blacks and Hispanics were accepted to higher tier schools such as University of California-Berkely and UCLA after Prop 209 passed, a legitimate argument could be made that some from these minority groups went to schools which were more commensurate with their skill levels and abilities.

Critics of Prop 209 argued in 1995 that a color-blind admissions process would decrease black enrollment 50 percent and that Hispanic enrollment would also decline. Three years after Prop 209 became law in California, the number of blacks admitted to the University of California system did drop slightly from 3,070 to 2,550, but the number of Hispanics rose steadily from 4,061 in 1995 to 4,373 in 2000.

Although overall the number of whites and Asians admitted has increased as a percentage of the total number from 19.1 percent prior to Prop 209 to 19.8 percent in 1997, this only reflects removing the bias which was once a part of the admissions process. In other words, when Hispanics and blacks with lower average scores and grades were not given preferential treatment based upon their race, it's only logical a certain percentage of the non-preferred groups (whites and Asians) with higher grades and test scores, would realize some degree of increased admittance.[8]

Minority enrollment has increased at the University of California's second-tier campuses—Irvine, Riverside and Santa Cruz. Because preferences have tended to force some schools to accept lesser-qualified students on the basis of race, underrepresented minorities have tended to fail college at disproportionately high rates. A Center of Equal Opportunity 2003 study found that at UC San Diego, only 41 percent of black freshman entering in 1998 graduated within five years, compared to 71 percent for whites.

The color-blind admissions process has redirected some members of disadvantaged ethnic groups away from elite schools such as UC Berkeley and UCLA which might be a disappointment. However, any employer would rather interview and hire a *graduate* of UC Irvine than a *dropout* from UC Berkely.[9]

CLAIM #5: "Affirmative action is necessary to promote diversity on college campuses and creates a better learning environment."

RESPONSE: Affirmative action focuses narrowly on racial diversity and ignores intellectual diversity which many would consider to be a more relevant and vital component of educational significance and value.

Individuals, as Dr. Martin Luther King argued, should be judged on the content of their character, not the color of their skin.

Achievement of diverse thoughts, opinions, beliefs and experiences should be the goal of any college or university, not a quasi-quota system based on skin pigmentation.

If the left genuinely wants more "diverse" campuses, they should begin by hiring more conservative professors. A recent Gallup poll revealed that approximately 90 percent of Ivy League college professors consider themselves to have a leftward leaning political ideology.[10]

Those who claim affirmative action promotes diversity conveniently ignore the lack of "diversity" in areas where blacks represent the majority.

For example, the NBA and NFL are approximately 90 percent black. Why don't the same advocates of affirmative action in state and federal hiring and admissions fail to demand more "diversity" in the NBA and NFL? Blacks earn hundreds of millions of dollars in these sports and command the vast majority of the income in their respective sports. Shouldn't these teams comprise a more representative cultural and racial cross section of America?

Or what about college athletic teams receiving federal funding? Where are the spokespersons demanding that basketball teams reflect a more diverse cultural and racial cross section of America? If there is a benefit to a more "diverse" classroom, couldn't the same argument be made for achieving similar diversity on the athletic field?

Advocates of affirmative action also conveniently ignore all black television networks such as BET and all black colleges and universities such as Howard, Grambling and Southern. Do those who support affirmative action also call for more whites and Asians on BET or on all-black college campuses?

There is no mention of "strict scrutiny," "diversity" or any other judicial creations in the 14th Amendment. We need more intellectual diversity—less government sanctioned racism.

CLAIM #6: "Affirmative action benefits society as a whole, even though 'more deserving' students and applicants are denied college admissions or jobs."

RESPONSE: Race-based admissions and hiring hurts society as a whole.

Denying admissions to applicants with superior test scores, grades and achievements, then accepting students with inferior records of achievement, dilutes the merit-based system which is intended to ensure the most highly skilled and talented lawyers, physicians and other professionals graduate from institutions of higher learning.

In addition, when students with inferior scores and achievements are admitted to the top graduate schools, largely based on race, society gets graduates who are not the most qualified and most skilled. It is dangerous for society as a whole when the physicians charged with the task of saving lives and lawyers discharged with the duty of ensuring their clients receive the best quality legal advice, are not the highest quality doctors and lawyers. The quality of medical care and legal advice is subsequently diluted. The physical health of our country, as well as the legal foundations, ultimately become weakened.

The Center of Equal Opportunity in 2000 analyzed six medical schools from every geographic region of the country and found that blacks and Hispanics were being admitted to medical school with substantially lower college grades and test scores than whites or Asians.

The odds of a black applicant being admitted over a white with the same grades at the University of Washington School of Medicine in 1997 was 30-to-1. At the University of New York, Brooklyn the ratio was 23-to-1 in 1996 and 9-to-1 in 1999. At the University of Maryland in 1999 the ratio was 21-to-1. At the Medical College of Georgia in 1996, the ratio was 19-to-1. And at the Michigan State University College of Human Medicine the ratio was 14-to-1 in 1999.

At every college, substantially more black students than white students failed their initial licensing exams and their subsequent licensing tests as well.[11]

At the six medical schools examined, 3,500 white and Asian students were not admitted, despite having higher grades and test scores than black and Hispanic students who were given preferential treatment.[12]

Our Constitution's "equal protection" clause (14th Amendment) ensures that state and federal governments cannot make laws which do not provide equal protection of the laws to each individual citizen regardless of his or her class, race, sex and religion.

Our Bill of Rights was enacted to protect individual citizens to ensure that even the smallest minority of citizens would be guaranteed fair and impartial treatment under the law.

Part of Section One of the 14th Amendment reads: "No State shall make or enforce any law which shall abridge the privileges or immunities of citizens of the United States; nor shall any State deprive any person of life, liberty, or property, without due process of law; nor deny to any person within its jurisdiction the equal protection of the laws."

Claiming that in the name of "greater diversity" it's acceptable to discriminate based on one's race blatantly violates the core protections of the 14th Amendment.

CLAIM #7: "Alumni legacies receive points for admission which is a form of preferences. Minority preferences are no different."

RESPONSE: At the University of Michigan, four points were awarded for being the child of an alumnus, 12 points for a perfect SAT score and 20 points for having black skin.

To conclude then that a minority is given the "same edge," as the *Washington Post* concluded in 2002, that an alumni child receives is disingenuous at best. The special scoring system at the University of Michigan awarded more points for skin color than achievement or "alumni status."[13]

Being allotted points for athletic achievement, artistic achievement, or any other special accomplishment the college or university deems worthy does not violate the "equal protection" clause of the 14th Amendment. Allocating points for an individual's race does.

The 14th Amendment was added to the original Bill of Rights in 1868 to ensure that no state could discriminate on the basis of race. In 1954, the Supreme Court upheld the Equal Protection Clause which prohibited the state from engaging in racial discrimination in education.

No such case law or legal precedent exists which prohibits colleges and universities from considering legacy status, extracurricular activities or even an applicant's extenuating circumstances.

CLAIM #8: "While it may not be legal for state colleges and universities to consider race in admissions decisions, private institutions—such as Harvard—can if they feel there is a compelling reason to do so."

RESPONSE: Private colleges and universities cannot discriminate on the basis of race if they accept federal funds.

The 1964 Civil Rights Act expanded the nondiscrimination principles of the Equal Protection Clause and prohibits any institution which receives federal funds (i.e. Harvard) from discriminating on the basis of race, color, religion or national origin.

CLAIM #9: "Affirmative action ensures that if two applicants have equivalent grades and test scores, blacks and Hispanics will be 'fairly' represented."

RESPONSE: The SAT scores for black students at the University of Michigan who were admitted to the school, were 230 points lower than for whites.

The high school grades of the black students admitted were nearly a half-a-point (on a four-point scale) below those of whites.[14]

The odds favoring a black applicant at the University of Michigan with identical test scores and grades of a white applicant was 174-to-1. (The second largest ratio found in the 47 public colleges and universities studied by Center for Equal Opportunity).[15]

When the rights of all citizens to compete for admissions to a college or university are protected, those who have the best grades, test scores and extra-curricular achievements will be admitted.

When special treatment is given to preferred groups in admissions based on skin color and race, other non-preferred groups are denied the same equality of opportunity under the law to which they are entitled.

Using race as a determinant in admissions, hiring or contracting, directly contradicts our Founding Fathers' declarations that all men are "created equal." Race-based preferences, quotas and set-asides blatantly contradict and violate that color-blind race neutral quality which is the cornerstone of our constitutional republican government.

Justice John Marshall Harlan's famous dissent in *Plessy* v. *Ferguson* (1897) in which the court upheld the constitutionality of racial segregation, argued, "our Constitution is color blind and neither knows, nor tolerates classes among its citizens."

Race-based preferences violate the spirit of the 1964 Civil Rights Act based on the principles of equal opportunity required by the 14th

Amendment's "equal protection" clause. Equal opportunity requires that the Constitution be "color-blind." According to the Civil Rights Act, "No individual could be discriminated against because of race, ethnicity, or sex, nor could anyone be preferred for public benefits based on race, ethnicity, or sex."

Race-based preferences lower standards of admission for select groups and perpetuates stereotypes that members of those select groups are inferior by nature to other groups not receiving preferential treatment.

Polls show that when the question is asked: "Should race be used in hiring and admissions decisions," blacks overwhelmingly oppose preferences. They don't want others to think the only reason somebody of color was able to attain admission into a college or university, or a certain job, was because of his or her skin color.

Race-based preferences imply some races are not as capable as others. At its core, race-based preferences perpetuate what President Bush calls the "soft bigotry of low expectations."

Preferences say certain minority groups cannot compete on their own and need government assistance to succeed. Most minorities reject this paternalism and are offended at the notion they need special assistance to compete and thrive.

Chapter 19

S is for Social Security:

How to Fix It

Claims:
1. "The GOP plan to privatize social security would endanger Social Security and is inherently 'risky'."
2. "If the stock market has a severe downturn as was the case in 2000-2002, 'privatizing' Social Security would destroy the retirement accounts of millions of seniors turning the system into a game of winners and losers."
3. "Benefit cuts in proposed personal retirement account plans would force workers to delay retirement."
4. "Privatization would mean that old people would be forced to invest their retirement savings in the stock market and end up broke like the Enron employees did."
5. "Privatization would help the 'rich' at the expense of the poor, minorities, and women."
6. "Privatization would devastate 'middle-class' working Americans."
7. "Social Security privatization with the wild market swings could adversely affect the economy."
8. "What if a person doesn't invest properly and loses everything?"
9. "Personal accounts would mean large benefit cuts for retirees."

10. "Personal accounts will drain money out of the Social Security trust fund."

11. "Personal accounts would mean higher administrative costs which would primarily go to Wall Street."

12. "Social Security is solvent and Republicans are only trying to scare the elderly by telling them of Social Security's imminent collapse."

Many consider Social Security reform to be the "third rail" of American politics. Because senior citizens comprise the largest voting block in the U.S., candidates must make a concerted effort to not antagonize or alienate them in any way.

The Baby Boomers will begin retiring (and collecting their SS benefits) in 2010. Every major prospective study, including President Bush's bipartisan Social Security Commission analysis, has shown that due to changing demographics, there will not be enough workers to sustain SS payments to recipients after 2018.

Those studies conclude benefits will have to be reduced, SS taxes increased, or retirement age increased unless something is done to ensure solvency for future beneficiaries.

The GOP and President Bush have studied the issue and have proposed individual voluntary retirement accounts as a way to reform and solidify the SS system to avert tax increases, reduced benefits and increasing the retirement age.

Democrats have almost unanimously opposed these proposals and have attempted to demagogue the issue by playing to older voters' fears. Democrats claim privatization will be too risky, will unfairly benefit the rich at the expense of the middle class and poor and will result in benefit cuts for current retirees.

The concept of a mixed retirement system—such as the one the president has proposed—is nothing new. In fact, many countries around the world have adopted such mixed retirement models in order to supplement workers' retirement benefits.

Chile has instituted privatization, permitting individuals to invest a portion of their payroll taxes in managed stock funds called PSAs.

"While I was Chile's Secretary of Labor and Social Security, from 1978 to 1980, we converted our national pension system to one based on ownership, choice and personal responsibility—just as George Bush proposes to change America's today," Jose Pinera, president of the International Center for Pension Reform and co-chairman of the Cato Institute's Project on Social Security Choice, wrote for the *American Enterprise Magazine*.[1]

Pinera also wrote, in an opinion piece for the *New York Times* on December 1, 2004, "Since the system started on May 1, 1981, the average real return on the personal accounts has been 10 percent a year. The pension funds have now accumulated resources equivalent to 70 percent of gross domestic product, a pool of savings that has helped finance economic growth and spurred the development of liquid long-term domestic capital markets. By increasing savings and improving the functioning of both the capital and labor markets, the reform contributed to the doubling of the growth rate of the economy from 1985 to 1997 (from the historic 3 percent to 7.2 percent a year)."[2]

Japan's legislature has approved tax-favored retirement saving plans similar to 401(k)s to supplement pensions provided by the government. Sweden, the leading welfare state in Europe, allows workers to shift two percent of earnings into individual retirement accounts. Australia adopted personal accounts in 1986 under a Labor government. In May 2001, leaders in socialist Germany announced there wasn't enough money to pay benefits projected under current law, but gave workers the opportunity to increase total benefits through personal retirement accounts.

If socialist countries—including Britain, which has had personal accounts since the 1980s—can have individual accounts, why can't citizens of the United States of America enjoy this same opportunity to invest a small portion of their own money in personal accounts to supplement their own retirement nest eggs?[3]

Tax-payer-financed, pay-as-you-go Social Security has been the cornerstone of the Democratic welfare state since the days of Franklin Roosevelt's "New Deal." Partisan opposition to personal accounts has been extremely vitriolic. A semi-free, market-based system which would ultimately make individuals less dependent upon government retirement by giving them personal ownership of their retirement benefits would restore solvency and allow individuals to earn higher market rates, build wealth, own their own accounts and bequeath them to their heirs.

Since the core voting block of the Democrat Party is comprised of voters who depend on government services, any program or initiative which would make them more autonomous poses a significant threat to the Democrat Party.

CLAIM #1: "The GOP plan to privatize Social Security would endanger Social Security and is inherently risky."

RESPONSE: Social Security is in serious danger now and is going bankrupt.

According to the 2000 report of the Social Security's Board of Trustees, the Social Security system will run a deficit in 2015. Unless the system is radically changed, solvency will require massive tax increases for future workers or benefit cuts for future retirees.

Social Security taxes have increased more than 30 times since its inception in 1935 and the fast-approaching deficit will mean taxes will need to rise again. The Social Security Administration reports taxes will need to be raised to 18 percent by 2032 if nothing is done to reform the current system.

The SSA estimates benefits will have to be reduced 33 to 35 percent. Since one in ten elderly people live in poverty, such benefit reductions would be disastrous.

Democrats didn't consider it risky when then-President Clinton proposed government-run retirement privatization in 1999. Clinton suggested we allow the federal government to invest Social Security revenues in private stocks and bonds. Allowing the federal government to own large portions of private industry was a proposed massive second step toward further socializing our national retirement system. (The first being the Clintons' attempt to nationalize U.S. health care—"Hillary-Care.")

Clinton was on the right track by acknowledging that one vital way to help restore solvency is to allow individual savings to be invested in the stock market. The market has historically returned significantly more than treasury bills. Clinton's support for having the government control the allocation of individual retirement funds instead of the individuals themselves, is a reflection of his and other elite liberals' belief that most Americans aren't smart enough to manage their own money.[4]

"We could give it all back to you and hope you spend it right," Clinton said of the government surplus in January 1999, shortly after his State of the Union speech. "But, I think, here's the problem. If you don't spend it right, here's what's going to happen. In 2013, that's just 14 years away, taxes people pay on their payroll for Social Security will no longer cover the monthly checks. So we have to get into the Social Security trust fund, the savings account. By 2032, it will be gone. After that, if we haven't done something, we can only pay a little over 70 percent of the benefits. By then, the cost of living will be higher and it will be devastating."[5]

Raising taxes and/or reducing benefits in the future is the real risk. According to the General Accounting Office (GAO), Social Security's total shortfall over the next 75 years is projected to total three trillion dollars. But, raising taxes is not the way to fix the problem.

During the past 20 years, Congress has raised payroll taxes seven times. Raising taxes again, many economists agree, will result in significant damage to the economy—especially for poor elderly recipients. The risk of maintaining the status quo is that taxes would be increased and retiree's wealth would diminish.[6]

Most Americans don't believe individual retirement accounts which *they* control and invest are risky. But the majority did oppose President Clinton's proposal to have the *federal government* invest Social Security in the stock market.

In fact, a 1999 CNN/USA/Gallup survey of 1,070 adults found only 33 percent of individuals surveyed approved of the *federal government* investing a portion of the Social Security Trust Fund in the stock market, while 65 percent disapproved; 64 percent approved of *individuals* investing a portion of their savings or taxes in the stock market, while 33 percent disapproved."[7]

What's the difference between individuals and the federal government investing your retirement in the stock market? When the government invests in corporations, it becomes a shareholder in those American corporations. The larger the shares the government holds, the more potential it has to control certain businesses. Not only that, but political parties could influence where the government invests, which would mean the federal government would be manipulating the stock market.

Shortly after the November 2002 mid-term national elections—when attacks against personal accounts were at their peak—a CNN/USA Today/Gallup poll found 57 percent of the people polled supported allowing people to put a portion of their Social Security payroll taxes into personal retirement accounts which would be invested in private stocks and bonds.[8]

A 2002 post-election poll, conducted for the United Seniors' Association, found by a margin of 59 to 35 percent, respondents prefer a system "with the option to invest part of your Social Security money" to a "system where the government holds all of your Social Security money."[9]

Millions of Americans are already successfully investing for their own retirement. In fact, approximately 50 percent of all American workers now currently manage their own retirement accounts through privately held 401(k) plans. The voluntary individually controlled retirement accounts are not fundamentally different from the defined contribution plans half of all Americans are currently enrolled in.

Since Americans can closely monitor their own individualized 401(k) portfolios and tailor them to their individual needs, they tend to have more of a vested interest. The great numbers of Americans who currently benefit from a 401(k) plan demonstrates Americans are smart enough to invest and manage their own money for their own retirement and don't consider these financial vehicles too "risky."

Federal government employees in the U.S. are allowed to invest in several types of stock or bond funds through the Thrift Savings Plan—a long-term, tax deferred, retirement savings plan. If these accounts aren't too risky for bureaucrats—whose salaries we pay—why should they pose a risk to average citizens? (Of course, average Americans don't get the life-long pension of about $15,000 per month for the rest of their lives that members of Congress do, but that's another matter.)

Individual retirement accounts would be voluntary, not mandatory. Individuals under Bush's plan would be given the choice to invest in their own retirement accounts, which they would control throughout their working lives. If individuals are really concerned about the long-term viability of the stock market and the associated risk, they could invest in less risky, lower yielding vehicles such as treasury bills and municipal bonds or insurance annuities.

The real risk is to do nothing and allow a failed system to get worse. It is irresponsible for our elected representatives to ignore the imminent failure of the current system. Successful reform will require individuals to invest a small portion of their own money in higher yielding stocks.

Liberal Democrats have tried to demagogue this issue by claiming Republicans want to invest old peoples' money in the "volatile" stock market. But Republicans have consistently advocated ensuring current benefits for current beneficiaries, while giving younger workers the ability to invest a small portion of their own money in a government-authorized, managed fund to earn a superior rate of return similar to the individual accounts government employees already have.

Seniors recognized this in the 2002 mid-term election and voted in candidates such as Elizabeth Dole (R-NC) and Jim Talent (R-Missouri) who publically advocated these reforms.

Profitable investing is a long-term process with very limited risk. According to Ibbotson Associates, a Chicago financial consultancy, an analysis of the Standard & Poors 500 over the past 76 years showed a 29 percent chance an investor would lose money if he invested for only one year. The risk dropped to ten percent over a five-year period, to three percent over a ten-year period and zero percent over fifteen years.

Long-term investors have always fared better with stocks than any other investment. According to the Ibbotson study, investors who held stocks for 20 years realized compound annual returns of about 11 percent compared to 5.3 percent for government bonds and 3.8 percent for Treasury bills. While there are always market risks, long-term investors saving and investing for their retirement are far less prone to wild swings in the market. Not investing in it for the long term, means a risk of losing significant wealth.[10]

The current pay-as-you go Social Security system poses far more "risk" for seniors than voluntary personal accounts would.

Because of the Supreme Court decision *Fleming* v. *Nestor*, Congress can raise taxes or cut benefits at any time by any amount for any reason.

The longer we wait to enact reform, the more expensive it will be for retiree's in the future. It's estimated every two-year delay increases the 75-year cost of Social Security by almost two trillion dollars (in 2005 dollars). Preserving the status quo is far more risky than reforming the system. In addition to earning higher long-term rates of return, the creation of individual personal accounts would also mean workers have a legal right to their accumulated assets.[11]

CLAIM #2: "If the stock market has a severe downturn, as was the case in 2000-2002, privatizing Social Security would destroy the retirement accounts of millions of seniors, turning the system into a game of winners and losers."

RESPONSE: The value of a retirement account is the sum total of about 45 years of saving and investing (assuming a 65-year-old retiree has been saving and investing since the age of 20).

This long-term view takes into consideration the inevitable and periodic market swings. Yet, the long-term return on stocks over the past 30 years has been approximately seven percent (counting inflation) versus government bonds which had a 3.5 percent return.

Jeremy Siegel, a finance professor from the Wharton School, concluded that, in the long run, stocks have been very safe investments which have not only experienced higher long-term returns, but also less long-term variations and instability in both price and return.[12]

Most financial advisors would say it's unwise to invest entirely in just one stock during your lifetime. (Note the case of Enron where investors lost everything.) Most 65-year-old workers only have about 35 percent of their retirement assets invested in stocks. During the 2001 market downturn, they would have fared very well. Although the S&P 500 dropped about 25 percent, the 13 percent increase in the Lehman Brothers U.S. Aggregate Bond Index would have resulted in gains.[13]

CLAIM #3: "Benefit cuts in proposed personal retirement account plans would force workers to delay retirement."

RESPONSE: The exact opposite is true.

According the President Bush's Commission to Reform Social Security (Plan number two), a 25-year-old woman would only have to work until age 65 to receive the benefits she would normally not receive under the current system until age 70.

Workers could still retire at age 62, as they can under current law, but with personal accounts they would be able to retire earlier with better benefits.[14]

CLAIM #4: "Privatization would mean old people would be forced to invest their retirement savings in the stock market and end up broke like the Enron employees did."

RESPONSE: Personal retirement accounts would be voluntary.

Individual workers have the ability to stay in the current program if they wish, or to open an individual account. All workers 55 years of age and older would remain in the current system and receive every penny they paid into it, including cost-of-living adjustments.

Individual voluntary personal retirement accounts would enable individual investors to enjoy the same retirement plans federal government employees currently have. The personal accounts the President's Commission has recommended have modeled their plans after the Federal Thrift Savings Plan. Workers would only be able to invest in government-approved, low-cost, diversified stock and bond mutual funds which federal workers already utilize, earning higher returns than the current Social Security system.[15]

Most Americans, including elderly voters, support personal accounts, according to many reputable and credible polls. A recent National Public Radio poll showed 55 percent of respondents said the Enron case strengthened the need for personal accounts.

A May 2001 McLaughlin &Associates poll found 63 percent of seniors would support personal accounts for younger workers if their own benefits would still be paid.[16]

CLAIM #5: "Privatization would help the 'rich' at the expense of the poor, minorities and women."

RESPONSE: Personal retirement accounts would help all workers, but would be especially advantageous for the poor, minorities and women.

Currently, low-wage workers who pay about one-eighth of their wages into Social Security can still retire below the poverty level. By contrast, personal savings account plans recommended by the President's Commission ensure that low-wage workers would retire above the poverty line and could lift up to one million seniors out of poverty.[17]

Individual voluntary retirement accounts would benefit black males the most. One third who enter the workforce don't live long enough to collect a dime of Social Security benefits given the current system. Personal account plans would enable black males to pass on $70,000 or more to their families if they die before they are legally eligible to collect Social Security benefits.

Additionally, former Clinton Administration official and Harvard professor Jeffery Liebman, who sits on President Bush's Commission to Strengthen Social Security, concluded that blacks "receive nearly $21,000 less on a lifetime basis from Social Security's retirement program than whites with similar income and marital status."

Since black males only live an average of 70.2 years versus 75.9 years for white males, and black females live an average 76.4 years compared to white females who live an average of 80.8 years, the current Social Security system transfers money from blacks to whites.

Unlike the current system, an individual in a system of personal retirement accounts owns his retirement savings. If the owner dies prior to reaching retirement, he can leave his money for his family members. Moreover, the greater benefits which are generated in a funded system would be particularly important to the black community. Currently, 30 percent of all blacks over the age of 65 live under the poverty level. The greater monthly payments would significantly enhance the lives of these individuals. How could the liberal lefties, who claim to make up the party which best represents blacks, continue to advocate maintaining a system, which is so harmful to them?[18]

Support for personal accounts exists among minorities. According to a February 2001 Zogby survey for the CATO Institute, 53.5 percent of blacks favor personal accounts. This number should rise as more Republicans become comfortable selling the benefits of the plan and are able to debunk the myths, which the left promulgates to demonize personal account reform.[19]

Personal retirement accounts also benefit poor women. Currently 12 percent of women retire into poverty compared with seven percent of men. The current system is biased in favor of men. Poverty rates for widows, divorcees and never-married women are about 25 percent. The President's Commission's plans would give new legal rights to divorced women (divorced women would receive 50 percent of all money that has been deposited into personal accounts called "earnings sharing") and increase benefits for two million to three million widows. Personal accounts will free many women from poverty in their later years.[20]

Cato Institute Social Security analyst Andrew G. Biggs wrote in June 2002, "Social Security's independent actuaries confirm that personal-account plans from the commission would pay higher benefits at lower costs than the current program, enhance the program's financing, strengthen the Social Security safety net and reduce poverty, while giving all workers the chance to build wealth and pass it on in voluntary personal accounts."[21]

Voluntary individual retirement accounts would increase the "progressivity" of the Social Security system. Commission plans provide progressive personal accounts which provide larger account balances to low-wage workers. In addition to the enhanced safety-net, progressivity would increase. In 2005, a low-wage retiree's monthly benefit is about 46 percent of a high-wage retiree's. That number would increase to 56 percent under one of the commission's plans.[22]

Personalizing the retirement system is the best possible way to stimulate real asset accumulation for low-income workers.

CLAIM #6: "Privatization would devastate middle-class working Americans."

RESPONSE: Personal retirement accounts benefit the middle class.

A union laborer who earns an average $33,200 a year can expect $1,559 per month from Social Security when he retires. But under President Bush's plan for individual accounts, this same average working American would enjoy a minimum of $411,052 when he retires—and that's at a conservative three percent rate of return. That translates into a monthly retirement payment of $2,671, significantly more than the current system.

Middle class Americans through personal accounts would be able to receive higher retirement benefits, would benefit from an improved economy and would have personal ownership of their retirement funds.[23]

CLAIM #7: "Social Security privatization with the wild market swings could adversely affect the economy."

RESPONSE: Personal retirement accounts would significantly increase GDP, employment and earnings.

Martin Feldstien of Harvard, a world renowned economist, estimates that personal accounts could have a value of $10 to $20 trillion to the U.S. economy. A boost like that would permanently increase our GDP by five percent, which would result in about one million new jobs and an increase of $5,000 annually for a family of four. Hundreds of billions of dollars would be invested in personal accounts each year which would also increase the national investment rate (with more private capital freed up) and increase productivity, wages and jobs.[24]

CLAIM #8: "What if a person doesn't invest properly and loses everything?"

RESPONSE: There would be restrictions

governing the use of personal retirement account funds for other purposes prior to age 65, and the government would provide insurance to the small percentage of individuals who for some reason lose everything.

Virtually all of the legislative proposals for individual personal accounts include a safety net to protect workers. If a worker has not accumulated adequate funds by retirement, then the government would "top off" the worker's account. This guaranteed benefit would ensure a minimum retirement income which is at or above the poverty level. This safety net could be financed out of the general tax revenues.[25]

CLAIM #9: "Personal accounts would mean large benefit cuts for retirees."

RESPONSE: Social Security's actuaries certify all existing voluntary personal account reform plans would pay higher benefits than the current system can pay.

Opponents of personal accounts incorrectly say personal accounts would lead to benefit cuts.

They compare benefits to those the current system promises to pay in the future. However, they fail to include the future reduction in benefits and tax increases in this calculation. Then they fail to include a significant part of the personal account plan benefit. They don't fairly measure the two plans against each other.

Let's compare a 25-year-old woman who earns $30,000 a year and will retire in 2042. Her "promised" benefit is $896 per month (in 2005 dollars) from the current Social Security program. The program will only be able to pay her $655 per month (the amount by law the government is required to pay with larger cuts in future years) because Social Security is projected to be insolvent in the year 2042.

The same woman under the President's Commission proposal would anticipate receiving $611 in traditional benefits from the government plus $375 from her personal account for a total of

$986 per month ($331 more per month than the current Social Security system will pay.) Hardly the benefit cut the critics claim.[26]

CLAIM #10: "Personal accounts will drain money out of the Social Security trust fund."

RESPONSE: There are no real assets in the "trust fund," despite Al Gore's rhetoric about protecting the "lock box" during the 2000 Election.

The trust fund contains IOU's which can only be repaid by raising taxes or cutting other government programs. Personal accounts in essence replace these IOUs with real assets, which pay benefits without raising taxes or cutting current government programs.[27]

According to the President's three plans, which incorporate optional voluntary personal retirement accounts, retirees would receive higher benefits compared to the current system and the Social Security deficit would be significantly reduced.

If full benefits were paid to employees under the current system, by 2076 the deficit in Social Security would be $3.23 trillion (2005 value taking into account annual compounding). Alternatively, under each of the President's Commission's plans, the deficit would be significantly reduced. The deficit under Plan one would be reduced to $2.75 trillion. Under Plan two, Social Security would have net assets of $1.67 trillion and under Plan three, $1.79 trillion.

Contrary to the reform opponents' claims that personal accounts "drain" money from the trust fund, it's clear that under all the non-partisan President's Commission's plans, the Social Security deficit is reduced and benefits increased.[28]

CLAIM #11: "Personal accounts would mean higher administrative costs, which would primarily go to Wall Street."

RESPONSE: Personal account plans currently under consideration have administrative costs of one-fifth of the costs of an average mutual fund.

Additionally, the administrative costs of personal plans are significantly cheaper than 401(k)s and IRAs. The average cost of a mutual fund is about 1.5 percent of managed assets. The independent Social Security actuaries have calculated that the administrative costs of personal accounts would be about 0.3 percent of assets managed. That means personal accounts would enable retiree's to keep more of their own retirement nest egg.[29]

Other countries which have individual retirement accounts have been able to reduce their administrative costs. In Chile, annual costs for workers' personal retirement accounts average $12.68. Australia's administrative costs for retirement accounts are 0.8 percent.

It is reasonable to assume that if these countries can achieve such low administrative costs, the USA, with the most advanced capital markets in the world, can do the same.

"It depends on how you design the system," says William Shipman of Carriage Oak Partners and co-chair of the Cato Institute's Social Security Project. Shipman designed a personal account system with State Street Global Advisors with asset management costs less than 0.3 percent. The State Street plan considered everything from investment management to the cost of mailing account statements.[30]

CLAIM #12: "Social Security is solvent and Republicans are only trying to scare the elderly by telling them Social Security will collapse."

RESPONSE: The system is broken.

Those were the exact words of former Senator Daniel Patrick Moynihan (D-NY), the chair of the bipartisan Commission to Strengthen Social Security. The liberal Democrat said, "The system is broken and unless we move boldly and quickly, the promise of Social Security to future retirees cannot be met without eventual resort to benefit cuts, tax increases or massive borrowing. The time to act is now."

"Individual accounts can be part of the answer," stated former House Minority Leader Dick Gephardt (D-MO), adding, "In my view, they should be a supplement, not a replacement to Social Security."

Former Senate Minority Leader, Senator Tom Daschle (D-SD) also admitted Social Security is in a precarious state and supported the idea of government investments in the markets.

Former President Clinton in his 1999 State of the Union said, "Today the state of Social Security is strong, but by 2013, payroll taxes will no longer be sufficient to cover monthly payments. And by 2032, the trust fund will be exhausted and Social Security will be unable to pay out the full benefits older Americans have been promised."

Clinton also urged bi-partisanship with regard to individual personal accounts stating: "Our ears and minds must remain open to any good idea and to any person of good will."[31]

The bottom line is:

The current Social Security system created under FDR in the 1930s is scheduled to be bankrupt by 2018. At that time, either payroll taxes will have to be raised, retirement age increased, or benefits reduced to make up for the deficit. Democrats have offered no plan of their own to strengthen Social Security.

Personal retirement account plans would enable workers to realize increased benefits, build individual wealth and own their assets which could be passed down to their heirs.

Chapter 20

T is for Taxes:

Cut Your Way to Financial Freedom

Claims:

1. "Tax cuts- such as the Reagan and Bush tax cuts- cause budget deficits."
2. "During Reagan's administration, the rich didn't pay their fair share of taxes."
3. "Reagan's tax cuts and military spending caused enormous deficits."
4. "The sluggish economy from 2002-2003 proves that the 'huge' Bush tax cut did nothing to boost growth. Bush has the worst economic record since Herbert Hoover."
5. "Tax cuts increase the money supply, which drives up interest rates and inflation, increasing the budget deficit."
6. "The Bush tax cuts squandered the tax surplus."
7. "Cutting taxes will endanger the long term viability and solvency of social security."
8. "To achieve fiscal discipline (balance the budget) it is sometimes necessary to increase taxes."
9. "Tax cuts, such as the Bush Tax Cuts, benefit the wealthy disproportionately on the backs of the poor."
10. "'Tax holidays' and other 'tax rebates' provide stimulus

to a sagging economy by putting money in consumers' pockets without risking long-term budget deficits."

11. "We need targeted tax cuts for middle class '"working families."'"
12. "We cannot 'afford' tax cuts."
13. "We should use the tax surplus to pay down the debt. Debt retirement reduces interest rates and thus encourages capital investment, producing good economic growth."
14. "Supply-Side economic theory ('trickle-down economics') is inflationary and the middle and lower classes never receive their fair share of benefits."
15. " JFK's tax cut in 1962 was responsible. Bush's tax cuts, in contrast are fiscally irresponsible."
16. "JFK's tax cut was for the middle class. Bush's tax cut only benefits the 'rich'."
17. "Cutting the dividend tax on stock unfairly benefits the rich."
18. "Responsible tax cuts are phased in over time so that budget deficits and entitlement programs are not adversely affected."
19. "Capital Gains Tax cuts reduce tax revenues for the government and are unfairly slanted toward the rich."
20. "The rich are getting richer, the poor are getting poorer."
21. "Because they have more money, rich people in this country should pay higher taxes."
22. "Higher marginal tax-rates for the rich are only fair. Progressive taxation levels the playing field."
23. "We need to maintain the estate/inheritance (death) tax as a way to 'level the playing field' so

that individuals in our society don't gain the unfair advantage of inherited wealth."

Liberals and conservatives continue to vigorously debate the form and function of taxation in our country.

Liberals argue taxes should be fair, and favor the poor and middle classes. They continue to advocate and promote progressive taxation which they claim levels the playing field and closes the gap between rich and poor. Many liberals also claim it is fiscally conservative and prudent to invest these tax dollars in areas such as health care and education.

Conservative Republicans, on the other hand, reject the theory of redistributive taxation. George W. Bush's tax cuts made the system more progressive, virtually absolving the bottom 50 percent of workers from paying any federal taxes, while simultaneously increasing the tax burden on the top ten percent.

Fiscal conservatives generally favor relatively low tax rates across the board. President Bush has proposed extensive tax simplification and some Republicans have proposed scrapping the income tax in favor of either a consumption-based tax or a flat tax.

Fiscal conservatives have demonstrated that reducing taxes provides incentive for people to work, save and invest—especially the most productive wealth creators who liberals smugly refer to as "the rich." Conservatives have demonstrated that high taxes penalize entrepreneurial risk taking and investment and that robust economic growth is generated from the top down, not the bottom up.

Conservatives have proven that lowering tax rates on the wealthiest, most productive members of society gives them the incentive to invest their money in new business ventures instead of diverting their money into tax-free shelters. When the tax burden is kept low, economic activity increases.

But liberals still mock trickle-down economics. Although they probably mean well by advocating redistributive progressive taxation to achieve economic justice, liberals' policies and ideas inhibit economic growth—and that hurts the poor the most.

The more any good or service is taxed, the less of it will be produced or supplied. When marginal tax rates are increased, the incentives to work are decreased. If workers know the more they work, the more their income will be taxed, it's only logical to assume they'll forgo working more.

Similarly, the more gains on investments are taxed, the less investment you'll have. The more savings are taxed, the less savings you'll have.

High tax economies have experienced stagnant economic activity, depressed wages, high unemployment and more volatile price fluctuations. No high-tax command style communist or socialist-style economy has ever been able to outperform the United States' robust, low, tax-free, market economy.

While liberals have for years claimed that lowering taxes produces deficits and higher interest rates, conservatives such as Ronald Reagan and George W. Bush, as well as Democrats such as John F. Kennedy, have shown that immediate and substantial tax cuts actually generate more tax dollars to the federal treasury—not less—while keeping interest rates and inflation low.

The liberal rhetoric and slogans sound alluring, but low taxes promote risk taking, investment, jobs, economic growth and an overall higher standard of living across the board.

The liberal left successfully preys on people's economic ignorance—demonizing tax cuts, free trade and the conservative Republicans who act as their primary advocates.

Conservatives differ among themselves on many issues, but one issue which unanimously unites nearly all is taxes. Most conservatives believe capital is most productive in the hands of the people who earned it.

Liberal Democrats, in contrast, believe the government, when acting as a partner with private business, is a far better arbiter of how capital should be allocated. That's why Democrats have favored heavy taxation to fund massive government programs.

<u>CLAIM #1</u>: "Tax cuts—such as the Reagan and Bush tax cuts—cause budget deficits."

<u>RESPONSE</u>: Tax cuts have increased tax revenues to the federal treasury.

In the 1920s, '60s, '80s, and 2003, taxes were cut across the board. All three cuts stimulated the economy substantially and immediately and resulted in tax dollar increases to the federal treasury.

Under the administrations of Presidents Warren Harding (1921-23) and Calvin Coolidge (1923-29), Treasury Secretary Andrew Mellon increased tax dollars to the federal treasury through what were really the first supply-side tax cuts in American history.

As part of the Revenue Acts of 1921, 1924 and 1926, taxes where cut across the board. Top marginal rates decreased from 73 percent to 58 percent in 1922, to 50 percent in 1923, to 46 percent in 1924, to 25 percent in 1925 and finally to 24 percent in 1929.

IRS data shows these across-the-board tax cuts resulted in greater tax payments, especially by those in the highest tax brackets. When taxes were reduced from 60 percent to 25 percent on top income earners, taxes paid increased from $300 billion to $700 billion a year. During this period, top income earners also increased their share of the overall tax burden from one-third of all taxes paid in the early 1920s to approximately two-thirds by the late '20s.

Of note, from 1922 to 1928, average income of those earning greater than $100,000 increased by 15 percent. Those earning between $10,000 and $100,000 increased by 84 percent! Clearly, tax cuts helped everyone, not just the rich.

During President John F. Kennedy's administration (1961-63), tax dollars to the federal treasury increased when income tax rates were cut across the board by 20 percent in 1962. JFK also proposed a ten percent reduction in corporate income taxes to spur economic growth and job creation. His brother, freshman Senator Ted Kennedy supported the legislation, though in 2003 he was one of the most vocal opponents of the Bush tax cuts, which, incidentally, have increased federal tax receipts and reduced the deficit.

From 1962 to '66, employment grew by more than one million jobs, while the economic growth rate increased from 4.3 percent to 6.6 percent. Additionally, tax receipts to the federal treasury grew from $48.7 billion in 1964 to $68.7 billion in 1968.

JFK acknowledged tax cuts did not cause deficits. When he proposed his tax cut legislation to the Congress in 1962, Republicans said the cuts were "fiscally irresponsible."

JFK's response was, "Our true choice is not between tax reduction on the one hand and the avoidance of large federal deficits on the other. It is between two kinds of deficits—a chronic deficit of inertia, as the unwanted result of inadequate revenues and a restricted economy—or a temporary deficit of transition, resulting from a tax cut designed to boost the economy, produce revenues and achieve a future budget surplus. The first type of deficit is a sign of waste and weakness—the second reflects an investment in the future."

In his 1962 speech to the Economic Club of New York, Kennedy declared, "It is a paradoxical truth that tax rates are too high today and tax revenues too low...An economy constrained by high tax rates will never produce enough revenue to balance the budget, just as it will never create enough jobs or enough profits."[1]

Tax cuts during the administration of President Ronald Reagan (1981-'89) also increased tax dollars to the federal treasury.

In 1981, Reagan cut marginal tax rates across the board. As a result, income taxes to the federal treasury doubled from approximately $500 million per year in 1983 to more than $1 billion per year in 1989.[2]

Tax revenues during the Reagan years increased 28 percent, but spending increased 36 percent. Liberal Democrats often imply Reagan's tax cuts were irresponsible because they caused the massive deficits of the 1980s. They fail to acknowledge the fact that tax revenues doubled as a result of the cuts. The primary reason for the budget deficits was inflation-adjusted federal spending which increased by a greater percentage than the increase in tax revenues to the federal treasury.

In order for Reagan to get the Democratic Congress to pass his tax cuts—which resulted in the most sustained economic expansion in history—and increase defense spending—which ultimately resulted in our winning the Cold War—he had to compromise and agree to new domestic social spending. It was this massive increase in non-defense spending which primarily fueled the budget deficit, not Reagan's tax cuts.[3]

Similarly, according to the US Treasury Department, the 2003 Bush Tax Cuts ignited an economic expansion that has resulted in year after year increases in federal revenues to the treasury from about $1.9 trillion in FY 2004, to $2.1 trillion in FY 2005, to $2.4 trillion in FY 2006, to $2.5 trillion in FY 2007, the exact opposite of what the liberal Democrats predicted would occur!

CLAIM #2: **"During Reagan's administration, the rich didn't pay their fair share of taxes."**

RESPONSE: **The rich paid more as a percent of what they earned and actually paid too much in taxes.**

According to Congressional Budget Office figures, the top one percent paid more than 25 percent of all federal income taxes in 1990, a 40 percent increase over what this income bracket paid in 1980 under Carter.

The bottom 60 percent paid 11 percent of federal taxes in 1990, 20 percent less than they paid in 1980. The poor actually paid less in federal taxes under Reagan than under Carter.[4]

CLAIM #3: **"Reagan's tax cuts and military spending caused enormous deficits."**

RESPONSE: **Although the federal deficit increased under Reagan, it wasn't due to tax cuts.**

The increase in the deficit of $230 billion from 1985 to 1986 was due to continued growth in entitlement spending. Inflation adjusted spending increased by 36 percent which resulted from deals whereby Democratic Congresses permitted increased defense spending if Reagan agreed to increase federal domestic spending. While tax cuts and deficits did occur together, there is no evidence which demonstrates the deficits were the result of the tax cuts. Correlation does not guarantee causation.[5]

Tax cuts have always resulted in improved long-term economic growth producing more tax revenue. The deficits of the 1980s were not the result of Reagan's tax cuts. The democratically controlled Congress continued to spend more than it collected in tax revenues! For every $1 of new tax revenues collected, the Democrat Congress spent $1.29. (Hence the term "tax and spend liberal.")

From 1987 to 1989 when economic growth reached its fastest pace, the deficit fell to $150 billion. The decline in the budget deficit resulted from stronger underlying economic growth emenating from a larger tax base which resulted in more tax revenues. During the last three years of Reagan's presidency, the deficit actually decreased from a high of $221 billion in 1986 to $150 billion in 1987.[6]

Reagan's tax bill cut marginal rates across the board. Top rates were cut from 70 percent to 28 percent, which resulted in a doubling of tax revenues from $519 billion in 1980 to $1 trillion in 1989.[7]

It was the liberal Democrats' wanton domestic spending, not the Reagan tax cuts, which were primarily responsible for the deficits of the 1980s.

CLAIM #4: "The sluggish economy from 2002 to 2003 proves the 'huge' Bush tax cut did nothing to boost growth. Bush has the worst economic record since Herbert Hoover."

RESPONSE: The recession began during Clinton's last term.

The economy began to weaken a year before the tax cuts were enacted. According to Commerce Department statistics, the economy began to weaken in mid-2000. Growth averaged less than one percent in the final six months of the year. The economic decline began in the last three months of 2001 while Bill Clinton was still in office—well before the approval of the Bush tax cut legislation.

The devastation to our economy had more to do with Clinton's inability to capture Osama bin Laden when he had the opportunity than Bush's early stage tax cut.

The rampant corporate corruption, culminating with the bursting of the high-tech bubble, also occurred during Clinton's eight years and had a significant negative impact on the economy.

Third quarter 2003 economic statistics demonstrate the Bush tax cuts worked. The result was 7.2 percent growth, the fastest growth since 1984; consumer spending increased by 6.6 percent—the fastest pace in 15 years; business spending increased 11.1 percent—the fastest rate since the first quarter of 2000; exports increased 9.3 percent; federal spending was up only 1.4 percent; unemployment was down, with varying estimates from 50,000 to 500,000 new jobs created. These bullish figures have continued through FY 2007 (4.5% unemployment, 7.5 million new jobs, rising hourly wages, and 23 consecutive quarters of economic growth).

CLAIM #5: "Tax cuts increase the money supply, which drives up interest rates and inflation, increasing the budget deficit."

RESPONSE: **Interest rates have decreased.**

They actually decreased from 6.03 percent in 2000 to 3.87 percent in 2002, even though the U.S. experienced a mid-size deficit (about $160 billion in 2002, which is just a fraction of our $13 trillion Gross Domestic Product [GDP]).

Larger deficits don't necessarily cause interest rates to fall. However, it is incorrect to assert that rising budget deficits cause interest rates to increase.

CLAIM #6: "The Bush tax cuts squandered the tax surplus."

RESPONSE: **The weak economy, which began under the Clinton Administration, is the main reason for the deficit.**

According to the Congressional Budget Office's accounting figures, lower tax revenues from the Bush tax cut accounted for only 8 percent of the change in the fiscal balance in 2002. The majority of the change could rightly be attributed to unrealistically "rosy" forecasting, spending increases for domestic programs, the bursting of the Clinton high tech "bubble" and the laggard economy.[8]

CLAIM #7: "Cutting taxes will endanger the long term viability and solvency of Social Security."

RESPONSE: **The long-term viability of Social Security is already "endangered."**

Democratic Congresses raided the so-called Social Security trust fund for 25 of the last 40 years to pay for mandatory entitlement spending and new discretionary spending. All government estimates conclude Social Security will be insolvent by 2015 and taxes will have to either increase or benefits will have to decrease to keep the system solvent.

The Bush Plan guarantees 100 percent Social Security benefits to current beneficiaries and is unaffected by any tax cuts. The president's bipartisan Commission to Strengthen Social Security has advanced three proposals (discussed in greater detail in the

Social Security chapter) which guarantee current beneficiaries receive 100 percent of their benefits while allowing younger workers to invest a small portion of their payroll taxes in voluntary personal retirement accounts.

Liberal Democratic opposition to Social Security reform endangers the system. All of the proposed bipartisan plans make the system solvent by increasing the benefits future retirees will receive without raising taxes or increasing the retirement age. (Both conditions would be required if the system were to remain in its current format.)

Democratic opposition to viable Republican Social Security reforms does more to threaten the long-term viability of Social Security than lowering marginal rates on federal income taxes.

Tax cuts to those on the political left always pose a threat to one government entitlement program or another. Rarely is there a situation where allowing individuals to keep more of their own money is a worthy endeavor. If reducing taxes doesn't threaten Social Security, it will be endangering either education, the environment or health care. Practicing this divisive brand of class warfare has been the primary manner in which liberals justify their opposition to tax cuts.

Liberals ignore the stimulative impact of tax cuts on economic growth. When the left has considered the subsequent effects of tax cuts, they have ignored the dynamic stimulative effects which tax cuts have on economic behavior. This tends to underestimate the actual tax revenue which will be collected to fund government spending programs.

The CBO uses a static-scoring model to calculate the cost of tax cuts. There is an effort underway by the Bush Administration and other Republicans in Congress to institute a dynamic scoring system, which considers the behavioral and stimulative effects tax cuts have on economic growth.

Dynamic models have forecast much larger economic growth and tax receipts, reducing the costs of proposed tax reductions. Those on the left have generally opposed a dynamic model because it diminishes their argument that tax cuts reduce money to the government and endangers programs such as Social Security and Medicare. Actually, when taxes are cut, there is more money for these programs, not less.

CLAIM #8: "To achieve fiscal discipline and balance the budget, it is sometimes necessary to increase taxes."

RESPONSE: Fiscal discipline is better achieved through spending restraint—coupled with tax cuts—than through tax increases.

In 2001, Russia cut personal income taxes to a flat rate of 13 percent from a top marginal rate of 30 percent. As a result, tax revenues rose by more than 50 percent in the first seven months of 2001, relative to the previous year.

This action stood in contrast to the International Monetary Fund's (IMF) earlier advice advising Russia to raise taxes to balance its budget.

Eric Enger of the Federal Reserve and Jonathan Skinner of Dartmouth College found that a five percent across-the-board reduction in marginal tax rates would raise the economy's growth rate by about 0.3 percent points. Raising the growth rate of the GDP from 3.1 percent per year to 3.4 percent per year would raise the GDP by six percent after 20 years, the equivalent of roughly $600 billion today.[9]

An example of why raising taxes can backfire is the luxury tax Congress imposed on cars, boats, jewelry, planes and furs beginning in 1991. It was a way for Democrats such as Senator Ted Kennedy and then-Majority Leader George Mitchell to impose a tax on the rich. They claimed the tax on the wealthy would force them to pay their fair share of the taxes.

The tax took in $97 million *less* than was expected in the first year as people decreased their purchases of these items.

Yacht retailers and boat builders were hardest hit. Yacht retailers reported a 77 percent drop in sales that year and boat builders laid off an estimated 25,000 workers.

Subsequently, the tax was phased out by a Republican-led congressional effort in 1993 and 1996.[10]

Tax cuts increase tax revenues to the federal treasury and result in surpluses. The left's assertion that tax increases somehow reduce deficits and increase surpluses is false.

Budget surpluses are the result of a strong underlying private economy, not vice versa. Harvard University professor Martin Feldstein conducted an analysis of Clinton's economic policies and found the 75 percent rise in revenues was the result of a strong economy, not the Clinton tax increases in 1993.[11]

CLAIM #9: "Tax cuts, such as the Bush Tax Cuts, benefit the wealthy disproportionately on the backs of the poor."

RESPONSE: Cutting taxes for the most productive citizens benefits the middle classes and the poor the most.

Taxes are a penalty imposed on productive behavior. High marginal tax rates serve to discourage work. When marginal rates (tax rates imposed on the next dollar earned) are high, workers have the incentive to forego work or spend more time on vacation. To stimulate long-term growth, it's particularly important to cut the top rates of the most productive citizens. When tax rates are exceedingly high at the top rates, the wealthy tend to divert money into shelters instead of job-creating investments.

The rest of society benefits when those with capital invest in new ventures creating wealth and opportunity for working families. The maxim that "nobody who's poor offers you a job" is true in our free market capitalist system.

More than two-thirds of the top 0.5 percent of all taxpayers report small business income. Because small businesses, unlike corporations, pay individual tax rates, they tend to be in the higher tax brackets. When liberal Democrats propose higher taxes on the rich who they say don't pay their fair share, they're primarily talking about small business owners.

Businesses with less than 100 employees represent about 98 percent of all businesses and create about 37 percent of all jobs. They are primarily responsible for generating the jobs which employ poor and middle class Americans. Proposing higher taxes on these "wealthy" small businesses would only eliminate jobs.

The wealthiest one percent of taxpayers—mostly small businesses—earned 21 percent of the income in 2000 and paid 37 percent of all individual income taxes. This figure doesn't include the 15.3 percent payroll tax of which businesses bear almost all of the cost. In contrast, the bottom 50 percent of all taxpayers earn 13 percent of all income and pay merely four percent of all individual income taxes.[12]

Whether an individual is rich or poor depends on the stage of his or her life. More than half of all taxpayers change tax brackets (up and down) within a ten-year period. The economy, over the long run, expands and wealth increases. People often move across income ranges. Most of those in the bottom are younger, unmarried workers who eventually enter the top income bracket.

Of the bottom 20 percent of wage earners in 1975, 97 percent had moved out of that lower income bracket within 16 years and of those, 39 percent had moved into the top 20 percent income earners.[13]

The Bush 2003 Tax Cuts have been among the most "progressive" in history in that the tax burden has shifted significantly to the wealthiest Americans. From 1979-2003 the total tax burden on the top quintile earning 52 percent of all income rose from 56 percent to 66 percent of all taxes. From 2003-2006 the top quintile's taxes paid rose to 85 percent from 66 percent. In 2003 the bottom quintile paid a net effective tax rate of −5.9 percent. These workers actually received a subsidy from Washington on April 15 because of the Earned Income Tax Credit and Child Tax Credit. The 2001 and 2003 Bush Tax Cuts have resulted in an increase of 10 million tax filers with zero or negative tax liabilities.

Under G.W. Bush total anti-poverty spending increased by 39%. Healthcare spending on the Children's Health Insurance Program (S-CHIP) increased by 39%. From 2001 to 2005 housing programs received a 26 percent increase. The Housing Certificate Fund/Rental Assistance (the largest low income housing program in the country) received a 39 percent budget increase since 2001. Food stamps spending increased 71 percent to $33 billion. School Breakfasts and Lunches have experienced a 24 percent increase since 2001. Funding for Women, Infants, and Children (WIC) is up 22 percent and total food assistance spending increased by 49 percent from 2001 through 2005. SSI spending since 2001 has increased by 36 percent to $41 billion. The Earned Income Tax Credit outlays increased from $26 billion to $35 billion since 2001. The Child Tax

Credit has increased from $1 billion in 2001 to a record $14.6 billion in 2005 significantly reducing the tax burden on low wage workers.[14]

The bottom line is that the highest income earners pay increasingly more in taxes while the poor pay increasingly less and receive more of the spending- the exact opposite of what the liberals claim.

<u>CLAIM #10</u>: "'Tax holidays' and other 'tax rebates' provide stimulus to a sagging economy by putting money in consumers' pockets without risking long-term budget deficits."

<u>RESPONSE</u>: Tax holidays and rebates have never stimulated long-term sustained economic growth.

Incentives depend upon permanent tax changes—or at least those perceived to be permanent. Any incentive involved in suspending a tax will be offset by disincentives which impose it again.

Consider the 1974 federal and state tax rebates which didn't raise consumer spending much. Nor did the Bush 2001, $300 rebates which most economists concur had little to no positive impact on the economy long-term.

Consumer spending increased, but investment spending decreased by a corresponding amount. No new wealth was created. Since individual investors were not required to work, save or invest in order to receive a tax rebate check in the mail, no new wealth was actually created. Wealth was merely transferred from government to individual citizens, many of whom paid little or no federal taxes to begin with.[15]

Across-the-board, permanent and immediate tax cuts which create incentives to work, save and invest have been the best way historically to generate long-term sustained economic growth. Economists refer to this as the "permanent income hypothesis." It says individuals increase their spending only in response to permanent increases in income. Temporary increases from rebates and tax holidays only marginally change spending patterns.

When marginal rates were reduced across the board in the 1920s, '60s and '80s, GDP increased by 59 percent from 1921 to 1929, 42 percent from 1961 to 1968 and 34 percent from 1982 to 1989.[16]

Tax credits and tax rebates for workers who don't pay taxes are welfare payments—something liberals and some so-called moderate Republicans have advocated. The role of the federal government is not to take private property from one group of individuals and redistribute it to another group. That's called communism. Democrats call it the "third way." Either way, it represents an anti-American and anti-capitalist position.

Everybody who pays taxes should get a tax cut. Conservative Republicans have consistently asserted that everybody who pays taxes would benefit from tax cuts. Select groups should not be singled out and treated preferentially at the expense of others.

The most productive members of our society should not be exempted from tax cuts. Cutting taxes on the highest income brackets has proven to generate the most sustained and powerful, long-term economic growth for all income levels.

CLAIM #11: "We need targeted tax cuts for middle-class, working families."

RESPONSE: Income redistribution is called communism.

When liberal Democrats call for tax cuts only for the middle-class (families with a combined income of less than about $70,000) and tax increases for the rich (those families with combined incomes above $70,000), they advocate taking more money from one group of citizens and, in essence, giving it in the form of tax cuts, rebates and credits to other groups of citizens.

Liberal Democratic advocates of this position echo the same economic philosophy as Karl Marx who asserted there was a moral imperative to redistribute wealth for the good of society. Liberals call it progressive taxation. In the final analysis, taking property from one group and redistributing it to another group is called communism.

According to liberal Democrats, firemen and teachers are rich and don't need a tax cut. The implication is that families who are rich—those families in the top five percent who earn more than $80,000 combined gross income—are not "working."

According to liberals, a man who makes $40,000 as a fireman

and his wife who earns $40,000 as a teacher are not a working family and don't need a tax cut. This type of rhetoric is misleading, insulting and demagogic.

Targeted tax cuts are unfair and discriminatory. They ultimately penalize the most productive citizens by making them pay a higher percentage of taxes while only government-selected groups get to keep more of their own income. Our elected officials don't have the constitutional authority to capriciously dictate which group of Americans can keep more of their property (income) than others. This progressive form of taxation is immoral. Targeted tax cuts for working Americans only exacerbate the inequality.

CLAIM #12: "We cannot afford tax cuts."

RESPONSE: The peoples' money belongs to the people, not government bureaucrats!

When the government over-taxes its citizens, the money should be returned to the people who paid the taxes initially. Period. Taxes, which bureaucrats in Washington D.C. collect, are the product of the labor of individuals who work to make a better life for themselves and their families. Any surplus beyond taxes appropriated for constitutionally mandated functions of the federal government needs to be returned to the citizens who generated the money.

To fund a liberal welfare state, we can't afford not to have tax cuts. Aside from their elitist stand on not being able to afford tax cuts, liberals also betray their ignorance of basic economics. They claim returning money to citizens threatens other more pressing societal needs which only those in Washington can understand. However, here again the left fails to acknowledge that every time across-the-board marginal tax cuts have been enacted, tax revenues have increased.

Instead, liberals should be saying, "We can't afford to not cut taxes."

CLAIM #13: "We should use the tax surplus to pay down the debt. Debt retirement reduces interest rates and encourages capital investment, producing good economic growth."

RESPONSE: Our national debt serves a purpose—it stabilizes our economy.

Our national debt level is normal. The debt, in fact, serves a positive role for economic growth. It's about 35 percent of our Gross Domestic Product, half the average of other industrialized countries. This percentage is also well below 50 percent—the point at which most economists believe the size becomes worrisome.[17]

Our national debt or treasury securities represent claims against the US government and are considered stable and risk-free assets. These securities serve as benchmarks against which other assets can be priced and are used to diversify bank accounts, pension funds and individual retirement accounts. They serve to make international financial markets more stable and efficient.[18]

Liberals argue that paying down the debt is analogous to Americans paying off their individual mortgages. This comparison is flawed. The American family can't print money or tax citizens like the federal government can.

Capital is more productive in the private sector. The national debt also frees money to be directed by the market into productive endeavors. If surplus tax dollars are returned to taxpayers instead of paying off the national debt, the economy could be several trillion dollars richer when the boomers start to retire.

Paying down the national debt completely would be dangerous to free market capitalism. The government would invest any tax surpluses in private accounts. Potentially, the government would invest enormous sums of money in private companies.

Liberals are not really interested in fiscal responsibility or paying down the national debt. Tax-and-spend liberals use this bogus assertion to hide their real purpose: which is to ensure that government continues to control tax dollars to spend on the welfare state.

At their core, liberals believe they know better than the average American how to spend and invest their money. They know if surplus revenues are returned to taxpayers via tax cuts, the money will never make it to Washington in the future. Reducing the amount of money coming into the federal treasury, they believe, would inhibit their ability to earmark this money for spending on social welfare programs.

Advocating the use of tax surplus dollars to pay down the debt makes liberals seem fiscally responsible, but they only advocate this position as a last resort to ensure taxes don't get reduced.

As evidence, Bill Clinton often bragged about the overflowing surplus of tax dollars in Washington during his administration and, yet, instead of returning the money to the taxpayers or even paying down the debt, spending increased substantially every year Clinton was in office (for everything except defense).

Fiscal conservatives, in contrast, understand that fiscal responsibility is vital to maintaining limited government, but understand surplus money should be returned primarily to the individuals who earned the money.

The connection between deficit reduction and economic growth is bogus. The economy enjoyed higher growth rates under Reagan (averaging 4.5 percent) when deficits were higher than it did under Clinton who, in an effort to obtain smaller budget deficits, slashed defense and intelligence spending to dangerously low levels.

The liberals have it backwards. Higher growth has led to deficit reduction, not the other way around. There is no evidence to support the claim that deficit reduction causes lower interest rates and economic growth. Economic studies disprove the low debt/high economic growth myth. John Barry, chief economist from the Tax Foundation, examined ten-year treasury rates and publicly held federal debt as a percentage of GDP from 1953 through 2001.

Barry found there appears to be a negative correlation between ten-year interest rates and publicly held federal debt. (When rates increase, debt decreases.)

He also found there is no correlation between publicly held debt and long-term interest rates for the past five years. From 1998 to 2000, a period of substantial budget surpluses and public debt reduction, long-term interest rates rose from 5.3 percent to 6 percent.[19]

CLAIM #14: "Supply-side economic theory ('trickle-down economics') is inflationary, and the middle and lower classes never receive their fair share of benefits."

RESPONSE: Workers are the first to benefit from supply-side tax cuts.

Free market supply-side economics is not about distributing anything to anyone. It is about people earning whatever they can from voluntary transactions with others.

When an individual, or group of investors, starts a business, the first money spent goes to workers. After expenses are paid, if the owners are fortunate enough, they realize a profit (taking into account the excessively high failure rate for new businesses in their first year of operation). The trickle-down theory liberals denounce is actually reversed. It tends to benefit the workers before any profit is realized from the owners.

Supply-side economic theory is not about the distribution and receipt of economic benefits to specific groups. The concept of the trickle-down economic theory is grounded in keeping marginal tax rates relatively low for taxpayers so wealthy citizens will not be penalized for investing their capital in new business ventures. The trickle-down theory is about freeing economic capital so it can be used for investing in new business ventures. This creates economic benefits for workers new businesses employ and for other businesses with whom these new businesses conduct transactions.

All four major supply-side tax cuts of the 1920s, '60s, '80s, and 2003 produced sustained long-term economic growth and income increases at all levels of the socioeconomic spectrum. Trickle-down economics has produced and sustained economic growth every time it has been enacted.

The Kemp-Roth across-the-board tax-cuts President Reagan signed into law in the early 1980s as an antidote to the stagflation of the Carter years, resulted in more than 20 million new jobs and the longest and most sustained economic expansion in our history. The result was also a massive decrease in inflation from 12.5 percent under Carter in 1980 to four percent throughout the '80s.[20]

CLAIM #15: "JFK's tax cut in 1962 was responsible. Bush's tax cuts, in contrast, are fiscally irresponsible."

RESPONSE: JFK's tax cuts in 1962 were much larger than Bush's.

As a share of national income and the budget, President Bush's 2003 tax cut was about one-third of JFK's.[21]

In 1963, the national debt was higher than in 2003. The debt in 1963 was 42 percent of the GDP versus 36 percent of the GDP in 2003.[22]

CLAIM #16: "JFK's tax cut was for the middle class. Bush's tax cut only benefits the rich."

RESPONSE: JFK's tax cut reduced the top rate from 91 percent to 70 percent.

Bush cut the top rate from 39 percent to 35 percent. JFK's tax cut gave a larger break to the rich than either Bush's or Reagan's tax cuts.[23]

CLAIM #17: "Cutting the dividend tax on stock unfairly benefits the rich."

RESPONSE: JFK proposed reducing the dividend tax from 91 percent to 70 percent for the richest Americans.

In JFK's own words: "The tax cut on capital gains directly affects investment decisions, the mobility and flow of risk capital…the ease or difficulty experienced in new ventures in obtaining capital and thereby the strength and potential for growth in the economy."[24]

CLAIM #18: "Responsible tax cuts are phased in over time so that budget deficits and entitlement programs are not adversely affected."

RESPONSE: The most effective tax cuts are broad, deep, immediate and permanent.

In order to gain support of congressional Democrats in 2001, Bush had to gradually phase in his relatively small tax cut over ten years. As a result, the $300 rebate check alongside one to two percent reductions in the marginal tax rates for the first two years of the tax cut had a relatively small positive impact on economic growth.

JFK's tax cut was enacted immediately across-the-board which resulted in significant and sustained economic growth.

Economic behavior is dictated by future economic expectations. When tax cuts are phased in, individuals tend to delay new business ventures.

Small, phased in tax cuts have a negligible effect on increasing the very same tax revenues which fund entitlement programs. To ensure adequate tax dollars are collected by the government to fund entitlement programs such as Medicare, welfare and Social Security, it is vital meaningful tax reduction takes place to increase economic activity.

Vibrant economic expansion and output increase tax revenues, not tax increases which tend to stifle economic opportunity and growth.

CLAIM #19: "Capital gains tax cuts reduce tax revenues for the government and are unfairly slanted toward the rich."

RESPONSE: Tax revenues to the federal government increase when rates are cut!

For example, in 1997, the capital gains tax rate was reduced from 28 percent to 20 percent. Critics claimed this would "cost" the government $100 billion over five years. Instead, capital gains receipts doubled.[25]

President John F. Kennedy was right! He said cutting the capital gains tax (as he did in 1963) doesn't reduce tax revenues, but rather creates businesses and jobs. The bull market of the-mid 1960s demonstrated he was correct.[26]

Moreover, capital gains taxation is an unfair double tax on money which has already been taxed. Capital gains on investments was never intended to be considered income since the 16th amendment became federal law.

When money is first earned by an individual, it's taxed at the individual marginal tax rate by the federal (and sometimes state) government. Taxing it again penalizes individuals who choose to risk their own capital on investments, while those who choose to spend their money are exempted from this double taxation. Additionally, if a person invests his money after it has already been taxed and loses money, he can only deduct a very small portion of the losses (about $3,000 per year) from his taxes.

Capital gains tax cuts benefit most working Americans who aren't rich. The vast majority of Americans either own stock or a home. Therefore, a capital gains cut won't just benefit the rich, but will benefit a broad and diverse group of working Americans whose retirement savings are at risk.

According to the New York Stock Exchange 2003 data, the median stockholder in the U.S. is 44 years old with an annual household income of $57,000 and a $28,000 average stock portfolio. This is hardly your typical rich family.[24]

CLAIM #20: "The rich are getting richer, the poor are getting poorer."

RESPONSE: The rich are shouldering a disproportionately high percentage of the taxes.

That's according to the May 2001 Congressional Budget Office. The report also states that raising taxes on the rich would not reduce inequalities in income distribution.

For the past 20 years, effective federal tax rates (taxes as a percentage of income) have fallen from 8.3 percent in 1981 to 5.3 percent in 2001. Those in the middle 40 percent of income earners have seen their tax burdens drop from 21.9 percent to 20 percent. The bottom 20 percent have experienced decreases while the wealthiest 20 percent have seen their tax rate increase from 27.1 percent to 27.4 percent. Those in the top five percent saw their effective tax rates rise from 28.5 percent in 1985 to 39.4 percent in 2001.[28]

The rich (those in the top five percent of workers) pay 56.5 percent of all federal income taxes. The top-half of all workers pay 96.1 percent of all federal income taxes. In other words, the top 50 percent of workers in our country fund our government and all of its entitlement programs from which the bottom half directly benefits. The top half are actually tax slaves who are exploited by the bottom half.[29]

Workers benefited the most in the high-tech boom of the 1990s. An article in *Business Week* in 2003 reported, "The biggest winners from the faster productivity growth of the 1990s were workers, not investors."[30]

Because of the tight labor markets and welfare reform, workers saw their wages increase an average of 12 percent, making them major beneficiaries of the 1990s boom. The poorest citizens in our country enjoy a better standard of living than the vast majority of people in the world.

In 1994, in households defined as at or below the poverty line by the U.S Bureau of the Census, 71.8 percent had one or more cars (up from 64.5 percent in 1984); 59.7 percent had a VCR (up from 3.4 percent in 1984); 71.7 percent had a washing machine (up from 58.2 percent in 1984); and 60 percent had a microwave (up from 12.5 percent in 1984). The list goes on, all reflecting a similar trend.

In terms of material goods and life's conveniences, "many of today's poorest households have ... more even than the general population had two decades ago," according to an article in the *Dallas Business Review*.[31]

There is tremendous economic mobility that liberals often ignore when they speak of rich and poor. The 2001 CBO reported that in one year 12.5 percent of people will move up at least one quintile and 12.5 percent will move down. Since individuals, depending on the stage of their careers, are in flux, it is meaningless for those on the left to speak of the rich as some monolithic entity which has an eternal stronghold on all the wealth in our country.

W. Michael Cox, the chief economist for the Federal Reserve Bank in Dallas and Richard Alm, a business writer for the *Dallas Morning News* conclude in their book *Myths of Rich and Poor: Why We're Better Off Than We Think* that only five percent of the 1975 poor were still poor in 1990—and 29 percent of them were rich.[32]

CLAIM #21: "Rich people in America should pay higher taxes because they have more money."

RESPONSE: Taxing the most productive citizens is anti-American.

The rich have more wealth because they created that wealth, not because they unfairly took more. As history has demonstrated, when the rich have more wealth in our free market capitalist system, the overall amount of wealth to society increases.[33]

Higher marginal tax rates reduce the reward for the most productive members of our society, while reducing the incentive for poor Americans to strive to become wealthy.

The notion of taxing the rich is rooted in Marxist class envy ideology and is contrary to the tenets of free market capitalism—along with the rule of law—the foundation to a free and prosperous representative democracy. People come to the U.S. to achieve the American Dream of unfettered economic opportunity and prosperity, not cradle to grave taxation and government handouts.

Our Constitution guarantees equal opportunity, not equal outcomes. Taxing those who make the most in an effort to level the playing field is not the duty of government. Government is merely supposed to ensure the playing field is level for all those who compete in the free market by discouraging anti-competitive behavior and fraud. There is no legitimate constitutional basis for their acting as arbiters of "fairness." Governments which engage in this behavior are either communist or socialist systems.

As Walter E. Williams, professor of economics at George Mason University, states, "In a free society, income is neither taken nor distributed. It is earned. Income is earned by pleasing one's fellow man. The greater one's ability to please his fellow man, the greater is his claim on what his fellow man produces. This claim is represented by the size of his income."[34]

CLAIM #22: "Higher marginal tax rates for the rich are only fair. Progressive taxation levels the playing field."

RESPONSE: Progressivity is regressive in nature.

Progressive taxation (marginal tax rates which increase as individuals earn more income) penalizes the most productive in our society. The maxim, "The more an individual makes, the more the government takes," strips incentive from poorer individuals who strive to become rich.

High progressive rates reduce investment and job creation. When tax rates are disproportionately high on the most productive members of society, the incentive to risk investment capital for new job creation is significantly reduced.

The ultimate reward to entrepreneurial investors is their net return on investment. Usually investors are the last ones to recognize their reward, while workers and creditors are usually the first to be paid when a new business is established. The higher the tax on income from an investment, the less the reward for the investor. Thus, the more progressive the system (i.e. the higher the marginal tax rates on the top income levels), the less the potential reward. As the tax increases, the willingness of the investor to take the risk decreases. He or she is more inclined to keep capital in less risky tax shelters.

Reagan's tax cuts disproved the progressive myth. This is why Reagan's slashing of the top rates from 70 percent under Carter to 28 percent had such an enormously positive impact on the economy.

The decreased top rates provided strong incentive for the wealthiest Americans to withdraw their capital from tax shelters and to invest them in new businesses. When taxes are kept disproportionately high on the most productive citizens, those who would benefit the most from investments and job creation end up being hurt the most.

Progressive taxation reduces the reward for achieving the American Dream. People from all around the world come to our country for a shot at the American Dream. Many escape communist and socialist tyrannies to provide a better life for their families. Their reward for risking their lives to come to the U.S. should be a shot at becoming successful and rich. The perception that there is no limit to what can be achieved in the United States is what has enabled our country to achieve the highest standard of living and most individual freedom and liberty of any country the world has ever known. When the incentive and reward for high achievement is diminished, the American Dream becomes more difficult to attain.

High progressive tax rates stifle economic opportunities for the poor. If taxes are as high as they now are on the most productive (the top five percent pay almost two-thirds of all taxes in our country), why should somebody in the poor or middle class aspire one day to become a tax-slave? One of the most negative aspects of progressivity is that it reduces the incentive for the poor and middle class to become rich.

Fairness is a highly subjective and arbitrary standard on which to base tax policy. Who is the arbiter of how much money one group of workers should have to pay to the government? What might seem fair to one individual may not seem fair and reasonable to another. The fairest tax policy is the one where every taxpayer pays the same percentage of taxes. This way government can't arbitrarily pick winners and losers.

CLAIM #23: "We need to maintain the estate/inheritance (death) tax as a way to 'level the playing field' so individuals in our society don't gain the unfair advantage of inherited wealth."

RESPONSE: Two-thirds of Americans believe the death tax should be abolished.

Opposition to the death tax is pervasive and cuts across political party and economic lines. Inheritance taxes can be as high as 50 percent—and that's unfair.[35]

According to Dr. James P. Smith, a senior economist at the Rand Corporation, only eight percent of wealth is inherited in our country—92 percent is earned. That means nine out of ten Americans don't inherit a dime![36]

Most of the super wealthy already know how to avoid inheritance tax through careful estate planning prior to their deaths. They don't pay a dime of inheritance tax. The working middle class are the ones who get hit with it.

Not everyone is as savvy as the rich about estate planning prior to their death. So who gets penalized with the inheritance tax? Usually the children of Americans who built their fortunes through hard work and prudent savings—the people who had family farms or small businesses, or those really good at pinching a dime and saving their money, the people who didn't take advantage of estate planning.

So what happens when they die and their heirs are hit with a 50 percent tax bill? Their children have to sell the small businesses and farms their parents and maybe grandparents worked so hard to run their entire lives.

Family farms which have been maintained for generations must liquidate the assets of the business because, upon death of the owner, they can't afford the tax due the government. The reduction in human capital (of the families who have run the businesses and know them best) resulting from these forced sales is another negative consequence of the tax.

The people stuck having to pay this tax are the ones who are least able to afford it because usually the businesses are just barely clearing a profit. Take away half the equity and the businesses are doomed to be sold to pay the tax.[37]

Stephen J. Entin, president of the Institute for Research on the Economics of Taxation, wrote in the *Wall Street Journal* that if income is "saved, the returns are taxed as interest, dividends and capital gains, and, if put into corporate shares, there is the corporate income tax too. Even if the saving was in a tax-deferred retirement account, it will be subject to the heirs' income tax in the years following inheritance. Consequently, every penny in an estate has either been subject to income taxes, often more than once, or is about to be subject to income taxes. The death tax is always an extra layer of punishment."[38]

The death tax violates the Fifth Amendment, which states an individual in the United States has a God-given right to private property. Read it for yourself: "…Nor shall private property be taken for public use without just compensation."

Liberals can't, according to the law, take from one group arbitrarily and give to another group. Whether they justify such confiscatory actions as fair is irrelevant. To quote the economist and noted author, Frederic Bastiat from his famous book *The Law*, "The law can be an instrument of equalization only as it takes from some persons and gives to other persons. When the law does this, it is an instrument of plunder."[39]

The estate tax is rooted in communist ideology. Karl Marx was a leading original proponent of the confiscation of land or estate tax in *The Communist Manifesto*. Edward Bellamy, an influential Socialist, in his book *Looking Backward* describes a utopian society without "private property to speak of, no disputes between citizens, over business relations, no real estate to divide and no debts to collect." Bellamy also advocated a society where there is no inherited money or land.

Liberal Democratic claims that repeal of the death tax would decrease tax revenues is false. In a report issued by the Joint Committee on Taxation in 2002, liberals opposed to repealing the death tax asserted that doing so would result in a reduction in government revenues by more than 150 percent of what the tax now collects.

This assertion is wrong because the committee fails to use a dynamic scoring model which correctly estimates the economic and budget gains of repeal. In the past, this same commission also suggested raising the tax by 50 percent would increase revenues collected from $26 billion in 1985 to $65 billion in 1991. However, $25 billion was raised in 1991.[40]

The death tax hurts the economy by giving wealthy people incentive to avoid the punitive double tax by sheltering the money. Putting their money in tax-free shelters reduces capital available to finance business investment, which reduces job creation and the overall standard of living. The people who get hurt are poor and middle class individuals who would benefit from the jobs and opportunities normally created by capital and human investment. (Note: accountants and tax attorneys continue to prosper.)

The tax is a punitive tax on income already taxed. The tax was collected first on the income when it was originally earned. Why should any individual who invests his money—which has already been taxed when it was earned—be taxed again when he dies?

The death tax is unconstitutional. Unlike the federal income tax, which taxes income directly, the death tax is a direct tax (up to 50 percent) on the value of the private property which is inherited. Our Constitution guarantees the U.S. government cannot lay claim to private property without either "due process" or "just compensation." By imposing a tax on private property the government is in essence stealing private property.

The death tax unfairly penalizes those who invest and save while giving unfair advantage to those who consume. Since the tax rates are so excessive on inherited wealth, individuals who desire to pass on a family business or home to other family members are discouraged from doing so. Instead they are given incentive to spend as much as they can before they die. The tax encourages excessive consumption at the expense of family members who would otherwise benefit from the inheritance.

The death tax violates government's primary role: to protect individual property rights. While governments do have an obligation to create a fair business environment and ensure individuals have equal opportunity, they have no right to be the arbiters of results. By claiming that inheritance taxes level the playing field, they assume it's legally and morally permissible to take property from one group and distribute it to another. Our government is charged with the duty of protecting individual property rights, not violating them.

Chapter 21

U is for the United States:

What Makes Us Great

Claims:

1. "The Pilgrims confiscated America from Native Americans and Mexicans. America is an imperialist nation."
2. "We live in a pluralistic society now with many different religions and are no longer a Christian nation."
3. "America is a racist, homophobic, and sexist nation."
4. "Western civilization and American culture in particular is not superior to any other civilization. All cultures are basically equal."
5. "American export of our capitalist system threatens the cultural identity of foreign cultures and results in ill will toward our country."
6. "America is the most violent nation on earth."

To those on the liberal left, America is often viewed as the root of all of the evil in the world. Following the 9/11 terrorist attacks, some on the left in academia, entertainment and the elite media asked what the U.S. had done to provoke the attacks and wanted to determine the root causes of the enmity toward America. These same blame-America-first people—as Jeanne Kirkpartick called them in 1984—assert America's founding was fraudulent, that aristocratic white males confiscated America from Native American Indians and Mexicans, that the U.S. was founded on slavery, that the words "under God" don't belong in the Pledge of Allegiance and that many of our founding documents are outdated and require revision which will reflect the multi-cultural nation into which we have evolved.

In sharp contrast to those on the left who claim the United States poses the greatest threat to its people and the rest of the world, conservatives believe America is a strong but fragile liberal democracy, whose longstanding traditions and documents must be revered and preserved. America, they argue, is the most enduring constitutional democracy in the history of the world, with the highest standard of living and most diverse citizenry who live together in general peace and prosperity.

Even though, those on the left accuse America of being racist and homophobic, it's clear by any measure, American minorities, women, handicapped and homosexuals enjoy more individual liberties and legal protections than in any other country in the history of the world. After all, it was America who ended the 3,000-year-old practice of slavery which is still being practiced today in many other parts of the world.

Although liberals claim America is an imperialist nation, history has demonstrated the exact opposite—the U.S. has liberated countless nations from imperialist threats and tyrannical dictators.

Conservatives argue the United States should only involve itself militarily in the affairs of other nations if there is a clear and present danger to America or our national security interests. Historically it becomes clear the U.S. has been a great liberator—not the imperialist occupiers liberals assert.

Those on the left say America is a multi-cultural nation and we must respect one another's differences. Conservatives appreciate and recognize the enormous cultural diversity of America, but unlike the multiculturalists on the left, conservatives understand that a nation without a common language and culture creates divisions among its citizens—those who are proficient in English who enjoy a relatively high standard of living and those only proficient in their own native language who are destined to a life of low skilled, low wage jobs and a permanently low standard of living.

America opens her arms to those from other countries, but requires that in order to promote the general welfare of all her citizens, they become proficient in English and knowledgeable about our shared history. Conservatives point out that a healthy respect for our cultural differences is vital to our rich heritage, but it's more crucial to focus on the things which unite us as Americans.

Without those common threads such as our shared language, borders, history, traditions and culture uniting us, conservatives argue we will become a sharply divided nation.

Defining America and what it represents could be the most important issue of our times. While those on the left claim our nation's founding was fraudulent, and our traditions and constitutional laws are outmoded, those on the right continue to defend America.

CLAIM #1: "The Pilgrims confiscated America from Native Americans and Mexicans. America is an imperialist nation."

RESPONSE: Colonialism/imperialism has not been unique to America and the West, and has been standard practice throughout world history.

The British ruled India for more than two centuries. Prior to that, India was invaded by the Persians, Afghans, Alexander the Great, the Arabs, the Mongols and the Turks. The Persian, Macedonian, Islamic, Mongol, Chinese, Inca and Aztec empires existed long before the British colonization of America.

Will wealthy liberals such as Teddy Kennedy, John Kerry and Warren Buffet give back all their property and possessions to the Native Americans? If those on the left who make this claim really believe America belongs to Native Americans and Mexicans, then they should put there money where their mouth is and relinquish all their property and possessions to them. If John Kerry's ancestors—some of whom came to this country on the Mayflower—stole land from the Indians, shouldn't Kerry give it back, starting with his $10 million mansion on Beacon Hill in Boston?

New scientific evidence has revealed the first people in North America were not Indians from Asia who walked across the Bering Strait Land Bridge, but were Caucasoids from Europe. These Caucasoids came over on boats along the North Atlantic ice sheets and into the eastern seaboard of what today is called the United States. Because these new archeological finds are not politically correct and because they disprove the notion the Indians were the first to occupy the United States, the political and academic left continue to conceal and ignore these facts.[1]

Western civilization and America became dominant because they invented three institutions: science, democracy and capitalism. In his book *What's So Great About America*, Dinesh D'Souza argues that the interaction between these three specific institutions alone primarily led to the success of Western civilization, that colonialism and imperialism were not the cause of the West's success, but the result of that success. D'Souza makes the convincing case America didn't grow rich from stolen goods, but by creating its own wealth.

Regarding science, D'Souza argues the invention of invention is distinctly a Western concept, a progress which is uniquely Western and born from Christianity. Science, which led to the West's—and particularly America's—technological explosion, has done more to enhance the overall standard of living and quality of life for those around the world than any other country in history.

Regarding democracy, D'Souza points out it's based on the human aspiration "to be heard and to participate in decision-making." The ideals of representative governments, separation of powers, and checks and balances are uniquely Western ideas—ideas which have done more to advance individual liberty and freedom than any other political institution in history.

Regarding capitalism, D'Souza argues that's founded on the universal human impulse to barter and trade. He points out that money is not uniquely Western, but property rights, contracts, courts to enforce them and free trade are Western in origin and have created the highest standard of living the world has ever known.[2]

CLAIM #2: "We live in a pluralistic society now with many different religions and are no longer a Christian nation."

RESPONSE: While America does have a plurality

of religions and cultures, we are primarily a Christian nation.

Although the United States is a beacon of religious tolerance and does not have any state-sponsored religion, we do have a predominant view: Judeo-Christianity. We respect those who may not be Christians and don't impose traditional Judeo-Christian beliefs and values on any of our citizens. However, the foundation of our society (our republican government, rule of law and free market capitalism) is indeed firmly rooted in traditional Judeo-Christian morality and values, which come from the Bible.

Most polls show that around 80 percent of Americans consider themselves Christians. Although, citizens are free to practice their own religion or not to practice at all, our country has always been and continues to be mainly comprised of Christians. Many would argue it's principally due to the high percentage of Christians in our country that so many others of different faiths from around the world can practice their faith as freely as they do in America. In most Arab countries those who don't convert to Islam are routinely tortured and killed.

CLAIM #3: "America is a racist, homophobic and sexist nation."

RESPONSE: **Minorities, homosexuals and women live more freely and enjoy a higher standard of living in the United States than in any other country in the world.**

The fact that so many diverse groups of people can live together in relative peace and harmony in the United States further disproves this assertion. In fact, no other nation can make this claim. America is the most tolerant and diverse nation on earth.

Minorities in other countries are routinely persecuted (Muslims in Serbia, the Kurds in Iraq and Christians in many African countries) and their human rights routinely violated.

Homosexuals in Muslim countries are beheaded and women in most Muslim countries are treated as second-class citizens with very few, if any, individual rights or freedoms. If they are raped they, according to Muslim law, must have four male witnesses—that virtually assures the rapist will not be convicted.

Women earn more in the United States than in any other country on earth.

Aside from random and isolated "hate crimes," homosexuals live freely in our country and in some states now have the legal right to marry. Orlando Patterson, a black Harvard sociologist, wrote that American blacks have more freedom and civil liberties than blacks anywhere else in the world, including black Africa.³

CLAIM #4: "Western civilization and American culture in particular are not superior to, or better than, any other civilization. All cultures are basically equal."

RESPONSE: In terms of overall individual liberty, freedom and economic opportunity, the United States is by far superior to any other country in the world.

The West has the highest standard of living in the world, enjoys the highest per capita income and owns 85 percent of all real estate in the world.⁴

Western industrialized nations—especially the United States—are more generous than any in the world, accounting for the majority of financial aid, food and medicine donated to the Third World.

The West adopted Eastern inventions such as the printing press, gunpowder and the compass from the Chinese, and the numerical system from the Hindus (erroneously called Arabic numerals), utilizing these to produce the most significant advancements in technology and science the world has ever seen.

In the past 500 years, great Western inventors have revolutionized and improved the way people around the world live—inventors such as: French physicist and mathematician Andre Ampere, who developed the science of electromagnetism; Scottish-American Alexander Graham Bell, who invented the telephone; American Thomas Edison, whose inventions included the electric light and the phonograph; German physicist Georg Ohm, who developed the theory and application of electrical current; German-American physicist Albert Einstein, who discovered the Theory of Relativity; American physicist Edward Teller, the father of the hydrogen bomb; German physicist Gustav Hertz, noted for his work on the atom; Italian physicist Guglielmo Marconi, who developed the world's first system of wireless telegraphy; American Samuel Morse, who invented the telegraph; American industrialist Henry Ford, who pioneered the automobile and assembly line production; Italian physicist and inventor Alessandro Volta, famous for work with electricity; Scotsman John Dunlop, who created the first usable pneumatic tire; German engineer Rudolf Diesel, who invented the pressure-ignited heat engine; and Italian astronomer, mathematician and physicist Galileo Galilei, who invented the first telescope.

This uniquely Western explosion of ideas and technology has improved the overall quality of life for billions around the world. If all cultures are the same, why has there not been one major invention or discovery from any Muslim nation in the past century?

The West has been responsible for representative democracy, popular sovereignty and human rights, the Renaissance, Enlightenment and the Scientific Revolution (all of which have been largely ignored by the rest of the world—especially the Muslim world).

In sharp contrast, the vast majority of non-Western countries—especially Arab countries—comprise the least free and tolerant societies in the world, characterized by enormous disparities between rich and poor, very few, if any, basic individual legal protections or rights, substandard health care, high illiteracy rates and high violent crime.

Citizens in Western countries enjoy far more individual liberties and freedoms than those in non-Western countries. Chinese couples are forced to sign "one child agreements" and are not permitted to have that child until they receive a "government quota." Couples who violate this rule are fined heavily, publically humiliated and sterilized. This "one child" policy has resulted in tens of millions of forced abortions and sterilizations.[5]

Similarly, in most Muslim nations, women have virtually no rights at all. They're viewed as property and can be summarily killed for not wearing appropriate clothing. In Saudi Arabia, they can even be imprisoned merely for driving a car.

CLAIM #5: "America's export of our capitalist system threatens the cultural identity of foreign cultures and results in ill will toward our country."

RESPONSE: The left hates capitalism because it competes with their socialist utopian vision for America.

Their shared disdain for free market capitalism has nothing to do with the perceived threat to another country's cultural identities.

Our capitalist free market system is predicated upon consumer demand. If there is no demand for a business, chances are investors will not risk their capital to create one. The reason American businesses, products and services thrive around the world is because most people, especially those living under oppression and tyranny in foreign countries, dream about the freedom and high standard of living the vast majority of Americans enjoy.

If there is a Burger King in China, chances are there are a lot of Chinese who like American hamburgers. Eating a Whopper is as much of a threat to the Chinese cultural identity as eating Chinese food would be for an American.

Why aren't similar claims made when foreign companies and chains open businesses here in America? Why don't those on the left assert foreigners are threatening our uniquely American cultural identity? Because of the double standard of the left. It's okay and, in fact, lauded when the U.S. becomes more diverse and multi-cultural, welcoming foreign traditions. But why don't those on the left support, instead of denounce, the export of American businesses abroad?

The reason is the left in our country despise America and all she stands for. They understand freedom and democracy are contagious and if they are to successfully promote their socialist ideas (including wealth redistribution, cradle to grave health care, socialized retirement and universal day care), they must destroy the free-market capitalist system which stands in their way.

The left's claim also ignores that American businesses abroad provide jobs for citizens in those countries and increases the overall standard of living around the world. That's what the U.S. exports—jobs and products people want to buy.

For many, especially in poorer nations, a job is the fastest way to economic freedom and a better life for them and their families. Why should the ability to earn money and provide more for their family necessarily threaten the cultural identity of that family? Nobody is coercing those in foreign countries to work for American companies or purchase American goods or services. Moreover, who says capitalism is incompatible with maintaining someone's cultural traditions?

The world doesn't hate Americans as the left would like everybody to believe. Support for America and our way of life around the world has never been higher, especially in oppressed Muslim nations.

Oppressive dictators hate America because our way of life inspires their people to desire freedom for themselves. Dictators maintain power by oppressing their people. The more people who live under the yoke of tyranny, the more easily they can be controlled while their rich leaders live in their palaces guarded by their private armed guard. Since these dictators routinely kill their own citizens even for minor crimes, they're not particularly interested in exposing them to freedom and democracy. Unfortunately, the left in our country help the dictators' cause by denouncing the American export of our way of life abroad.

The less exposure oppressed people have to freedom and liberty, the less they will demand it in their own countries. While many of the French, German and U.N. elites may not like the U.S., millions risk their lives to come to America.

The majority of the world's countries oppress their people and violate and deny basic human rights such as rule of law, equality under the law, freedom of speech and trial by a jury.

In countries such as China, Cuba, Afghanistan, Iran, Iraq and countries in sub-Saharan Africa, women have very few rights, if any. Citizens in many of these countries are routinely tortured, forced to work in slave labor camps or placed under surveillance. To claim these human rights violations and abuses are the result of American capitalism is ridiculous.

The U.S. didn't murder 100 million innocent people. Stalin did.

Mao killed 30 million of his citizens. Countless millions of others have died throughout the world at the hands of brutal dictators and tyrants of all persuasions—including Communists, Nazis and Fascists.

The U.S. has exported freedom and democracy throughout the world and has been the main contributor to the unparalleled increase in the standard of living worldwide during the past two centuries while dictatorial regimes may "hate" the U.S., millions of people around the world living under tyranny and oppression dream of one day living in America.

CLAIM #6: "America is the most violent nation on earth."

RESPONSE: The U. S. didn't even make the top 17 democidal states of the 20th century.

In the 20th century, according to Rudolph J. Rummel in *Death by Government*, collective or inter-group violence killed 12,000 people in the U.S.[6]

America's death toll pales when compared to that of communist dictators who murdered 100 million people, or the communist Chinese who murdered 61 million, or Yugoslavia's communist Tito regime which murdered one million.[7]

Chapter 22

V is for Vouchers and Public Schools:

How We Can Fix Education

Claims:

1. "Democrats are the party of education."
2. "Democrats represent the best educational interests of minorities."
3. "Republicans are against spending money on public schools. Democrats care more about education than Republicans."
4. "Spending more money on our public schools will improve results."
5. "Vouchers unfairly benefit the wealthy."
6. "We need to pay teachers more to strengthen public education."
7. "Vouchers help private schools at the expense of public education."
8. "Even though vouchers have been relatively successful on a limited basis, it would be too much of a 'risk' to try them on a national level."
9. "Giving public money to private religious schools violates the 'separation of church and state' clause of the Bill of Rights."
10. "Private institutions are not directly accountable for their actions. There is no way to make sure that they act responsibly."
11. "Additional money to strengthen public schools is lost

> because of the billions of dollars in tax cuts for the rich, bailouts for corporations and the war in Iraq."

The U.S. government-run public school system has been an abysmal failure. In spite of billions in increased funding every year for public education, student performance in reading, math and science has either declined or remained flat. American minorities trapped in under-performing public schools continue to be at the greatest disadvantage.

Students from other industrialized countries continue to outperform American students in math and science—and those governments spend less money achieving it.

Liberal Democrats claim school choice reforms President Bush and the GOP members of Congress have proposed are unproven, risky and will unfairly benefit rich kids at the expense of minorities.

The president wants to increase funding for charter schools, require merit-based testing for teachers' pay and institute federal and state testing for students. Spending on education under Bush has increased more than 40 percent since 2001—twice what Clinton budgeted for education—but that doesn't dissuade liberal Democrats from blaming the crisis on lack of funding. When parents are offered a choice of schools for their children, the end results are lower costs and better quality education.

Conservatives advocate the superiority of a free-market approach to education versus the "one size fits all" state-controlled educational monopolies which the National Education Association—the Democratic Party's main financial constituency—supports. NEA members represented one out of every ten delegates at the 2004 Democratic National Convention in Boston.

Why don't those on the left support choice in education as vehemently as they support "choice" in other areas of our lives?

The vast majority of Americans—especially minority parents—support school choice, accountability, standardized testing, merit pay for teachers and charter schools. But the vast majority of liberal Democratic politicians overwhelmingly oppose these reforms.

Democrats sit on the majority of school boards, comprise the majority of administrations and constitute the majority of teachers. You would think that would make our public schools top-notch, especially since the Democratic party is one the NEA chooses to support politically and financially with contributions.

How well have public schools done their jobs over the decades? What kind of grade do they rate? Not great.

Even as spending on education has increased nationwide, test scores among the poor are significantly worse than they were ten years ago.[1]

Nearly two-thirds of Hispanic and black fourth graders in the U.S. are illiterate, according to statistics from the 2004 National Assessment of Educational Progress. That suggests the billions we spend on education rarely result in greater student achievement.[2]

Liberals who dominate the vast majority of public schools are directly responsible for the under-performing schools over which they have presided for the past 50-plus years. They continue to advocate the status quo and oppose any proposal to add choice and accountability to the system.

Even though the vast majority of parents want to have a choice in the schools their children attend, the NEA and Democrats don't want to allow it.

The NEA, in a concerted effort to retain its own power, has consistently opposed school choice reform, in spite of the fact these reforms have significantly helped students in the worst performing government schools across the country.

Instead of representing the most disadvantaged in our society, as Democrats claim to do, they've made the decision to put political campaign contributions from the NEA above supporting the very reforms which have proven to help the most disadvantaged students.

Democrats are out of touch with the vast majority of mainstream American voters on educational reform issues. President Bush has proposed educational reforms as part of his administration's No Child Left Behind Act—the law which requires all students by 2014 be proficient in reading and math based on state-adopted standards. The Act has the overwhelming support of large majorities of Americans, but most of the liberal left opposes it.

The Democratic Party which claims to have blacks' best interests at heart, opposes school choice reform. In essence, liberal Democrats have manipulated blacks in this country by championing symbolic issues such as hate crimes legislation and race-based preferences. At the same time, they've ignored and overtly impeded the very educational reforms such as charter schools, vouchers for children attending the worst performing government schools, more local control and teacher/student testing which have helped black students the most.

The reality is the Democratic Party has presided over the failure of our current government school system and, given their track record, should have limited input on how to reform it.

CLAIM #1: "Democrats are the party of education."

RESPONSE: **The Democratic Party consistently opposes school choice programs such as vouchers and charter schools.**

Liberal elites such as the Clintons, Gores and Kennedys sent their kids to private schools, but they have consistently denied the same opportunity to the least privileged children.

Who could be more disadvantaged in our society than an illiterate, minority teenager without the requisite reading, writing and verbal skills to advance in our high-tech global economy—doomed to a life of low-skilled and low-wage jobs?

But where overcrowded public schools have failed poor urban minority students, vouchers and charter schools have helped them more than any other single group in America.

School choice reform has proven to be overwhelmingly successful in Cleveland, Milwaukee, Washington, D.C. and elsewhere.

About 57 percent of all blacks support vouchers—and that goes up to 75 percent among blacks under the age of 35, according to the Joint Center for Political and Economic Studies.[3]

But even though black parents overwhelmingly support voucher programs and charter schools, the liberal left and NEA uniformly oppose them, falsely claiming vouchers violate the separation of church and state, siphon funds from public schools and weaken public schools overall.

CLAIM #2: "Democrats best represent the educational interests of minorities."

RESPONSE: **The vast majority of establishment Democrats oppose school choice for kids trapped in failing public schools across the nation.**

Nearly two-thirds of our country's Hispanic and African-American fourth graders are illiterate.

Liberal Democrats have sided with the NEA and consistently opposed English immersion programs for Hispanic students, even though it's been demonstrated these programs lead to higher achievement in reading and math for minorities.

English immersion has been highly successful, but Democratic support for bilingual education has been a complete and utter failure. Test results demonstrate that Hispanic children achieve higher scores in reading and math when they're immersed in English. In California, where bilingual education ended in 1998, the share of Hispanic students scoring above the median in math tests is 46 percent (as of 2002), up from 27 percent. In reading, the number scoring above median, is 35 percent (as of 2002), up from 21 percent.

In spite of the overwhelming evidence that English immersion produces higher academic achievement and results among Hispanic students, it's strongly opposed by leftist groups such as the NEA, The Hispanic-American Chamber of Commerce and the white hate group La Raza. These organizations claim children learn more quickly in their own language and English should be taught incrementally.

One reason those in the bilingual lobby oppose English immersion is because bilingual programs create jobs for Spanish teachers who are part of teachers' unions. Those in favor of maintaining the failed bilingual system care more about union money and protection of bureaucratic jobs than opportunity for Hispanic children. They're guilty of what President Bush called the "soft bigotry of low expectations."[4]

There's nothing wrong with children knowing their own native language. However, to be successful in America, you need to be fluent in English. Students not proficient in English are doomed to a life of low-paying, low-skilled jobs. It's also important that those coming to our country learn our common language so they can assimilate into our culture.

Americans favor increasing the number of hours children spend in school on education basics such as math, science, history and English. The NEA has largely opposed these reforms.[5]

According to Public Opinion Strategies in 1998 and 1999, more than 80 percent of Americans want to require teachers to pass a standardized test before they're allowed to teach and to be retested and certified every five years.

The same polls found that: more than 70 percent of Americans want principals to fire under-performing teachers without a long wait; 85 percent favor an education reform package which includes more stringent teacher standards and more local control over schools and expands the use of computers and new technology in the classroom; and 80 percent favor tougher teacher standards and more local control over schools. The NEA has consistently opposed these initiatives.[6]

Eighty percent favor requiring all state education spending to go directly into classrooms—not to teacher union bureaucrats. The NEA opposes this reform.[7]

Almost 65 percent believe charter schools should be expanded and parents should be given school choice programs. They also believe children should have more options to attend the highest quality school which best meets their needs. The NEA opposes this reform.[8]

CLAIM #3: "Republicans are against spending money on public schools. Democrats care more about education than Republicans."

RESPONSE: President Bush proposed to spend more money on education than the biggest tax and spender in Congress—Ted Kennedy.

Republicans are opposed to wasting money on public schools. However, they support more money for the teachers and students, not the bureaucrats in the NEA.

Republicans also advocate annualized testing for teachers and students, requirement of an annual increase in student performance tests, abolishment of bilingual programs which fail to teach English, teaching children phonics-based reading and requiring expulsion for disruptive students.

It's absurd to claim Republicans oppose educational spending because education spending growth under the Bush Administration exceeded educational spending under the Clinton Administration. Republicans, however, have tied increased spending to actual results—something Democrats, for many years, have failed to do. Democrats pay lip service to "caring" about education, but they're directly responsible for the educational catastrophe in our country.

"In most major urban areas, there is hardly a single elected Republican on any school board or in charge of administering any district," writes author, civil rights activist and commentator David Horowitz, who is president of the Freedom Center. "Democrats, liberals and not a few Marxists have controlled most of the big city school systems in America for the last 60 years, including those in the big metropolitan districts: New York, Chicago, Los Angeles, Baltimore, Boston and Washington, D.C."[9]

He adds, "Democrats have crippled and nearly destroyed the public education system through fifty years of bureaucratic bungling and selfish policies that benefit the unions. In major cities, the public schools are failing to graduate nearly fifty percent of their minority students. Lack of education usually leads to a lifetime of poverty. In the past, the public schools were the path to success for America's immigrants and poor. Now they are dead ends for kids with no future. No Democrat in Congress sends his or her own children to public schools. Why should they be allowed to condemn the children of minorities and the poor to a failed system to whom they wouldn't entrust their own children? It's time to end the social tragedy, to give these kids a shot at the American dream."[10]

Students from other industrialized countries continue to outperform American students in math and science despite spending significantly less money. American minorities trapped in under-performing public schools continue to be at the greatest disadvantage.

Liberal Democrats claim Bush's proposed school choice reforms, such as funding for charter schools, merit-based testing and pay for teachers and federal and state testing for students endanger education, are unproven, risky and will unfairly benefit rich kids at the expense of minorities—even though poor urban minorities benefit the most from these very school choice initiatives.

Under the Bush administration, spending on education has increased more than 40 percent, but that doesn't dissuade liberal Democrats from blaming the education crisis on lack of funding.

CLAIM #4: "Spending more money on our public schools will improve results."

RESPONSE: In the last three decades, spending per-pupil nationwide has doubled, but less than three-fourths of high school students ever graduate.

Spending more money has not been the answer. America has the worst elementary and secondary (K-12) education system in the civilized world, despite the highest per pupil spending of any industrialized nation in the world.

During a ten-year period, from 1991 to 2002, even though spending per student increased, graduation rates remained about the same with 72 percent of students graduating in 1991 and 71 percent graduation in 2002, according to a study by the Manhattan Institute.[11]

For minority students in the U.S., the figures are worse. Only 56 percent of black students and 52 percent of Hispanic students in the class of 2002, graduated from high school with a diploma, compared to about 78 percent of white students.[12]

In the Third International Mathematics & Science Study (TIMSS) in 1998, American students scored near the bottom in math—a dismal 19th out of 21 nations—behind Sweden, Switzerland, Germany, the Netherlands, Norway, Canada, New Zealand, Russia, Italy and the Czech Republic. Americans only outperformed students from Cyprus and South Africa.[13]

In New York City, per-pupil spending increased 20 percent over the last decade, yet half the students didn't graduate.[14]

On the NAEP (National Assessment of Educational Progress) exams, only 38 percent of fourth graders demonstrated a proficiency in reading.[15]

The Brookings Institute, a liberal think tank, in 1993 admitted, "Funding is not related to school quality."[16]

The District of Columbia spends more than $500 million a year on public schools—number three in per-pupil expenditures in the nation ($10,836 per student). D.C. teachers' salaries rank eighth. Yet student performance ranked the lowest in the country in math and reading for fourth graders—and in math, reading and science for eighth graders.

Catholic schools in the area surrounding D.C. spend per pupil less than two-thirds what public schools do. Yet, in a study the Manhattan Institute's Education Research Office conducted on black graduation rates in the nation's top 50 districts, Fairfax, Prince George and Montgomery Counties surrounding Washington, D.C. were ranked at number two, three and four respectively while spending significantly less money per pupil than the District.[17]

Despite a 49 percent increase in educational spending under Bush for elementary and secondary schools, reading proficiency among 9- to 13-year-olds has declined even further. Only 24 percent of high school seniors were at or above proficiency in writing in 2002, and half of them were below basic proficiency in science, according to the National Center for Education Statistics. Only 29 percent of eighth graders in 2003 were at or above math proficiency and about 32 percent were at or above proficiency in reading.[18]

CLAIM #5: "Vouchers unfairly benefit the wealthy."

RESPONSE: Test scores for low-income students increase when they have a choice in schools.

The scores especially increase for low-income students when a choice is offered for their schooling, according to a Canadian study by William Robson and Claudia R. Hepburn, entitled *Learning from Success: What Americans Can Learn from School Choice in Canada*.

"Choice has been particularly advantageous for poor and middle income families," writes researchers from the Frasier Institute in British Columbia who studied the impact of choice in Canada. "Achievement test scores have gone up, particularly among low-income students, in the provinces that offer school choice."

Interestingly the study also found, "Independent schools tend to be more socially diverse than public schools, which often draw from economically homogenous neighborhoods."[19]

Voucher programs have almost exclusively benefited *poor minority* students. The vast majority of voucher programs have almost exclusively enabled minorities in cities such as Washington, D.C.,

Cleveland, Ohio and Milwaukee, Wisconsin to transfer from their under-performing public school to a superior charter school where, on average, grades and test scores have risen dramatically at a lower per-pupil expenditure.

Liberal Democratic politicians overwhelmingly choose private and parochial schools for their children, but hinder minorities from having the same opportunities. Instead, they side with the teachers' unions, NEA and the American Federation of Teachers (AFT), which happen to be their largest financial contributors.

Private schools are the choice of 14 percent of Americans, including those in Congress. Fifty percent of U.S. senators and 34 percent of House members send their kids to private schools.

Forty-five percent of the Congressional Hispanic Caucus send their kids to private schools compared to only eight percent of Hispanics overall.

Only eight percent of blacks send their kids to private schools compared to 32 percent of the Congressional Black Caucus.

Why can't the most underprivileged minorities have equal access to the same high quality schools where liberal bureaucrats routinely send their own children?

CLAIM #6: "We need to pay teachers more to strengthen public education."

RESPONSE: Relatively speaking, teachers are well paid for the work they perform.

On a national average, teachers make about $42,000 for nine months of work—or about $4,667 a month—plus have long vacations (including winter and spring breaks, plus three months every summer), enormous benefits and retirement.[20]

We need to pay more qualified teachers better salaries. We need to make sure salaries for teachers are competitive, while also raising the standards to ensure the best-qualified teachers are entering the profession.

While there are certainly some top-notch teachers, statistics show that many who enter the profession are usually from the bottom third of their class, have a C+ average in high school, have not majored in the subjects they teach, score 50 points below average on the SAT and score the lowest on the GRE of eight professional groups tested.[21]

Teacher pay should be contingent upon merit like every other profession. The free market is the most effective and efficient arbiter of goods and services. In a free market educational system, ideally, those teachers most proficient in the subjects they teach would receive the highest salaries. It is axiomatic in the free market that price almost always reflects intrinsic value. The higher the perceived value, the greater the price one can charge for the services he or she performs.

When teacher compensation is primarily the result of seniority and tenure, performance becomes less significant by comparison, which ultimately dilutes competition among the teachers affecting the education students receive.

Because private, parochial and charter schools promote competition among teachers and students, teacher quality and student performance have been consistently higher than their public school counterparts. Allowing teachers to freely compete against each other will improve education. Merit-based testing and pay have been vital in improving the quality of education. It's unfortunate the establishment left and the teachers' unions oppose such an important reform.

CLAIM #7: "Vouchers help private schools at the expense of public education."

RESPONSE: Vouchers help students—not schools.

First, the ultimate purpose of choice is to allow parents the ability to send their children to the best possible schools.

Second, with more students in private schools, public taxpayer money is freed up, allowing it to go farther for those still attending public schools.

"When students who cost $8,000 a year to educate in the public schools transfer to a private school with a $4,000 voucher the total cost of educating all these students does not go up. It goes down," writes Dr. Thomas Sowell, a senior fellow at Stanford University's Hoover

Institution, in *Vouchers Vindicated*. "Far from reducing per capita spending in the public schools, the departure of voucher students leaves more money per pupil for those left behind."[22]

The voucher system, to the dismay of the public school bureaucrats, is already a huge success which has actually improved the standards in many public schools.

Milwaukee Mayor John O. Norquist, writing in the *Wall Street Journal*, noted that his city offers more tax-supported school choices than any other city in America. He noted that one-third of the 11,000 Milwaukee students who opted to choose their schools in 2002 were being educated in inner-city private schools.

Norquist said there have been numerous benefits to having educational choices. Milwaukee public school administrators and the teachers' unions worked together to institute a new program which "counsels out" problem teachers.

Public school officials found they had the money to increase half-day kindergarten classes to full day and expand before- and after-school child care.

The Democrat-at-large of the Milwaukee School Board of Directors found, "Students have made significant academic gains between 1997 and 2001, the period of the most rapid expansion of school choice."[23]

Public-school students improved on 11 of 15 tests where their performance was compared to a national sample and the dropout rate is declining.

But one of the most positive outcomes of having a choice in selecting schools is that the competition encourages public schools to improve and reform.

"Overall, an evaluation of Milwaukee suggests that public schools have a strong, positive response to competition from vouchers," writes Harvard economist Caroline M. Hoxby, who investigated the impact of the city's vouchers.[24]

CLAIM #8: "Even though vouchers have been relatively successful on a limited basis, it would be too much of a 'risk' to try them on a national level."

RESPONSE: **School choice has already been successful on a national level in Canada.**

As a result of the government-funded choice program, 92 percent of Canadians now live in areas with school choice.

Scores have risen dramatically, for minorities and the poor. Subsequently, choice in Canada has led to more educational equality across socioeconomic boundaries. Costs of educating students has decreased. (Independent schools now receive 60 percent of what public schools spend and special needs students receive 100 percent of what public schools would spend.)

These positive educational results have been the result of a national choice and government-subsidized voucher system—the same one that liberals, such as those from the powerful teaching unions like the NEA and elite liberal politicians oppose and claim can't work here in the United States nationally.[25]

Independent non-public schools are not new in the United States. In fact, private and parochial schools predated public schools. Using public funds for independent private education is not novel either. Public money such as Pell grants and the G.I Bill have been used to finance non-public school educations for millions.

Most Americans—including 65 percent of minority parents—support having more options to attend high quality schools which best meet their needs, according to a February 2004 Public Opinions Strategies poll. These parents don't believe such programs would be too "risky."

Yet, the liberal Democratic educational establishment opposes this vast public support for expanding choices to parents and their children.[26]

In another poll conducted by the Washington-based Center for Education Reform, 70 percent of black parents earning less than $15,000 a year said they supported school choice.[27]

CLAIM #9: "Giving public money to private religious schools violates the 'separation of church and state' clause of the Bill of Rights."

RESPONSE: **The words "separation of church**

and state" do not appear anywhere in the U.S. Constitution.

In fact, the very first sentence of the First Amendment reads, "Congress shall make no law respecting an establishment of religion, or prohibiting the free exercise thereof."

There is no body of case law which says public money cannot be used for private school tuition. In fact, there is probably more evidence to support the notion that it would be unconstitutional for government to discriminate against parents who voluntarily chose to spend public money on parochial education versus a secular public education.

When Thomas Jefferson used the phrase "separation of church and state" 11 years after the First Amendment was written, his purpose was to convey to the Danbury Baptists in a letter he had written to them that the federal government would not mandate a national religion or church, as was the case in England. None of the Founders, especially those responsible for the debate and final drafting of the Bill of Rights, ever said anything about prohibiting public tax money for religious schools. In fact prior to 1960, the Bible was the centerpiece of American education.

We have for years given "public" federal money to religious institutions in the form of student aid (Pell Grants for students attending Notre Dame for example). Never before did the left object to this purported "violation of church and state."

The "church and state violation" argument is merely a smokescreen meant to conceal their underlying opposition to school choice in general.

<u>**CLAIM #10**</u>**: "Private institutions are not directly accountable for their actions. There is no way to make sure they act responsibly."**

<u>**RESPONSE**</u>**: If this were true, then why do so many liberal politicians who oppose school choice send their kids to private schools?**

If accountability was really a concern, wouldn't liberals send their own kids to public schools instead of to all those "unaccountable" private schools?

V IS FOR VOUCHERS AND PUBLIC SCHOOLS: *HOW WE CAN FIX EDUCATION*

Private schools are accountable to parents. In fact, the reason private schools provide a superior education is because parents expect more and get more out of them, including the fact that private schools continue to send more students to the top colleges and universities.

It's public schools which, for years, have not been accountable for their inferior results. Public schools and the liberal Democratic educators who run them have failed to account for their failure to educate our children—especially minorities and the poor. Public schools and the teachers' unions need to be held accountable for their failures.

In President Bush's No Child Left Behind Act, which was signed into law in 2001, measures were added for greater accountability in the form of teacher and student testing. More local control was also given to parents so decisions could be made at the local level. The bill left out a vital component of reform—a national voucher program—but it did at least include some modest testing and accountability measures. For years the teachers' unions have opposed every reform which would have held teachers themselves accountable for results in the classroom.

Those who impede school choice reforms must be accountable for their staunch opposition, especially in denying minorities the same opportunities which liberal Democratic politicians routinely take advantage of for their own children. Liberals should have to answer for why they have consistently opposed the very educational reforms which have been most effective.

CLAIM #11: "Additional money to strengthen public schools is lost because of the billions of dollars in tax cuts for the rich, bailouts for corporations and the war in Iraq."

RESPONSE: The Bush administration has spent more on public education than Clinton did.

Congress authorized $26.3 billion for public education for President Bush's No Child Left Behind Act which was co-authored by Ted Kennedy, one of the most renowned liberals ever to serve in the United States Senate. This amount represented eight billion dollars more than Clinton's last education bill. Did the left accuse Clinton of not spending enough on education?

Increased funding has not been the answer. Again the implication is that Republicans don't invest enough in education. Even think-tanks on the left, such as the Brookings Institute, conclude funding is not related to school quality.

It's ludicrous to say that because the United States spends tax dollars on defense and allows Americans to keep more of what they make to stimulate the economy, that education is somehow ignored. We are funding public education at record levels.

Chapter 23

W is for Welfare:

What's Wrong With It

Claims:

1. "Welfare levels the playing field for those who fail to make it on their own."
2. "Conservatives oppose welfare because they have no concern for the poor."
3. "Welfare reform has led to more poverty for women, children, and the elderly resulting in more homelessness and hunger."

President Lyndon B. Johnson launched the War on Poverty in 1965. The primary intent of the program initially was to reduce poverty by providing a safety net.

The annual amount spent on federal welfare assistance to the poor—through Medicare, Medicaid, food stamps and public housing—grew from $8.9 billion in 1965 to $434 billion in 2000. The cost of these programs now represents nearly one half of all money spent by the federal government. As a percentage of gross domestic product (GDP), welfare spending has increased from 1.2 percent in 1965 to 4.4 percent today. Over the past 40 years, the United States has spent at least $8.9 trillion (in 2003 dollars) on the War on Poverty.[1]

President Clinton reluctantly signed into law the Personal Responsibility and Work Opportunity Reconciliation Act in 1996, welfare legislation which replaced the failed Aid To Families With

Dependent Children (AFDC) with the more work-oriented Temporary Assistance to Needy Families (TANF).

The primary objective for ending the historic cash entitlement was to reduce welfare dependence by: increasing employment and self-sufficiency; reducing child poverty and illegitimacy; and strengthening marriage. (More than 80 percent of children who live in long-term poverty live in single-parent families where their parents either never married or divorced.)

Under the new law, states were given broad flexibility in determining how to best use those funds to achieve the goals of increased employment, marriage, abstinence and poverty reduction.

When this legislation was signed into law, many liberal groups, such as the Children's Defense Fund, claimed the reforms would cast millions of children into poverty and hunger.[2] In fact, the exact opposite occurred. Today, 2.9 million fewer children live in poverty than in 1995.[3]

Since the reform law was enacted, welfare cases in the Temporary Assistance to Needy Families have plummeted more than 50 percent, employment of single mothers who otherwise would have become dependent on welfare has increased more than 50 percent and child hunger has decreased substantially. Most striking has been the dramatic reduction in poverty among black children.

Liberal groups and organizations still assert child poverty has increased since welfare reform, even though it's the exact opposite. Left-of-center think tanks such as the Brookings Institute want Congress to draft legislation which would: increase availability of food stamps to the poor; provide higher benefits for families with three or more children; increase the five-year limit on welfare and provide more government-incentive funding for states to help families work toward self-sufficiency.

They advocate a mixture of "federal and state policies that encourage individual effort and then subsidize work and perhaps marriage." In other words, more government programs and "perhaps" marriage—as if marriage were not one of the most crucial elements of the debate.[4]

Conservatives, on the other hand, believe considerably more can be done to further reduce poverty and increase self-sufficiency.

Groups such as the conservative think-tank The Heritage Foundation suggest the government needs to require more from those receiving TANF welfare aid, such as encouraging marriage and abstinence among non-marrieds, as well as requiring increased hours for work.

Although welfare reform has generated some early signs of success, it's only been moderate at best. The reason millions of welfare recipients made the successful transition from welfare to work was because of the booming economy.

Spending in the four years after welfare reform went into effect in 1996 continued to rise steadily. From 1996 to 2000 more than nine billion dollars was spent on work-support programs which provided welfare recipients with non-cash benefits.

The country still spends approximately $80 billion per year on cash income supplements such as The Earned Income Tax Credit (EITC) and childcare for low-income workers. Even though six million welfare recipients have been eliminated from the welfare rolls (representing a 47 percent reduction in caseloads from August 1999 to December 1999), many of those have been individuals who in the short-term have been the easiest to employ.

The Cato Institute evaluated how every state has implemented welfare reform since 1996 and studies show long-term dependence continues to be problematic.

States such as Missouri and Vermont have experienced the least amount of success decreasing government assistance and dependence due in part because they've never implemented real welfare reform, choosing instead to almost reward people for not working. Missouri increased benefits to those who had more children while they were receiving welfare. Vermont didn't put into effect a single program to help welfare recipients become self-sufficient.

But there were success stories in some of the states. Idaho and Ohio have experienced the most significant declines in caseloads since implementation of welfare reform. Idaho had an 85 percent decline in welfare caseloads since reforms were implemented and by 2000, 78 percent of those who had been on welfare had found jobs—the highest rate in the U.S. In Ohio, federal officials turned welfare administration over to the state and county officials, giving the local level the authority to determine how best to deliver social services. Both states require welfare recipients to show personal responsibility and work for benefits. There is a strict time limit—they can only receive welfare temporarily.[5]

Conservatives have also stressed the importance of funding programs which encourage abstinence or marriage since the poverty rate among never married mothers is seven times higher than in intact married families. A recent Zogby poll found that 79 percent of parents with children age 17 and under want their children to be taught to abstain from sex until marriage or near marriage. Unfortunately, the government currently spends $4.50 to encourage the use of contraceptives among teens for every one dollar spent on promoting abstinence.[6]

Liberals have consistently argued it is the obligation of the government to provide a safety net for poor citizens, regardless of whether they're able to work or not. Even though welfare has been one of the most colossal failures of the federal government in our nation's history, liberal Democrats continue to insist welfare reform has been harmful, Republicans don't care for the poor and that we should follow the example of other more "enlightened" European countries who provide welfare to any citizen in need.

While both sides disagree on future remedies, both generally agree the 1996 welfare reform law requires some major restructuring if we are ever going to truly end welfare.

CLAIM #1: "Welfare levels the playing field for those who fail to make it on their own."

RESPONSE: Since the mid-1960s, welfare has been the primary cause of the rapid rise in illegitimacy, crime and long-term government dependency, experienced mainly by blacks.

This government safety net called welfare has cost American taxpayers more than eight trillion dollars in government social service spending.

Since welfare was enacted, illegitimacy, crime and welfare rolls have increased significantly. In the 1960s, only 7.7 percent of Americans were born out of wedlock, according to The Centers for Disease

Control, National Health Statistics, Division of Vital Statistics. By 2002, that figure had increased dramatically to 34.5 percent.[7]

More taxpayer funded welfare—which was originally intended to provide a temporary safety net—has only led to increased illegitimacy, single-parenthood and long-term government dependence, especially for blacks.

While most Americans would agree there should be some sort of federal insurance safety net for formerly productive law abiding citizens, most would agree that assistance should only be reserved for extreme circumstances and should not take the place of work and personal responsibility.

While welfare may have benefited people in need over the past 40 years, no government program should have as one of its primary goals, a system of wealth redistribution. There is no legitimate constitutional foundation for that. That concept is called socialism and it's contrary to the American ideal of individual liberty and freedom—the cornerstones of our republic.

Abraham Lincoln argued that the very foundation of kingship and tyranny is, "You work and I eat." Any system which perpetuates dependence by encouraging able-bodied individuals to not work is morally and ethically wrong, regardless of the purported justification.

The only long-term solution to end welfare is to permanently discontinue the program so it's no longer a viable option and fall-back for teenage women who choose to have babies out of wedlock. Three quarters of single teenage mothers end up on welfare before their first child turns five. Long-term dependency is almost always the result of out-of-wedlock pregnancy.

The 1996 welfare reforms did alleviate welfare dependency to a certain extent. However, long-term dependency continues to inhibit any long-term solutions to welfare, primarily among unmarried women who have children out of wedlock. Until welfare is no longer a viable alternative for these women who continually choose to make bad decisions, we will continue to subsidize this behavior. Only by removing the financial safety net will we make it clear that out-of-wedlock births are socially unacceptable and something taxpayers won't continue to tolerate and subsidize.[8]

CLAIM #2: "Conservatives oppose welfare because they have no concern for the poor."

RESPONSE: Conservatives don't measure compassion for the poor in terms of how many tax dollars they can collect and redistribute to welfare recipients.

Conservatives measure compassion for the poor in terms of how many poor and dependent individuals they can help lift out of poverty, not through government programs or assistance. Good paying jobs lead to wealth creation and self sufficiency. Conservatives oppose welfare in general because one of the primary tenets of conservatism is individual self-reliance.

Although well-meaning liberals who support welfare may be concerned for the poor, they may want to consider the devastation poverty has had on millions of Americans (especially blacks) during the past 40 years. They should also consider the high cost to society of their welfare-state utopian experiment.

Republican legislation (via the 1996 welfare reform bill) has primarily been responsible for lifting more than 1.2 million black children out of poverty.[9] President Clinton only reluctantly signed welfare reform into law to appeal to vital white suburban swing voters in a calculated effort for reelection in 1996.

A Republican Congress was primarily responsible for the ultimate drafting and passage of the '96 welfare reform bill which dramatically reduced welfare rolls and poverty. While President Clinton took the credit for ending welfare as we know it, it was conservatives in Congress who led the charge for welfare reform amidst a great deal of opposition and obstruction from the Democratic minority and a liberal Democratic administration.

CLAIM #3: "Welfare reform has led to more poverty for women, children and the elderly—resulting in more homelessness and hunger."

RESPONSE: Welfare reform has, in almost every year since its enactment in 1996, resulted in a

sharp decline in welfare rolls. Employment among single mothers has increased substantially and child hunger has declined.

The decrease in child poverty, especially among black children, has been significant. Since welfare reform was enacted, the poverty rate among black children has declined by one-fourth (falling from 41.5 percent in 1995 to 30 percent in 2001.) More than 1.2 million black children have been lifted out of poverty since welfare reform.[10]

The vast majority of those families who are still living in extreme poverty are currently unemployed and receiving TANF benefits. The fact that many of the children of these parents who choose not to seek employment are living in extreme poverty doesn't mean welfare reform, per se, has caused them to live in these conditions. It means states with high caseloads need to strongly consider instituting more austere work requirement standards to reduce the incentive to remain unemployed and to encourage self-sufficiency through work.

Welfare reform has been most successful reducing caseloads in states which emphasize work and personal responsibility. The Cato Institute conducted a study in 2004 which evaluated all 50 states and the District of Columbia on how successfully they have implemented welfare reform since 1996. The study specifically evaluates the reduction in the number of caseloads and poverty rates, but also considers how effectively individual states have been in aiding recipients in achieving self-sufficiency. Four states received A's, seven received B's, twenty scored C's, eleven had D's and nine received F's. Every New England "blue" state received a D or an F—except for Connecticut.[11]

The study found that the states which were most successful implementing welfare reforms reduced welfare dependence long-term, required work for benefits and encouraged students to prevent teenage pregnancy and finish high school.

States least successful in reducing poverty and caseloads failed to reduce illegitimacy and didn't encourage either work, personal responsibility or marriage.

According to the USDA's annual Household Food Security Survey, on a typical day, less than one American in 200 will experience hunger due to a lack of money to buy food. In 2003, according to the report, 92 percent of those who experienced hunger were adults and only eight percent were children, meaning that, in a typical month, one child in 400 skipped one or more meals because his or her family lacked funds to purchase food. Overall, the report concluded hunger has declined slightly since the measurement began.

The U.S. Department of Agriculture defines hunger as the physical discomfort caused by food shortages due to a lack of funds to obtain food. The USDA clarifies that hunger is not the same as malnutrition and that most hunger experienced in the United States is short-term.

In 1995, 4.1 million households experienced hunger at some point during the year. By 2003, the number had dropped to 3.9 million households. Among children, hunger was cut in half between 1995 and 2003, according to USDA data. In 1995, there were 887,000 hungry children. By 2003, the number had declined to 420,000 representing 0.6 percent of children who the USDA classifies as hungry.[12]

Chapter 24

X is for Xenophobia:

Why Illegal Immigration is Hurting Us

Claims:

1. "Republicans are anti-immigration."
2. "We should provide amnesty to all illegal aliens who have been in the U.S. for a certain period of time. It is the compassionate thing to do."
3. "We should concentrate our efforts on stopping terrorists from entering our country illegally, not migrant workers from Mexico."
4. "Illegal immigrants do the jobs Americans won't do."
5. "The economy would be harmed without the steady flow of cheap illegal immigrant labor."
6. "We are a nation of immigrants. Preventing those seeking economic opportunity from entering our country, even those who cross the border illegally, is immoral and contrary to what we stand for as Americans."
7. "America is a multi-cultural nation which is good for society."

Both Democrats and Republicans have been relatively quiet about illegal immigration because the large Hispanic minority in this country represents a key voting constituency for both parties.

Hispanics have become the largest minority in America and have subsequently become a highly-coveted voting block. Indeed, without the large Hispanic turnout on election day 2004, George W. Bush would not be in the White House today.

While large majorities of Americans believe the United States should seal the borders and oppose amnesty for the more than 14 million undocumented workers already in the United States today, many politicians, business interests and labor unions view the issue in a different way.

Many Republicans support the notion of guest worker programs because of the powerful business interests which favor a steady supply of cheap labor. Republican political operatives such as Karl Rove also believe that for Republicans to govern long-term, they must be able to win large majorities of Hispanics in states such as New Mexico, Arizona, Colorado, Florida, North Carolina and California.

Democrats maintain a similar view. Leftward leaning labor unions have also recently favored guest worker programs and other amnesty type proposals to legalize "undocumented workers" as a way to increase membership and union dues within their dwindling organizations. Other political organizations, such as the Democratic National Committee, also recognize the significance of attracting Hispanic votes.

Some courageous conservatives such as Congressman Tom Tancredo of Colorado and James Sensenbrenner of Wisconsin have argued passionately against illegal immigration, amnesty, guest worker programs and issuing driver's licenses to illegals—all things President Bush has supported.

While conservatives such as Tancredo and Sensenbrenner unequivocally oppose illegal immigration and have advocated sealing off the border as a security measure, liberals continue to claim Republicans are anti-immigrant, that illegals are not posing a national security threat and are just doing the jobs Americans won't do.

When the economic, cultural and national security ramifications of illegal immigration are considered, it's evident the left's pleasant sounding rhetoric and notions about multiculturalism and diversity is dangerously idealistic and misguided.

<u>CLAIM #1</u>: "Republicans are anti-immigration."

<u>RESPONSE</u>: Republicans are anti-illegal immigration.

The United States has the most generous legal immigration policy in the world and accepts more legal immigrants than any other country, taking in approximately 800,000 foreigners each year. But the U.S. should always oppose *illegal* immigration. There is no constitutional right for foreigners to immigrate to the United States. We allow immigrants to enter our country and become U.S citizens, but that's a privilege, not a right.

We need to be discriminating when considering how many and what type of immigrants we allow in our country—especially post 9/11 and during a time of a global terror when immigration has a direct impact on national security.

Conservatives, especially, should advocate immigration policies based upon national security considerations and should demand that anyone entering our country illegally be immediately deported to their country of origin.

If conservative Republicans claim to be strict constitutionalists, then they have a vital obligation to enforce all the laws of our nation. Our elected representatives and government employees don't have a constitutional right to selectively enforce our immigration laws. Once we fail to enforce our laws, we send a direct message to the world that the United States is no longer a nation of laws.

Lee Malvo—the 2002 Washington "beltway sniper"—came to this country illegally from Jamaica and was arrested in 2001. Instead of being deported as he should have been, Malvo was released without bond and went on a killing spree murdering ten and injuring three others, inciting a national panic. If Malvo had been immediately deported, ten Americans would still be alive today. Those who condone and encourage illegal immigration are, in essence, increasing the chance of more Lee Malvos committing more terrorist acts on U.S. soil.

Republicans who claim to be conservative should favor *legal* immigration which makes sense. They should advocate immigration policy which favors granting citizenship to those who want to become Americans—immigrants who want to learn English, respect our unique and diverse American culture and contribute to the economic prosperity and defense of our nation.

Conservatives should demand our immigration laws be faithfully executed and our borders secured. During a time of war, our country is most vulnerable from terrorists entering through our porous borders.

CLAIM #2: "We should provide amnesty to all illegal aliens who have been in the U.S. for a certain period of time. It's the compassionate thing to do."

RESPONSE: Amnesty rewards illegal behavior and only encourages increased illegal immigration.

The Democratic Congress voted to grant amnesty in 1986 to more than three million illegal aliens. Since then, illegal aliens, mostly from Mexico, have been flooding our borders, with 8,000 each day entering illegally.

We know that granting amnesty only sends the message to other illegal aliens that if they can successfully sneak into our country, there will be few, if any, penalties and a great many rewards, including taxpayer-subsidized health care, education, welfare and social security, as well as a good paying job.

Households headed by illegal aliens used ten billion dollars more in government services than they paid in taxes in 2002, according to a 2004 Center for Immigration Studies—one of the first to estimate the impact of illegal immigration on the federal budget. If illegal aliens are given amnesty, the study concludes, the fiscal burden at the federal level will grow to nearly $29 billion.

Illegal alien households use approximately $2,700 more in services than they pay in taxes, which in 2002 created a fiscal burden of nearly $10.4 billion on the federal budget. If illegal aliens were legalized under an amnesty program, according to the study, the annual federal deficit would increase from $2,700 per household to nearly $7,700, for a total federal deficit of $29 billion.

Not only does amnesty erode our immigration laws rendering them ineffective, but it exacerbates an already enormous deficit which would burden future generations.[1]

The other problem is crime. Some illegal aliens come to this country, commit crimes—including murder—then flee back to their native country and escape justice. Many of those countries refuse to extradite or cooperate with the U.S. More than 60 Mexican illegal aliens accused of murder in the Los Angeles area have fled across the border to hide in Mexico. Mexican authorities know their whereabouts, but they refuse to extradite them.[2]

CLAIM #3: "We should concentrate our efforts on stopping terrorists from entering our country illegally, not blocking migrant workers from Mexico."

RESPONSE: We should prevent both terrorists and illegal immigrants from crossing the borders into our country.

Securing our borders is paramount to preventing anybody from entering our country illegally. All that's required to launch a terrorist attack is a few individuals sneaking across the border with chemical, biological or nuclear weapons. We need to protect and secure our borders from all individuals who seek to enter illegally-especially during a time of war.

If migrant workers from Mexico, or any other country for that matter, want to come to America to make a living, they should enter legally. They should do what every other individual seeking admission to our country does—apply for a visa and go through the legal normalization process.

"Border Patrol officers and local investigative journalists in the Southwest reported on increasing numbers of Middle Eastern males entering illegally from Mexico," wrote noted syndicated columnist and author Michelle Malkin in an article titled *Homeland Insecurity: 2004 in Review*. "Muslim prayer books and Arabic diaries were discovered in 'Terrorist Alley' in southwest Arizona. Suspected al Qaeda operative Adnan Shukrijumah, a fugitive Saudi pilot...is believed to be in Mexico."[3]

In 1980, there were fewer than 9,000 criminal aliens in our state and federal prisons. By 1999, that number had grown to 68,000. In Orange County, California alone, there are 275 street gangs, with 17,000 members—98 percent Mexican or Asian.[4]

Even though those who perpetrated the 9/11 attacks were all Muslim males, not everybody who commits acts of terrorism and violent crime in America are Muslims. The presumption which often goes unchallenged in the mainstream media that those who cross the southern border illegally are basically just harmless migrants ignores the millions of South American MS-13 gang members who sneak into our country. They're well-versed in weapons, drug and alien smuggling. Gang members from MS-13 have been linked to numerous killings, car-jackings, extortions and gang rapes. The gang has also aided al Qaeda members in illegally crossing into the U.S. from Mexico.[5]

There are probably many individuals who sneak into our country to find work and a better life. But by encouraging an open border policy, the U.S. is making it easier for criminals and terrorists to enter as well. This threat to our national security is not worth the cheap labor. It's not easy to determine who's entering our country to pick vegetables and who's coming to kill Americans.

Seal the borders and ensure a system of lawful and orderly immigration. Period!

CLAIM #4: "Illegal immigrants do the jobs Americans won't do."

RESPONSE: Illegal immigrants do the jobs Americans would do if wages were not artificially depressed.

If Americans can earn more money collecting unemployment or working under the table in the black market, who could really blame them? Illegal aliens, especially from Mexico, come to our country and perform work at significantly lower wages than employers have to pay American citizens. Illegals from Mexico are only too happy to earn three or four dollars per hour under the table when the alternative would be fifty cents per hour in Mexico. It's not that we need illegal aliens to perform jobs most Americans deem beneath themselves to perform. It's that most illegals will perform these jobs at well below free market wage rates.

The open borders business lobby—which primarily consists of the agriculture, fast food, hotel and construction industries—are only too happy to have a steady flow of cheap labor to keep their labor costs as low as possible. Liberal Democratic politicians and even some so-called conservative Republicans have done little to seal our borders and send illegals back to their countries of origin because these undocumented workers represent new sources of union dues and potential votes.

If it were true Americans won't perform certain jobs, then the market would adjust as free markets always do. When labor shortages exist, expanding businesses respond by offering more money to a limited labor pool. Businesses could alternatively purchase new equipment and technology in response to low labor supply. That's how businesses exercise rational behavior in response to external economic conditions.

Condoning and even rewarding the intentional breaking of our immigration laws by granting illegals amnesty, temporary worker permits or U.S. driver's licenses, will only encourage others in Mexico to enter our country illegally and further depress wages.

President Bush says his plan "will match willing workers with willing employees." Yet, since there are no limits placed on the number of willing employees, isn't it reasonable to assume there would also not be any limits on the number of willing workers who would flood the borders to fill many more millions of jobs at lower wages?

Illegal immigrants impose significant costs to the economy. The Federation for American Immigration Reform concluded that illegal aliens cost the State of California alone $10.5 billion annually, or about $1,200 per year for every native born family. That's $7.7 billion to educate the children of illegals (15 percent of K-12 enrollment), $1.4 billion for illegals' health care and the same amount to incarcerate alien lawbreakers.[6]

CLAIM #5: "The economy would be harmed without the steady flow of cheap illegal immigrant labor."

RESPONSE: Illegal immigration is draining our economy.

That's because illegals use considerably more government services—including health care, education, social security and welfare—and most don't pay income taxes. Illegal aliens used ten billion dollars more in government services than they paid in taxes in 2002, according to the Center for Immigration Studies (CIS) in a report entitled *The High Cost of Cheap Labor: Illegal Immigration and the Federal Budget.*

Based on data taken from the Census Bureau, the study concluded, "Illegal alien households on average are estimated to use $2,700 a year more in services than they pay in taxes, creating a total fiscal burden of nearly $10.4 billion on the federal budget in 2002.

CIS's study estimated that in 2002, illegals cost: Medicaid an additional $2.5 billion; health care and hospitals $2.2 billion; food assistance programs $1.9 billion; education expenses $1.4 billion; not to mention putting an additional $1.6 billion strain on the federal and prison court systems.

The study adds that nearly two-thirds of illegals don't have their high school diploma, meaning even if they were granted amnesty, they would still be an unskilled workforce, not paying much in taxes, but using more government services.[7]

CLAIM #6: "We are a nation of immigrants. Preventing those seeking economic opportunity from entering our country, even those who cross the border illegally, is immoral and contrary to what we stand for as Americans."

RESPONSE: The United States is a nation of laws.

Conservative Republicans support legal immigration and recognize the importance of fostering a diverse nation of productive citizens.

However, illegal immigration sets a precedent for breaking the law. We are a nation of laws. Our whole system of self-government is contingent upon the underpinnings of the rule of law. We should protect those immigrants who come to this country legally and follow the letter and spirit of the law. When people from other countries break our laws with hubris and impunity and are not punished, then the rule of law becomes meaningless, useless and weak.

Rewarding lawbreakers and giving taxpayer funds to those who break the law is immoral and unethical at its very core. Immigration has been vital to the success of our great nation. To ensure it continues, immigration must be conducted in an orderly, controlled and legal fashion, upholding the rule of law equally so our country's security is in no way threatened by undocumented aliens. The federal government has a constitutional responsibility to "protect and defend the borders" of our country from foreign attack. Anybody not legally entering our country is, in essence, breaking federal law and should be considered an enemy of the United States of America.

In order to help secure the American Dream for all new American citizens, we must ensure they learn our language and history with special emphasis on the Declaration of Independence and the U.S. Constitution.

It's unfair to penalize immigrants who wait for years to enter our nation *legally* while we silently condone and pardon others who have *illegally* cut in line ahead of them.

We are, in essence, rewarding law-breakers while penalizing those who abide by the letter of the law. While we should take pride in our rich ethnic and cultural diversity which is America, we must ensure our immigration policies are based on the rule of law and not politically correct whim and caprice.

CLAIM #7: "America is a multi-cultural nation which is good for society."

RESPONSE: America is an aggregation of people from around the world who come from different cultures to form a nation of laws.

However, America is not a nation of different cultures. America is a nation of laws. We accept people from all over the world from different countries and cultures with the expectation that they assimilate to the American culture and family. What makes our country unique is that we value other ethnic cultures and celebrate them. However, we don't place foreign cultures above our own uniquely American culture. We pledge allegiance to the United States of America that is "one nation under God… indivisible with liberty and justice for all."

Chapter 25

Y is for Yankee Doodle Founding Fathers:

They Really Got It Right

Claims:

1. "The Founding Fathers were aristocratic, slave owning white male racists who only paid lip service to the 'equality of all men' by virtue of the fact that blacks used to only count for three-fifths of a person."

2. "America's founders such as Jefferson, Paine, Washington, and Franklin were enlightenment humanists and Deists not Evangelical Christians."

3. "Thomas Jefferson, who favored the separation of church and state, was a moving force behind the creation of the Bill of Rights and a primary authority on the First Amendment."

4. "The Founders didn't intend the Constitution to be a religious document founded on Judeo-Christian principles."

In the second floor parlor of a house in Philadelphia during June 1776, thirty-three-year-old Thomas Jefferson wrote, edited and re-edited his manuscript.

While he worked, a British invasion force headed for New York Harbor, eager to squash whatever ideas of rebellion and independence their fledgling thirteen-state colony was dreaming up.

Within weeks, Jefferson had a finished document.

"In Congress, July 4, 1776," it began in large letters across the top. "The unanimous Declaration of the thirteen United States of America."

More than just a piece of parchment, the Declaration of

Independence was so profound in its simplicity that it has inspired millions of people down through the centuries to rise up against oppression.

"When in the Course of human Events, it becomes necessary for one People to dissolve the Political Bands which have connected them with another and to assume among the Powers of the Earth, the separate and equal Station to which the Laws of Nature and of Nature's God entitle them..."

In Jefferson's neat handwriting, the words which had been discussed, approved and embellished by members of that first Congress, came together. People weren't to be judged by their rank or birth, but by their talent, hard work and ability.

"We hold these Truths to be self-evident, that all Men are created equal, that they are endowed by their Creator with certain unalienable Rights, that among these are Life, Liberty and the Pursuit of Happiness..."

John Hancock signed first. Fifty-five of America's Founding Fathers followed his lead, putting their names to the Declaration of Independence. With the strokes of their pens, they changed the course of history.

"We have it in our power to begin the world over again. A situation, similar to the present, hath not happened since the days of Noah until now. The birthday of a new world is at hand," Thomas Paine had written earlier that year.

Eleven years later, the war with Britain won, delegates met again in Philadelphia to revise the Articles of Confederation—and draft America's Constitution, penning those immortal words, "We the People of the United States, in Order to form a more perfect Union, establish Justice, insure domestic Tranquility, provide for the common defense, promote the general Welfare and secure the Blessings of Liberty to ourselves and our Posterity, do ordain and establish this Constitution for the United States of America..."

In an effort to advance their "progressive" agenda, the liberal left has attempted to demonstrate that our founding documents are constantly evolving documents which are outmoded. Many on the left claim the men responsible for writing them were not necessarily the Bible following benevolent men many believe them to be. Since increasing numbers of activist liberal judges seek to impose their ideological leftist agenda on America via judicial fiat—usurping the law-making responsibilities of the legislative branch of government—it's vital that Americans understand the truth about our Founding Fathers and the documents they wrote.

> **CLAIM #1**: "The Founding Fathers were aristocratic, slave-owning, white male racists who only paid lip service to the 'equality of all men' by virtue of the fact that blacks used to only count for three-fifths of a person."
>
> **RESPONSE**: While slavery was a dark spot on American history, it was the United States that abolished slavery.

The Founders differed in their opinions of slavery, but it was ultimately Republican President Abraham Lincoln who ended slavery.

Today, slavery is still practiced in parts of Africa and other countries. Where are the calls from Jesse Jackson and the NAACP to end slavery in Africa and other parts of the world?

James Madison, the primary author of the Constitution, vehemently opposed slavery and stated at the 1787 Constitutional Convention, "We have seen the mere distinction of colour made in the most enlightened period of time, a ground of the most oppressive dominion ever exercised by men over men."

In a separate letter, he wrote to Francis Wright on September 1, 1825, "The magnitude of this evil (slavery) among us is so deeply felt and so universally acknowledged; that no merit could be greater than that of devising a satisfactory remedy for it."

The issue of slavery was a tricky political issue which took some time to end. Although some of the Founding Fathers were wealthy aristocrats, it was primarily the money these wealthy men risked to secure the blessings of liberty and prosperity which would eventually end slavery in the coming years.

The Constitution's framers in Philadelphia faced a difficult dilemma with how to abolish slavery outright because for millennia it had been accepted in so many societies throughout the world. The Founders had to maintain the central premise of the Declaration that governments derive their legitimacy from the consent of the governed. Even though a great many of the Founders were opposed to slavery on moral grounds, the democratic process still had to be preserved and maintained.

Because the slave population was so large, the delegates in the North came up with the "Three-Fifths Compromise," counting blacks as only three-fifths of a person to limit the South's political representation in Congress and ensure an anti-slavery majority.

The compromise merely enabled the Founders to maintain the core principles of the democratic process outlined in our founding documents, without giving any moral approval of the practice itself. Without maintaining the democratic process, slavery would not have been able to be outlawed by that very same democratic process.[1]

CLAIM #2: "America's founders such as Thomas Jefferson, Thomas Paine, George Washington and Benjamin Franklin were enlightenment humanists and deists, not evangelical Christians."

RESPONSE: The vast majority of the signers of the Declaration and Constitution were strong practicing Christians, not secular humanists.

Fifty-two of the 56 signers of the Declaration of Independence were Christians.

Deists are those who believe in God, but don't define Him with sacred texts or organized religion. Ben Franklin was the only Deist who signed the Constitution, but he was also a devout Christian who called for public prayer and tithed to all denominations.[2]

Thomas Jefferson said, "I am a real Christian, that is to say, a disciple of the doctrine of Jesus."[3] He referred to himself as a Christian and was probably a Unitarian, not a Deist.

Jefferson "believed in the creative, sovereign and superintending God of Scripture," according to journalist M. Stanton Evans.[4]

Jefferson did pen the first draft of the Declaration of Independence, but the document was not entirely reflective of his unique individual beliefs.

"Neither aiming at originality of principles or sentiment, nor yet copied from any particular or previous writing, it was intended to be an expression of the American mind," he wrote.[5]

Members of that first Congress made more than 80 changes to Jefferson's original draft and deleted nearly 500 words.

"No nation has ever existed or been governed without religion. Nor can be," said Jefferson when he was president. "The Christian religion is the best religion that has ever been given to man and I as chief Magistrate of this nation am bound to give it the sanction of my example."[6]

In a ten-year study analyzing 15,000 political writings of the founding era (1760-1805), 34 percent of direct source quotations were from the Bible—four times as many as philosophers Baron de Montesquieu and Sir William Blackstone, who were thought to be secularists.[7] Yet Montesquieu and Blackstone were both strong Christians.

Montesquieu wrote *The Spirit of Laws* which stated God was the primary source of all law.[8] Blackstone wrote *Commentaries on the Laws of England* which served as the primary legal source for American lawyers in the early days of the Republic. He believed all law was derived from the God of the Bible.

"The doctrines thus delivered we call the revealed of divine law and they are to be found only in the Holy Scriptures," Blackstone wrote. "Upon these two foundations, the law of nature and law of [biblical] revelation, depend all human laws; that is to say, no human law should be suffered to contradict these."[9]

According to author and historian David Barton, the basis of the Declaration was John Locke's book *Two Treatises of Civil Government*, which quotes the Bible 1,700 times.[10]

Some have claimed Locke was a Deist, but James Wilson, one of the original signers of the Declaration and one of the original Supreme Court justices, rebutted the claim, saying Locke was "one of the most sincere and most amiable assertors of Christianity and true philosophy…"[11]

George Washington was not a Deist. He was a dedicated Christian who served as a vestryman in the Episcopal Church and who publicly promoted the Christian faith. Washington wrote a twenty-four-page prayer book called the *Daily Sacrifice* in which he prays directly to his Lord and Savior Jesus Christ.

John Marshall who served as Chief Justice of the Supreme Court from 1801 to 1835 said of Washington, "Without making ostentatious professions of religion, he was a sincere believer in the Christian faith and a truly devout man."

Washington himself said, "True religion affords to government its surest support."[12]

Alexander Hamilton, who was one of the three authors of the *Federalist Papers* which provided a defense of the principles of the Constitution was not a Deist. He was a devout Christian. With the aid of Reverend James Bayard, Hamilton formed the Christian Constitutional Society whose goals were "the support of the Christian religion" and "support for the United States."[13]

James Madison, the "Father of the Constitution" and fourth president of the United States, who spoke 161 times at the Constitutional Convention, was not a Deist. He was a devout Christian. Madison stated, "Religion [is] the basis and foundation of Government."[14]

John Jay, the third author of the *Federalist Papers* and first Supreme Court Chief Justice was not a secular Deist. He, too, was a committed Christian.

He said on October 12, 1816, "Providence has given to our people the choice of their rulers and it is the duty, as well as the privilege and interest of our Christian nation to select and prefer Christians for their rulers."[15]

John Adams was not a secular Deist. He was a strong Christian and said, "We have no government armed with the power capable of contending with human passions unbridled by morality and religion... Our Constitution was made only for a moral and religious people. It is wholly inadequate for the government of any other."[16]

CLAIM #3: "Thomas Jefferson, who favored the separation of church and state, was a moving force behind the creation of the Bill of Rights and a primary authority on the First Amendment."

RESPONSE: Jefferson himself denied any significant involvement in drafting either the Constitution or Bill of Rights.

Jefferson was ambassador in France when the Constitution was framed and only provided vague direction with regard to the drafting of the Bill of Rights.

"One passage in the paper you enclosed me must be corrected. It is the following, 'And all say it was yourself more than any other individual, that planned and established it,' i.e. the Constitution. I was in Europe when the Constitution was planned and never saw it till after it was established," Jefferson wrote to Dr. Joseph Priestly in a June 19th, 1802 letter.[17]

Since Jefferson was not present when the Constitution and First Amendment were drafted and ratified, the specifics of what he may or may not have intended for the document are primarily hearsay and subject to interpretation.[18]

Thomas Jefferson's statement regarding a wall of separation between church and state was made in a personal and private letter on January 1, 1802, written to the Danbury Baptist Association of Connecticut (13 years after the First Amendment was debated in the first congressional session of 1789). The Baptists had heard rumors Congregationalism was going to become the national religion and were quite alarmed since most had fled from the persecution of the state-established church of England. Jefferson merely assuaged their fears by assuring the Baptists the U.S. government would not establish any type of state-sponsored religion such as the "Church of the United States."

The words Jefferson used on that occasion actually acknowledged the first amendment rights, "I contemplate with sovereign reverence that act of the whole American people which declared that their Legislature should 'make no law respecting an establishment of religion, or prohibiting the free exercise thereof,' thus building a wall of separation between Church and State."[19]

Historians have concluded the reason Jefferson chose the words "separation of church and state" was to establish common ground with the Baptists to whom he was addressing. Jefferson actually borrowed the words from Roger Williams, a very prominent Baptist preacher at the time. Initially Williams had used the term "wall." However the meaning of this term was understood to be one-directional in that the "wall's" ultimate purpose was to protect the church from the state.

The people who escaped religious persecution in England under King George desired freedom *of* religion, not, as the left often claims, freedom *from* religion. This distinction is vital in understanding the intent of the Founders and the true meaning and nature of the establishment clause of the First Amendment.[20]

Jefferson wrote a letter to Dr. Benjamin Rush several months after the Danbury letter to further reveal the true nature and intent of his address to the Danbury Baptists.

"My views…are the result of a life of inquiry and reflection and very different from the anti-Christian system imputed to me by those who know nothing of my opinions," he wrote. "To the corruption of Christianity I am, indeed, opposed; but not to the genuine precepts of Jesus himself. I am a Christian in the only sense in which He wished anyone to be; sincerely attached to His doctrines in preference to all others."[21]

Jefferson was not in favor of removing religion from government. When he was Governor of Virginia, he decreed a day of "public and solemn thanksgiving and prayer to Almighty God."[22]

In 1798, at the occasion of the Kentucky Revolution, Jefferson wrote, "no power over the freedom of religion, freedom of speech, or freedom of the press [was] delegated to the United States by the Constitution nor prohibited by it to the States."[23]

During his presidency, he chaired the school board for the District of Columbia, where he used the Bible and Isaac Watts' Hymnal as the books to teach reading to students.

As president, he signed bills which appropriated financial support for chaplains in Congress and in the armed services as well as signing the Articles of War in which he "earnestly recommended to all officers and soldiers, diligently to attend divine services."[24]

While those on the left assert Jefferson should be considered the authority on the Constitution and the First Amendment, it is vital to consider the Founders who actually were present and directly involved in the drafting and ratification of the Constitution and Bill of Rights. They are far more relevant and legitimate spokesmen for those documents.

Consider George Washington, Fisher Ames of Massachusetts and Governor Morris of Pennsylvania. Washington was the president of the Constitutional Convention where the Constitution was initially framed and was primarily responsible for monitoring the formation of the Bill of Rights. Washington never used the term "separation of church and state" in any of his writings or public speeches.

In fact, in his Farewell Address, he advocated the inclusion of religious principles in governmental and national policies, "Of all the dispositions and habits which lead to political prosperity, religion and morality are indispensable supports...And let us with caution indulge the supposition that morality can be maintained without religion. Whatever may be conceded to the influence of refined education on minds...reason and experience both forbid us to expect that national morality can prevail in exclusion of religious principle."[25]

Fisher Ames, on September 20, 1789, provided the wording of the First Amendment which was passed by the House of Representatives. If anyone should be considered an authority regarding the First Amendment, it should be Fisher Ames. Yet he never used the term "separation of church and state" in any of his writings or public speeches. He did, however, advocate the Bible should be the primary textbook in America's classrooms.

"Why...should not the Bible regain the place it once held as a school book?" Ames wrote. "Its morals are pure, its examples captivating and noble. The reverence for the sacred book that is thus early impressed in infancy, never takes firm hold of the mind."[26]

Governor Morris, the most active member of the Constitutional Convention, spoke 173 times on the floor of the Convention and is the man who authored the Constitution. Morris synthesized all disparate and diverse ideas from the Convention floor and formed them into the language which now appears in the document. He, too, must be considered an "authority" who knew the Constitution's "intent." Yet Morris never used the term "separation of church and state" in either his own writings or speeches. In contrast, he states religious principles form the basis for morality and must be included in education.

"Religion is the only solid basis of good morals," Morris wrote. "Therefore education should teach the precepts of religion and the duties of man towards God."[27]

The Founders were clear the U.S. government would never have the legal right to establish any state-sponsored religion. It's clear from the annals of history that one of the primary motivations of the original settlers was to escape religious persecution which confronted them in England.

The Founders who drafted our earliest documents—the Mayflower Compact, the Declaration of Independence and the U.S. Constitution—were God-fearing men who understood that a system of self-government would be dependent upon the virtue of the people. They recognized virtue was based upon the morality which was taught from the Bible.

The words the Founders chose and our earliest documents reflect their belief that God-given "natural rights" were the very basis of our constitutional republic.

In the Declaration of Independence, the Founders used the term "unalienable" rights.

"We hold these truths to be self-evident, that all men are created equal, that they are endowed by their Creator with certain *unalienable Rights,* that among these are Life, Liberty and the pursuit of Happiness..."

Unalienable rights are those which man can neither grant nor take away. Unalienable rights are rights each individual is born with. These rights are their birthright! Since our legal rights emanate from God and are predicated upon "natural law," then how can an argument be made that, there must be a separation of church (God and the Bible) and state (our courts, schools and government bodies) if the very laws which govern these institutions are based on God-given natural law?

Consider evidence to the contrary. Lincoln in his Gettysburg Address said, "… this nation under God shall have a new birth of freedom and that government of the people, by the people and for the people shall not perish from the earth."

The Pilgrims' Mayflower Compact read, "Having undertaken, for the glory of God and the advancement of the Christian Faith and honor of our King and country, a voyage to plant the first colony in the northern parts of Virginia."

The New Hampshire Constitution, written in 1776, reads, "That morality and piety, rightly grounded on evangelical principles, would give the best and greatest security to government...therefore the legislature is empowered to adopt measures for the support and maintenance of public Christian teachers of piety, religion and morality."

William Penn, the founder of Pennsylvania, said, "If we will not be governed by God, we must be governed by tyrants."

Benjamin Rush, a signer of the Declaration of Independence, wrote, "Let the children...be instructed in the principles and obligations of the Christian religion. This is the most essential part of education. The great enemy of the salvation of man, in my opinion, never invented a more effectual means of extirpating Christianity from the world than by persuading mankind that it was improper to read the Bible at schools."

Noah Webster, who was a translator of the Bible wrote, "Almost all the civil liberty now enjoyed in the world owes its origin to the principles of the Christian religion...The religion which has introduced civil liberty, is the religion of Christ and his apostles...This is genuine Christianity and to this we owe our free constitution and government."

The Pledge of Allegiance (with "under God" added by an Act of Congress 1954) states, "I pledge allegiance to the flag of the United States of America and to the republic for which it stands, one nation under God, indivisible, with liberty and justice for all."

"In God We Trust" is the motto on all of our paper currency by an Act of Congress in 1955 and chosen as our national motto by an Act of Congress in 1956.

The inscription on the top of the Liberty Bell comes from the Bible, Leviticus 25:10, "Proclaim liberty throughout the land and to all the inhabitants thereof."

John Adams said, "The general principles on which the Fathers achieved independence were the general principles of Christianity."

Adams later told his wife Abigail that the Fourth of July marking the Declaration of Independence, "ought to be commemorated as the day of deliverance by solemn acts of devotion to God Almighty." In other words, Adams wanted the Fourth of July to be primarily a religious holiday.

John Quincy Adams, in 1837 while addressing a Fourth of July crowd in Newburyport, Massachusetts, asked, "Is not that the Declaration of Independence first organized the social compact on the foundation of the Redeemer's mission upon earth? That it laid the cornerstone of human government upon the first precepts of Christianity?"

Adams also wrote, "On the Fourth of July, the Founders simply took the precepts of Christ, which came into the world through His birth and incorporated those principles into civil government."

Does this sound like the Founders set up a government, which was intended to build a wall of separation between church and state?

CLAIM #4: "The Founders didn't intend the Constitution to be a religious document founded on Judeo-Christian principles."

RESPONSE: In fact, the Bible was the primary source behind the writing of the U.S. Constitution.

Thirty-four percent of all citations came from the Bible, which represented the most often quoted source.

Sixty percent of all the quotes came from the men who used the Bible to form their conclusions.

Ninety-four percent of all the quotes used by the Founding Fathers came from the Bible.

For example, Isaiah 33:22 reads, "For the Lord is our judge, the Lord is our lawgiver and the Lord is our king..." This passage was the basis for the three major branches of our government: judicial, legislative and executive.

The Founders knew since man is corrupt by nature that the government must be set up with these three divisions of "checks and balances" to avoid the tyranny which could result from consolidating power in a single authority (such as a king in a monarchy).

"God grant that in America true religion and civil liberty may be inseparable and that unjust attempts to destroy the one may in the issue tend to the support and establishment of both," wrote John Witherspoon, a signer of the Declaration, president of Princeton University and huge advocate for religious freedom.[28]

Witherspoon's comments are a mirror of how the Founding Fathers planned for religion to be an integral part of our society as well as the basis for our government and laws.

Chapter 26

Z is for Zealot Terrorists:

How Can We Fight Them?

Claims:

1. "The Patriot Act violates civil liberties."
2. "Section 215 of the Patriot Act means the 'thought police' can target individuals for what they choose to read or websites they visit, which violates the First and Fourth Amendments."
3. "The Patriot Act expands terrorism laws to include 'domestic terrorism' that subjects political organizations to wiretapping, surveillance, harassment, and criminal actions for political advocacy."
4. "Section 213 of the Patriot Act entitled 'Authority for Delaying Notice of the Execution of a Warrant,' also known as the 'sneak and peak' section, gives federal agents the ability to enter and search your home without any probable cause."
5. "There is no accountability in the Patriot Act."
6. "You can't profile at airports and single out only individuals resembling the 9/11 hi-jackers since terrorism has also been perpetrated by white males in the past too. Profiling is discriminatory and racist."

Americans have struggled to understand not only *how* zealot Muslim terrorists could attack this country, but *why*.

Terrorism is rooted in a fundamental hatred of Western-style liberal democracy. Those in the Muslim and Arab world who sponsor terrorism against the U.S. and other Western Democracies, such as Israel, are threatened by the values we promote.

In his book *What's So Great About America*, Dinesh D'Souza explains that Islamic countries view the United States as a "subversive idea," which poses a threat to the existence of Islam.[1]

Islam means "submission." In order for Islam to thrive, there must be a total submission to Allah. Since Western-style democracy promotes religious freedom and toleration, radical Islam cannot peacefully co-exist. Therefore terrorism is the weapon that the Islamo-terrorists have chosen to destroy our Westernized free way of life.

Islamo-fascists have declared jihad (holy war) on America and have vowed to destroy our country and our way of life.

Although it's preferable for America to fight the terrorists on their soil, the reality is that terrorist cells exist in our country. In order to combat domestic terrorism by disrupting these terror cells, it's crucial that law enforcement be able to acquire the best intelligence information possible.

Prior to 9/11, the Clinton Administration's Attorney General Janet Reno led the Justice Department to construct a "wall" of separation between intelligence agencies. This "wall" stifled communication and information sharing between criminal intelligence and criminal terror investigators. Before 9/11, if two investigators were pursuing the same terrorist cell in the United States, the intelligence agent couldn't share intelligence information with the criminal agent. Failure to gather terror related intelligence rendered the FBI feckless in thwarting the 9/11 attacks.

Congress overwhelmingly enacted the USA Patriot Act into law (98-1 in the Senate and 357-66 in the House) and removed the major legal barriers which inhibited intelligence, law-enforcement and national defense communities from sharing terror specific intelligence in an effort to combat future terrorist attacks on U.S. soil.[2]

Yet, civil libertarians on the left like the ACLU and some on the libertarian right have complained the Patriot Act and other practices such as terrorist profiling violate individual civil liberties and are unconstitutional.[3]

CLAIM #1: "The Patriot Act violates civil liberties."

RESPONSE: The United States now needs to take extraordinary precautions to prevent another terrorist attack.

Democratic Senator Diane Feinstein of California stated at an oversight hearing in 2003, "I have never had a single abuse of the Patriot Act reported to me. My staff e-mailed the ACLU and asked them for instance of actual abuses. They e-mailed back and said they had none."[4]

Not a single instance of abuse under the Act has been cited by any court, the Congress or the Justice Department's own Inspector General.[5] There have been 1,073 complaints filed with the DOJ's Inspector General. Of those, only 34 complaints appeared to state a claim even remotely related to the Patriot Act and only two of the 34 have been substantiated. Both of these complaints involved verbal taunts of detainees by prison guards.[6]

But that hasn't stopped liberal Democrats from vehemently opposing virtually every section of the Patriot Act, despite the fact that many of it's provisions were already available to investigate organized crime and drug trafficking. Even Democratic Senator Joe Biden, no friend of the Bush administration, explained during the floor debate about the Act in 2001, "The FBI could get a wiretap to investigate the mafia, but they could not get one to investigate terrorists. To put it bluntly, that was crazy!" What's good for the mob should be good for terrorists."[7]

Any discussion of "civil liberty" violations is meaningless in a society which can't adequately defend itself from those who want to annihilate it. If the United States is to win the war on Islamo-fascist terrorism, it's vital all Americans, regardless of political affiliation, understand the main provisions of the USA Patriot Act.

Since 9/11, U.S. intelligence and law enforcement agents, armed with the Patriot Act, have been able to charge more than 360 individuals with terror related crimes and almost 200 have been convicted, sparing thousands and potentially millions of innocent American lives.[8]

Even former Attorney General Janet Reno credited the Patriot Act with updating the law to deal more effectively with terrorists.[9]

Former North Carolina Democratic Senator and Vice-Presidential aspirant John Edwards said about the Patriot Act, "We simply cannot prevail in the battle against terrorism if the right hand of our government has no idea what the left hand is doing."[10]

CLAIM #2: "Section 215 of the Patriot Act means the 'thought police' can target individuals for what they choose to read or websites they visit, which violates the First and Fourth Amendments."

RESPONSE: The Patriot Act specifically protects Americans' First and Fourth Amendment rights.

Under section 215 of the Patriot Act, the FBI is only able to access business or other records upon permission of a federal judge or court (The Foreign Intelligence Surveillance Court). It's highly unlikely that a judge charged with overseeing espionage and counterterrorism investigations would approve a records request because the person wrote an e-mail critical of government policy as groups such as the ACLU have claimed.

Since terrorists and spies have historically used libraries to research, plan and execute activities which pose a threat to national security, the Patriot Act aids investigators in uncovering intelligence information to prevent terrorist attacks.

For example, a grand jury recently served a subpoena on a bookseller to obtain records which demonstrated that a suspect had purchased a book describing how to construct an unusual detonator used in several bombings. This particular evidence was crucial in identifying the suspect as the actual bomber.[11]

Once an individual has disclosed information to someone else, the Constitution no longer protects that information. Once an individual checks out a library book, he forfeits any constitutional protections he may have had with regard to his reading habits. Government has always had the authority to subpoena library records and internet logs without seeking a warrant or any judicial approval at all. Section 215 merely gives anti-terror investigators the same access to such records as criminal grand juries with the added protection of judicial oversight.

Documents under section 215 are not private, which means they're not governed by the Fourth Amendment's warrant requirement. The Supreme Court has long held that records in third party hands enjoy no constitutional privacy protections.[12]

Furthermore, the Congress reviews the government's use of business records under the Act. Every six months the Attorney General has to "fully inform" Congress on how the Act has been implemented. On October 17, 2002, the House Judiciary Committee concluded in a press release that it was satisfied with the Department's use of Section 215: "The Committee's review of classified information related to FISA orders for tangible records, such as library records, has not given rise to any concern that the authority is being misused or abused."[13]

CLAIM #3: "The Patriot Act expands terrorism laws to include 'domestic terrorism' which subjects political organizations to wiretapping, surveillance, harassment and criminal actions for political advocacy."

RESPONSE: Section 802 of the Patriot Act specifically bars targeting political groups which exercise free and peaceful dissent.

Under the Patriot Act, domestic terrorism is limited to conduct that violates criminal laws and endangers human life. Political organizations which don't fit this description will not be subject to the Patriot Act.[14]

CLAIM #4: "Section 213 of the Patriot Act entitled 'Authority for Delaying Notice of the Execution of a Warrant'—also known as the 'sneak and peak' section—gives federal agents the ability to enter and search your home without any probable cause."

RESPONSE: Section 213 does not require investigators to forever conceal they've conducted a

search. It requires notice after a reasonable period of time.

Delayed notice of a search is not a novel "vast expansion of government power," but one which the appellate courts have granted for decades. The Patriot Act merely codifies the authority that law enforcement has had for decades. Courts have long upheld delayed notification search warrants in organized crime, drug and child pornography cases.

The dangers of unnecessary delays in obtaining vital, terror related information was made clear in the Zacarias Moussaoui case. Because of the wall created by the Reno Justice Department, FBI agents were prohibited from searching the al Qaeda operative's computer just weeks prior to 9/11. Had the wall not been erected, terror investigators might have been able to prevent the 9/11 attacks.

In certain cases it's vital that law enforcement be able to delay notification of a search warrant to prevent the criminal from being tipped off, destroying evidence or fleeing.

Section 213 of the Patriot Act only allows the government to delay notice of a terrorism search with the approval of a terrorism court. This provision of the Act is based on longstanding legal precedent which allows the government to delay notice of a search. Section 213 merely codifies this precedent.[15]

It's vital to recognize that section 213 is preemptive. It would be virtually impossible to foil the next terrorist attack if the government was to notify terror cell members that they were under investigation.

The Supreme Court has long held that the Fourth Amendment does not require law enforcement to provide immediate notice of the execution of a search warrant. The Court emphasized in *Dalia* v. *U.S.* in 1979 that "covert entries are constitutional in some circumstances, at least if they are made pursuant to a warrant." In fact, the Court stated that an argument to the contrary was "frivolous."[16]

CLAIM #5: "There's no accountability in the Patriot Act."

RESPONSE: There has never been a time during our history where government has safeguarded

Z IS FOR ZEALOT TERRORISTS: *HOW CAN WE FIGHT THEM?*

the individual rights of aliens, immigrants and enemy-combatant suspects with such great care.

All alleged civil rights abuses by Justice Department employees have to undergo review. Also, a Special Operations Branch staffed by an FBI Special Agent in Charge, two assistant Special Agents in Charge and two investigative specialists has been established to investigate complaints. Moreover, the Justice Department's Civil Rights Division has established the Initiative to Combat Post 9/11 Discriminatory Backlash and a National Origin Working Group.[17]

CLAIM #6: "You can't profile only individuals resembling the 9/11 hijackers. White males have committed terrorism in the past, too. Profiling is discriminatory and racist."

RESPONSE: Muslim males have committed the vast majority of domestic terrorism.

It's possible a white male could potentially commit acts of airline terrorism, but it's not possible to search every passenger entering security.

Muslim males committed: the 1972 Munich Olympic Massacres; the 1979 U.S. Embassy takeover; the 1980s kidnappings in Lebanon; the 1983 U.S. Marine barracks bombing; the 1985 cruise ship Achille Lauro hijacking where terrorists murdered a crippled 70-year old American passenger by throwing him overboard; the 1985 TWA flight 847 hijacking in Athens resulting in the murder of a U.S. Navy officer; the 1998 Pan Am flight 103 bombing; the February 1993 World Trade Center bombing; the 1998 bombings of the U.S. Embassies in Kenya and Tanzania; the 9/11 hijacking of four airliners which were intentionally flown into buildings resulting in the murder of more than 3,000 Americans; the 2002 kidnapping and beheading of *Wall Street Journal* reporter Daniel Pearl; the Beslan School hostage crisis which left 344 dead; the 2004 Madrid train bombings which left 192 dead; the 2005 London Underground bombings which left 50 dead; and the 2006 Bombay train bombings which left 200 dead.

The common denominator in all these terrorist acts has been Muslim males between the ages of 18 and 40. Since we have limited resources at airports, it only makes sense to screen passengers who resemble the physical description of those who have committed almost 100 percent of airline terrorism acts during the last 20 years.

It's absurd to suggest that law enforcement officials disregard physical appearance when attempting to screen airport passengers given the fact that 20 of the 20 hijackers in the 9/11 attacks fit the same physical description.

Even the left-leaning *New York Times* has publicly endorsed racial profiling as a vital tool in the war on terror.

In a lead editorial, the *Times* suggested the 9/11 attacks may have been prevented if airports had used "threat profiling" to screen out Muslim terrorists after receiving a CIA warning in August 2001 that al Qaeda was preparing to hijack U.S. airplanes.

The editorial read, "After receiving that briefing memo entitled 'Bin Laden Determined To Strike in U.S.' Bush should have rushed back from his Crawford ranch and assembled all his top advisors and demanded to know what in particular, was being done to screen airline passengers to make sure people who fit the airlines' threat profiles were being prevented from boarding American planes."[18]

Since the terrorists mentioned in the memo were Middle Eastern radical Muslims, it's reasonable to assume the *Times* endorsed screening passengers of Middle Eastern appearance who "fit the airline profile."

If terrorist profiling is racist, then evidently large majorities of Americans—including African Americans—are racists.

A 2001 Gallup poll concluded that African-Americans are more likely than any racial or ethnic groups to support profiling and tight airport security checks for Arabs and Arab-Americans. The poll results, reported in *The Boston Globe* September 30, 2001, showed 71 percent of blacks—versus 57 percent of whites—believe Arabs and Arab-Americans should "undergo special, more intensive security checks before boarding airplanes." John Zogby, president and CEO of Zogby International and an Arab-American, obtained similar results in a poll he conducted.[19]

Another *Boston Globe* article about the Zogby and Gallup polls reported, " A majority of Americans now support ethnic profiling measures aimed at Arab-Americans, and a significant minority now views Arabs in the United States even more poorly than they did before Sept. 11, when a majority of Americans already associated Arabs with terrorism."[20]

A 2001 Fox News Poll showed that nearly 70 percent of respondents support racial profiling as a method of curbing terrorism.[21]

Consideration of someone's physical appearance has been a key component law enforcement has used to identify criminals. If a bank robber is identified as a "hispanic male approximately 30 years of age fleeing the scene in a red Corvette" it's only logical to assume that such a physical description of the assailant will be used to alert other law enforcement officials and citizens. The notion of intentionally disregarding physical descriptions in criminal investigations is preposterous.

Since all of the 9/11 terrorists were Middle Eastern males, it's only logical to assume that paying more attention to Middle Eastern males as opposed to 70-year-old Asian grandmothers is in the best national security interests of our country and overall safety for airline travelers in general.

Of course, when profiling for potential terrorists, if anyone else displays suspicious behavior such as being fidgety, nervous or has indirect eye contact, then security should take extra precautions to screen those passengers—even if they don't resemble Middle Eastern males. The job of airport security should be to determine who are the most suspicious and likely potential terrorist threats. Common sense must transcend political correctness when it comes to screening airline passengers in an effort to ensure the safety and security of Americans.

If the FBI received credible intelligence that eight Middle Eastern males were planning to hijack four planes in the United States on a certain date, wouldn't it be reasonable to assume security would "profile" by checking all Middle Eastern males?

Consider the alternative. If after receiving the same warning, security failed to "profile," but instead continued to just randomly search little old ladies, the likelihood of preventing the planned hijackings would be dramatically reduced since security checks would be "random" instead of specifically focused on Muslim males.

"Thus searches should not be 'random' but deliberate," wrote

James Q. Wilson, Ronald Reagan Professor of Public Policy at Pepperdine University, and Heather Higgins, vice president of the Independent Women's Forum, in a *Wall Street Journal* article. "The profile should not be based exclusively on race, but on hints—that is, useful stereotypes based on judgments made by rational people...The more we study terrorists the more we will learn about them and the better our screening profiles—our stereotypes—will become. If we apply that knowledge, fewer innocent people will face any burden and more real terrorists will be caught. We will overcome slogans about 'racial profiling' and instead become a bit safer."[22]

If the government can sanction legalized discrimination (i.e. race based preferences) in the name of "diversity," then they can surely sanction consideration of race as one component of terrorist profiling in the name of national security.

Endnotes

Chapter 1
A is for Abortion: A Woman's Right to Choose Murder?

1. Gallup Poll, 21 January 2001.
2. Janice Shaw Crouse, Ph.D., "Unsafe, Deadly & Legal: On Abortion 30 Years After *Roe v. Wade*," *Touchstone: A Journal of Mere Christianity*, January/February 2003, pp. 15-16.
3. Janet E. Gans Epner, Ph.D., et al., "Late Term Abortion," *Journal of the American Medical Association*, Vol. 280, No. 26 (August 1998), pp. 724-729.
4. Catherina Hurlburt, *Christ Hospital Attempts to Save Face: New Policy Announced, But Old Habits Continue* (Washington, DC: Concerned Women for America, 22 October 1999), <http://www.cwfa.org/articledisplay.asp?id=1410&department=CWA&categoryid=life>.
5. David C. Reardon, Ph.D., *Aborted Women: Silent No More* (Westchester, IL: Crossway Books, 1987), p. 96.
6. National Center on Child Abuse and Neglect (Department of Health, Education and Welfare), *National Analysis of Official Child Abuse and Neglect Reporting: 1977* (Washington, DC: U.S. Department of Health and Human Services, Administration for Children and Families, Clearinghouse on Child Abuse and Neglect Information, 1979).
7. Philip G. Ney, M.D., "Relationships Between Abortion and Child Abuse," *Canadian Journal of Psychiatry*, Vol. 24, pp. 610-620.
8. Ney, pp. 610-620.
9. Antonio J. Ferreira, "The Pregnant Woman's Emotional Attitude and its Reflection in the Newborn," *American Journal of Orthopsychiatry*, Vol. 30, July 1960, pp. 553-561.
10. Paul Cameron, Ph.D., et al., "How Much Do Mothers Love Their Children," paper presented to Rocky Mountain Psychological Association, 12 May 1972. Indexed in *Research in Education*, ERIC/ECE, 1976.
11. Philip Elmer-Dewitt, "A Bitter Pill to Swallow," *Time Magazine*, Vol. 135, No. 9, 26 February 1990, p. 94.
12. Carol Everett, "A Walk Through An Abortion Clinic," *About Issues Magazine*, August-September 1991, p. 117.
13. Vanderbilt Students for Life, *Abortionists Speak: Personal Stories: Carol Everett*, (Nashville, TN: Vanderbilt University, 2005), <http://www.vanderbilt.edu/SFL/carol_everett.htm>.

14. James Tunstead Burtchaell, *Rachel Weeping and Other Essays About Abortion* (Kansas City, KS: Andrews & McMeel, 1982), p. 34.
15. Gloria Williamson, "The Conversion of Kathy Sparks," *Christian Herald*, January 1986, p. 28.
16. Bernard Nathanson, M.D., "Deeper into Abortion," *New England Journal of Medicine*, November 1974, p. 1189.
17. Marilee C. Allen, M.D., et al., "The Limit of Viability," *New England Journal of Medicine*, Vol. 329, No. 22, 25 November 1993, pp. 1597-1601.
18. Mona Z. Browne, "19-Week-Early Preemie Wins Life Struggle," *Miami Herald*, 4 October 1985, p. A1.
19. Dorian Friedman, "A Nation of Significant Change," *U.S. News & World Report*, 14 August 1995, p. 9.
20. Associated Press, "France Hopes Incentives Will Keep Birth Rate From Falling" *Minneapolis Star Tribune*, 22 September 2005.
21. William D. Montalbano, "Italians' Baby Boom Goes Bust," *Los Angeles Times*, 24 June 1994, pp. A1, A6.
22. Montalbano, pp. A1, A6.
23. Paul E. Waggoner, *How Much Land Can Ten Billion People Spare for Nature?*, (Ames, IA: Council for Agricultural Science and Technology, Task Force Report, No. 121, February 1994).
24. Mary Calderone, M.D., "Illegal Abortion as a Public Health Problem," *American Journal of Public Health*, July 1960, Vol. 50, No. 7, pp. 948-54. Dr. Calderone is founder of Sexuality Information and Education Council of the United States (SIECUS) and medical director for Planned Parenthood Federation of America.
25. Bernard Nathanson, M.D., *Aborting America: The Case Against Abortion* (New York: Pinnacle Books, 1979), p. 193.
26. National Center for Health Statistics, (Hyattsville, MD: U.S. Department of Health and Human Services, Centers for Disease Control and Prevention, 2004).
27. U.S. Vital Statistics, (Hyattsville, MD: U.S. Department of Health and Human Services, Centers for Disease Control and Prevention, 2004).
28. Calderone, pp. 948-954.
29. U.S. Vital Statistics, 2004.
30. William Robert Johnston, *Abortion Statistics and Other Data*, September 2005, <http://www.johnstonsarchive.net/policy/abortion/ab-poland.html>.
31. Milka Gissler, et al. "Pregnancy-Associated Deaths in Finland 1987-1994: Definition Problems and Benefits of Record Linkage," *Acta Obstetrica et Gynecologica Scandinavica*, Vol 76, 1997, pp. 651-657.
32. Brenda Major, et al., "Psychological Responses of Women After First-Trimester Abortions," *Archives of General Psychology*, Vol. 57, August 2000, pp. 777-784.
33. Weijin Zhou, M.D., et al., "Induced Abortion and Low Birth Weight in the Following Pregnancy," *International Journal of Epidemiology*, Vol. 29, January 2000, pp. 100-106.

34. Ann Aschengrau Levin, M.D., "Association of Induced Abortion with Subsequent Pregnancy Loss," *Journal of American Medical Association*, Vol. 243, No. 24, 1980, pp. 2495-2499.

35. Kenneth Schultz, et al., "Measures to Prevent Cervical Injury During Suction Cutterage Abortion," *The Lancet*, Vol. 28 May 1983, pp. 1182-1184.

36. Joel Brind, Ph.D., et al., "Induced Abortion as an Independent Risk Factor for Breast Cancer: A Comprehensive Review and Meta-Analysis," *Journal of Epidemiology and Community Health*, Vol. 50, 1996, pp. 481-496.

37. Katrina Armstrong, M.D., et al., "Assessing the Risk of Breast Cancer," *New England Journal of Medicine*, Vol. 342, No. 8, 2000, pp. 564-571.

38. David C. Reardon, et al., "Abortion and Subsequent Substance Abuse," *American Journal of Drug and Alcohol Abuse* Vol. 26, No. 1, 2000, pp. 61-75.

39. Brenda Major, et al., "Psychological Responses of Women After First Trimester Abortions," *Archives of General Psychology*, Vol. 57, August 2000, pp. 777-784.

40. Hanna Soderberg, M.D., Ph.D., et al., "Emotional Distress Following Induced Abortion: A Study of its Incidence and Determinants Among Abortees in Malno, Sweden," *European Journal of Obstetrics & Gynecology and Reproductive Biology*, Vol. 79, No. 2, 1998, pp. 173-178.

41. Christopher Morgan, "Mental Health May Deteriorate as a Direct Effect of Induced Abortion," *British Medical Journal*, Vol. 314, 1997, p. 902.

42. The Physicians' Ad Hoc Coalition for Truth, public statement, September 1996.

43. David Brown, "Head of Abortion Group Admits Lying in Interview," *Washington Post*, 27 February 1997, p. A4.

44. Gloria Steinem interview, *USA Today*, 1985.

45. "'Jane Roe' Recants Rape Claim," *Washington Post*, 9 September 1987, p. D10.

46. David Mall & Walter F. Watts, eds., *The Psychological Aspects of Abortion* (Washington, DC: University Publications of America, 1979), p. 58.

47. Sandra Mahkorn, M.D. & William Dolan, M.D., "Sexual Assault and Pregnancy," *New Perspectives on Human Abortion*, eds. Thomas Hilgers, M.D., et al, (Frederick, MD: Aletheia Books, 1981), pp.182-199; and Sandra Mahkorn, M.D., "Pregnancy and Sexual Assault," *The Psychological Aspects of Abortion*, eds. David Mall & Walter F. Watts, (Washington, DC: University Publications of America, 1979), pp. 53-72.

48. John Hart Ely, "The Wages of Crying Wolf: A Comment on *Roe v. Wade*," *Yale Law Journal*, Vol. 82, No. 5, April 1973, p. 920-949.

Chapter 2
Bill Clinton: Sex, Lies, and Blind Devotees

1. [Editorial], *Wall Street Journal*, 25 March 2002, p. A18.

2. Rich Lowery, *Legacy: Paying the Price for the Clinton Years* (Washington, DC: Regnery Publishing, 2003).
3. United States Department of Commerce, 2004.
4. "Doctor Quizzed in Death of McDougal," *Fort Worth Star Telegram*, 16 September 1998, p. 1 Metro.
5. Sari Horwitz and John W. Fountain, "Coffee Shop a Fateful Stop on Three Career Paths," *The Washington Post*, 13 July 1997, p. A1; and "Full Text: Starbucks Affidavit," *The Washington Post*, 17 March 1999, <http://www.washingtonpost.com/wp-srv/local/daily/march99/affidavit18.htm>.
6. "Once Upon a Time in Arkansas: Foster's Journal," joint production of *Frontline & Nightline*, PBS/WGBH, Boston, MA & ABC News, Washington, DC, 16 January 2001,
<http://www.pbs.org/wgbh/pages/frontline/shows/arkansas/etc/foster.html>.
7. Christopher Ruddy, "Second Expert: Brown's Wound Appeared to be From Gunshot," *Pittsburgh Tribune-Review*, 9 December 1997.
8. Geoff Metcalf, "The Clinton Body-Count," September 2005, <http://www.geoffmetcalf.com/397.html>
9. Metcalf.
10. Metcalf.
11. Metcalf.
12. Metcalf.
13. The Counter Clinton Library, "People Bill Didn't Need to Pardon," 28 January 2004,
<http://www.counterclintonlibrary.com/cgi-data/news/files/8.shtml>
14. Day R. Williams, Esq., "A List of Clinton-Related Deaths," September 2005, <http://www.daywilliams.com/clinton-related_deaths.html>
15. Metcalf.
16. Metcalf.
17. Metcalf.
18. Metcalf.
19. Metcalf.
20. Metcalf.
21. Metcalf.
22. Metcalf.
23. Metcalf.
24. Metcalf.
25. Metcalf.
26. The Paper Source, "Bill Clinton-Related Deaths: The Unfolding Story," September 2005, <http://www.papersourceonline.com/deaths.htm>
27. The Paper Source.
28. The Paper Source.
29. The Paper Source.
30. The Paper Source.
31. The Paper Source.

32. The Paper Source.
33. The Paper Source.
34. The Paper Source.
35. The Paper Source.
36. The Paper Source.

Chapter 3
Separation of Church and State: What Our Constitution Says About Religion

1. David Barton, *The Truth About Thomas Jefferson and the First Amendment*, (Aledo, TX: WallBuilder Press, 1992), <http://www.Wallbuilders.com>
2. Vic Bilson, "Separation of Church and State," *The Jeremiah Project*, 25 June 2000, <http://www.jeremiahproject.com/culture/ch_state.html>.
3. Paul Johnson, *A History of the American People* (New York: Harper Collins, 1997), p. 30.
4. D. James Kennedy and Jerry Newcombe, *What if the Bible Had Never Been Written* (Nashville, TN: Thomas Nelson Publishers, 1998), p. 85.
5. Dr. David C. Gibbs, Jr. with Jerry Newcombe, *One Nation Under God: Ten Things Every Christian Should Know About the Founding of America* (Seminole, FL: The Christian Law Association, 2003), p. 36.
6. Gallup Polling Organization, 2004.
7. David Limbaugh, *Persecution: How Liberals Are Waging War Against Christianity* (Washington, DC: Regnery Publishing, 2003), p. 308.
8. Gary Amos, "The Philosophical and Biblical Perspectives That Shaped the Declaration of Independence," *The Christian and American Law, Christianity's Impact on America's Founding Documents and Future Direction*, ed. H. Wayne House (Grand Rapids, MI: Kregel Publications, March 1998), p. 51.
9. Amos, pp. 53-54.
10. William L. Shirer, *The Rise and Fall of the Third Reich* (New York: Gramercy, 1 June 1994), p. 240.

Chapter 4
D is For Democrats: Why They're Usually Wrong About Everything

1. David Maraniss and Ellen Nakashima, "Gore's Grades Belie Image of Studiousness; His High School Transcripts Are a Lot Like Bush's," *Washington Post*, 19 March 2000, p. A1.
2. Maraniss and Nakashima, p. A1.
3. Maraniss and Nakashima, p. A1.
4. Adam Nagourney, "We Must Go Forward Together: Clinton Team Capitalizes on the Limelight," *USA Today*, 18 January 1993, p. A1.

5. Larry Elder, "If Bush is Dumb...?" *Townhall.com*, 23 July 2005, <http://www.townhall.com/columnists/larryelder/le20050623.shtml>.
6. Larry Elder, "Bush to NAACP: Maybe Next Year," *Human Events*, January 2003.
7. Jeffrey M. Jones, "How Americans Voted," *Gallup News Service*, 5 November 2004; and Marjorie Connelly, "How Americans Voted: A Political Portrait," *The New York Times*, 7 November 2004.
8. Center for Responsive Politics, Federal Election Committee data, 1999-2000.
9. Karl Zinsmeister, "Dem de la Crème" *Wall Street Journal*, 2 September 2004, p. A12.
10. Zinsmeister, p. A12.
11. OpenSecrets.org, "The Big Picture: Top Overall Donors," September 2005, <http://www.opensecrets.org/bigpicture/topcontribs.asp>.
12. OpenSecrets.org, "Party Preferences," September 2005, <http://www.opensecrets.org/pubs/toporgs/party.asp>.
13. OpenSecrets.org, "Top Individual Contributors to 527 Committees," September 2005, <http://www.opensecrets.org/527s/527indivs.asp?>.
14. OpenSecrets.org, "Top Individual Contributors..."

Chapter 5
E is for Economics: Why it Really is About the Economy, Stupid!

1. National Taxpayers Union, "NTU's Taxpayer Friends in the Senate," September 2005, <http://www.ntu.org/main/page.php?PageID=36>; and National Taxpayers Union, "NTU's Taxpayer Friends in the House," September 2005, <http://www.ntu.org/main/page.php?PageID=35>.
2. National Taxpayers Union.
3. Walter Block and Edgar Olsen, eds., *Rent Control, Myth and Realities, International Evidence of the Effects of Rent Control in Six Countries* (Vancouver, BC: Fraser Institute, 1981).
4. William Tucker, *The Excluded Americans: Homelessness and Housing Policies* (Washington, DC: Regnery Gateway, 1990).
5. Paul Niebanck, *Rent Control and the Rental Housing Market in New York City*, (New York: Housing and
Development Administration, Department of Rent and Housing Maintanance, 1968).
6. Block and Olsen.
7. Block and Olsen.
8. Block and Olsen.
9. Michael S. Berliner, "Why Rent Control is Immoral," *Capitalism Magazine*, 29 August 2003; and <http//www.aynrand.org>.
10. Brian M. Riedl, *Ten Common Myths about Taxes, Spending, and Budget Deficits* (Washington, DC: The Heritage Foundation, Backgrounder No. 1660, 13 June 2003), <http://www.heritage.org/Research/Budget/BG1660.cfm>.
11. Riedl.

12. Richard McKenzie, *What Went Right in the 80s* (San Francisco: Pacific Research Institute, 1994).
13. Larry Elder, "Did Reagan Torture Blacks? Exposing the Myths of Reagan's 'Anti-Civil Rights' Record," *Human Events*, 21 June 2004.
14. Elder.
15. Alan Reynolds, "The Real Reagan Record," *National Review Online*, 31 August 1992.
16. Reynolds.
17. Elder.
18. R. Glenn Hubbard, "Tax Cuts Won't Hurt the Surplus," *Wall Street Journal*, 22 August 2001; and Silvia Ardagna, et al, *Fiscal Policy, Profits and Investment* (Cambridge, MA: National Bureau of Economic Research, March 1999, rev. June 2001), <http://www.nber.org/papers/W7207>.
19. Lowell E. Gallaway and Richard K. Vedder, *Government Size and Economic Growth* (Washington, DC: Study prepared for U.S. Congress, Joint Economic Committee, December 1998).
20. Riedl.
21. Thomas Sowell, "Low Taxes Do What?" *Wall Street Journal*, 24 February 2004, p. A18.
22. Sowell, p. A18.
23. Sowell, p. A18.
24. Sowell, p. A18.

Chapter 6
F is for Females: Which Group Really Supports Them?

1. Susan B. Anthony, *The Revolution*, Vol. 4, No. 1, 8 July 1869, p. 4.
2. Anthony, p. 4.
3. Anthony, p. 4.
4. Elizabeth Cady Stanton, *The Revolution*, Vol. 1, No. 5, 5 February 1868, p. 1; and Stanton's personal letter to Julia Ward Howe, 16 October 1873, recorded in Howe's diary, Harvard University Library.
5. Matilda Gage, *The Revolution*, Vol. 1, No. 14, 9 April 1868, pp. 215-216.
6. Matilda Gage, *The Revolution*, Vol. 3, No. 9, 2 September 1869, pp. 138-139.
7. Victoria Claffin Woodhull, *Woodhull's and Claffin's Weekly*, Vol. 2, No. 6, 24 December 1870, p. 4.
8. Caroline Elizabeth Sarah Norton, *Woodhull's and Claffin's Weekly*, 19 November 1870.
9. Victoria Claffin Woodhull, *Evening Standard*, 17 November 1875.
10. Emma Goldman, "The Hypocrisy of Puritanism," *Mother Earth*, 1911.
11. *Feminists for Life*, Winter 1992, Sisterlife edition, <http://feministsforlife.com/text/news/alicepaul.htm>.
12. Michael W. McConnell, "*Roe v. Wade* at 25: Still Illegitimate," *The Wall Street Journal*, 22 January 1998, p. A18.

Chapter 7
G is for Gun Control: Why We Have a Second Amendment

1. Richard Poe, *The Seven Myths of Gun Control: Reclaiming the Truth About Guns, Crime, and the Second Amendment* (Roseville CA: Prima Publishing, 2001), p. 10.
2. Richard E. Gardiner, *The 5th Circuit Court Gets It Right*, Law Enforcement Alliance of America, September 2005, <http://www.leaa.org/Shield%202003/5thcircuitcourt.html>; and National Rifle Association, "Fables, Myths & Other Tall Tales about Gun Laws, Crime and Constitutional Rights: Fable II," September 2005, <http://www.nraila.org/media/misc/fables.htm>.
3. Gardiner.
4. John Ashcroft, "Setting the Record Straight," *America's 1st Freedom*, July 2001, p. 37.
5. Ashcroft, p. 37.
6. Ashcroft, p. 37.
7. Poe, pp. 94-103.
8. Poe, pp. 72-74.
9. Poe, pp. 18-22.
10. FBI data on gun related crimes and survey research on gun ownership.
11. Poe, pp. 193-203.
12. Poe, p. 20.
13. Data on file at the Metropolitan Police Department of the District of Columbia.
14. National Archive of Criminal Justice Data, *Chicago Homicide Dataset: Homicides in Chicago, 1965-1995* (Washington, DC: National Archive of Criminal Justice Data, September 2005), <http://www.icpsr.umich.edu/NACJD/SDA/chd95d.html>.
15. National Rifle Association, Fable IV & V.
16. National Rifle Association, Fable IV & V.
17. National Rifle Association, Fable IV & V.
18. National Rifle Association, Fable IV & V.
19. National Rifle Association, Fable IV & V.
20. United States Department of Justice, *Historical Statistics on Prisoners in State and Federal Institutions, Year end 1925-1986* (Washington, DC: United States Department of Justice, Bureau of Justice Statistics); and United States Department of Justice, *Correctional Populations in the United States, 1987-1994* (Washington, DC: United States Department of Justice, Bureau of Justice Statistics).
21. Department of Justice, *Probationer and Parole Violators in State Prison* (Washington, DC: Department of Justice, 1991).
22. Federal Bureau of Investigation, *Uniform Crime Reports: Law Enforcement Officers Killed and Assaulted*, (Washington, DC: Federal Bureau of Investigation, 2000), <http://www.fbi.gov/ucr/ucr.htm>.
23. FBI, *Uniform Crime Reports*...
24. Poe, p. 21.

25. John R. Lott, *More Guns Less Crime: Understanding Crime and Gun Control Laws* (Chicago: University of Chicago Press, 1997), pp. 50-96.
26. Lott, pp. 50-96.
27. Lott, pp. 50-96.
28. Lott, pp. 50-96.
29. Lott, pp. 50-96.
30. Lott, pp. 50-96.
31. Lott, pp. 50-96.
32. Florida Department of State, <http://www.dos.state.fl.us/>.
33. Gary Kleck, *Targeting Guns: Firearms and Their Control* (New York: Aldine de Gruyter, December 1997).
34. James D. Wright, Peter H. Rossi, *Armed and Considered Dangerous: A Survey of Felons and Their Firearms*, (New York: Aldine de Gruyter, December 1986).
35. Gary C. Lawrence, *National Survey of Registered Voters*, (Santa Ana, CA: Lawrence Research, 1998).
36. FBI, *Uniform Crime Reports...*
37. FBI, *Uniform Crime Reports...*
38. David McDowell, *Preventative Effects of Firearm Regulations on Injury Mortality*, prepared for the annual meeting of the American Society of Criminology, 1993.
39. *Gun Control: Implementation of the Brady Handgun Violence Protection Act: Report to the Judiciary, U.S. Senate and the Committee on the Judiciary, House of Representatives* (Washington, DC: U.S. General Accounting Office/GGD-96-22, January 1996) pp. 8, 44-45.
40. Federal Bureau of Investigation data.
41. Clifford Krauss, "New York Sees Steepest Decline in Violent Crime Rate Since '72: Analysts Begin to Credit New Police Strategies," *The New York Times*, 31 December 1995, p. 32.
42. U. S. Department of Justice, *Correctional Populations in the United States, 1997* (Washington, DC: U.S. Department of Justice, Bureau of Justice Statistics, November 2000).
43. Krauss, p. 1.
44. National Center for Health Statistics.
45. National Center for Health Statistics.
46. Alan Travis, "England and Wales Top Crime League," *The Guardian*, 23 February 2001.
47. David Kopel, *The Samurai, The Mountie and the Cowboy: Should America Adopt the Gun Controls of Other Democracies?* (Buffalo, NY: Prometheus Books, July 1992), pp. 431-32.
48. Jeffery R. Snyder, "A Nation of Cowards," *The Public Interest*, No. 113, Fall 1993.
49. Lott, p. 11.
50. Lott, p. 9.
51. David Kopel, "An Army of Gun Lies: How the Other Side Plays," *National Review*, Vol 52, 17 April 2000, pp. 32-33.

52. Tanya Metaksa, "Gun Grabbers Use the 'Safety' Scam," *FrontpageMagazine.com*, 15 February 2001.

53. Poe, p. 31.

54. Walter Williams, "What About Hate Crimes by Blacks?" *Cincinnati Enquirer*, 22 August 1999, p. D2; and e-mail interview with John Perazzo, 5 May 2001.

55. Gary Kleck and Marc Gertz, "Armed Resistence to Crime: The Nature and Prevalence of Self Defense With a Gun," *The Journal of Criminal Law and Criminology*, Fall 1995, p. 164.

56. Marvin E. Wolfgang, "Tribute to a View I Have Opposed," *The Journal of Criminal Law and Criminology*, Fall 1995, pp. 188-192.

57. National Center for Health Statistics, 1999.

58. George Washington, et al, *Constitution of the United States of America, Bill of Rights, Article the Fourth (Amendment II)*, 17 September 1787. Ratification on first 10 Amendments completed 15 December 1791.

59. Phillip Cook, "The 'Saturday Night Special:' An Assessment of Alternative Definitions from a Policy Perspective," *Journal of Criminal Law and Criminology*, 1981, p. 1737.

60. Gary Kleck, *Point Blank: Guns and Violence in America* (New York: Aldine de Gruyter, 1991), pp. 85-86.

61. National Institute of Justice.

62. U.S. Department of Justice, *FBI Uniform Crime Reporting Handbook* (Washington, DC: U.S. Department of Justice, Federal Bureau of Investigation, 2003).

63. FBI, *Uniform Crime Reports...*

64. FBI, *Uniform Crime Reports...*

65. Lott, pp. 50-96.

66. National Center for Health Statistics.

67. National Center for Health Statistics.

68. *U.S. Code: Title 18: Section 921: (a)(17)(B)(i) and (C)* (Washington, DC: Office of the Law Revision Counsel, U.S. House of Representatives).

69. *U.S. Code: Title 18: Section 921*.

70. House of Representatives, Reps. William Hughes and Rep. Bill McCollum, *Hughes-McCollum Bill*, 99th Congress, H.R. 4768.

71. NRA, *Fables, Myths...*

72. NRA, *Fables, Myths...*

73. *U.S. Code: Title 18: Section 922(g), Section 922(x), and Section 922(t)*.

74. NRA, *Fables, Myths...*

Chapter 8
H is for Health Care: Do You Really Want Eighty Percent National Taxation?

1. Holman W. Jenkins, Jr., "Wanna Fix Health Care? Stop Hiding the Cost!" *Wall Street Journal*, 13 October 2004, Opinion, p. A17.

2. Newt Gingrich and Vince Haley, "Small Businesses are Saving Money and Insuring More People Today With Health Savings Accounts," *Medical Progress Today*, 1 November 2004,
<http://www.medicalprogresstoday.com/spotlight/spotlight_indarchive.php?id=365>.
3. Leonard Peikoff, Ph.D., "Health Care Is Not A Right," *Capitalism Magazine*, 23 January 1998, <http://capmag.com/article.asp?ID=9>.
4. [Editorial], "Health and Poverty," *Wall Street Journal*, 27 August 2004, p. A12.
5. [Editorial], A12.
6. [Editorial], A12.
7. [Editorial], A12.
8. Charles W. Jarvis and Merrill Mathews, Jr., Ph.D., "Can 7,700 Doctors Be Wrong About Health Care?" *Human Events*, 29 September 2003, p. 7, <http://www.humaneventsonline.com/article.php?id=1926>.
9. Jarvis and Mathews, Jr., p. 7.
10. Jarvis and Mathews, Jr., p. 7.
11. Jarvis and Mathews, Jr., p. 7.
12. Jarvis and Mathews, Jr., p. 7.
13. James Frogue, "A High Price for Patients: An Update on Government Health Care in Britain and Canada," The Heritage Foundation, 26 September 2000, <http://www.heritage.org/Research/health care/BG1398.cfm#pgfId-1109235>.
14. Center for Health Transformation, "Transforming Examples," accessed 6 October 2005,
<http://www.healthtransformation.net/Transforming_Examples/Transforming_Examples_Resource_Center/>.
15. Gingrich and Haley.
16. Gingrich and Haley.
17. [Editorial], "Hillary's Vaccine Shortage," *Wall Street Journal*, 15 August 2003.
18. [Editorial], *Wall Street Journal*.
19. [Editorial], *Wall Street Journal*.
20. [Editorial], *Wall Street Journal*.

Chapter 9
I is for Independent Israel: Why We Need to Support the Only Middle East Democracy

1. Joseph Farah, "An Unconventional Arab Viewpoint," *WorldNetDaily*, 24 February 2003,
<http://worldnetdaily.com/news/article.asp?ARTICLE_ID=31194>.
2. Farah.
3. Farah.
4. Mark W. Smith, *The Official Handbook of the Vast Right-Wing Conspiracy*

(Washington, DC: Regnery Gateway Inc, March 2004) p. 49.
 5. William J. Bennett, "Moral Clarity and the Middle East: Why We Support Israel," *National Review*, 24 July 2003, <http://www.nationalreviewonline.com>.

Chapter 10
J is for Justice: Why Criminals Need Discipline

 1. FBI statistics 2004.
 2. The John Locke Foundation, "Crime and Punishment," accessed 3 October 2005. <http://www.johnlocke.org/agenda2004/crimepunishment.html>.
 3. The John Locke Foundation.
 4. 2002 U.S. Department of Justice Statistics.
 5. Patrick F. Fagan, *The Real Root Causes of Violent Crime: The Breakdown of Marriage, Family, and Community* (Washington, DC: The Heritage Foundation, Policy Research Analysis, Backgrounder No. 1026, 17 March 1995), <http://www.heritage.org/Research/Crime/BG1026.cfm>.
 6. 2002 U.S. Department of Justice Statistics.
 7. U.S. Bureau of the Census staff, eds., *The American Almanac 1997-1998: Statistical Abstract of the United States, 117th Ed.* (Austin, TX: Hoover's, Incorporated, 1997), pp. 285-288.
 8. Fagan.
 9. Fagan.
 10. Fagan.
 11. Fagan.
 12. Fagan.
 13. Paul G. Cassell and Richard Fowles, "Handcuffing the Cops? A Thirty Year Perspective on Miranda's Harmful Effects on Law Enforcement," *Stanford Law Review*, Vol. 50, 1998, pp. 1055-1145.
 14. Charles Murray, "And Now for the Bad News," *Wall Street Journal*, 2 February 1999, p. A22.
 15. Murray.
 16. H. Naci Mocan and R. Kaj Gittings, *Pardons, Executions and Homicide*, National Bureau of Economics Research Working Paper No. 8639, December 2001, <http://papers.nber.org/papers/W8639>.
 17. James S. Liebman, et al., *Broken System: Error rates in Capital Cases, 1973-1995*, paper prepared for U.S. Senate Committee on the Judiciary, June 2000, <http://www2.law.columbia.edu/instructionalservices/liebman/>.
 18. Thomas R. Eddlem, "Ten Anti-Death Penalty Fallacies," *The New American*, Vol 18, No. 11, 3 June 2002,
 <http://www.thenewamerican.com/tna/2002/06-03-2002/vo18no11_fallacies.htm>.
 19. Roger Clegg, "The Color of Death: Does the Death Penalty Discriminate?" *National Review*, 11 June 2001,
 <http://www.nationalreview.com/contributors/clegg061101.shtml>.

20. Clegg.
21. Clegg.
22. Clegg.
23. Clegg.
24. Clegg.

Chapter 11
K is for Kids: The Leftist Indoctrination of our Children

1. U.S. Department of Health and Human Services, Health Resources and Services Administration, Maternal and Child Health Bureau, *Child Health USA 2004* (Rockville, MD: U.S. Department of Health and Human Services, 2004), <http://www.mchb.hrsa.gov/mchirc/chusa_04/pages/0462sa.htm>; and Hillard Weinstock, et al., "Sexually Transmitted Diseases Among American Youth: Incidence and Prevalence Estimates, 2000," *Perspectives on Sexual and Reproductive Health*, Volume 36, Number 1, January/February 2004, pp. 6-10, <http://agi-usa.org/pubs/journals/3600604.html> and <http://agi-usa.org/tables/360104/3600604t2.pdf>.

2. National Institutes of Health, National Institute of Child Health & Human Development, *America's Children: Teen Birth Rate Continues Decline*, 20 July 2005, <http://www.nichd.nih.gov/new/releases/americas_children05.cfm> and <http:childstats.gov>.

3. Amanda Gardner, *Kids in Single-Parent Homes Have Worse Health: At Higher Risk for Mental Illness, Substance Abuse and Suicide*, HealthScoutNews, 24 January 2003, <http://www.hon.ch/News/HSN/511438.html>.

4. Mary Eberstadt, *Home Alone America: The Hidden Toll of Day Care, Behavioral Drugs and Other Parent Substitutes* (New York: Sentinel [Penguin Group], 4 November 2004); and Mary Eberstadt, "Home Alone America," *The American Enterprise Magazine*, <http://www.taemag.com/issues/articleid.18298/article_detail.asp>.

5. Jay Belsky, Ph.D., "Parental and Nonparental Child Care and Children's Socioemotional Development," *Journal of Marriage and the Family*, November 1990, p. 890.

6. Belsky, p. 890.

7. J. Conrad Schwarz, Ph.D., et al., "Infant Day Care: Behavioral Effects of Preschool Age," *Developmental Psychology*, Vol. 10, 1974, pp. 502-506.

8. Brenda Hunter, Ph.D., "Attachment and Infant Daycare," *Who Will Rock the Cradle? The Battle for Control of Child Care in America*, Phyllis Schlafly, ed. (Nashville, TN: W Publishing Group [Thomas Nelson], March 1990), pp. 62-63, 75; and Kerby Anderson, "National Child Care," Probe Ministries, 14 July 2002, <http://www.leaderu.com/orgs/probe/docs/childcar.html>.

9. Hunter, pp. 62-63, 75.

10. Karl Zinsmeister, "The Problem with Daycare," *The American Enterprise Magazine*, May/June 1998, pp. 14-15, <http://www.taemag.com/issues/articleid.16929/article_detail.asp>.

11. Zinsmeister, pp.14-15.

12. Urie Bronfenbrenner, "Discovering What Families Do," David Blankenhorn, et al., eds., *Rebuilding the Nest: A New Commitment to the American Family* (Milwaukee, WI: Family Service America, 1990), p. 31.

13. Reed Bell, M.D., "Health Risks from Daycare Diseases," *Who Will Rock the Cradle? The Battle for Control of Child Care in America*, Phyllis Schlafly, ed. (Nashville, TN: W Publishing Group [Thomas Nelson], March 1990), p. 116.

14. Ron Haskins, M.D. and Jonathan Kotch, M.D., "Day Care and Illness: Evidence, Cost, and Public Policy," *Pediatrics*, Volume 77, Issue 6, 1 June 1986, pp. 951-982.

15. Haskins and Kotch, pp. 951-982.

16. Stanley H. Schuman, M.D., "Day-Care-Associated Infection: More Than Meets the Eye," *Journal of American Medical Association*, Vol. 249, No. 1, 7 January 1983, p. 76.

17. National Institute of Child Health and Human Development, *Infant Child Care and Attachment Security: Results of the NICHD Study of Early Child Care* (Washington, DC: National Institute of Child Health and Human Development, Department of Health and Human Services, 20 April 1996), pp. 11-14.

18. Douglas Foster and David Beers, "Clout," *Mother Jones,* May/June 1991, p. 36.

19. Joe S. McIlhaney, Jr., *Safe Sex* (Grand Rapids, MI: Baker Book House, 1991), p. 86.

20. Kerby Anderson, "Condoms, Clinics, or Abstinence,"17 July 2005, <http://www.probe.org/content/view/101/152/>.

21. Anderson.

22. Anderson.

23. Anderson.

24. Anderson.

25. Anderson.

26. Anderson.

27. Anderson.

28. Anderson.

29. Meg Meeker, M.D., *Epidemic: How Teen sex is Killing Our Kids* (Washington DC: Life Line Press, 2002), p. 107.

30. National Institute of Allergy and Infectious Diseases, National Institute of Health, Department of Health and Human Services, *Workshop Summary: Scientific Evidence On Condom Effectiveness for Sexually Transmitted Disease (STD) Prevention*, 20 July 2001. Summary prepared 12-13 June 2000 at workshop held at Hyatt Dulles Airport, Herndon, Virginia.
<http://www.niaid.nih.gov/dmid/stds/condomreport.pdf>.

31. NIAID, NIH, *Workshop Summary: Scientific Evidence On Condom Effectiveness...*

32. Ceci Connolly, "Report Questions Condoms' Disease Prevention Ability," *The Washington Post*, 20 July 2001, p. A1.

33. Saifuddin Ahmed, et al., "HIV Incidence and Sexually Transmitted Disease Prevalence Associated With Condom Use: A Population Study in Rakai, Uganda." *AIDS*, Vol. 15, Issue 16, 9 November 2001, pp. 2171-2179.

34. NIAID, NIH, *Workshop Summary: Scientific Evidence On Condom Effectiveness...*

35. Anna Wald, M.D., et al., "Effect of Condoms on Reducing the Transmission of Herpes Simplex Virus Type 2 from Men to Women." *Journal of the American Medical Association*, Vol. 285, No. 24, 27 June 2001, pp. 3100-3106.

36. Jared M. Baeten, et al., "Hormonal Contraception and Risk of Sexually Transmitted Disease: Results from a Prospective Study," *American Journal of Obstetrics and Gynecology*, Vol. 185, No. 2, August 2001, pp. 380-385.

37. Baeten, pp. 380-85.

38. Leighton Ku, Ph.D., et al., "The Dynamics of Young Men's Condom Use During and Across Relationships." *Family Planning Perspectives*, Vol. 26, No. 6, November/December 1994, pp. 246-251.

39. Gabriela Paz Bailey, M.D., et al., *Condom Protection Against STD: A Study Among Adolescents Attending a Primary Care Clinic in Atlanta*, Abstract B9D, Department of Health and Human Services, Centers for Disease Control and Prevention, presented at the 2002 National STD Prevention Conference, San Diego, CA, 4-7 March 2002.

40. J. Thomas Fitch, M.D., *How Effective Are Condoms in Preventing Pregnancies and STDs in Adolescents?*, Medical Institute for Sexual Health, July 1997, pp. 4-11.

41. Stephen J. Sondheimer, M.D., *OB/GYN Diagnosis*, Vol. 6, No. 3, 1987.

42. Jeff Jacoby, "A Left-Wing Monopoly on Campuses," *Boston Globe*, 2 December 2004, A19, <http://www.boston.com/news/globe/editorial_opinion/oped/articles/2004/12/02/a_left_wing_monopoly_on_campuses/>.

43. Karl Zinmeister, "Diversity on Campus? There is None," *The American Enterprise*, January/February 2005, <http://www.taemag.com/issues/articleid.18346/article_detail.asp>.

44. Zinmeister.

45. Luntz Research, Center for the Study of Popular Culture, "Professor Survey," January 2002,
<http://studentsforacademicfreedom.org/reports/LUNTZ.html>.

Chapter 12
L is for Liberal Media: Agenda, Agenda, Agenda

1. Bernard Goldberg, *Bias: A CBS Insider Exposes How the Media Distort the News* (Washington, DC: Regnery Publishing, 2002), p. 123-124.

2. Goldberg, p. 125.

3. Goldberg, p. 123.

4. Goldberg, p. 125.

5. Goldberg, p. 126.
6. Peter Hannaford, "Dissecting Liberal Media Bias," *Human Events*, 4 October 2004, p. 24.
7. Brent Bozell III, *Weapons of Mass Distortion: The Coming Meltdown of the Liberal Media*, (NY: Crown Forum, 2004).
8. Peter Hannaford, p. 24.

Chapter 13
M is for Megga Watt Energy: Oil, Tree Huggers, and Environmental Yappers

1. Paul R. Ehrlich and Anne H. Ehrlich, "Too Many Rich Folks," *Populi*, Vol. 16, No. 3, September 1989. pp. 20-29.
2. Ronald Bailey, "Earth Day, Then and Now," *Reason Magazine*, 1 May 2000, pp. 18-28, <http://reason.com/0005/fe.rb.earth.shtml> and Kenneth E. F. Watt, Earth Day lecture given at Swarthmore College, 19 April 1970.
3. Sallie Baliunas, "The Kyoto Protocol and Global Warming," *Imprimis*, March 2002, Vol. 31, No. 3, p. 6,
<http://www.hillsdale.edu/imprimis/2002/march/>.
4. "Capital Briefs: Cold Globaloney," *Human Events*, 21 January 2002, p. 2.
5. Michael Fumento, *Science Under Siege* (New York: William Morrow and Co., Inc., January 1993), p. 362.
6. S. Fred Singer, "NAS Report on Climate Change Was Severely Flawed," *Human Events*, 18 June 2001, p. 4.
7. Baliunas, p. 6.
8. Baliunas, p. 6.
9. Thomas Gale Moore, "Warmer Earth Might Be Welcome Trend," Cato Institute, 28 April 1998, <http://www.cato.org/dailys/4-28-98.html>.
10. Baliunas, p. 7.
11. Gary W. Yohe, Ph.D., "Climate Change Policies, the Distribution of Income and U.S. Living Standards," Special Report, American Council for Capital Formation Center for Policy Research, November 1996.
12. Alexander F. Annett, "The Department of Energy's Report On the Impact of Kyoto: More Bad News For Americans," The Heritage Foundation, Backgrounder No. 1229, 23 October 1998,
<http://www.heritage.org/Research/EnergyandEnvironment/BG1229.cfm>.
13. Bjorn Lomborg, *The Skeptical Environmentalist* (Oxford, England: Cambridge University Press, 2001), p. 4.
14. Environmental Protection Agency, "What Is the Quality of Drinking Water?" *Draft Report on the Environment* (Washington, DC: Environmental Protection Agency, 23 June 2003),
<http://www.epa.gov/indicators/roe/html/roeWaterDr.htm>.
15. Lomborg, p. 4.
16. Lomborg, p. 4.
17. Lomborg, p. 4.

18. David Limbaugh, "ANWR: Bush Should Give Greens the Red Light," *Townhall.com*, 25 April 2001,
<http://www.townhall.com/opinion/columns/davidlimbaugh/2001/04/25/166266.html>
19. Limbaugh.
20. Thomas L. Torget, *The Attwater's Prairie Chicken and the Gas Well*, Spring 2000,
<http://www.exxonmobil.com/Corporate/Newsroom/Publications/c_spring00_lamp/c_page6.html>.
21. "Do the Caribou Really Care?" Arctic National Wildlife Refuge, <http://www.anwr.org/features/pdfs/caribou-facts.pdf>; and U.S. Department of the Interior, *ANWR Talking Points*, (House Republican Conference, 2001), <http://www.doi.gov/news/010801a.html>.
22. Jim Peron, *Exploding Population Myths* (Chicago: Heartland Institute, 1995).
23. Nicholas Eberstadt, "The Myth of Overpopulation," *Washington Times*, 6 April 2001; and Nicholas Eberstadt, "The World Population 'Crisis:' American Philanthropy's long, fruitless affair with population control," *Philanthropy Magazine*, November/December 1998, <http://www.philanthropyroundtable.org/magazines/1998/november/index.html>.
24. Eberstadt.
25. Eberstadt.
26. Eberstadt.
27. Roger A. Sedjo, "Forests: Conflicting Signals," *Issue Analysis*, 1 January 1995, <http://www.cei.org/gencon/025,01438.cfm>.
28. Sedjo.
29. Sedjo.
30. Sedjo.

Chapter 14
N is for 9/11 Attacks: A New Kind of War

1. The Associated Press, "Missed Opportunities,"
USA Today, 24 March 2004,
<http://www.usatoday.com/news/washington/2004-03-24-sept-11-timeline_x.htm>.
2. The Associated Press.
3. The Associated Press.
4. Gerald L. Posner, *Why America Slept: the Failure to Prevent 9/11* (New York: Random House, 2 September 2003) and Dave Eberhart, "Clinton's Negligence Led to 9/11," *Newsmax.com*, 4 September 2003, <http://www.newsmax.com/archives/articles/2003/9/4/03534.shtml>.
5. Posner and Eberhart.
6. The Associated Press.

7. The Associated Press.
8. The Associated Press.
9. The Associated Press.
10. The Associated Press.
11. The Associated Press.
12. The Associated Press.
13. Lisa Myers, *Osama bin Laden: Missed Opportunities*, NBC News, 17 March 2004, <http://www.msnbc.msn.com/id/4540958/>.
14. Myers.
15. Myers.
16. Myers.
17. National Commission on Terrorist Attacks, "Responses to Al Qaeda's Initial Assaults," *The 9/11 Commission Report* (New York: W. W. Norton & Company; 22 July 2004), pp. 108-144.
18. National Commission on Terrorist Attacks, pp. 108-144.
19. National Commission on Terrorist Attacks, pp. 108-144.
20. Myers.
21. National Commission on Terrorist Attacks, pp. 108-144.
22. National Commission on Terrorist Attacks, pp. 108-144.
23. National Commission on Terrorist Attacks, pp. 108-144.
24. Condoleeza Rice, Ph.D., testimony before 9/11 Commission on 8 April 2004, *Transcript of Rice's 9/11 Commission Statement*, CNN, 19 May 2004, <http://www.cnn.com/2004/ALLPOLITICS/04/08/rice.transcript/>.
25. Rice.
26. Rice.
27. Rice.
28. Rice.
29. Rice.
30. Mark W. Smith, *The Official Handbook of the Vast Right Wing Conspiracy* (Washington, DC: Regnery Publishing Inc, March 2004), p. 49.
31. William J. Bennett, "Moral Clarity and the Middle East: Why We Support Israel," *National Review*, 22 July 2003, <http://www.nationalreview.com/comment/comment-bennett072203.asp>.
32. Dinesh D'Souza, *What's So Great About America* (Washington, DC: Regnery Publishing, Inc., 24 April 2002), p. 133.

Chapter 15
O is for Operation Iraqi Freedom: Why We Had to Fight This War

1. Richard Spertzel, "Have War Critics Even Read the Duelfer Report?" *The Wall Street Journal*, 14 October 2004.
2. Spertzel.
3. Spertzel.
4. Spertzel.

5. Vin Weber, "As They Were Saying..." *The Wall Street Journal*, 13 August 2003.
6. Weber.
7. Weber.
8. Weber.
9. Richard Butler, *The Greatest Threat: Iraq, Weapons of Mass Destruction, and the Growing Crisis of Global Security* (New York: Public Affairs, 2001), p. xvii.
10. Weber.
11. Susan Schmidt, "Plame's Input Is Cited on Niger Mission: Report Disputes Wilson's Claims on Trip, Wife's Role," *Washington Post*, 10 July 2004, p. A09, <http://www.washingtonpost.com/wp-dyn/articles/A39834-2004Jul9.html>.
12. Joseph C. Wilson IV, *The Politics of Truth: Inside the Lies that Led to War and Betrayed My Wife's CIA Identity: A Diplomat's Memoir* (New York: Carroll & Graf Publishers, 2004).
13. [Editorial], "Of 'Lies' and WMD," *The Wall Street Journal*, 12 July 2004.
14. British Prime Minister Tony Blair, speech before British Parliament, London, England, 24 September 2002.
15. [Editorial], *The Wall Street Journal*.
16. [Editorial], *The Wall Street Journal*.
17. Blair.
18. Conclusion 83 of the Senate Intelligence Committee report on pre-war intelligence on Iraq, August 2004.

Chapter 16
P is for President George W Bush: The Man for the Hour

1. [Editorial], "The Florida Myth," *Wall Street Journal*, 28 September 2004, <http://www.opinionjournal.com/editorial/feature.html?id=110005682>.
2. [Editorial], *Wall Street Journal*.
3. Pat Caddell interview on *Hardball with Chris Mathews*, MSNBC, 27 November 2000.
4. Bill Sammon, *At Any Cost: How Al Gore Tried to Steal the Election* (Washington, DC: Regnery, 2001), p. 20.
5. John R. Lott, Jr., *Documenting Unusual Declines in Republican Voting Rates in Florida's Western Panhandle Counties in 2000*, unpublished paper, 10 December 2000, revised 8 May 2001.
6. *2004 Election Results*, CNN, November 2004,
<http://www.cnn.com/ELECTION/2004/pages/results/states/US/P/00/epolls.0.html>.

Chapter 17
Q is for Queer Eye for the Same Sex Marriage: Why the Family is in Jeopardy

1. Maggie Gallagher, "What Marriage Is For," *The Weekly Standard*, Vol. 8, No. 45, 4 August 2003, <http://www.weeklystandard.com/Content/Public/Articles/000/000/002/939pxiqa.asp>.
2. Sue Bohlin, "Homosexuality: Questions and Answers," *Probe.org*, accessed October 2005, <http://www.probe.org/content/view/697/72/>.
3. Gallagher.
4. Jeffery B. Satinover, M.D. and Ph.D., "The Gay Gene?" *The Journal of Human Sexuality*, 1996, pp. 3-10.
5. Joe Dallas, *A Strong Delusion: Confronting the "Gay Christian" Movement* (Eugene, OR: Harvest House Publishers, September 1996).
6. David Blankenhorn, *Fatherless America: Confronting Our Most Urgent Social Problem* (New York: Basic Books, February 1995); and Kyle D. Pruitt, M.D., *Fatherneed: Why Father Care is as Essential as Mother Care*, (New York: Free Press, 2000).
7. Brenda Hunter, Ph.D., *The Power of Mother Love* (Colorado Springs, CO: Waterbrook Press, 1997).
8. Dawn M. Upchurch, et al., "Neighborhood and Family Contexts of Adolescent Sexual Activity," *Journal of Marriage and Family*, Vol. 61, No. 4, 1999, pp. 920-933.
9. Upchurch. See also, Timothy J. Dailey, Ph.D., "Breaking the Ties That Bind: The APA's Assault on Fatherhood," *Insight*, No. 213, 18 February 2000.
10. David T. Elwood, *Poor Support: Poverty in the American Family* (New York: Basic Books, 1988), p. 46.
11. Elaine Kamarck and William Galston, "Putting Children First: A Progressive Family Policy for the 1990s," white paper from the Progressive Policy Institute, 27 September 1990, p. 12.
12. James Q. Wilson, "Why We Don't Marry," *City Journal*, Winter 2002, <http://www.city-journal.org/html/12_1_why_we.html>.
13. Fiona Tasker, Ph.D. and Susan Golombok, Ph.D., "Adults Raised as Children in Lesbian Families," *American Journal of Orthopsychiatry*, Vol. 65, No. 2, April 1995, pp. 203-215.
14. Glenn T. Stanton, *Why Marriage Matters for Children*, CitizenLink, 22 May 2003, <http://www.family.org/cforum/fosi/marriage/facts/a0028317.cfm>.
15. Sara McLanahan and Gary Sandefur, *Growing Up With a Single Parent: What Hurts, What Helps* (Cambridge, MA: Harvard University Press, October 1994), p. 19.
16. Deborah Dawson, "Family Structure and Children's Health and Well Being: Data for the 1988 National Health Interview Survey on Child Health," *Journal of Marriage and the Family*, Vol. 53, August 1991, pp. 573-584.
17. Kamarck and Galston, pp. 14-15.
18. Ellen C. Perrin, MD, "Technical Report: Coparent and Second-Parent Adoption by Same-Sex Parents," *Pediatrics*, Vol. 109, No. 2, 2002, p. 341.
19. Elizabeth Hilton Thomson, Ph.D., et al., "Family Structure, Gender, and Parental Socialization," *Journal of Marriage and the Family*, Vol. 54, No. 2, 1992, pp. 368-378.

20. Nicholas Zill, "Understanding Why Children in Stepfamilies Have More Learning and Behavioral Problems Than Children in Nuclear Families," in *Stepfamilies: Who Benefits? Who Does Not?*, ed. Alan Booth and Judy Dunn (Hillsdale, NJ: Lawrence Eribaum Associates, 1994), p. 98.

21. Martin Daly and Margo Wilson, "Child Abuse and Other Risks of Not Living With Both Parents," *Ethology and Sociobiology*, Vol. 6, 1985, pp. 197-210.

22. Margo Wilson and Martin Daly, "Risk of Maltreatment of Children Living With Stepparents," *Child Abuse and Neglect: Biosocial Dimensions*, ed. Richard J. Gelles and Jane B. Lancaster (New York: Aldine de Gruyter, 1987), p. 230.

23. Michael N. Stiffman, M.D., et al., "Household Composition and Risk of Fatal Child Maltreatment," *Pediatrics*, Vol. 109, No. 4, April 2002, pp. 615-621.

24. Glenn T. Stanton, *Examining the Research Literature on Outcomes from Same-Sex Parenting* (Colorado Springs, CO: Focus on the Family, August 2004), <http://www.family.org/cforum/pdfs/fosi/marriage/examining_research_on_ss_parenting.pdf>.

25. Judith S. Wallerstein, Ph.D., et al., *The Unexpected Legacy of Divorce: The 25 Year Landmark Study* (New York: Hyperion, 6 September 2000), p. xxvii.

26. Judith S. Wallerstein, Ph.D., "The Long Term Effects of Divorce on Children: A Review," *Journal of the American Academy of Child and Adolescent Psychiatry*, Vol. 30, May 1991, pp. 349-360.

27. Wallerstein, 6 September 2000, p. xxiii.

28. Robert Lerner, Ph.D. and Althea K. Nagai, Ph.D., *No Basis: What the Studies Don't Tell Us About Same Sex Parenting* (Washington, DC: Marriage Law Project, Ethics and Public Policy Center, 2001).

29. Lerner and Negai.

30. Affidavit of Steven Lowell Nock, *Halpern et al. v. The Attorney General of Canada et al.*, Ontario Superior Court Justice, March 2001, Court File No. 684/00, par. 130-31.

31. Linda J. Waite and Maggie Gallagher, *The Case for Marriage: Why Married People are Happier, Healthier, and Better Off Financially* (New York: Doubleday, 3 October 2000), p. 64.

32. Catherine Kohler Riessman, Ph.D. and Naomi Gerstel, Ph.D., "Marital Dissolution and Health: Do Males or Females Have Greater Risk?" *Social Science and Medicine*, Vol. 20, 1985, pp. 627-635.

33. James Q. Wilson, *The Marriage Problem: How Our Culture Has Weakened Families* (New York: Harper Collins, March 2002), p. 16

34. Robert Coombs, "Marital Status and Personal Well-Being: A Literature Review," *Family Relations*, Vol. 40, 1991, pp. 97-102.

35. Coombs, pp. 97-102.

36. I. M. Joung, et al., "Differences in Self Reported Morbidity by Marital Status and by Living Arrangement," *International Journal of Epidemiology*, Vol. 23, February 1994, pp. 91-97.

37. Linda J. Waite, *Does Marriage Matter?*, presidential address to the American Population Association of America, 8 April 1995; and Linda J. Waite, "Does Marriage Matter?" *Demography*, Vol. 32, 1995, pp. 483-507.

38. David R. Williams, Ph.D., et al., "Marital Status and Psychiatric Disorders Among Blacks and Whites," *Journal of Health and Social Behavior,* Vol. 33, No. 2, June 1992, pp. 140-157.

39. Steven Stack, Ph.D. and J. Ross Eshleman, "Marital Status and Happiness: A 17-Nation Study," *Journal of Marriage and the Family,* Vol. 60, May 1998, pp. 527-536.

40. Randy M. Page and Galen E. Cole, "Demographic Predictors of Self-Reported Loneliness in Adults," *Psychological Reports,* Vol. 68, 1991, pp. 939-945.

41. Jan E. Stets, "Cohabitation and Marital Aggression: The Role of Social Isolation," *Journal of Marriage and the Family,* Vol. 53, 1991, pp. 669-680.

42. Ronald J. Angel, Ph.D. and Jacqueline L. Angel, Ph.D., *Painful Inheritance: Health and the New Generation of Fatherless Families* (Madison, WI: University of Wisconsin Press, 1993), pp. 139, 148.

43. Janet Wilmoth and Gregor Koso, "Does Marital History Matter? Marital Status and Wealth Outcomes Among Pre-retirement Adults," *Journal of Marriage and Family,* Vol. 64, 2002, pp. 743-754.

44. Waite and Gallagher, pp. 483-507.

45. Peter LaBarbera, "The Gay Youth Suicide Myth," *The Journal of Human Sexuality,* 1996, pp. 65-72, <http://www.leaderu.com/jhs/labarbera.html>.

46. LaBarbera, pp. 65-72.

47. LaBarbera, pp. 65-72.

48. LaBarbera, pp. 65-72.

49. LaBarbera, pp. 65-72.

50. LaBarbera, pp. 65-72.

51. R. S. Hogg, et al., "Modeling the Impact of HIV Disease on Mortality in Gay and Bisexual Men," *International Journal of Epidemiology,* Vol. 26, 1997, pp. 657-661.

52. Paul Cameron, Ph.D., et al., "The Longevity of Homosexuals: Before and After the AIDS Epidemic," *Omega: Journal of Death and Dying,* Vol. 29, No. 3, 1994, pp. 249-272.

53. Alan P. Bell and Martin S. Weinberg, *Homosexualities: A Study of Diversity Among Men and Women* (New York: Simon & Schuster, 1978).

54. Lawrence Corey and King K. Holmes, "Sexual Transmission of Hepatitis A in Homosexual Men," *New England Journal of Medicine,* Vol. 302, No. 8, 21 February 1980, pp. 435-438.

55. Richard J. Estes, Ph.D. and Neil Alan Weiner, Ph.D., *The Commercial Sexual Exploitation of Children in the U.S., Canada and Mexico* (Philadelphia, PA: University of Pennsylvania, Center for the Study of Youth Policy, 10 September 2001), <http://caster.ssw.upenn.edu/~restes/CSEC.htm>.

56. W. D. Erickson, "Behavior Patterns of Child Molesters," *Archives of Sexual Behavior,* Vol. 17, 1988, p. 83.

57. Paul Cameron, Ph.D., et al., "Child Molestation and Homosexuality," *Psychological Reports,* Vol. 58, 1986, pp. 327-337.

58. Karla Jay and Allen Young, *The Gay Report: Lesbians and Gay Men Speak Out About Sexual Experiences and Lifestyles* (New York: Summit Books, 1979), p. 275.

59. "Gay Power, Gay Politics," *CBS Reports*, CBS News, New York, NY, 26 April 1980.

60. A. G. Lawrence and A. E. Singaratnam, "Changes in Sexual Behaviour and Incidence of Gonorrhoea," *Lancet*, Vol. 1, No. 8539, 25 April 1987, p. 982-83.

61. United States Congressional Record, 29 June 1989.

62. Centers for Disease Control and Prevention, *Taking Action to Combat Increases in STDs and HIV Risk Among Men Who Have Sex with Men* (Atlanta, GA: US Department of Health and Human Services, CDC, May 2001), <file http://www.cdc.gov/nchstp/od/news/92288_AED_CDC_report-0427c.pdf> and Dan Black, et al., "Demographics of the Gay and Lesbian Population in the United States: Evidence from Available Systematic Data Sources," *Demography*, Vol. 37, May 2000, p. 141.

63. Steven D. Wexner, M.D., "Sexually Transmitted Diseases of the Colon, Rectum, and Anus: The Challenge of the Nineties," *Diseases of the Colon & Rectum*, Vol. 33, No. 12, December 1990, pp. 1048-1062.

64. Centers for Disease Control and Prevention, "Hepatitis A Among Homosexual Men: United States, Canada and Australia," *Morbidity and Mortality Weekly Report*, Vol. 41, No. 9, 6 March 1992, pp. 155, 161-164, <http://www.cdc.gov/mmwr/preview/mmwrhtml/00016243.htm>.

65. Robert L. Spitzer, *Archives of Sexual Behavior*, Vol. 32, No. 5, October 2003, pp. 403-417.

Chapter 18
R is for Race-Based Preferences: What's Wrong With Affirmative Action

1. Larry P. Arnn, *America's 'Passion for Fairness:' How Quotas and Preferences Have Undermined True Equality, and What Can Be Done About It* (Claremont, CA: The Claremont Institute, 5 January 1997), <http://www.heartland.org/pdf/12001n.pdf>.

2. Linda Chavez, "Make College Admissions Colorblind," *Human Events*, 9 December 2002, <http://www.humaneventsonline.com/article.php?id=621>.

3. James Robinson, Ph.D., "Why Blacks Should Loathe Government," *Human Events*, 17 June 2002.

4. Robinson.

5. The Washington Post, Kaiser Family Foundation and Harvard University, *Race and Ethnicity in 2001: Attitudes, Perceptions and Experiences*, survey conducted 8 March-22 April 2001 and published August 2001,
<http://profile.kff.org/kaiserpolls/loader.cfm?url=/commonspot/security/getfile.cfm&PageID=13839>.

6. Ann Scales, "Polls Say Blacks Tend to Favor Checks," *The Boston Globe*, 30 September 2001; and Gallup Poll Data, September 2001.

7. Scales; and Zogby Poll Data, September 2001, <http://www.zogby.com>.

8. Chris Weinkopf, "Racial Preferences No Longer Important: Passing of Proposition 209 Proved UC Admissions Forecasts Wrong," *Los Angeles Daily News*, 12 April 2000, p. N15; and Chris Weinkopf, "Stumping the Racial Bean Counters," *FrontPageMagazine.com*, 10 April 2000,

<http://frontpagemag.com/articles/ReadArticle.asp?ID=2954>.
9. Center for Equal Opportunity Study, 2003 Data.
10. Bruce Bartlett, "Faculty Tilt: Our Teachers Lean Left by a Sizeable Majority," *National Review*, 15 September 2003, <http://nationalreview.com/nrof_bartlett/bartlett091503.asp>; and Frank Luntz, "Inside the Mind of an Ivy League Professor," *FrontPageMagazine.com*, 30 August 2002, <http://www.frontpagemag.com/articles/ReadArticle.asp?ID=2642>; and Gallup Poll, Fall 2002.
11. Linda Chavez, "Medical School Admissions Allow Race to Trump Qualifications," *Human Events*, 25 June 2001.
12. Chavez.
13. Ann Coulter, "Racial Profiling in University Admissions," *Human Events*, 5 April 2001.
14. Linda Chavez, "Make College Admissions Colorblind," *Human Events*, 9 December 2002.
15. Chavez.

Chapter 19
S is for Social Security: How to Fix it

1. José Piñera, "Personal Retirement Accounts Are Not Unproven," in *Be Not Afraid: Personal Accounts Are No Radical Idea*, Leon Aron, et al., *The American Enterprise Magazine*, March 2005, <http://www.taemag.com/issues/articleid.18420/article_detail.asp>.
2. José Piñera, "Retiring in Chile," *The New York Times*, 1 December 2004, p. A31.
3. Martin Feldstein, "Democrats Play Politics with Social Security," *Wall Street Journal*, 2 August 2001.
4. Eric V. Schlecht, *Private Savings Accounts: The Cure for What Ails Social Security*, National Taxpayers Union Foundation, Policy Paper, No. 110, 7 April 1999.
5. Bill Clinton made those remarks in January 1999 shortly after his State of the Union speech.
6. Schlecht.
7. Schlecht.
8. CNN/USA Today/Gallup poll conducted 8-10 November 2002.
9. United States Seniors Association post-election poll conducted November 2002, <http://www.usanext.org/blog.cfm>.
10. [Editorial], "The Great Retirement Scare," *Wall Street Journal*, 2 August 2002, p. A8.
11. Andrew G. Biggs, "Claims and Facts: Common Arguments Against SS Reform Featuring Voluntary Personal Retirement Accounts," Cato Institute, 9 July 2002, <http://socialsecurity.org/pubs/articles/art-biggs020709.pdf>.
12. Biggs.

13. Biggs.
14. Biggs.
15. Biggs.
16. Biggs.
17. Andrew G. Biggs, "Symposium: Social Security Reform: Will the President's Plan for Privatization Take the Security Out of Social Security?" *Insight Magazine*, 24 June 2002.
18. Deroy Murdock, "Social Security: Ripping Off African Americans," *Human Events*, 20 May 2002.
19. Biggs, *Insight Magazine*.
20. Biggs, *Insight Magazine*.
21. Biggs, *Insight Magazine*.
22. Biggs, *Insight Magazine*.
23. Social Security Administration, *FAQs About Social Security Choice* (Washington, DC: Social Security Administration, 2005), <http://www.socialsecurity.org/reformandyou/faqs.html>.
24. Peter Ferrara, "The Failed Critique of Personal Accounts," Cato Institute, Briefing Paper No. 68, 8 October 2001, <http://www.cato.org/pubs/briefs/bp68.pdf>.
25. Social Security Administration.
26. Biggs, "Claims and Facts..."
27. Biggs, "Claims and Facts..."
28. Biggs, "Claims and Facts..."
29. Biggs, "Claims and Facts..."
30. Biggs, "Claims and Facts..."
31. Matthew Robinson, "Democrats Hypocritical on Social Security," *Human Events*, 6 August 2001.

Chapter 20
T is for Taxes: Cut Your Way to Financial Freedom

1. John F. Kennedy, speech to Economic Club of New York, 14 December 1962.
2. Thomas Sowell, "Low Taxes Do What?" *Wall Street Journal*, 24 February 2004, p. A18.
3. Sowell, p. A18.
4. Larry Schweikart, "Myths of the 1980s Distort Debate Over Tax Cuts," Mackinac Center for Public Policy, 27 June 2001,
<http://www.mackinac.org/article.aspx?ID=3535>.
5. Larry Elder, "Did Reagan Torture Blacks? Exposing the Myths of Reagan's 'Anti-Civil Rights' Record," *Human Events*, 21 June 2004.
6. Brian M. Riedl, "Ten Common Myths about Taxes, Spending, and Budget Deficits," The Heritage Foundation, Backgrounder No. 1660, 13 June 2003, <http://www.heritage.org/Research/Budget/BG1660.cfm>.
7. R. Glenn Hubbard, "Tax Cuts Won't Hurt the Surplus," *Wall Street Journal*,

22 August 2001, p. A16.

8. Daniel J. Mitchell, Ph.D., "Debunking Four Election-Year Budget Myths," The Heritage Foundation, Policy Research & Analysis, Executive Memorandum No. 837, 17 October 2002,
<http://www.heritage.org/Research/Budget/em837.cfm>

9. Hubbard, p. A16.

10. George Will, "Yacht Tax's Failure," *This Week with George Stephanopoulos*, ABC News, Washington, DC, 12 January 2003,
<http://www.andromeda.rutgers.edu/~jhv/ABC's%20George%20Will%20on%20Yacht%20Tax's%20Failure.txt>.

11. Hubbard, p. A16.

12. Congressional Budget Office Data.

13. Thomas Sowell, *Basic Economics: A Citizen's Guide to the Economy* (New York: Basic Books, 2000), p. 137.

14. Congressional Budget Office, "Historical Effective Federal Tax Rates:1979-2003, December 2005 at www.cbo.gov/ftpdoc.cfm?index=7000&type=1 (Feb 4,2006) and anti-poverty spending on file with Office of Management and Budget, Historical Tables, Budget of the U.S. Government, FY 2007 p.55-72, table 3.2, and p.137-142, table 8.5 at Whitehouse.gov/omb/budget/fy2007/pdf/his.pdf(Feb 4,2006). Originally, this information derived from Brian M. Riedl, "The Myth of Spending Cuts for the Poor, and Tax Cuts for the Rich," no.1912, Feb 14, 2006, Heritage.org.

15. Bruce Bartlett, "Tax Rebates Won't Stimulate the Economy," *Wall Street Journal*, 1 November 2001.

16. Daniel J. Mitchell, Ph.D., "Lowering Marginal Tax Rates: The Key to Pro-Growth Tax Relief," The Heritage Foundation, Backgrounder No. 1443, 22 May 2001, <http://www.heritage.org/Research/Taxes/BG1443es.cfm>.

17. [Editorial], "When Debt is Good," *Wall Street Journal*, 27 March 2001, p. A30.

18. [Editorial], p. A30.

19. John S. Barry, "Fiscal Forecasting: A Perilous Task," Tax Foundation, January 2002,
<http://www.taxfoundation.org/files/ea74e1d478b91d4b7c463449b05ba957.pdf>

20. Bruce Bartlett, "Remember Reagan-Kemp-Roth Tax Cut," *Human Events*, 22 July 2002.

21. Stephen Moore, "Remembering the Real Economic Legacy of JFK," *Human Events*, 19 May 2003.

22. Moore.

23. Moore.

24. Moore.

25. Stephen Moore, "Bush Should Listen to Schwab: Cut Capital Gains Taxes," *Human Events*, 26 August 2002.

26. Bruce Bartlett, "Deeper Look at CBO Study and 'Rich Getting Richer,'" *Human Events*, 18 June 2001.

27. Bartlett.
28. Bartlett.
29. Bartlett.
30. Michael J. Mandel, "Restating the '90s," *Business Week*, 1 April 2002, pp. 51-58.
31. Bob McTeer, "Where We've Been and What's Ahead," *Dallas Business Review*, Spring 1996,
<http://www.dallasfed.org/htm/dallas/articles/spring96.html>.
32. Walter E. Williams, "Giving Back," *Capitalism Magazine*, 30 March 2002, <http://capmag.com/article.asp?ID=1515>
33. Williams.
34. Williams.
35. Stephen Moore and Greg Kaza, "'Dracula Tax' Won't Stay Dead," *Human Events*, 30 July 2001.
36. Stephen J. Entin, "Why the Death Tax Lives," *Wall Street Journal*, 19 June 2002, p. A18.
37. Gary Robbins, "Estate Taxes: An Historical Perspective," The Heritage Foundation, Backgrounder No. 1719, 16 January 2004,
<http://www.heritage.org/Research/Taxes/bg1719.cfm>.
38. Entin, p. A18.
39. Frederic Bastiat, et al., *The Law & Cliches of Socialism* (Whittier, CA: Constructive Action, Inc., 1964).
40. Entin, p. A18.

Chapter 21
U is for the United States of America: What Makes Us Great

1. B. Forrest Clayton, *Suppressed History: Obliterating Politically Correct Orthodoxies* (Cincinnati, OH: Armistead Publishing, 2003).
2. Dinesh D'Souza, *What's So Great About America* (Washington, DC: Regnery Publishing, Inc., 24 April 2002), pp. 64-66.
3. Dennis Prager, "Liberal Myths Fanned the Flames in Los Angeles," *The Orange County Register*, 22 May 1992.
4. D'Souza, p. 41.
5. John S. Aird, *Slaughter of the Innocents: Coercive Birth Control in China* (Washington, DC: American Express Institute Press, August 1990). It's estimated that between 1971 and 1985 there were some 100 million coercive birth-control "operations" in China, including forced sterilizations and forced abortions.
6. Richard Poe, *The Seven Myths of Gun Control: Reclaiming the Truth About Guns, Crime, and the Second Amendment* (Roseville, CA: Prima Lifestyles Publishing, July 2001), p. 23.
7. Poe, p. 23.

Chapter 22
V is for Vouchers and the Public Schools: How We Can Fix Education

1. Thomas Sowell, "Vouchers Vindicated," *Human Events*, 15 July 2002, <http://www.findarticles.com/p/articles/mi_qa3827/is_200207/ai_n9104341>
2. Martin Gross, "More Failed Federal Aid to Education," *Human Events*, 21 January 2002, <http://www.findarticles.com/p/articles/mi_qa3827/is_200201/ai_n9045519>.
3. Jennifer Garrett, "School Choice: A Lesson in Hypocrisy," The Heritage Foundation, 26 June 2002, <http://new.heritage.org/Press/Commentary/ed062602b.cfm>.
4. [Editorial], "Money and Class," *Wall Street Journal*, 9 January 2003, p. A10.
5. John O. Norquist, "Vouchers Aren't Just for Religious Schools," *Wall Street Journal*, 20 February 2002.
6. Norquist.
7. Norquist.
8. Marvin Olasky, "School Choice in Canada Now Thriving," *Human Events*, 26 August 2002.
9. Sowell.
10. Norquist.
11. Jay P. Greene, Ph.D. and Marcus A. Winters, "Public High School Graduation and College-Readiness Rates: 1991–2002," Manhattan Institute for Policy Research, Education Working Paper, No. 8, February 2005, <http://www.manhattan-institute.org/html/ewp_08.htm>
12. Greene and Winters.
13. Nanette Asimov, "U.S. Teens Rank Low in World Tests," *San Francisco Chronicle*, 25 February 1998, p. 1A, <http://www.sfgate.com/cgi-bin/article.cgi?file=/chronicle/archive/1998/02/25MN5403.DTL>.
14. Jay P. Greene, Ph.D., "Raise Standards, Not Money," *Wall Street Journal*, 7 October 2002.
15. Gross.
16. Eric A. Hanushek, Ph.D., *Making Schools Work: Improving Performance and Controlling Costs* (Washington, DC: Brookings Institution Press, 1993).
17. "Money and Class," *Wall Street Journal*.
18. National Center for Educational Statistics, <http://www.nces.ed.gov>.
19. Olasky.
20. Gross.
21. Gross.
22. Sowell.
23. Norquist.
24. Norquist.
25. Olasky.
26. Public Opinion Strategies, February, 2004.
27. Garrett.

Chapter 23
W is for Welfare: What's Wrong With It

1. Robert E. Rector, "Means Tested Welfare Spending: Past and Future Growth," testimony before The Committee on Budget, US House of Representatives, Washington, DC, 7 March 2001, <http://www.house.gov/budget/hearings/rectorstmnt.pdf>.
2. Children's Defense Fund, "How the Welfare Bill Profoundly Harms Children," Children's Defense Fund, 31 July 1996.
3. Robert E. Rector, "Welfare Reform: Progress, Pitfalls, and Potential," The Heritage Foundation, 10 February 2004, <http://www.heritage.org/Research/Welfare/wm421.cfm>.
4. Ron Haskins and Wendell Primus, "Welfare Reform and Poverty," The Brookings Institution, WR&B Brief No. 4, July 2001, <http://www.brookings.edu/dybdocroot/wrb/publications/pb/pb04.htm>.
5. Jenifer Zeigler, "Is Welfare the New 'Third Rail' of Politics?" Cato Institute, 20 October 2004, <http://www.catoinstitute.org/research/articles/zeigler-041020.html>.
6. Rector, "Welfare Reform..."
7. Stephanie J. Ventura and Christine A. Bachrach, Ph.D., *Nonmarital Childbearing in the United States, 1940–99* (Hyattsville, MD: U.S. Department of Health & Human Services, Centers for Disease Control and Prevention, National Center for Health Statistics, Vol. 48, No. 16, 18 October 2000, rev. 19 March 2001), <http://www.cdc.gov/nchs/data/nvsr/nvsr48/nvs48_16.pdf>.
8. Lisa E. Oliphant, "A Happy Anniversary for Welfare Reform?" Cato Institute, 22 August 2000, <http://www.cato.org/dailys/08-22-00.html>.
9. Bernadette D. Proctor and Joseph Dalaker, *Poverty in the United States: 2001,* Current Population Reports, Series P60-219 (Washington DC: U.S. Government Printing Office, U.S. Bureau of the Census, October 2002).
10. Proctor and Dalaker.
11. Zeigler.
12. Mark Nord, et al., *Household Food Security in the United States, 2003* (Washington, DC: Economic Research Service, U.S. Department of Agriculture, October 2004), p. 6, <http://www.ers.usda.gov/publications/fanrr42/>.

Chapter 24
X is for Xenophobia: Why Illegal Immigration is Hurting Us

1. Michael Reagan, "Immigration: The New Third Rail," *FrontPageMagazine.com,* 9 November 2004, <http://www.frontpagemag.com/Articles/ReadArticle.asp?ID=15864>.
2. Edward J. Erler, "Amnesty for Illegal Aliens," *The Washington Times,* 21 January 2004,

<http://www.washtimes.com/op-ed/20040121-090531-2669r.htm>.
 3. Michelle Malkin, "Homeland Insecurity: The Year in Review," *Human Events*, 29 December 2004, <http://www.humaneventsonline.com/article.php?id=6161>.
 4. Don Feder, "The Mexican-American War, Round 2," *FrontPageMagazine.com*, 10 January 2005, <http://www.frontpagemag.com/Articles/ReadArticle.asp?ID=16577>.
 5. Malkin.
 6. Feder.
 7. Steven A. Camarota, "The High Cost of Cheap Labor: Illegal Immigration and the Federal Budget," Center for Immigration Studies, August 2004, <http://www.cis.org/articles/2004/fiscal.html>.

Chapter 25
Y is for Yankee Doodle Founding Fathers: They Really Got it Right

 1. Dinesh D'Souza, *What's So Great About America* (Washington, DC: Regnery Publishing, 2002), p. 111.
 2. David Limbaugh, *Persecution: How Liberals Are Waging War Against Christianity* (Washington, DC: Regnery Publishing, 25 September 2003), p. 308.
 3. Thomas Jefferson, *The Writings of Thomas Jefferson*, ed. Albert Ellery Bergh (Washington, DC: The Thomas Jefferson Memorial Association, 1904), Vol. XIV, p. 385, to Charles Thompson on January 9, 1816.
 4. M. Stanton Evans, *The Theme is Freedom: Religion, Politics, and the American Tradition* (Washington, DC: Regnery Publishing, Inc., November 1994), p. 240.
 5. Evans, pp. 231-232.
 6. Limbaugh, p. 311.
 7. David Barton, *Original Intent: The Courts, the Constitution, & Religion* (Aledo, TX: WallBuilder Press, 30 May 2000), p. 225.
 8. Montesquieu, *The Spirit of the Laws* (New York: Hafner, 1949, 1962), quoted in John Eidsmoe, *Christianity and the Constitution, The Faith of our Founding Fathers* (Grand Rapids, MI: Baker Books, 1987), p. 55.
 9. Sir William Blackstone, "Commentaries of the Laws of England," quoted in John Eidsmoe, *Christianity and the Constitution: The Faith of our Founding Fathers* (Grand Rapids, MI: Baker Books, 1987), p. 58.
 10. Donald S. Lutz, *The Origins of American Constitutionalism* (Baton Rouge, LA: Louisiana State University Press, 1988).
 11. James Wilson, "Of the General Principles of Law and Obligation," *The Works of the Honourable James Wilson, L.L.D.*, ed. Bird Wilson (Philadelphia, PA: Lorenzo Press for Bronson and Chauncey, 1804), Vol. 1, pp. 67-68, <http://deila.dickinson.edu/cgi-bin/docviewer.exe?CISOROOT=/own-words&CISOPTR=15462>.
 12. Limbaugh, pp. 314-315.
 13. Limbaugh, p. 315.

14. Stephen K. McDowell and Mark A. Beliles, *America's Providential History* (Charlottesville, VA: Providence Foundation, 1 December 1989), p. 93; and David Barton, *The Myth of Separation* (Aledo, TX: WallBuilder Press, 1991), pp. 92, 93, 119.
15. Henry P. Johnston, ed., *The Correspondence and Public Papers of John Jay, 1763-1826* (New York: G. P. Putnam's Sons, 1890-93, reprint New York: Burt Franklin, 1970) Vol. IV, p. 393.
16. Richard Vetterli and Gary C. Bryner, *In Search of the Republic: Public Virtue and the Roots of American Government* (Totowa, NJ: Rowman and Littlefield, 1987), p. 70.
17. Thomas Jefferson, in a letter to Dr. Joseph Priestley, 19 Jun 1802. Thomas Jefferson, *The Writings of Thomas Jefferson,* Memorial Edition, eds. Lipscomb and Bergh, (Washington, D.C: 1903-04), Vol. 10, p. 325.
18. Jefferson.
19. Jefferson, Vol. 16, p. 281. Thomas Jefferson writing to Danbury Baptists, 1802.
20. John Eidsmoe, *Christianity and the Constitution,* (MI: Baker Book House, 1987), p. 243.
21. Thomas Jefferson, letter to Dr. Benjamin Rush on 21 April 1803.
22. Thomas Jefferson, *Proclamation Appointing a Day of Thanksgiving and Prayer,* 11 November 1779.
23. Jefferson, Vol. 17, p. 381. Draft of Kentucky Resolutions, 1798.
24. United States Continental Congress, *Articles of War,* 30 June 1775. Thomas Jefferson signed it in his second term as president, on 10 April 1806.
25. George Washington, "Farewell Address to the People of the United States," 17 September 1796. Washington never publicly read the address to the nation, but gave a copy to Claypoole's *American Daily Advertiser,* Philadelphia, PA, 19 September 1796. It was reprinted in *The Independent Chronicle,* 26 September 1796.
26. Fisher Ames, *The Works of Fisher Ames,* 1809.
27. Jared Sparks, *The Life of Gouverneur Morris* (Boston: Gray and Bowen, 1832), Vol. III, p. 483.
28. John Witherspoon, address at Princeton University, 17 May 1776.

Chapter 26
Z is for Zealot Terrorists: How Can We Fight Them?

1. Dinesh D'Souza, *What's So Great About America* (Washington, DC: Regnery Publishing, Inc., 24 April 2002).
2. United States Department of Justice, *What Is the USA Patriot Act?* (Washington, DC: United States Department of Justice, 2005), <http://www.lifeandliberty.gov/highlights.htm>; and United States Department of Justice, *Dispelling the Myths,* (Washington, DC: United States Department of Justice, 2005), <http://www.lifeandliberty.gov/subs/u_myths.htm>.

3. U. S. Department of Justice, *Dispelling the Myths*.
4. Susan Schmidt, "Patriot Act Misunderstood, Senators Say," *The Washington Post*, 22 October 2003, p. A4, <http://www.washingtonpost.com/ac2/wp-dyn/A61591-2003Oct21?language=printer>; and Robert Corrente, *The Patriot Act—Fear Not Porcupines in Tin Boxes* (Washington, DC: United States Department of Justice, U.S. Attorney's Office, District of Rhode Island), <http://www.usdoj.gov/usao/ri/patriot.html>.
5. John Ashcroft, "The Patriot Act: Wise Beyond Its Years," *Wall Street Journal*, 26 October 2004, p. A24.
6. Jamie Glazov, "The Un-PATRIOT-ic Left," *FrontpageMagazine.com*, 18 May 2004, <http://www.frontpagemag.com/Articles/ReadArticle.asp?ID=13430>.
7. United States Department of Justice, *USA Patriot Act Overview* (Washington, DC: United States Department of Justice), <http://www.lifeandliberty.gov:80/patriot_overview_pversion.pdf>.
8. Ashcroft, p. A24.
9. Ashcroft, p. A24.
10. DOJ, *USA Patriot Act Overview*.
11. DOJ, *Dispelling the Myths*.
12. Glazov.
13. DOJ, *Dispelling the Myths*.
14. DOJ, *Dispelling the Myths*.
15. DOJ, *USA Patriot Act Overview*.
16. *Dalia v. U.S.*, 441 U.S. 238 (1979).
17. Glazov.
18. [Editorial], "The Silent President," *The New York Times*, 12 April 2004, p. A18; and Carl Limbacher, "NY Times: Bush Should Have Used Racial Profiling to Prevent 9/11," *NewsMax.com*, 12 April 2004, <http://www.newsmax.com/archives/ic/2004/4/12/120947.shtml>.
19. Ann Scales, "Polls Say Blacks Tend to Favor Checks," *The Boston Globe*, 30 September 2001; and Gallup poll data, September 2001.
20. Michael Paulson, "U.S. Attitudes Toward Arabs Souring, According to Poll," *The Boston Globe*, 29 September 2001, p. A5.
21. Polling data on file at <http://www.foxnews.com>, 2001.
22. James Q. Wilson and Heather Higgins, "Profiles in Courage," *Wall Street Journal*, 10 January 2002.

BRING GREGG JACKSON
TO SPEAK AT YOUR CLUB, GROUP, ORGANIZATION OR CAMPUS

For more information contact Annie Fischer at annie@conservativecomebacks.com or go to www.greggjackson.com.